Bed & Breakfast USA

A GUIDE TO
Tourist Homes
AND
Guest Houses

Betty Revits Rundback
and
Nancy Kramer

Tourist House Association of America

E. P. Dutton, Inc. • New York

With love to Bob Rundback
because this whole project was his idea,
and to Ann Revits,
ever the proud mother and grandma, and to Rick.

Editor: Sandra W. Soule

Designer: Stanley S. Drate/Folio Graphics Co. Inc.

Cover photo: Green Trails, Brookfield, Vermont 05036, by William Brahmstedt

Published in the United States by E.P. Dutton, Inc., 2 Park Avenue, New York, N.Y. 10016

Library of Congress Catalog Card Number: 83-73723

ISBN: 0-525-48091-9

Published simultaneously in Canada by Fitzhenry & Whiteside Limited, Toronto and Vancouver

10 9 8 7 6 5 4 3 2 1

Contents

Preface

If you have read earlier editions of *Bed & Breakfast USA*, you know this book has always been a labor of love. It is personally gratifying to see how it has grown from the first 16-page edition, titled the *Guide to Tourist Homes and Guest Houses*, which was published in 1975 and contained 40 individual listings. Nine years later, the eighth revised edition lists 480 homes and 99 reservation agencies, giving travelers access to over 11,000 host homes. This spectacular success seems to strongly indicate that the revived concept of the guest house has recaptured the fancy of both travelers and proprietors.

All of the B&Bs described in this book are members of the Tourist House Association of America. All members are dedicated to the standards of "Cleanliness, Comfort, and Cordiality" and sincerely enjoy plumping up the pillows in anticipation of having visitors. THAA dues are $15 annually. We share ideas and experiences by way of our newsletter and arrange regional seminars and conferences.

Our biggest problem has been the attempt to include new listings in time for publication, since we are constantly deluged with applications from additional hosts who wish to be mentioned in *Bed & Breakfast USA*. We had to stop somewhere, so we have provided a form in the back of the book that you can use to order a list of B&Bs that joined our Association after we went to press.

BETTY R. RUNDBACK
Director, Tourist House Association of America
RD 2 Box 355A Greentown, Pennsylvania 18426

March, 1984

Acknowledgments

A special thanks to Michael Frome, who saw promise in the first sixteen-page "Guide" and verbally applauded our growth with each subsequent edition. And many thanks to all the other travel writers and reporters who have brought us to the attention of their audience.

Many hugs to family and friends who lovingly devoted time to the "office" chores. Among them are the best stamp lickers and envelope stuffers in the world! Mike and Peggy Ackerman, John Rundback, Fred Rundback, Ricky Costanzo, Sherry and Joyce Buzlowsky, Sharon Makler, Betty Neuer, Julie Cohen, Lisa Eagleston, Chris Sakoutis, Harry Revits, Susie Scher, Joan Smith, and Karen Zane. We are most grateful to Joyce Ackerman and James McGhee for their artwork.

Our appreciation goes to our editor, Sandy Soule. She exhausted her supply of blue pencils but never her patience.

1

Introduction

Whatever name you use—bed and breakfast, guest house, or tourist home—the idea is the same: private residences whose owners rent their spare bedrooms to travelers—places where travelers are treated more like welcome guests than paying customers.

The custom of opening one's home to travelers dates back to the earliest days of colonial America. Hotels and inns were few and far between in those days, and wayfarers relied on the kindness of strangers to provide a bed for the night. Which is why, perhaps, there is hardly a colonial-era home in the mid-Atlantic states that does not boast: "George Washington Slept Here!"

During the Depression, the tourist home provided an economic advantage to both the traveler and the host. Travelers always drove through the center of town; there were no superhighways to bypass local traffic. A house with a sign in the front yard reading "Tourists" or "Guests" indicated that a traveler could rent a room for the night and have a cup of coffee before leaving in the morning. The usual cost for this arrangement was $2. The money represented needed income for the proprietor as well as the opportunity to chat with an interesting visitor.

In the 1950s, the country guest house became a popular alternative to the costly hotels in resort areas. The host compensated for the lack of hotel amenities, such as private bathrooms, by providing comfortable bedrooms and bountiful breakfasts at a modest price. The visitors enjoyed the home-away-from-home atmosphere; the hosts were pleased to have paying houseguests.

The incredible growth in international travel that has occurred over the past 25 years has provided yet another stimulus. Millions of Americans now vacation annually in Europe and travelers have become enchanted with the bed and breakfast concept so popular in Britain, Ireland, and other parts of the continent. In fact, many well-traveled Americans are delighted to learn that we "finally" have B&Bs here. But, as you now know, they were always here . . . just a rose by another name.

Bed and breakfasts are for:

- **Parents of college kids:** Tuition is costly enough without the added expense of "Parents' Weekends." Look for a B&B near campus.

- **Parents traveling with children:** A family living room, play room, or backyard is preferable to the confines of a motel room.

- **"Parents" of pets:** Many proprietors will allow your well-behaved darling to come too. This can cut down on the expense and trauma of kenneling Fido.

- **Business travelers:** Being "on the road" can be lonely and expensive. It's so nice, after a day's work, to return to a home-away-from-home.

- **Women traveling alone:** Friendship and conversation are the natural ingredients of a guest house.

- **Skiers: Lift prices are** lofty, so it helps to save some money on lodging. Many mountain homes include home-cooked meals in your room rate.

- **Students:** A visit with a family is a pleasant alternative to camping or the local "Y."

- **Visitors from abroad:** Cultural exchanges are often enhanced by a host who can speak your language.

- **Carless travelers:** If you plan to leave the auto at home, it's nice to know that many B&Bs are convenient to public transportation. Hosts will often arrange to meet your bus, plane, train for a nominal fee.

- **Schoolteachers and retired persons:** Exploring out-of-the-way places is fun and will save you money.

- **Antique collectors:** Many hosts have lovely personal collections, and nearby towns are filled with undiscovered antique shops.

- **House hunters:** It's a practical way of trying out a neighborhood.

- **Relocating corporate executives:** It's more comfortable to stay in a real home while you look for a permanent residence. Hosts will often give more practical advice than a professional realtor.

- **Relatives of hospitalized patients:** Many B&Bs are located near major hospitals. Hosts will offer tea and sympathy when visiting hours are over.

- **Convention and seminar attendees:** Staying at a nearby B&B is less expensive than checking into a hotel.

And everyone else who has had it up to here with plastic motel monotony!

What It Is Like to Be a Guest in a B&B

The B&B descriptions provided in this book will help you choose the places that have the greatest appeal to you. A first-hand insight into local culture awaits you; imagine the advantage of arriving in New York City or San Francisco and having an insider to help you sidestep the tourist traps and direct you to that special restaurant or discount store. Or explore the countryside, where fresh air and home-cooked meals beckon. Your choice is as wide as the U.S.A.

Each bed and breakfast listed offers personal contact, a real advantage in unfamiliar environments. You may not have a phone in your room or a TV on the dresser. You may even have to pad down the hall in robe and slippers to take a shower, but you'll discover little things count:

- In Williamsburg, Virginia, a visitor from Germany opted to stay at a B&B to help improve her conversational English. When the hostess saw that she was having difficulty understanding directions, she personally escorted her on a tour of Old Williamsburg.

- In Pennsylvania, the guests mistakenly arrived a week prior to their stated reservation date and the B&B was full. The hostess made a call to a neighbor who accommodated the couple. (By the way, the neighbor has now become a B&B host!)

- In New York City, the guest was an Emmy Award nominee and arrived with his tuxedo in need of pressing. The hostess pressed it; when he claimed his award over nationwide TV, he looked well groomed!

Expect the unexpected, like a pot of coffee brewed upon your arrival or fresh flowers on the nightstand. At the very least, count on our required standard of cleanliness and comfort. Although we haven't personally visited all the places listed, they have all been highly recommended by Chambers of Commerce or former guests. We have either spoken to or corresponded with all the proprietors; they are a friendly group of people who enjoy having visitors. They will do all in their power to make your stay memorable.

Our goal is to enable the traveler to crisscross the country and stay only at B&Bs along the way. To achieve this, your help is vital. Please take a moment to write us of your experiences; we will follow up on every suggestion. Your comments will serve as the yardstick by which we can measure the quality of our accommodations. For your convenience, an evaluation form is included at the back of this book.

Cost of Accommodations

Bed and Breakfast, in the purest sense, is a private home where the owners rent their spare bedrooms to travelers. These are the backbone of this book.

However, American ingenuity has enhanced this simple idea to include more spectacular homes, mansions, small inns, and intimate hotels. With few exceptions, the proprietor is the host and lives on the premises.

Whether plain or fancy, all B&Bs are based on the concept that people are tired of the plastic monotony of motels and are disappointed that even the so-called budget motels can be quite expensive. Travelers crave the personal touch and they sincerely enjoy "visiting" rather than just "staying."

Prices vary accordingly. There are places in this book where lovely lodging may be had for $5 a night and others that feature a gourmet breakfast in a canopied bed for $75.

Accommodations vary in price depending upon the locale and the season. Peak season usually refers to the availability of skiing in winter and water sports in summer; in the sunbelt states, the winter months are usually the peak season. Off-season rate schedules are usually reduced. Resorts and major cities are generally more expensive than out-of-the-way places. However, B&Bs are always less expensive than hotels and motels of equivalent caliber in the same area. A weekly rate is usually less expensive than a daily rate. Special reductions are sometimes given to families or senior citizens. Whenever reduced rates are available, you will find this noted in the individual listings.

Meals

Breakfast: "Continental" refers to fruit or juice, rolls, and a hot beverage. Many hosts pride themselves on home-baked breads, homemade preserves, plus imported teas and cakes, so their continental breakfast may be quite deluxe. Several hosts have regular jobs outside the home so you may have to adjust your schedule to theirs. A "Full" breakfast includes fruit, cereal and/or eggs, breakfast meats, breads, and hot beverage. The table is set family-style and is often the highlight of a B&B's hospitality. Either a continental breakfast or full breakfast is included in the room rate unless otherwise specified.

Other Meals: If listed as "available," you can be assured that the host takes pride in his or her cooking skills. The prices for lunch or dinner are usually reasonable but are not included in the quoted room rate unless clearly specified as "included."

Making Reservations

- Reservations are a MUST or you may risk missing out on the accommodations of your choice. Reserve *early* and confirm with a deposit equal to one night's stay. If your plans change and you notify the proprietor well in advance, your deposit will be refunded. If you call to inquire about reservations, please remember the difference in time zones. When dialing outside of your area, remember to dial the digit "1" before the area code.
- Many individual B&Bs now accept charge cards. This information is indicated in the listings by the symbols "MC" for Master Card, "AMEX" for American Express, etc. A few have a surcharge for this service so inquire as to the policy.

- Cash or traveler's checks are the accepted method of paying for your stay. Be sure to inquire whether or not tax is included in the rates quoted so that you will know exactly how much your lodging will cost.
- We have requested that each B&B described in this book *guarantee* the rates quoted for 1984 to anyone making a reservation as a result of reading about the B&B *in this book.* This may not have been possible in all cases, but if you find a place whose prices have increased in excess of 15%, please advise us immediately.
- Rates are based on single or double occupancy of a room as quoted. Expect that an extra person(s) in the room will be charged a small additional fee. Inquire when making your reservation what the charge will be.
- If a listing indicates that children or pets are welcome, it is expected that they will be well behaved. All of our hosts take pride in their homes and it would be unfair to subject them to circumstances where their possessions might be abused or the other houseguests be disturbed by an unruly child or animal.
- Please note that many hosts have their own resident pets. If you are allergic or don't care to be around animals, inquire before making a reservation.
- In homes where smoking is permitted, do check to see if it is restricted in any of the rooms. Most hosts object to cigars.
- Where listings indicate that social drinking is permitted, it usually refers to your bringing your own beverages. Most hosts will provide ice; many will allow you to chill mixers in the refrigerator, and others offer complimentary wine and snacks. A few B&B inns have licenses to sell liquor. Any drinking should not be excessive.
- If "Yes" is indicated in the listings for airport pickup, it means that the host will meet your plane for a fee. If you are arriving by bus or train, ask if this service can be arranged.
- Feel free to request brochures and local maps so you can better plan for your visit.
- Do try to fit in with the host's house rules. You are on vacation; he isn't!
- A reservation form is included at the back of this book for your convenience; just tear it out and send it in to the B&B of your choice.

B&B Reservation Services

There are many host families who prefer not to be individually listed in a book, and would rather have their houseguests referred by a coordinating agency. The organizations listed in this book are all members of the Tourist House Association. They all share our rigid standards regarding the suitability of the host home as to cordiality, cleanliness, and comfort.

The majority do a marvelous job of matching host and guest according to age, interests, language, and any special requirements. To get the best match, it is practical to give them as much time as possible to find the host home best tailored to your needs.

Many have prepared descriptive pamphlets describing the homes on their rosters, the areas in which the homes are located, and information regarding special things to see and do. If you send a self-addressed, stamped, business-size envelope, you will receive a descriptive directory by return mail along with a reservation form for you to complete. When returning the form, you will be asked to select the home or homes listed in the brochure that most appeal to you. (The homes are usually given a code number for reference.) The required deposit should accompany your reservation. Upon receipt, the coordinator will make the reservation and advise you of the name, address, telephone number, and travel instructions for your host.

A few agencies prepare a descriptive directory and *include* the host's name, address, and telephone number so that you can contact the host and make your arrangements directly. They charge anywhere from two to five dollars for the directory.

Several agencies are *membership* organizations, charging guests an annual fee ranging from $5 to $25 per person. Their descriptive directories are free to members and a few of them maintain toll-free telephone numbers for reservations.

Most reservation services have a specific geographic focus. The coordinators are experts in the areas they represent. They can often make arrangements for car rentals, theater tickets, and touring suggestions, and offer information in planning a trip best suited to your interests.

Most work on a commission basis with the host, and that fee is included in the room rates quoted in each listing. Some make a surcharge for a one-night stay; others require a two- or three-night minimum stay for holiday periods or special events. Some will accept a credit card for the reservation but the balance due must be paid to the host in cash or traveler's checks.

All of their host homes offer continental breakfast and some may include a full breakfast.

Many reservation services in the larger cities have, in addition to the traditional B&Bs, a selection of apartments, condominiums, and houses *without hosts in residence*. This may be appealing to those travelers anticipating an extended stay in a particular area.

The statewide services are listed first in the section for each state. City or regionally-based organizations are listed first under the heading for that area. A few agencies are nationwide and their addresses are listed below. For a complete description of their services, look them up under the city and state where they're based.

NOTE: When calling, do so during normal business hours (for that time zone), unless otherwise stated. Collect calls are not accepted.

EVA, *317 Piedmont Road, Santa Barbara, California 93105.*

HOME SUITE HOMES, *1470 Firebird Way, Sunnyvale, California 94087.*

THE INTERNATIONAL SPAREROOM, *P.O. Box 518, Solana Beach, California 92075.*

THE BED AND BREAKFAST LEAGUE, *2855 29th Street, N.W., Washington, D.C. 20008.*

BED & BREAKFAST REGISTRY—NORTH AMERICA, *P.O. Box 80174, St. Paul, Minnesota 55108-0174.*

2

How to Start Your Own B&B

What It's Like to Be a Host

Hosts are people who like the idea of accommodating travelers and sharing their home and the special features of their area with them. They are people who have houses too large for their personal needs and like the idea of supplementing their income by having people visit. For many, it's a marvelous way of meeting rising utility and maintenance costs. For young families, it is a way of buying and keeping that otherwise-too-large house and furnishing it, since many of the furnishings may be tax deductible. Another advantage is that many state and local governments have recognized the service that some host families perform. In browsing through this book you will note that some homes are listed in the National Historic Register. Some state governments allow owners of landmark and historical houses a special tax advantage if they are used for any business purpose. Check with the Historical Preservation Society in your state for details.

If you have bedrooms to spare . . . if you sincerely like having overnight guests . . . if your home is clean and comfortable . . . this is an opportunity to consider. It is a unique business because *you* set the time of the visit and the length of stay. (Guest houses are not boarding homes.) You invite the guests at *your* convenience, and the extras, such as meals, are entirely up to you. You can provide a cup of coffee, complete meals, or just a room and shared bath.

Although the majority of hosts are women, many couples are finding pleasure in this joint venture. The general profile of a typical host is a friendly, outgoing, flexible person who is proud of her home and hometown. The following information and suggestions represent a guideline to consider in deciding whether becoming a B&B host is really for you.

There are no set rules for the location, type, or style of a B&B. Apartments, condos, farmhouses, town houses, beach houses, vacation cottages, houseboats, mansions, as well as the traditional one-family dwelling are all appropriate. The important thing is for the host to be on the premises. The setting may be urban, rural, or suburban; near public transportation or in the hinterlands. Location is only important if you want to have guests every night. Areas where tourism is popular, such as resort areas or major cities, are often busier than out-of-the-way places. However, if a steady stream of visitors is not that important or even desirable, it doesn't matter where you are. People will contact you if your rates are reasonable and if there is something to see and do in your area, or if it is near a major transportation route.

Setting the Rates

Consider carefully four key factors in setting your rates: location, private vs. shared bath, type of breakfast, and your home itself.

Location: If you reside in a traditional resort or well-touristed area, near a major university or medical center, or in an urban hub or gateway city, your rates should be at least 40% lower than those of the area's major motels or hotels. If you live in an out-of-the-way location, your rates must be extremely reasonable. If your area has a "season"—snow sports in winter, water sports in summer—offer off-season rates when these attractions are not available. Reading through this book will help you to see what is the going rate in a situation similar to yours.

The Bath: You are entitled to charge more for a room with private bath. If the occupants of two rooms share one bath, the rate should be less. If more than five people must share one bathroom, you may have complaints, unless your rates are truly inexpensive.

The Breakfast: Figure the approximate cost of your ingredients, plus something for your time. Allow about $1 to $1.50 for a continental breakfast; $2 to $3 for a full American breakfast; then *include* it in the rate.

Your Home: Plan on charging a fair and reasonable rate for a typical B&B home, one that is warm and inviting, clean and comfortable. If your home is exceptionally luxurious, with king-size beds, Jacuzzi baths, tennis courts, or hot tubs, you will find guests who are willing to pay a premium. If your home is over 75 years old, well restored, with lots of antiques, you may also be able to charge a higher rate.

The Three 'B's—Bed, Breakfast, and Bath

The Bedroom: The ideal situation for a prospective host is the possession of a house too large for current needs. The children may be away at college most of the year or may have left permanently, leaving behind their bedrooms and, in some cases, the extra bath. Refurbishing these rooms does not mean refurnishing; an extraordinary investment need not be contemplated for receiving guests. Take a long hard look at the room. With a little imagination and a little monetary outlay, could it be changed into a bedroom *you'd* be pleased to spend the night in? Check it out *before* you go any further. Are the beds comfortable? Do the pillows or mattresses need replacement? Would the bed linens be appropriate if your fussy aunt slept overnight? Is the carpet clean? Are the walls attractive? Do the curtains or shades need attention? Are there sturdy hangers in the closet? Would emptying the closet and bureau be an impossible task? Is there a good light to read by? A writing table and comfortable chair? A mirror? Peek under the bed and see if there are dust balls or old magazines tucked away. While relatives and friends would "understand" if things weren't perfect, a paying guest is entitled to cleanliness and comfort.

If the idea of sprucing up the room has you overwhelmed, forget the idea and continue to be a guest rather than a host! If, however, a little "spit and polish," replacement of lumpy mattresses, sagging springs, and freshening the room in general presents no problem . . . continue! In short, your goal should be the kind of a room *you'd* be pleased to spend the night in and be willing to pay for.

The Breakfast: Breakfast time can be the most pleasant part of the guest's stay. It is at the breakfast table with you and the other guests that suggestions are made as to what to see and do, and exchanges of experiences are enjoyed. From a guest's point of view, the only expected offering is what is known as continental breakfast, which usually consists of juice, roll, and coffee or tea.

Breakfast fare is entirely up to you. If you are a morning person who whips out of bed at the crack of dawn with special recipes for muffins dancing in your head, to be drenched with your home-made preserves followed by eggs Benedict, an assortment of imported coffee or exotic tea . . . hop to it! You will play to a most appreciative audience. If, however, morning represents an awful intrusion on sleep and the idea of talking to anyone before noon is difficult, the least you should do is to prepare the breakfast table the night before with the necessary mugs, plates, and silverware. Fill the electric coffee pot and leave instructions that the first one up should plug it in; you can even hook it up to a timer, so that it will brew automatically!

Most of us fall somewhere in between these two extremes. Remember that any breakfast at "home" is preferable to getting dressed, getting into the car, and driving to some coffee shop. Whether you decide upon "continental breakfast" or a full American breakfast, consisting of juice or fruit, cereal or eggs, possibly bacon or sausage, toast, rolls, coffee, or tea, is up to you. It is most important that whatever the fare, it be included in your room rate. It is most awkward, especially after getting to know and like your guests, to present an additional charge for breakfast.

The Bath: This really is the third "B" in "B&B." If you are blessed with an extra bathroom for the exclusive use of a guest, that's super. If guests will have to share the facilities with others, that really presents no problem. If it's being shared with your family, the family must always be "last in line." Be sure that they are aware of the guest's importance; the guest, paying or otherwise, always comes first. No retainers, or used bandaids, or topless toothpaste tubes are to be carelessly left on the sink. The tub, shower, floor, and toilet bowl are to be squeaky clean. The mirrors and chrome should sparkle and a supply of toilet tissue, fresh soap, and unfrayed towels go a long way in reflecting a high standard of cleanliness. Make sure that the grout between tiles is free of mildew and that the shower curtain is unstained. Cracked ceilings should be repaired, the paint free of chips, and if your bath is wallpapered, make certain no loose edges mar its beauty.

Most guests realize that in a share-the-bath situation they should leave the room ready for the next person's use. It is a thoughtful reminder for you to leave tub cleanser, a cleaning towel or sponge, and bathroom deodorant handy for this purpose. A wastepaper basket, paper towels, paper cups, should be part of your supplies. Needless to say, your hot water system should be able to accommodate the number of guests you'll have without being taxed. And a plumber should make certain that there aren't any clogged lines or dripping faucets to spoil things for you or your visitors. If more than one guest room is sharing the same bath, it makes sense to have a supply of different colored towels and to assign a color for each guest. There should be enough towel bars and hooks to accommodate the towels. You might even want to supply each guest room its own soap in its own covered soap dish. This is both popular and economical.

The B&B Business

Money Matters: Before embarking upon any business, it's a good idea to discuss it with an accountant and possibly an attorney. Since you'll be using your home for a business enterprise there are things with which they are familiar that are important for you to know. For instance, you may want to incorporate, so find out what the pros and cons are. Ask about depreciation. Deductible business expenses may include refurbishing, furnishings, supplies, printing costs, postage, etc. Although an occasional paying guest may not necessarily subject you to the state tax applicable to hotels, your B&B income is taxable. An accountant will be able to guide you with a simple system of record keeping. Accurate records will help you analyze income and expense, and show if you are breaking even, or operating at a profit or a loss.

Insurance: It is important to call your insurance broker. Many home-owner policies have a clause covering "an occasional overnight paying guest." See if you will be protected under your existing coverage and, if not, what the additional premium would be.

Every home should be equipped with smoke detectors and fire extinguishers. All fire hazards should be eliminated; stairways and halls should be well lit and kept free of clutter. If you haven't already done so, immediately post prominently the emergency numbers for the fire department, police, and ambulance service.

Regulations: If you have read this far and are still excited about the concept of running a B&B, there are several steps to take at this point. First, visit the local Chamber of Commerce to see if there are any zoning restrictions concerning this sort of operation in your neighborhood. Bring along your copy of *Bed & Breakfast USA* to illustrate what you have in mind, in case they are unfamiliar with B&Bs. Generally, in residential areas, you are not permitted to display a sign indicating that you are operating a B&B, since the idea of attracting strangers might be objectionable to your neighbors. There might also be parking problems if you expect too many guests with automobiles at the same time. Most Chambers of Commerce are enthusiastic, because additional visitors mean extra business for local restaurants, shops, theaters, and businesses. This is a good time to inquire what it would cost to join the Chamber of Commerce.

As of this writing, there don't seem to be any specific laws governing B&Bs. Since guests are generally received on an irregular basis, B&Bs do not come under the same laws governing hotels and motels. And since B&Bs aren't inns where emphasis is on food rather than on lodging, no comparison can really be made in that regard either. As the idea grows, laws and regulations will probably be passed. Refer to the back of *Bed & Breakfast USA* and write to your state's office of tourism for information. The address and phone number is listed for your convenience. You might even call or write to a few B&Bs in your state and ask the host about her experience in this regard. Most hosts will be happy to give you the benefit of their experience, but keep in mind that they are busy people and it would be wise to limit your intrusion upon their time.

The Name: The naming of your B&B is most important and will take some time and consideration because this is the moment when dreams become reality. It will be used on your brochures, stationery, and bills. (If you decide to incorporate, the corporation needs a name!) It should somehow be descriptive of the atmosphere you wish to convey.

Brochure: Once you have given a name to your house, design a brochure. The best ones include a reservation form and can be mailed to your prospective guests. The brochure should contain the name of your B&B, address, phone number, best time to call, your name, a brief description of your home, its ambience, a brief history of the house if it is old, the number of guest rooms, whether or not baths are shared, the type of breakfast served, rates, required deposit, minimum stay requirement if any, dates when you'll be closed, and your cancellation policy. A deposit of one night's stay is acceptable and the promise of a full refund if cancellation is received at least two weeks prior to arrival is typical. If you have reduced rates for a specific length of stay, families, senior citizens, etc., mention it.

If you can converse in a foreign language, say so, because many visitors from abroad seek out B&Bs; it's a marvelous plus to be able to chat in their native tongue. Include your policy regarding children, pets, or smokers, and whether you offer the convenience of a guest refrigerator or barbecue. It is helpful to include directions from a major route and a simple map for finding your home. It's a good idea to include a line or two about yourself and your interests, and do mention what there is to see and do in the area as well as proximity to any major university. A line drawing of your house is a good investment since the picture can be used not only on the brochure, but on your stationery, postcards, and greeting cards as well. If you can't have this taken care of locally, write the Tourist House Association. We have a service that can handle it for you.

Take your ideas to a reliable printer for his professional guidance. Don't forget to keep the receipt for the printing bill since this is a business expense.

Confirmation Letter: Upon receipt of a paid reservation, do send out a letter confirming it. You can design a form letter and have it offset by a printer, since the cost of doing so is usually nominal. Include the dates of the stay, number of people expected, the rate including tax, as well as explicit directions by car and, if applicable, by public transportation. A simple map reflecting the exact location of your home in relation to major streets and highways is most useful. It is a good idea to ask your guests to call you if they will be traveling and unavailable by phone for the week prior to their expected arrival. You might even want to include any of the house rules regarding smoking, pets, or whatever.

Successful Hosting

The Advantage of Hosting: The nicest part of being a B&B host is that you aren't required to take guests every day of the year. Should there be times when having guests would not be convenient, you can always say you're full and try to arrange an alternate date. But most important, keep whatever date you reserve. It is an excellent idea at the time reservations are accepted to ask for the name and telephone number of an emergency contact should you have to cancel unexpectedly. However, *never* have a guest come to a locked door. If an emergency arises and you cannot reach your prospective guests in time, do make arrangements for someone to greet them and make alternate arrangements so they can be accommodated.

House Rules: While you're in the "thinking stage," give some thought to the rules you'd like your guests to adhere to. The last thing you want for you or your family is to feel uncomfortable in your own home. Make a list of House Rules concerning arrival and departure during the guests' stay and specify when breakfast is served. If you don't want guests coming home too late, say so. Most hosts like to lock up at a certain hour at night, so arrange for an extra key for night owls. If that makes you uncomfortable, have a curfew on your House Rules list. If smoking disturbs you, confine the area where it's permitted.

Some guests bring a bottle of their favorite beverage and enjoy a drink before going out to dinner. Many hosts enjoy a cocktail hour too, and often provide cheese and crackers to share with the guests. B&Bs cannot sell drinks to guests since this would require licensing. If you'd rather no drinks be consumed in your home, say so.

Many hosts don't mind accommodating a well-behaved pet. If you don't mind or have pets of your own, discuss this with your guests before they pack Fido's suitcase. Your House Rules can even be included in your brochure. That way both the host and the guest are aware of each other's likes and dislikes, and no hard feelings are made.

Entertaining: One of the most appealing features of being a guest at a B&B is the opportunity of being able to visit in the evening with the hosts. After a day of sightseeing or business, it is most relaxing and pleasant to sit around the living room and chat. For many hosts, this is the most enjoyable part of having guests. However, if you are accommodating several people on a daily basis, entertaining can be tiring.. Don't feel you'll be offending anyone by excusing yourself to attend to your own family or personal needs. The situation can be easily handled by having a room where you can retreat and offering your guests the living room, den, or other area for games, books, magazines, and perhaps the use of a television or bridge table. Most guests enjoy just talking to each other since this is the main idea of staying at a B&B.

The Telephone: This is a most important link between you and your prospective guests. As soon as possible, have your telephone number included under your B&B name in the White Pages. It is a good idea to be listed in the appropriate section in your telephone directory Yellow Pages. If your home phone is used for a lot of personal calls, you should think about installing a separate line for your B&B. If you are out a lot, give some thought to using a telephone answering device to explain your absence and time of return, and record the caller's message. There is nothing more frustrating to a prospective guest than to call and get a constant busy signal or no answer at all. Request that the caller leave his name and address, "at the sound of the beep," so you can mail a reservation form. This will help eliminate the necessity of having to return long distance calls. If the caller wants further information, he will call again at the time you said you'd be home.

B&B guests don't expect a phone in the guest room. However, there are times when they might want to use your phone for a long distance call. In your House Rules list, suggest that any such calls be charged to their home telephone. Business travelers often have telephone charge cards for this purpose. In either case, you should keep a telephone record book and timer near your instrument. Ask the caller to enter the city called, telephone number, and length of call. Thus, you will have an accurate record should a charge be inadvertently added to your bill. Or, if you wish, you can add telephone charges to the guest bill. The telephone operator will quote the cost of the per-minute charge throughout the country for this purpose.

Maid Service: If you have several guest rooms and bathrooms, you may find yourself being a chambermaid as part of the business. Naturally, each guest gets fresh linens upon arrival. If a guest stays up to three days, it isn't expected that bed linen be changed every day. What is expected is the room be freshened and the bath be cleaned and towels replaced every day. If you don't employ a full-time maid you may want to investigate the possibility of hiring a high school student on a part-time basis to give you a hand with the housekeeping. Many guests, noticing the absence of help, will voluntarily lend a hand, although they have the right to expect some degree of service, particularly if they are paying a premium rate.

Keys: A great many hosts are not constantly home during the day. Some do "hosting" on a part-time basis, while involved with regular jobs. There are times when even full-time hosts have to be away during the day. If the guests are to have access to the house while you are not on the premises, it is wise to have extra keys made. It is also wise to take a key deposit of $50 simply to assure return of the key. Let me add that in the 10 years of my personal experience, as well as in the opinions of other hosts, B&B guests are the most honest people you can have. No one has ever had even a washcloth stolen, let alone the family treasures. In fact, it isn't unusual for the guest to leave a small gift after a particularly pleasant visit. On the other hand, guests are sometimes forgetful and leave belongings behind. For this reason it is important for you to have their names and addresses so you can return their possessions. They will expect to reimburse you for the postage.

Registering Guests: You should keep a regular registration ledger for the guest to complete before checking in. The information should include the full names of each guest, their home address, phone number, business address and telephone, and auto license number. It's a good idea to include the name and phone number of a friend or relative in case of an emergency. This information will serve you well for other contingencies, such as the guest leaving some important article behind, or an unpaid long distance phone call, or the rare instance of an unpaid bill. You may prefer to have this information on your guest bill which should be designed as a two-part carbon form. You will then have a record and the guest has a ready receipt. (Receipts are very important to business travelers!)

Settling the Bill: The average stay in a B&B is two nights. Since a deposit equal to one night's lodging is the norm, when to collect the balance is up to you. Most guests pay upon leaving, but if they leave so early that the settling of the bill at that time is inconvenient, you can request the payment the previous night. You might want to consider the convenience of accepting a major credit card but contact the sponsoring company first to see what percentage of your gross is expected for this service. If you find yourself entertaining more business visitors than vacationers, it might be something you should offer. Most travelers are aware that cash or traveler's checks are the accepted modes of payment. Accepting a personal check is rarely risky but again, it's up to you. You might include your preference in your brochure.

Other Meals: B&B means that only breakfast is served. If you enjoy cooking and would like to offer other meals for a fee, make sure that you investigate the applicable health laws. If you have to install a commercial kitchen, the idea might be too expensive for current consideration. However, allowing guests to store fixings for a quick snack or to use your barbecue can be a very attractive feature for families traveling with children or for people watching their budget. If you can offer this convenience, be sure to mention it in your brochure. (And, be sure to add a line to your House Rules that the guest is expected to clean up.) Some hosts keep an extra guest refrigerator on hand for this purpose.

It's an excellent idea to keep menus from your local restaurants on hand. Try to have a good sampling, ranging from moderately priced to expensive dining spots, and find out if reservations are required. Your guests will always rely heavily upon your advice and suggestions. After all, when it comes to your town, you're the authority! It's also a nice idea to keep informed of local happenings that might be of interest to your visitors. A special concert at the university or a local fair or church supper can add an extra dimension to their visit. If parents are visiting with young children they might want to have dinner out without them; try to have a list of available baby-sitters. A selection of guide books covering your area is also a nice feature.

The Guest Book: These are available in most stationery and department stores, and it is important that you buy one. It should contain designated space for the date, the name of the guest, home address, and a blank area for the guest comments. They generally sign the guest book before checking out. The guest book is first of all a permanent record of who came and went. It will give you an idea what times during the year you were busiest and which times were slow. Secondly, it is an easy way to keep a mailing list for your Christmas cards and future promotional mailings. You will also find that thumbing through it in years to come will recall some very pleasant people who were once strangers but now are friends.

Advertising: Periodically distribute your brochures to the local university, college, and hospital, since out of town visitors always need a place to stay. Let your local caterers know of your existence since wedding guests are often from out of town. If you have a major corporation in your area, drop off a brochure at the personnel office. Even visiting or relocating executives and salesmen enjoy B&Bs. Hotels and motels are sometimes overbooked; it wouldn't hurt to leave your brochure with the manager for times when there's no room for their last-minute guests. Local residents sometimes have to put up extra guests so it's a good idea to take an ad out in your local school or church newspaper. The cost is usually minimal. Repeat this distribution process from time to time, so that you can replenish the supply of brochures.

The best advertising is being a member of the Tourist House Association since all member B&Bs are fully described in this book, which is available in bookstores, libraries, and B&Bs throughout the U.S. and Canada. In addition, it is natural for THA members to recommend each other when guests inquire about similar accommodations in other areas. The most important reason for keeping your B&B clean, comfortable, and cordial is that we are all judged by what a guest experiences in any individual Tourist House Association home. The best publicity will come from your satisfied guests who will recommend your B&B to their friends.

Additional Suggestions

Extra Earnings: You might want to consider a few ideas for earning extra money in connection with being a host. If you enjoy touring, you can plan and conduct a special outing, off the beaten tourist track, for a modest fee. In major cities, you can do such things as acquiring tickets for theater, concert, or sports events. A supply of *Bed & Breakfast USA* for sale to guests is both a source of income and gives every THA member direct exposure to the B&B market.

Several hosts tell me that a small gift shop is often a natural offshoot of a B&B. Items for sale could include handmade quilts, pillows, potholders, and knitted items. One host has turned his hobby of woodworking into extra income. He makes lovely picture frames, napkin rings, and foot stools that many guests buy as souvenirs to take home. If you plan to do this, check with the Small Business Administration to inquire about such things as a resale license and tax collection; the Chamber of Commerce can advise in this regard.

Transportation: While the majority of B&B guests arrive by car, there are many who rely on public transportation. Some hosts, for a modest fee, are willing to meet arriving guests at airports, train depots, or bus stations. Do be knowledgeable about local transportation schedules in your area and be prepared to give explicit directions for your visitors' comings and goings. Have phone numbers handy for taxi service, as well as information on car rentals.

Thoughtful Touches: Guests often write to tell us of their experiences at B&Bs as a result of learning about them through this book. These are some of the special touches that made their visit special: fresh flowers in the guest room; even a single flower in a bud vase is pretty. One hostess puts a foil-wrapped piece of candy on the pillow before the guest returns from dinner. A small decanter of wine and glasses, or a few pieces of fresh fruit in a pretty bowl on the dresser are lovely surprises. A few one-size-fits-all terry robes are great to have on hand, especially if the bathroom is shared. A small sewing kit in the bureau is handy. Writing paper and envelopes in the desk invites the guest to send a quick note to the folks at home. If your house sketch is printed on it, it is marvelous free publicity. A pre-bed cup of tea for adults or cookies and milk for children is always appreciated.

By the way, keep a supply of guest-comment cards in the desk, both to attract compliments as well as to bring your attention to the flaws in your B&B that should be corrected.

Join the Tourist House Association: If you are convinced that you want to be a host, and have thoroughly discussed the pros and cons with your family and advisers, complete and return the membership application found at the back of this book. Our dues are $15 annually. As a member, the description of your B&B will be part of the next issue of the book *Bed & Breakfast USA,* as well as in the interim supplement between printings. You will also receive the THA's newsletter; regional seminars and conferences are held occasionally and you might enjoy attending. And, as an association, we will have clout should the time come when B&B becomes a recognized industry.

Affiliating with a B&B Reservation Agency: Over 100 agencies are listed in *Bed & Breakfast USA.* If you do not care to advertise your house directly to the public, consider joining one in your area. Membership and reservation fees, as well as the degree of professionalism, vary widely from agency to agency, so do check around.

Prediction for Success: Success should not be equated with money alone. If you thoroughly enjoy people, are well organized, enjoy sharing your tidy home without exhausting yourself, then the idea of receiving compensation for the use of an otherwise dormant bedroom will be a big plus. Your visitors will seek relaxing, wholesome surroundings, and unpretentious hosts who open their hearts as well as their homes. Being a B&B host or guest is an exciting, enriching experience.

3

B&B Recipes

The recipes that follow are not to be found in standard cook-books. Some are original and the measurements are sometimes from the school of "a smidgen of this," "according to taste," and "till done." But they all indicate the host's desire to pamper guests with something special. The most important ingredient is the heartful of love that is as unmeasured as the handful of flour.

We had an overwhelming response to our request for host-contributed favorite breakfast recipes. Although we could not publish them all this time, we will use most of them in future editions. The following represent, as much as possible, regional or ethnic recipes that impart the flavor and variety of B&Bs across the country.

Apple 'n Fruit Bake

1½ c. apple cider (or apple juice)
½ c. raisins
½ c. cut-up dates
½ c. sliced almonds
½ c. sunflower seeds
cinnamon

(Allow at least 1 large fruit (sliced thick) per person.) Apples, pears, peaches, nectarines, whole seedless grapes, and bananas.

In a large, shallow casserole, mix the apples with the liquid and sprinkle lightly with cinnamon. Bake at 350° for 10 minutes. Add remaining fruit (except bananas) and bake an additional 10 minutes. Do not overcook. Remove from oven and gently toss with sliced bananas. Serve hot or cold. (Delicious hot with French toast or pancakes!)

NOTE: The liquid portion suggested above is enough for a dozen pieces of whole fruit. The fruit should not be swimming in juice and should keep its identity and shape.

The Turning Point, Great Barrington, Massachusetts

Blueberry-Raspberry Soup

> 2 c. water
> 3 tbsp. quick-cooking tapioca
> 2 1½" cinnamon sticks
> ½ c. sugar
> ¼ tsp. salt
> 1 tsp. lemon peel (grated)
> ⅓ c. lemon juice
> 8 oz. fresh or frozen blueberries
> 2 packages frozen raspberries (16 oz.)

In a saucepan, combine water, tapioca, sugar, salt, cinnamon, lemon peel, lemon juice, and blueberries. Over medium-high heat, bring to a boil, stirring constantly. Reduce heat and simmer, stirring occasionally, for 5 minutes. Remove from heat and stir in raspberries. Cover and refrigerate until well chilled. Remove cinnamon sticks. Serve cold and pass bowl of sour cream. (Makes 6 large or 12 small servings)

NOTE: Tastes great hot, too!

Barnard Good House, Cape May, New Jersey

Cheese-Baked Eggs

> 1 tsp. melted butter
> 1 tbsp. cream
> 1 large egg
> Havarti cheese (grated)

Butter a 3½ oz. ramekin or custard dish. Add cream. Gently crack egg into dish. Season with salt and pepper. Sprinkle cheese on top. Bake in pre-heated oven at 350° for 8 to 10 minutes.

Chanticleer, Ashland, Oregon

Cheese Pudding

$1/2$ c. sharp cheese (grated)
4 eggs
$1/4$ c. melted butter
$1/2$ tsp. salt
$1/2$ tsp. pepper
$1/2$ tsp. Dijon mustard
$1/2$ tsp. paprika
$2^2/3$ c. milk
12 slices firm bread—remove crusts and cut in 1" cubes

Beat eggs and add butter, milk, and spices. Alternate layers of bread and cheese in a greased 9" X 13" baking pan. Pour egg mixture over the layers and refrigerate overnight. Preheat oven at 350° and bake for 1 hour. (Serves 6 to 8) Great with sausage!

Bed & Breakfast of Delaware, Wilmington, Delaware

Bev's Chili Relleno Souffle

1 4-oz. can diced green chilis
$1/2$ lb. sharp cheddar cheese (grated)
5 eggs (separated)
2 c. milk
$1/2$ c. flour

Place chilis in 7" X 11" baking dish and cover with cheese. Beat egg yolks, add flour and milk, and pour over cheese. Beat egg whites, fold in, and bake for 45 minutes at 350° or until custard sets. (Serves 4)

Megan's Friends, Los Osos, California

Eierkuchen (German Egg Cakes)

$1/2$ c. cake flour
$1/4$ tsp. baking soda
$3/4$ tsp. baking powder

1 tbsp. sugar
salt (dash)
½ c. buttermilk
6 eggs (separated)
cream of tartar (pinch)
2 tbsp. sour cream
1 tsp. vanilla

In a large bowl, mix flour, baking soda, baking powder, sugar, and salt. Add egg yolks and vanilla, then beat. In a separate bowl, add cream of tartar to egg whites and beat until stiff. Carefully fold into the yolk mixture. Preheat griddle and grease with sweet butter. Spoon onto griddle, spreading mixture slightly with side of spoon to make small round pancakes. When golden brown on one side, flip over and bake the underside. Top with fresh berries or applesauce. (Serves 4) *Guten Appetit!*

Elk Cove Inn, Elk, California

Dutch Baby (Oven Pancake Puff)

6 eggs
1 c. flour
1 c. milk
4 tbsp. butter
½ tsp. salt

Preheat oven to 425°. Put butter into 9" X 13" pan and melt in oven. In blender, combine eggs, flour, milk, and salt. Turn oven down to 400° and pour mixture into pan. (Do not stir!) Bake 25 minutes. (Delicious served with pure maple syrup or cinnamon sugar. Serves 4 to 6)

Lake Pateros B&B, Washington
Vermont B&B, Jericho, Vermont
Miss Anne's B&B, Nashville, Tennessee
B&B Center City, Philadelphia, Pennsylvania
Nashville Bed & Breakfast, Nashville, Tennessee

Whole-Wheat Pancakes with Orange Syrup

1 c. unbleached flour
¾ c. whole-wheat flour

1 tbsp. sugar
1/2 tsp. salt
1 tsp. baking powder
1 tsp. baking soda
1 2/3 c. buttermilk
3 tbsp. melted butter
3 eggs (separated)

Combine flours, sugar, salt, baking powder, and baking soda. In a separate bowl, beat buttermilk, melted butter, and egg yolks with rotary beater. Add egg mixture all at once to dry ingredients. Mix well. Gently fold in stiffly beaten egg whites. Drop batter by spoonfuls (2 to 3 tbsp.) onto lightly greased hot griddle. Bake until cakes are full of bubbles on top. Turn with spatula and brown on other side. (Yields 16 to 20 4" pancakes)

Orange Syrup

1 12-oz. can of frozen juice concentrate
1 1/2 c. sugar

Mix together in a small saucepan. Heat to boiling, stirring occasionally.

Beach House, Ocracoke Island, North Carolina

Buttermilk Pancakes

4 c. flour
1 tsp. baking soda
1 tsp. salt
4 eggs (beaten)
1/2 c. melted butter
2 tsp. vanilla
4 c. buttermilk

Mix dry ingredients. Add milk, vanilla, and melted shortening to eggs. Combine mixtures and stir until smooth. Bake on hot griddle until bubbles break. Turn over and bake until golden brown. Delicious with homemade jam or pure maple syrup!

Pittsfield Inn, Pittsfield, Vermont

Maine Blueberry Scones

2 c. all-purpose flour
2 tbsp. sugar
3 tsp. baking powder
nutmeg (dash)
3/4 tsp. salt
1/2 stick sweet butter
1 egg (beaten)
1 c. blueberries
1/2 c. medium cream

Sift dry ingredients. Cut in shortening. Add berries. Combine egg with milk. Add to dry ingredients. Stir just enough to moisten. Pat out dough quickly and gently into a circle about 3/4" thick. Cut into pie-shaped wedges. Brush with cream and sprinkle with sugar. Place on cookie sheet and bake in 450 ° oven for 15 minutes or until golden brown. Serve warm.

Bed & Breakfast Down East, Eastbrook, Maine

Fresh Fruit Bran Muffins

1 1/2 c. whole bran cereal
1 c. milk
1 egg
1/4 c. cooking oil
1 c. all-purpose flour
1/4 c. sugar (use slightly more if you want to)
2 tsp. baking powder
1/2 tsp. baking soda
1/2 tsp. salt
1/2 tsp. finely shredded lemon peel
1/2 tsp. cinnamon
1 c. fresh fruit (choice of apples, peaches, blueberries, raspberries, dark cherries)

Combine bran and milk, and let stand for 4 minutes or until liquid is absorbed. Stir in egg and oil; set aside. In a separate bowl, stir together flour, sugar, baking powder, baking soda, salt, lemon peel, and cinnamon. Add bran mixture and stir just until moist. Fold in fruit. Fill greased muffin tins ²/₃ full. Bake in 400° oven for 20 to 25 minutes. (Yields 12 to 15 muffins)

Cheney House, Ashland, New Hampshire

Jalapeño Muffins

  3 c. corn bread mix
  2½ c. milk
  ½ c. salad oil
  3 eggs (beaten)
  1 large onion (grated)
  2 tbsp. sugar
  ½ c. finely chopped peppers
  1½ c. sharp cheese (shredded)
  ¼ lb. bacon (fried and crumbled)
  ¼ c. chopped pimentos
  ½ clove garlic (crushed)

Mix first four ingredients, then add remainder. Bake in heavily greased muffin tins, or in tins with paper liners. Bake at 400° for approximately 35 minutes. (Yields 4 dozen muffins)

NOTE: These may be frozen in packages of three. Take out the night before and heat the next morning for a delicious treat.

VARIATION: Decrease milk by ¼ c. and add 2 c. creamed-style corn.

Bed & Breakfast Texas Style, Dallas, Texas

Skyline Apple Muffins

  1½ c. brown sugar
  ²/₃ c. oil
  1 egg
  1 c. buttermilk
  1 tsp. salt
  1 tsp. baking soda
  1 tsp. vanilla
  2 c. all-purpose flour
  1½ c. chopped apples (tart)
  ½ c. chopped pecans or walnuts

In a mixing bowl, mix the sugar, oil, and egg. In a measuring cup, mix the buttermilk, salt, soda, and vanilla. Stir this into the sugar mixture. Add the flour and stir thoroughly. Add the apples and nuts. Bake in greased muffin tin at 350° for 30 minutes.

The Lords Proprietors' Inn, Edenton, North Carolina

B. J.'s Apple Cake

    2 c. sugar
    4 c. chopped apples (pared)
    2 c. flour
    1½ tsp. baking soda
    1 tsp. salt
    2 tsp. cinnamon
    2 eggs (beaten)
    1 c. cooking oil
    2 tsp. vanilla
    1 c. nuts (optional)

Sprinkle sugar over apples in large bowl. Sift together dry ingredients twice. Add to apples. Add remaining ingredients. Stir only until mixed (by hand), not longer. Pour into greased 9" X 13" pan. Bake at 350° for 45 to 50 minutes. Serve hot or cold.

Kenwood Inn, St. Augustine, Florida

Grandma Nettie's Bread Pudding

    4 kaiser rolls or half-pound challah bread
    4 eggs (large)
    ½ c. white raisins
    1 tart apple
    1 qt. milk
    4 c. corn flakes
    ½ c. sugar
    1½ tsp. vanilla

Topping: 2 tsp. cinnamon and 3 tsp. sugar (mixed)

Soak bread in water and cover. Pour boiled water over raisins and cover. Squeeze water from bread and add slightly beaten eggs. Add sugar, milk, corn flakes, grated apple, and vanilla. Drain raisins and add. Mix together. Spread into 9″ X 13″ baking pan that has been well greased with butter or margarine. Sprinkle with topping and bake at 350° for 1 hour.

Serve warm with sweet cream. Enjoy!

A Bit o' the Apple, New York City

Cheddared Walnut Bread

2½ c. all-purpose flour
2 tbsp. sugar
2 tsp. baking powder
½ tsp. baking soda
1¼ tsp. salt
½ tsp. dry mustard
dash of cayenne
¼ c. shortening
1 c. grated sharp cheddar cheese
1 egg
1 c. buttermilk
½ tsp. Worcestershire sauce
1 c. chopped walnuts
several whole walnut pieces (for garnish)

In a bowl, sift first 7 ingredients together. Cut in the shortening. Mix in cheese with a fork. Beat egg slightly; add the buttermilk and Worcestershire sauce. Stir into dry mixture just until moistened. Add walnuts and mix through. Turn the stiff dough into a greased 8½″ X 4½″ loaf pan and smooth the top. Gently press large walnut pieces into top of loaf. Bake at 350° for 55 minutes or until it tests done. Let stand for 10 minutes, then turn out to cool on wire rack.

NOTE: Delicious toasted with butter!

Feller House, Naples, Florida

Lemon Yogurt Bread

3 c. flour
1 tsp. salt
1 tsp. baking soda
1/2 tsp. baking powder
3 eggs
1 c. oil
1¾ c. sugar
2 c. lemon yogurt
1 tbsp. lemon extract
1 c. finely chopped almonds (optional)

Sift dry ingredients; stir in nuts; set aside. Beat eggs in a large bowl; add oil and sugar; cream well. Add yogurt and extract. Spoon into 2 well-greased loaf pans, or 1 large well-greased bundt pan. Bake in preheated oven at 325° for 1 hour. (Blue Ribbon Winner at '82 Mendocino County Fair!)

The Grey Whale Inn, Fort Bragg, California

Zucchini Raisin Bread

3 eggs
1 c. sugar
2 c. grated raw zucchini (peeled)
1 c. vegetable oil
3 tsp. vanilla
3 c. flour
1 tsp. salt
1½ tsp. baking soda
1 tsp. baking powder
3 tsp. cinnamon
1 c. raisins

Beat eggs until light and foamy. Add sugar, oil, zucchini, and vanilla. Beat well. Combine flour, salt, soda, powder, and cinnamon, then add to egg mixture. Stir until well blended. Add raisins and pour into two 9" X 5" loaf pans. Bake at 350° for 1 hour. Let cool in pans for 7 minutes. Turn out on wire rack.

The Wedgwood Inn, New Hope, Pennsylvania

Easy Sausage Patties

  1 lb. bulk sausage meat
  1 lb. freshly ground lean pork
  1 tsp. garlic powder
  1 tsp. sage (or Bell's Seasoning)
  2 tsp. fresh parsley (chopped)
  1 tsp. fresh chives (chopped)

Mix ingredients thoroughly. Make patties ½ inch thick. Dust with flour. Heat skillet. (No fat required.) Brown quickly on both sides. Cover with a lid. Reduce heat and cook 8 minutes. Pour off excess fat. Turn and cook 8 minutes. Great with scrambled eggs!

Grane's Fairhaven Inn, Bath, Maine

Judy's Breakfast Ideas

Prepare your favorite hot cereal with apple juice or sweet cider instead of water. Sprinkle with cinnamon.

Keep hot cereals hot in a crock pot during a leisurely breakfast. Late arrivals can help themselves.

Heat a favorite jam or jelly with an equal amount of maple syrup and a pat of butter to create a new pancake topping.

Use leftover eggnog for a quick French toast batter.

Loch Lyme Lodge, Lyme, New Hampshire

Bed & Breakfast on the Ocean

KEY TO LISTINGS

Location: As specified, unless B&B is right in town, or its location is clear from address as stated.

No. of Rooms: Refers to the number of guest bedrooms.

Double: Rate for two people in one room.

Single: Rate for one person in a room.

Suite: Can either be two bedrooms with an adjoining bath, or a living room and bedroom with private bath.

Guest Cottage: A separate building that usually has a mini-kitchen and private bath.

pb: Private bath.

sb: Shared bath.

Breakfast: Included, unless otherwise noted.

Air-Conditioning: If "no" or "unnecessary" is stated, it means the climate rarely warrants it.

Children: If "crib" is noted after the word "welcome," this indicates that the host also has a high-chair, baby-sitters are available, and the B&B can accommodate children under the age of three.

Smoking: If permitted, this means it is allowed *somewhere* inside the house.

Social Drinking: Some hosts provide a glass of wine or sherry; others provide setups for bring-your-own.

Please enclose a self-addressed, stamped, business-size envelope when contacting Reservation Services.

Remember the difference in time zones when calling for a reservation.

4
State-by-State Listings

ALABAMA

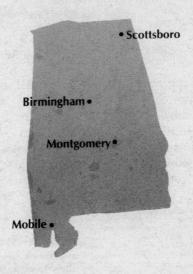

• Scottsboro

Birmingham •

Montgomery •

Mobile •

Bed & Breakfast—Birmingham
P.O. BOX 31328, BIRMINGHAM, ALABAMA 35222

Tel: (205) 591-6406
Coordinator: **Ruth Taylor**
States/Regions Covered:
  Birmingham, Franklin

Rates (Single/Double):
  Modest: **$25**   **$28**
  Average: **$28**   **$32**
  Luxury: **$32**   **$40**
Credit Cards: **No**

Birmingham is the site of the 1984 PGA Tournament and is also directly en route to the 1984 World's Fair in New Orleans. See where Bear Bryant coached, Martin Luther King led, and where the Old and New South blend in a unique way that never fails to surprise and please first-time visitors.

Kraft's Korner
90 CARLILE DRIVE, MOBILE, ALABAMA 36619

Tel: (205) 666-6819
Host(s): **Estelle and Allen Kraft**
Location: **5 miles from I-10**
No. of Rooms: **2**
No. of Private Baths: **1**
Maximum No. of Guests Sharing
  Bath: **2**
Double/pb: **$30**
Single/pb: **$25**
Double/sb: **$25**
Single/sb: **$20**

Suites: **$50 (for 4)**
Months of Operation: **All year**
Reduced Rates: **10%, seniors**
Breakfast: **Full**
Other Meals: **Available**
Air-Conditioning: **Yes**
Pets: **No**
Children: **Welcome**
Smoking: **No**
Social Drinking: **No**
Airport Pickup: **Yes**

This is a contemporary home in a residential section, where the temperate climate allows the flowers to bloom all year long. Nearby Bellingrath Gardens, called the Charm Spot of the South, is a must on your itinerary. Estelle and Allen love to spoil guests with southern hospitality. Estelle is a fine cook and the emphasis is on natural goodness and healthy dining.

Travellers' Rest
3664 KELLY LANE, MONTGOMERY, ALABAMA 36105

Tel: (205) 281-2772
Host(s): **Joan Sullivan**
Location: **2 miles from I-65**
No. of Rooms: **2**
Maximum No. of Guests Sharing
  Bath: **4**
Double/sb: **$25**
Single/sb: **$18**
Months of Operation: **All year**

Reduced Rates: **6%, seniors**
Breakfast: **Full**
Air-Conditioning: **Yes**
Pets: **Sometimes**
Children: **Welcome**
Smoking: **Permitted**
Social Drinking: **No**
Airport Pickup: **Yes**
Foreign Languages: **German**

This single-story brick home is located ten minutes from downtown. Furnished in Colonial decor, it is warm and inviting. It is minutes away from the Governor's House and the First White House of the Confederacy. Joan offers a hearty Southern breakfast, including grits.

The Brunton House
P.O. BOX 1006, 112 COLLEGE AVENUE, SCOTTSBORO, ALABAMA 35768

Tel: **(205) 259-1298**
Host(s): **Norman and Jerry Brunton**
Location: **1 mile from Route 72**
No. of Rooms: **7**
Maximum No. of Guests Sharing
  Bath: **6**
Double/sb: **$24**
Single/sb: **$19**
Months of Operation: **All year**

Reduced Rates: **10%, seniors**
Breakfast: **Full**
Air-Conditioning: **Yes**
Pets: **Sometimes**
Children: **Welcome**
Smoking: **Permitted**
Social Drinking: **Permitted**
Airport Pickup: **Yes**

This fine old home is located on historic College Avenue. At Courthouse Square, two blocks away, an old-time drugstore with its original soda fountain is a treat. Swimming, boating, and fishing are close by on the Tennessee River. Norman and Jerry invite you to watch TV in the living room, or use the kitchen for light snacks. The first six weeks in summer feature Monday Trade Day, an extravaganza of antique dealers from all over the country.

ALASKA

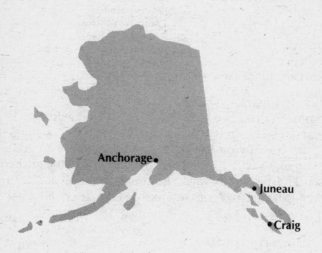

Anchorage•

•Juneau

•Craig

Stay with a Friend

BOX 173, 3605 ARCTIC BOULEVARD, ANCHORAGE, ALASKA 99503

Tel: **(907) 274-6445**	Rates (Single/Double):
Coordinator: **Irene Pettigrew**	Modest: **$30–$36** **$36–$41**
States/Regions Covered: **Anchorage,**	Average: **$36–$46** **$41–$47**
Homer	Luxury: **$51–$56** **$56–$60**
	Credit Cards: **No**

Host homes are located convenient to shopping malls, restaurants, churches, and near enough downtown to get to the starting point for tours to McKinley, Portage Glacier, or the Kenai Peninsula. If you are watching your budget, consider that a home in the downtown area is the most expensive and the peak demand for all lodging is from June 15 to September 15. If you are 60 years old or over, you may use the People Mover Bus at no charge. The depot is at 6th and G Street.

Alaska Bed and Breakfast
526 SEWARD STREET, JUNEAU, ALASKA 99801

Tel: (907) 586-2959
Coordinator: **Pat Denny**
States/Regions Covered: **Haines, Juneau, Petersburg, Sitka**

Rates (Single/Double):

	Single	Double
Modest:	$30	$40
Average:	$35	$45
Luxury:	$40	$50

Credit Cards: No

Visitors can enjoy southeast Alaskan hospitality in an historic inn, a log cabin in the woods, a modern home overlooking the water, or an old Indian village. For the adventuresome, there's an old homesteader's cabin on the banks of Lynn Canal with a striking view of the Chilkat Mountains; you'll be met at the end of the road by your host, who will take you home in his boat and cook a gourmet dinner of freshly caught king crab or salmon.

Karta Inn
P.O. BOX 114, CRAIG, ALASKA 99921

Tel: **Marine Phone: WYE 7600 Darmi J II Ratz Mt.**
Host(s): **Karen and David Gubser**
Location: **40 miles from Ketchikan**
No. of Rooms: **2**
No. of Private Baths: **2**
Suites: **$75**
Months of Operation: **All year**
Reduced Rates: **10%, non-smokers; $37.50, children under 16**

Breakfast: **Full**
Other Meals: **Included**
Air-Conditioning: **Unnecessary**
Pets: **Sometimes**
Children: **Welcome**
Smoking: **Permitted**
Social Drinking: **Permitted**
Airport Pickup: **Yes**
Foreign Languages: **German**

If you want to get away from everything and enjoy superb home cooking, ride the float plane taxi to the eastern shore of Prince of Wales Island ($76 round-trip fare) and stay with Dave and Karen. The rate of $75 per person per day includes three meals, the use of the skiff and motor boat for halibut and king salmon fishing, and the company of fourth generation Alaskans. There are several hiking trails and uninhabited beaches for you to explore.

ARIZONA

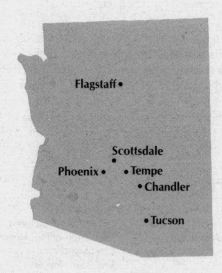

Bed & Breakfast in Arizona
8433 N. BLACK CANYON, SUITE 160, PHOENIX, ARIZONA 85021

Tel: **(602) 995-2831**
Coordinator: **Bessie Thompson
Lipinski**
States/Regions Covered: **Arizona
(statewide)**

Rates (Single/Double):
  Modest: **$15–$20**   **$25–$30**
  Average: **$25–$30**   **$35–$40**
  Luxury: **$35–$60**   **$45–$75**
Credit Cards: **MC, VISA**

Bessie offers you local color and local customs explained by friendly hosts. Arizona is a spectacular state with every kind of scenery and climate you can imagine. This is the land of the spellbinding Grand Canyon, Indian and Mexican cultures, cowboys and cattle ranches, gold mines, ghost towns, majestic mountains, and awesome deserts. Plan to spend several days to truly get the most out of your visit.

Mi Casa Su Casa Bed & Breakfast
1456 N. SCOTTSDALE ROAD, SUITE 110, TEMPE, ARIZONA 85281

Tel: **(602) 990-0682**
Coordinator: **Ruth T. Young**
States/Regions Covered: **Apache Junction, Benson, Flagstaff, Mesa, Nogales, Payson, Paradise Valley, Phoenix, Prescott, Scottsdale, Sedona, Sun City, Tucson**

Rates (Single/Double):
Modest:	**$20**	**$25**
Average:	**$25**	**$35**
Luxury:	**$50**	**$50–$110**

Credit Cards: **MC, VISA**

Ruth's guest houses are located statewide; the above is only a partial listing. They are located in cities, suburbs, and rural settings, all of which are within easy driving range of canyons, national parks, Indian country, Colorado River gem country, the Mexican border area, historic mining towns, and water recreation areas.

Cone's Tourist Home
2804 WEST WARNER, CHANDLER, ARIZONA 85224

Tel: **(602) 839-0369**
Host(s): **Howard and Beverly Cone**
Location: **15 miles southeast of Phoenix**
No. of Rooms: **2**
No. of Private Baths: **1**
Maximum No. of Guests Sharing Bath: **2**
Double/pb: **$26**
Single/pb: **$26**
Double/sb: **$22**
Single/sb: **$22**
Months of Operation: **October 1 to May 31**
Reduced Rates: **Weekly**
Breakfast: **Continental**
Air-Conditioning: **Yes**
Pets: **Welcome**
Children: **Welcome**
Smoking: **Permitted**
Social Drinking: **Permitted**

This beautiful home is situated on two acres in the Arizona countryside. Howard and Beverly offer horseback riding for experienced riders, a large parlor for relaxing, a recreation room with Ping-Pong and pool tables, and kitchen and barbecue facilities. It is three miles from fine restaurants and eight miles from Arizona State University for cultural events; Phoenix is close too.

Rainbow Ranch
2860 NORTH FREMONT, FLAGSTAFF, ARIZONA 86001

Tel: **(602) 774-3724**
Host(s): **Miriam Pederson**
Location: **¼ mile from Highway 180**
No. of Rooms: **3**
Maximum No. of Guests Sharing
  Bath: **6**
Double/sb: **$40**
Single/sb: **$20**
Months of Operation: **All year**

Reduced Rates: **No**
Breakfast: **Full**
Air-Conditioning: **Unnecessary**
Pets: **Sometimes**
Children: **Welcome (crib)**
Smoking: **Permitted**
Social Drinking: **Permitted**
Airport Pickup: **Yes**
Foreign Languages: **French (limited)**

Miriam's 90-year-old farmhouse stands on seven acres, is comfortably furnished with lovely antiques, and is accented with Miriam's good humor. After a hearty breakfast featuring home-grown eggs and herbs, plus homemade breads and jams, you'll be ready to explore the Grand Canyon (75 miles away), Oak Creek Canyon, Sunset Crater, or the Navajo and Hopi Indian reservations. There's something doing in every season, including hiking and skiing; the tennis court is a few steps from the door. This is Southwestern hospitality at its finest, and you will discover special touches that convert a guest into an instant friend.

Bed & Breakfast Scottsdale—Carefree
6502 NORTH 83RD STREET AND LINCOLN DRIVE, SCOTTSDALE, ARIZONA 85253

Tel: (602) 998-7044
Host(s): Lois O'Grady
Location: 5 miles north of Scottsdale (Old Town)
No. of Rooms: 3
No. of Private Baths: 1
Maximum No. of Guests Sharing Bath: 2
Single/sb: $30
Suites: $50 (for 2)

Months of Operation: November to May
Reduced Rates: 10%, 7 days or more
Breakfast: Continental
Air-Conditioning: Yes
Pets: No
Children: Welcome, school-age
Smoking: No
Social Drinking: No

This special home typifies Southwestern style, accented with wicker, plants, a fireplace for chilly times, and a breakfast area that overlooks the palm-shaded pool and patio. Located close to shops, galleries, Paolo Soleri's "City of the Future," and Indian reservations. Lois is an artist, and she will arrange special tours to suit your interests, from jeeping to archeological digs. She'll be happy to serve wine and cheese before you dine at the fine restaurants in the area.

The Bird's Nest
6201 N. PIEDRA, SECA, TUCSON, ARIZONA 85718

Tel: (602) 299-9164
Host(s): Vic and Betty Hanson
Location: 10 miles from I-10
No. of Rooms: 1
No. of Private Baths: 1
Double/pb: $35
Single/pb: $35
Months of Operation: January 1 to May 31; September 1 to November 30

Reduced Rates: No
Breakfast: Continental
Air-Conditioning: Yes
Pets: No
Children: No
Smoking: No
Social Drinking: Permitted

Located in the foothills of the Catalina Mountains, this one-story adobe home has a patio. It's furnished in a pleasant blend of colonial and Southwestern styles, decorated with lovely plants and original art, and it features beautiful views. Vic and Betty enjoy people and will be happy to help you with your touring plans. They'll also identify the large variety of birds that visit their backyard.

Myers' Blue Corn House
4215 EAST KILMER, TUCSON, ARIZONA 85711

Tel: (602) 327-4663
Host(s): **Barbara and Vern Myers**
Location: **5 miles from I-10**
No. of Rooms: **2**
Maximum No. of Guests Sharing
  Bath: **4**
Double/sb: **$30**
Single/sb: **$20**
Months of Operation: **All year**

Reduced Rates: **7th night free; 20%,**
  seniors (minimum 2 nights); families
Breakfast: **Full**
Air-Conditioning: **No**
Pets: **Sometimes**
Children: **Welcome (crib)**
Smoking: **No**
Social Drinking: **Permitted**
Airport Pickup: **Yes**

Located on a quiet residential street, it's convenient to downtown Tucson and the University of Arizona via city buses. The family room, decorated with Indian arts and crafts, and filled with history books, has bumper pool and TV. Close to seasonal recreation, it is also handy for tours of Old Tucson, Saguaro National Monument, Kitt Peak Observatory, and Nogales, Mexico. Barbara and Vern will allow you to use the kitchen for light snacks, and to use the washing machine, dryer, and barbecue.

KEY TO LISTINGS

Location: As specified, unless B&B is right in town, or its location is clear from address as stated.
No. of Rooms: Refers to the number of guest bedrooms.
Double: Rate for two people in one room.
Single: Rate for one person in a room.
Suite: Can either be two bedrooms with an adjoining bath, or a living room and bedroom with private bath.
Guest Cottage: A separate building that usually has a mini-kitchen and private bath.
pb: Private bath.
sb: Shared bath.
Breakfast: Included, unless otherwise noted.
Air-Conditioning: If "no" or "unnecessary" is stated, it means the climate rarely warrants it.
Children: If "crib" is noted after the word "welcome," this indicates that the host also has a high-chair, baby-sitters are available, and the B&B can accommodate children under the age of three.
Smoking: If permitted, this means it is allowed *somewhere* inside the house.
Social Drinking: Some hosts provide a glass of wine or sherry; others provide setups for bring-your-own.

Please enclose a self-addressed, stamped, business-size envelope when contacting Reservation Services.

Remember the difference in time zones when calling for a reservation.

ARKANSAS

• Eureka Springs

• Little Rock
• Hot Springs

Devon Cottage
26 EUREKA STREET, EUREKA SPRINGS, ARKANSAS 72632

Tel: (501) 253-9169
Host(s): **Laura and Ed Cantrell**
No. of Rooms: **2**
No. of Private Baths: **1**
Maximum No. of Guests Sharing
  Bath: **4**
Double/pb: **$38**
Single/pb: **$32**
Double/sb: **$38**
Single/sb: **$32**

Months of Operation: **All year**
Reduced Rates: **No**
Breakfast: **Full**
Air-Conditioning: **Yes**
Pets: **Sometimes**
Children: **Welcome**
Smoking: **Permitted**
Social Drinking: **Permitted**
Foreign Languages: **Spanish, French**

This Edwardian frame cottage, just a block from the historic downtown, is decorated with antiques and graced with wicker, plants, brass, and art. Laura is a psychotherapist and craftsperson; Ed is an attorney active in amateur theatricals; they look

45

forward to sharing the delights of their area with you. Surrounded by the beautiful Ozarks, there are many lakes and rivers where fishing and bird-watching are fun to do.

Harvest House
104 WALL STREET, EUREKA SPRINGS, ARKANSAS 72632

Tel: **(501) 253-9363**	Breakfast: **Full**
Host(s): **Margaret and Jim Conner**	Air-Conditioning: **Yes**
No. of Rooms: **2**	Pets: **Sometimes**
No. of Private Baths: **2**	Children: **Welcome**
Double/pb: **$35**	Smoking: **Yes**
Months of Operation: **All year**	Social Drinking: **Permitted**
Reduced Rates: **No**	

This green and white Victorian house is furnished with antiques, collectibles, and family favorites. The guest rooms are downstairs and have private entrances. Located in the Ozark Mountains, the scenery is lovely. Homemade surprise snacks are always available. Margaret and Jim are wonderful hosts and will do everything possible to make your stay pleasant.

Williams House Bed & Breakfast Inn
420 QUAPAW, HOT SPRINGS, ARKANSAS 71901

Tel: **(501) 624-4275**	Suites: **$60–$65**
Host(s): **Mary and Gary Riley**	Guest Cottage: **$75 sleeps 5**
Location: **50 miles southwest of Little Rock**	Months of Operation: **All year**
	Reduced Rates: **$5, weekly; 10%, seniors**
No. of Rooms: **5**	
No. of Private Baths: **3**	Breakfast: **Full**
Maximum No. of Guests Sharing Bath: **4**	Air-Conditioning: **Yes**
	Pets: **No**
Double/pb: **$50–$65**	Children: **Welcome, over 6**
Single/pb: **$40–$60**	Smoking: **Permitted**
Double/sb: **$40–$45**	Social Drinking: **Permitted**
Single/sb: **$35–$40**	Airport Pickup: **Yes**

This Victorian mansion, with its stained glass and beveled glass windows, is a nationally registered landmark. The atmosphere is friendly and intimate, and the marble fireplace and grand piano invite congeniality. There's a choice of menu at breakfast which may include quiche, toast amandine, or exotic egg dishes. Gary and Mary will spoil you with special iced tea, snacks, and mineral

spring water. Health experts around the world recognize the benefits of the hot mineral baths in Hot Springs National Park. The inn is within walking distance of Bath House Row.

Davis Bed & Breakfast
5705 N. HILLS BOULEVARD, NORTH LITTLE ROCK, ARKANSAS 72116

Tel: **(501) 835-2083**	Reduced Rates: **No**
Host(s): **Mick and Andrea Davis**	Breakfast: **Continental**
Location: **1 mile from I-30**	Air-Conditioning: **Yes**
No. of Rooms: **2**	Pets: **No**
Maximum No. of Guests Sharing Bath: **4**	Children: **Welcome**
	Smoking: **No**
Double/sb: **$30**	Social Drinking: **Permitted**
Single/sb: **$20**	Airport Pickup: **Yes**
Months of Operation: **All year**	Foreign Languages: **German**

Mick and Andrea are world travelers and love to meet people. Their home is spacious and modern, with a circular rock fireplace in the center of the great room. Located on a quiet street, it is close to shops and restaurants. Less than an hour away are many recreational lakes and the town of Hot Springs, famous for its hot mineral springs and horse racing. Guests are welcome to use the kitchen and laundry facilities.

CALIFORNIA

Eureka● ●Murphys

Westport●
　　　● Fort Bragg
Elk●
　　Oroville● Grass Valley
Healdsburg●　　●　●Sutter Creek
Cloverdale ●　　●Sacramento
Pt. Reyes●　　●Ione

San Francisco ● Kensington
Santa Cruz●　●San Jose

Pebble Beach●
　　　　●Carmel
San Simeon●
San Luis Obispo●　●Cambria ●Orosi
Arroyo Grande●　●Lancaster
Santa Barbara ●　Montecito

Seal Beach　Los Angeles●　● Santa Ana
Newport Beach　Laguna Beach●
　　　San Clemente●　● Julian
　　　　　●La Jolla
San Diego●

GOLD COUNTRY

The Heirloom

P.O. BOX 322, 214 SHAKLEY LANE, IONE, CALIFORNIA 95640

Tel: **(209) 274-4468**	Months of Operation: **All year**
Host(s): **Melisande Hubbs and Patricia Cross**	Reduced Rates: **No**
	Breakfast: **Full**
Location: **35 miles east of Sacramento**	Air-Conditioning: **Some**
No. of Rooms: **5**	Pets: **No**
No. of Private Baths: **2**	Children: **Welcome, over 12**
Maximum No. of Guests Sharing Bath: **6**	Smoking: **Permitted**
Double/pb: **$65**	Social Drinking: **Permitted**
Double/sb: **$45**	Airport Pickup: **Yes**
Guest Cottage: **$55–$75 sleeps 2 to 3**	Foreign Languages: **Portuguese**

48

Nestled in the Sierra foothills yet close to the historic gold mines, wineries, antique shops, and museums, this 1863 mansion, with its lovely balconies and fireplaces, is a classic example of antebellum architecture. It is furnished with a comfortable combination of family treasures and period pieces. Patricia and Melisande's hearty breakfast includes such delights as quiche, crepes, soufflé, and fresh fruits. Afternoon refreshments are always offered.

Dunbar House
271 JONES STREET, P.O. BOX 1375, MURPHYS, CALIFORNIA 95247

Tel: **(209) 728-2897**
Host(s): **John and Barbara Carr**
Location: **55 miles east of Stockton**
No. of Rooms: **5**
Maximum No. of Guests Sharing
  Bath: **6**
Double/sb: **$50**
Single/sb: **$45**
Suites: **$55**
Months of Operation: **All year**

Reduced Rates: **15%, winter; 15%, midweek**
Breakfast: **Continental**
Air-Conditioning: **Yes**
Pets: **No**
Children: **Welcome, over two**
Smoking: **No**
Social Drinking: **Permitted**
Foreign Languages: **Portuguese**

This 19th-century Victorian house is located in the heart of one of the best-preserved Gold Rush towns. Guests are greeted with sherry and offered rooms with lace curtains, fresh flowers, pillow shams, and bed ruffles. A generous breakfast is served in the fireplaced dining room or on the sunny porch. Nearby attractions include Mercer Caverns and Calveras Big Trees State Park.

The Hanford House
P.O. BOX 847, 3 HANFORD STREET, SUTTER CREEK, CALIFORNIA 95685

Tel: **(209) 267-0747**
Host(s): **Ronald Van Anda**
Location: **35 miles east of Sacramento on Highway 49**
No. of Rooms: **9**
No. of Private Baths: **9**
Double/pb: **$45–$70**
Suites: **$100**
Months of Operation: **All year**
Reduced Rates: **10%, Sunday to Thursday (except holidays)**

Breakfast: **Continental**
Credit Cards: **MC, VISA**
Air-Conditioning: **Yes**
Pets: **No**
Children: **Welcome, over 12**
Smoking: **Permitted**
Social Drinking: **Permitted**
Airport Pickup: **Yes**

This charming home is elegant yet warm and comfortable. Ron is an antique dealer, and the furnishings reflect the graciousness of long-ago eras although the queen-size beds are new. A rooftop redwood deck provides breathtaking views of the countryside and the scenic Gold Rush town where you can still pan for gold in the streams. A complimentary bottle of wine is part of Ron's way of welcoming his guests. There is a barrier-free entrance and a special guest room for the handicapped.

LOS ANGELES AREA

Bed & Breakfast of Los Angeles
32074 WATERSIDE LANE, WESTLAKE VILLAGE, CALIFORNIA 91361

Tel: **(213) 889-8870 or 889-7235**	Rates: (Single/Double):
Coordinator: **Peg Marshall and Angie Kobabe**	Modest: **$24** **$30**
	Average: **$24** **$45**
States/Regions Covered: **30 communities in greater Los Angeles**	Luxury: **$42** **$75**
	Credit Cards: **No**

Peg and Angie can provide accommodations for you, from Ventura in the north to Laguna Beach in the south. There's a guest house in Hollywood, a luxury suite in Beverly Hills, and a contemporary loft in Balboa, to name a few choices. Peg and Angie publish a directory, so you can make your reservation directly. Please send a self-addressed envelope with 40 cents postage. Note that prices during the 1984 Olympics will range from $35 to $125 per couple for homes convenient to the Olympic sites.

California Houseguests International
6051 LINDLEY AVENUE, #6, TARZANA, CALIFORNIA 91356

Tel: **(213) 344-7878**	Rates: (Single/Double):
Coordinator: **Trudi Alexy**	Modest: **$35–$45** **$40–$50**
States/Regions Covered: **Greater Los Angeles Area, Agoura, the beach cities, San Diego, San Francisco, Ventura**	Average: **$45–$55** **$50–$60**
	Luxury: **$55–$65** **$60–$70**
	Credit Cards: **No**
	Minimum Stay: **2 days**

This is a membership organization with a five-dollar annual fee per person. Trudi has a huge roster of homes in preparation for the 1984 Olympics; traditional bed & breakfast, as well as absentee host homes, are available. Prices during the Olympics range from $70 for two for B&B to $1,000 per night for a large house that sleeps eight and has all the amenities, including a full staff to cater to your needs.

Brown's Guest House
1105 EAST NORWOOD PLACE, ALHAMBRA, CALIFORNIA 91801

Tel: **(213) 281-8853**
Host(s): **Opal Brown**
Location: **8 miles east of Los Angeles**
No. of Rooms: **1**
No. of Baths: **1**
Double/pb: **$30**
Single/pb: **$25**
Months of Operation: **All year**

Reduced Rates: **No**
Breakfast: **Continental**
Air-Conditioning: **Yes**
Pets: **No**
Children: **No**
Smoking: **No**
Social Drinking: **Permitted**

Opal's modern stucco home is in a residential area just 20 minutes from Los Angeles. The Pasadena Rosebowl is five miles away, and many restaurants are within walking distance. The comfortable guest room has a private entrance. Prices will be $10 higher during the summer Olympics only.

Shroff House
1114 PARK AVENUE, GLENDALE, CALIFORNIA 91205

Tel: **(213) 507-0774**
Host(s): **Spencer and Gerry Shroff**
Location: **10 miles northeast of downtown Los Angeles**
No. of Rooms: **3**
No. of Private Baths: **1**
Maximum No. of Guests Sharing Bath: **5**
Double/pb: **$40**
Single/pb: **$35**
Double/sb: **$25–$35**

Single/sb: **$20–$30**
Months of Operation: **All year**
Reduced Rates: **7th day free**
Breakfast: **Continental**
Air-Conditioning: **No**
Pets: **No**
Children: **Welcome**
Smoking: **Yes**
Social Drinking: **Permitted**
Airport Pickup: **Yes**

A Spanish-style stucco house with a red tile roof, it is furnished with 1930s motifs. It is comfortable in all seasons, being centrally heated and air-cooled. You are welcome to relax on the shaded patio or in the gazebo. It is convenient to the movie studio tours, art galleries, ethnic restaurants, the Pasadena Rose Bowl (site of the 1984 Olympic soccer games), as well as to Forest Lawn

The Shroffs'

Memorial Park. Spencer and Gerry are a semiretired couple and love visiting with their guests.

Avon Bed & Breakfast
1553 AVON TERRACE, LOS ANGELES, CALIFORNIA 90026

Tel: **(213) 663-4368**
Host(s): **Eileen Searson**
Location: **2 miles from Hollywood Freeway**
No. of Rooms: **2**
No. of Private Baths: **1**
Maximum No. of Guests Sharing Bath: **2**
Double/pb: **$30**
Double/sb: **$30**

Months of Operation: **All year**
Reduced Rates: **No**
Breakfast: **Full**
Air-Conditioning: **Yes**
Pets: **Welcome**
Children: **Welcome**
Smoking: **Permitted**
Social Drinking: **Permitted**
Airport Pickup: **Yes**

Eileen is a costume designer who likes nothing better than taking her houseguests on tours of "tinsel town" to meet the celebrities she knows. Her Swiss-chalet-style home has leaded glass windows, red flocked wallpaper, and is decorated with lovely antiques. It's 15 minutes to Universal Studios, Grauman's Chinese Theater, and the Civic Center.

Salisbury House

2273 WEST 20TH STREET, LOS ANGELES, CALIFORNIA 90018

Tel: **(213) 737-7817**
Host(s): **Kathleen Salisbury and Bill Washington**
Location: **3 miles west of downtown, 1 block from Freeway 10**
No. of Rooms: **5**
No. of Private Baths: **3**
Maximum No. of Guests Sharing Bath: **4**
Double/pb: **$60**
Single/pb: **$55**
Double/sb: **$50**

Single/sb: **$45**
Suites: **$65**
Months of Operation: **All year**
Reduced Rates: **No**
Breakfast: **Full**
Air-Conditioning: **Some**
Pets: **Sometimes**
Children: **Welcome, over 10**
Smoking: **Permitted**
Social Drinking: **Permitted**
Airport Pickup: **Yes**

Experience antique charm and ultimate luxury in this spacious, handcrafted home. Enjoy a cozy fire in the wood-beamed living room or a complimentary glass of sherry on the porch. Kathleen is a professional decorator and gourmet cook. Breakfast on exotic casseroles, crab quiche, or peach cobbler as well as homemade preserves and breads. It's minutes to the beaches and movie studios. Only 10 miles to C.C.L.A. (the Olympic site), rates will be substantially higher from July 1 to August 31, 1984, with a one-week minimum stay required.

Casa Larronde

P.O. BOX 86, MALIBU, CALIFORNIA 90265

Tel: **(213) 456-9333**
Host(s): **Jim and Charlou Larronde**
Location: **45 miles northwest of Los Angeles**
No. of Rooms: **3**
No. of Baths: **3**
Double/pb: **$75**
Single/pb: **$60**

Months of Operation: **All year**
Reduced Rates: **No**
Breakfast: **Full**
Air-Conditioning: **Unnecessary**
Pets: **Sometimes**
Children: **Welcome**
Smoking: **Permitted**
Social Drinking: **Permitted**

All the guest rooms have color TV, but if you walk down the beach you may get to see the stars live; Johnny Carson, Rich Little, Ann Margret, and Flip Wilson are the neighborhood people here on Millionaires' Row. This house is 4,000 square feet of spectacular living space. It has floor-to-ceiling glass, ocean decks, a private beach, and a planter that's two stories high. Jim and Charlou, world travelers, enjoy entertaining, and their gourmet breakfast ranges from Scotch eggs to French toast made with Portuguese sweet bread. Champagne, cocktails, and snacks are complimentary refreshments.

Hideaway House
8441 MELVIN AVENUE, NORTHRIDGE, CALIFORNIA 91324

Tel: **(213) 349-5421**
Host(s): **Dean and Dorothy Dennis**
Location: **20 miles northwest of Los Angeles**
No. of Rooms: **2**
No. of Private Baths: **1**
Maximum No. of Guests Sharing Bath: **2**
Double/pb: **$50**
Single/pb: **$35**
Double/sb: **$45**
Single/sb: **$30**

Months of Operation: **All year**
Reduced Rates: **No**
Breakfast: **Full**
Other Meals: **Available**
Air-Conditioning: **Yes**
Pets: **No**
Children: **Welcome, over 10**
Smoking: **Permitted**
Social Drinking: **Permitted**
Airport Pickup: **Yes**

Located in a beautiful Los Angeles suburb, this secluded country estate in the San Fernando Valley is a good base for exploring southern California. It's 30 minutes to the beach and 50 minutes to Disneyland. Dean and Dorothy welcome you to their art- and antique-filled home and will provide local guide service by prior arrangement.

By-the-Sea
4273 PALOS VERDES DRIVE SOUTH, RANCHO PALOS VERDES, CALIFORNIA 90274

Tel: **(213) 377-2113**
Host(s): **Ruth and Earl Exley**
Location: **5 miles southwest of Los Angeles**
No. of Rooms: **2**
No. of Private Baths: **2**
Double/pb: **$50**
Single/pb: **$35**
Months of Operation: **All year**
Reduced Rates: **20%, November 1 to May 1; 10%, seniors**

Breakfast: **Full**
Other Meals: **Available**
Air-Conditioning: **Unnecessary**
Pets: **Sometimes**
Children: **Welcome**
Smoking: **Yes**
Social Drinking: **Permitted**
Airport Pickup: **Yes**

This gracious ranch-style home in suburban Los Angeles has an unobstructed ocean view. Ruth and Earl belong to a private beach club across the road, and you can use the facilities there. It is close to Marineland, Disneyland, and Hollywood. Ruth's breakfast specialties include honey-baked ham, French toast, or quiche. Your hosts offer you *hors d'oeuvres* with other pre-dinner refreshments.

Seal Beach Inn
212 5TH STREET, SEAL BEACH, CALIFORNIA 90740

Tel: **(213) 493-2416**
Host(s): **Dr. and Mrs. Jack Bettenhausen**
Location: **1 block from Highway 101**
No. of Rooms: **24**
No. of Private Baths: **24**
Double/pb: **$60–$90**
Single/pb: **$60–$90**
Suites: **$90**
Months of Operation: **All year**
Reduced Rates: **15%, weekly (except July and August); 10%, seniors**
Breakfast: **Continental**
Credit Cards: **AMEX, MC, VISA**
Air-Conditioning: **Unnecessary**
Pets: **No**
Children: **Welcome, over 12**
Smoking: **Permitted**
Social Drinking: **Permitted**
Airport Pickup: **Yes**

At first glance you'll think you're at a French Mediterranean *auberge*. The canopies, antique street lamps, ornate fences, and profusion of flowers have romanced travelers for over 60 years. It is beautifully appointed with antiques and comfortable furnishings. The beach is 300 yards away, and there's a pool, if you prefer. Disneyland is close by.

A Home Away from Home
4724½ FORMAN LANE, TOLUCA LAKE, CALIFORNIA 91602

Tel: **(213) 769-5946 or 486-2307**
Host(s): **Sherry Silva**
Location: **North Hollywood**
No. of Rooms: **2**
No. of Private Baths: **1**
Maximum No. of Guests Sharing Bath: **2**
Double/pb: **$40**
Single/pb: **$35**
Double/sb: **$40**
Single/sb: **$35**
Months of Operation: **All year**
Reduced Rates: **No**
Breakfast: **Continental**
Air-Conditioning: **Yes**
Pets: **No**
Children: **Welcome**
Smoking: **Permitted**
Social Drinking: **Permitted**

Sherry's large home is surrounded by lovely landscaping on half an acre. There's a large patio for relaxing and a swimming pool to enjoy. It's conveniently located to all the TV studios, movie studios, the Universal Amphitheater, Magic Mountain, and the universities of Los Angeles and of Southern California. Reserve early for the Olympics.

Hazel's Habitat
2440 CABRILLO AVENUE, TORRANCE, CALIFORNIA 90501

Tel: **(213) 328-2375**
Host(s): **Hazel Virginia Gilliland**
Location: **22 miles south of Los Angeles**
No. of Rooms: **1**
No. of Baths: **1**
Maximum No. of Guests Sharing Bath: **n/a**
Double/pb: **$30–$40**

Single/pb: **$20–$25**
Months of Operation: **All year**
Reduced Rates: **7th night free**
Breakfast: **Continental**
Air-Conditioning: **No**
Pets: **Sometimes**
Children: **Welcome**
Smoking: **No**
Social Drinking: **No**

You can relax and enjoy the quiet of the suburbs while you are only a short distance from Marineland, Catalina Island, and the Olympics. The beach is 10 minutes away. The local shopping center is the largest in the U.S., so don't worry if you forgot your sunglasses. Hazel welcomes married couples and women year-round.

Noone Guest House
2755 SONOMA STREET, TORRANCE, CALIFORNIA 90503

Tel: **(213) 328-1837**
Host(s): **Betty and Bob Noone**
Location: **15 miles northeast of Los Angeles**
No. of Rooms: **1**
No. of Private Baths: **1**
Guest Cottage: **$30 sleeps 2**
Months of Operation: **All year**

Reduced Rates: **No**
Breakfast: **Continental**
Air-Conditioning: **No**
Pets: **Sometimes**
Children: **Welcome**
Smoking: **Permitted**
Social Drinking: **Permitted**
Airport Pickup: **Yes**

It's only 10 miles from this comfortable guest cottage to the 1984 Olympic Stadium. It has a bedroom, bath, kitchen, patio, and laundry facilities, but the special plus is the warm hospitality offered by Betty and Bob. They'll be pleased to direct you to Marineland, Disneyland, Knott's Berry Farm, or the beach—all close to "home."

The Venice Beach House
15 THIRTIETH AVENUE, VENICE, CALIFORNIA 90291

Tel: **(213) 823-1966**
Host(s): **Elaine Burke**
Location: **5 miles from I-10, 405 Freeway**
No. of Rooms: **8**
No. of Private Baths: **4**
Maximum No. of Guests Sharing Bath: **8**
Double/pb: **$55–$100**
Double/sb: **$50–$60**
Suites: **$125**

Months of Operation: **All year**
Reduced Rates: **20%, weekly; 25%, monthly; 15%, Monday to Thursday**
Breakfast: **Continental**
Credit Cards: **AMEX, MC, VISA**
Air-Conditioning: **No**
Pets: **No**
Children: **No**
Smoking: **No**
Social Drinking: **Permitted**
Airport Pickup: **Yes**

This landmark house was built in 1911 and has been carefully restored to reflect the charming atmosphere of that era. Some of the rooms have fireplaces, balconies, or Jacuzzi tubs, and all are attractively furnished with antiques. It's half a block to the beach, two miles to the marina, and the house is close to restaurants, museums, and shops.

Hendrick Inn
2124 E. MERCED AVENUE, WEST COVINA, CALIFORNIA 91791

Tel: **(213) 919-2125**
Host(s): **Mary and George Hendrick**
Location: **20 miles east of Los Angeles**
No. of Rooms: **4**
No. of Private Baths: **3**
Maximum No. of Guests Sharing Bath: **2**
Double/pb: **$30–$35**
Single/pb: **$25**
Double/sb: **$30–$35**
Single/sb: **$25**

Suites: **$40**
Months of Operation: **All year**
Reduced Rates: **No**
Breakfast: **Full**
Other Meals: **Available**
Air-Conditioning: **Yes**
Pets: **No**
Children: **Welcome, over 8**
Smoking: **Permitted**
Social Drinking: **Permitted**
Foreign Languages: **Spanish**

This lovely home is one hour from the mountains, seashore, and desert. It's less than an hour to Disneyland or the busy streets of downtown Los Angeles. The living rooms of this sprawling ranch-style house contain comfortable sitting areas and fireplaces where you may share a nightcap with your hospitable hosts. You will surely enjoy the lovely backyard swimming pool and the Jacuzzi after a day of touring.

MENDOCINO AREA

Bed & Breakfast Exchange
P.O. BOX 88, ST. HELENA, CALIFORNIA 94574

Tel: (707) 963-7756	Rates (Single/Double):
Coordinator: **Andee Beresini**	Modest: **$25** **$35**
States/Regions Covered: **Napa and**	Average: **$40** **$65**
Sonoma counties, Calistoga,	Luxury: **$75** **$85–$150**
Cloverdale, Healdsburg, Napa,	Credit Cards: **No**
Rutherford, Santa Rosa	

The homes on Andee's roster are all located convenient to the wineries and vineyards that have made this section of the state known as Wine Country. Wine-tasting tours are popular pastimes. The more expensive accommodations are on fabulous estates with pools, spas, and special services.

The Old Crocker Inn
26532 RIVER ROAD, CLOVERDALE, CALIFORNIA 95425

Tel: **(707) 894-3911**	Breakfast: **Full**
Host(s): **Ed and Deborah Lyons**	Credit Cards: **MC, VISA**
Location: **40 miles north of Santa Rosa**	Air-Conditioning: **No**
No. of Rooms: **10**	Pets: **No**
No. of Private Baths: **10**	Children: **Welcome**
Double/pb: **$50–$70**	Smoking: **Permitted**
Singe/pb: **$50–$70**	Social Drinking: **Permitted**
Months of Operation: **All year**	Airport Pickup: **Yes**
Reduced Rates: **No**	Foreign Languages: **German**

Situated on five acres in the Asti Hills of Sonoma Wine Country, this 1897 lodge consists of four redwood and brick buildings. Furnished with rural antiques, the guest rooms open directly on lush, landscaped gardens. Breakfast may be enjoyed on the spacious veranda or at poolside. After visiting the nearby wineries or enjoying the Russian River, you're invited to relax and enjoy the romantic fireplaces and complimentary wine and cheese.

Elk Cove Inn
6300 SOUTH HIGHWAY ONE, P.O. BOX 367, ELK, CALIFORNIA 95432

Tel: **(707) 877-3321**
Host(s): **Hildrun-Uta Triebess**
Location: **On Highway 1**
No. of Rooms: **9**
No. of Private Baths: **7**
Maximum No. of Guests Sharing
   Bath: **4**
Double/pb: **$52–$78**
Single/pb: **$46**
Double/sb: **$46–$48**
Single/sb: **$30**
Months of Operation: **All year**

Reduced Rates: **No**
Breakfast: **Full**
Other Meals: **Available weekends**
Credit Cards: **MC, VISA**
Air-Conditioning: **Unnecessary**
Pets: **No**
Children: **Welcome, over 8**
Smoking: **Permitted**
Social Drinking: **Permitted**
Airport Pickup: **Yes**
Foreign Languages: **French, Italian,
   German, Spanish**

This 1883 Victorian inn is attractively furnished, and the beds have the freshness of sun-dried linens. Cut flowers and hand-made accessories add to the loveliness. There's access to a driftwood beach as well as another secluded beach to explore. Spectacular views and beautiful gardens make this a romantic spot. On weekends and holidays, Hildrun-Ute includes French and German gourmet dinners, which she prepares, as well as breakfast. Weekend rates increase to between $126 and $139 (private bath) and $98 to $106 (shared bath).

Carter House Inn

1033 THIRD STREET, EUREKA, CALIFORNIA 95501

Tel: **(707) 445-1390**
Host(s): **Mark and Christi Carter**
No. of Rooms: **3**
No. of Private Baths: **1**
Maximum No. of Guests Sharing
  Bath: **4**
Single/pb: **$65**
Double/sb: **$65**
Single/sb: **$55**
Months of Operation: **All year**

Reduced Rates: **No**
Breakfast: **Full**
Credit Cards: **AMEX, MC, VISA**
Air-Conditioning: **Unnecessary**
Pets: **No**
Children: **Welcome, over 8**
Smoking: **Permitted**
Social Drinking: **Permitted**
Airport Pickup: **Yes**
Foreign Languages: **Spanish**

In 1982, this Victorian mansion was precisely reproduced from architectural plans drawn in 1884. The exterior is redwood, and the interior is done in redwood and oak. All trims and moldings are handmade and the chimneys rise to 50 feet. The rooms, each with a view, are furnished with authentic antiques, down comforters, Oriental rugs, original art, and fresh flowers. Christi and Mark want to pamper you with breakfasts that often include eggs Benedict or unusual pastries, *hors d'oeuvres* and complimentary wine before dinner, cookies and cordials before bedtime, and (by special arrangement with Mark) limousine service in his 1958 Bentley. Wow!

Colonial Inn

P.O. BOX 565, 533 EAST FIR STREET, FORT BRAGG, CALIFORNIA 95437

Tel: (707) 964-9979
Host(s): **Catherine and Donald Markham**
Location: **150 miles north of San Francisco**
No. of Rooms: **8**
No. of Private Baths: **8**
Double/pb: **$40–$48**
Single/pb: **$30–$37**

Months of Operation: **All year**
Reduced Rates: **No**
Breakfast: **No**
Air-Conditioning: **Unnecessary**
Pets: **No**
Children: **Welcome**
Smoking: **Permitted**
Social Drinking: **Permitted**

Located in a quiet, residential area, surrounded by a well-manicured lawn and lovely trees, the inn is convenient to antique shops, restaurants, museums, tennis, and other recreational activities. The beach is nearby and famous Mendocino is 12 miles away. Catherine and Donald have furnished their home with your comfort and convenience in mind, and they look forward to helping you get the most out of your visit.

Country Inn

632 NORTH MAIN STREET, FORT BRAGG, CALIFORNIA 95437

Tel: (707) 964-3737
Host(s): **Don and Helen Miller**
Location: **165 miles north of San Francisco**
No. of Rooms: **8**
No. of Private Baths: **8**
Double/pb: **$50**
Single/pb: **$45**
Months of Operation: **All year**

Reduced Rates: **10%, seniors**
Breakfast: **Continental**
Credit Cards: **AMEX, MC, VISA**
Air-Conditioning: **No**
Pets: **No**
Children: **No**
Smoking: **No**
Social Drinking: **Permitted**
Airport Pickup: **Yes**

Built in the 1800s, this two-story redwood town house has been attractively updated to contemporary standards. Don is an artist and Helen enjoys making stained glass. Breakfast features delicious fruit-and-nut breads; a bottomless decanter of wine is set out at 6:00 PM for your pre-dinner relaxation. The inn is within five blocks of the Skunk Railroad, Glass Beach, galleries, restaurants, and shops.

The Grey Whale Inn
615 NORTH MAIN STREET, FORT BRAGG, CALIFORNIA 95437

Tel: (707) 964-0640 (toll-free in
California: 1-800-FT BRAGG)
Host(s): John and Colette Bailey
Location: 165 miles northwest of San
Francisco
No. of Rooms: 13
No. of Private Baths: 11
Maximum No. of Guests Sharing
Bath: 4
Double/pb: $45–$70
Single/pb: $40–$60
Double/sb: $65

Single/sb: $60
Suites: $60–$70 (for 2); $90–$100
(for 4)
Months of Operation: All year
Reduced Rates: Available
Breakfast: Continental
Credit Cards: AMEX, MC, VISA
Air-Conditioning: Unnecessary
Pets: No
Children: Welcome, over 6
Smoking: Permitted
Social Drinking: Permitted

An imposing three-story weathered redwood inn, with beautifully landscaped grounds, can be your home away from home. It
is attractively furnished and boasts an extensive art collection.
The warm colors, varied woods, plump comforters, and collection of books make for a cozy environment. Area attractions
include the Noyo Harbor, Redwood Forest, and the Skunk Rail-
way. John and Colette will advise where and when to watch the
fascinating whales.

Camellia Inn
211 NORTH STREET, HEALDSBURG, CALIFORNIA 95448

Tel: (707) 433-8182
Host(s): Ray and Del Lewand
Location: 65 miles north of San
Francisco
No. of Rooms: 6
No. of Private Baths: 4
Maximum No. of Guests Sharing
Bath: 4
Double/pb: $47–$60
Single/pb: $47–$60
Double/sb: $37–$47

Single/sb: $37–$47
Months of Operation: All year
Reduced Rates: No
Breakfast: Full
Credit Cards: MC, VISA
Air-Conditioning: No
Pets: No
Children: No
Smoking: Permitted
Social Drinking: Permitted

This elegant Italianate Victorian town house (circa 1869) is an
architectural delight. It is convenient to the Russian River, wineries, golf, tennis, and more. Ray and Del serve a hearty breakfast
buffet in the dining room, and wine is served in the afternoon in

the grand parlor or on the pool terrace. You will be made to feel like visiting royalty in this regal setting.

The Victorian Farmhouse
7001 NORTH HIGHWAY 1, P.O. BOX 357, LITTLE RIVER, CALIFORNIA 95456

Tel: (707) 937-0697
Host(s): **Tom and Jane Szilasi**
Location: **2½ miles south of Mendocino**
No. of Rooms: **6**
No. of Private Baths: **6**
Double/pb: **$60**
Single/pb: **$60**

Months of Operation: **All year**
Reduced Rates: **No**
Breakfast: **Continental**
Air-Conditioning: **No**
Pets: **No**
Children: **No**
Smoking: **Permitted**
Social Drinking: **Permitted**

Built in 1877, this clapboard farmhouse has been completely renovated and furnished in period antiques to enhance its original beauty and Victorian charm. It's close to Mendocino with its many galleries, boutiques, and restaurants. There's an apple orchard and gardens, and the ocean is a short walk away. Whale-watching in the winter months is popular. Tom and Jane will pamper you with breakfast brought to your room, and will invite you to join them for an evening sherry.

Howard Creek Ranch Inn
P.O. BOX 121, 40501 NORTH HIGHWAY ONE, WESTPORT, CALIFORNIA 95488

Tel: (707) 964-6725
Host(s): **Sunny and Sally Lasselle**
Location: **3 miles north of Westport**
No. of Rooms: **3**
Maximum No. of Guests Sharing Bath: **3**
Double/sb: **$30**
Single/sb: **$25**
Suites: **$45–$65**
Months of Operation: **All year**

Reduced Rates: **Available**
Breakfast: **Full**
Air-Conditioning: **Unnecessary**
Pets: **Sometimes**
Children: **Sometimes**
Smoking: **Yes**
Social Drinking: **Permitted**
Foreign Languages: **Dutch, French, German, Italian, Spanish**

This 100-year-old redwood ranch borders the Pacific Ocean in a secluded valley. Glass skylights illuminate the decor of collectibles, antiques, handmade lace, quilts; the original fireplace still warms the parlor. A hot tub, sauna, and pool on the hillside form a unique health spa with privacy and dramatic views. Sally and Sunny offer refreshments of juice, tea, coffee, and wine.

MONTEREY PENINSULA

Bed & Breakfast—Monterey Peninsula
P.O. BOX 1193, PEBBLE BEACH, CALIFORNIA 93953

Tel: **(408) 372-7425**	Rates (Single/Double):
Coordinator: **Rosalie Adron**	Modest: **$40** **$40**
States/Regions Covered: **Carmel,**	Average: **$50** **$50**
Monterey, Pebble Beach, Pacific	Luxury: **$65** **$65**
Grove	Credit Cards: **No**

This area is an artists' and photographers' paradise. Homes are convenient to the Pebble Beach Golf Course, Carmel Village, Cannery Row, Fisherman's Wharf, and Big Sur. For five dollars, Rosalie will send you detailed information on all the homes she represents. After you've made your selection, she will provide you with the name, address, and phone number of the host so that you can make your arrangements directly.

Home Suite Homes
1470 FIREBIRD WAY, SUNNYDALE, CALIFORNIA 94087

Tel: **(408) 733-7215**	Rates (Single/Double):
Coordinator: **Rhonda Robins**	Modest: **$20** **$40**
States/Regions Covered: **Wine**	Average: **$30** **$45–$50**
Country, San Francisco, Santa Cruz	Luxury: **$35** **$50–$60**
	Credit Cards: **No**

As a member of this organization, you will be sent a directory of hosts which fully describes all the homes on Rhonda's roster. Select your destination, then make your reservation directly. The membership fee is $20 and is paid only once.

Happy Landing
P.O. BOX 2619, CARMEL, CALIFORNIA 93921

Tel: **(408) 624-7917**	Location: **120 miles south of San**
Host(s): **Bob Alberson and Dick**	**Francisco**
Stewart	No. of Rooms: **5**

No. of Private Baths: **5**
Double/pb: **$55–$65**
Single/pb: **$55–$55**
Suites: **$85**
Months of Operation: **All year**
Reduced Rates: **No**
Breakfast: **Continental**

Credit Cards: **AMEX, MC, VISA**
Air-Conditioning: **Unnecessary**
Pets: **Sometimes**
Children: **No**
Smoking: **Permitted**
Social Drinking: **Permitted**
Foreign Languages: **Japanese**

Located on Monte Verde between 5th and 6th, this early Comstock-style inn is a charming and romantic place to stay. Rooms with cathedral ceilings open onto a beautiful central garden with gazebo, pond, and flagstone paths. Lovely antiques and personal touches, including breakfast served in your room, make your stay special.

Holiday House
P.O. BOX 782, CARMEL, CALIFORNIA 93921

Tel: **(408) 624-6267**
Host(s): **Kenneth and Janet Weston**
Location: **1 mile from Highway 1**
No. of Rooms: **6**
No. of Private Baths: **2**
Maximum No. of Guests Sharing Bath: **8 (shower and toilet in separate rooms)**
Double/pb: **$58**
Single/pb: **$55**

Double/sb: **$50**
Single/sb: **$47**
Months of Operation: **All year**
Reduced Rates: **No**
Breakfast: **Full**
Air-Conditioning: **Unnecessary**
Pets: **No**
Children: **Welcome, over 6**
Smoking: **No**
Social Drinking: **Permitted**

Centrally located on Camino Real (near 7th Street), three blocks from the beach and town, this 73-year-old grande dame of guest houses is the perfect spot to relax and reflect. All the bedrooms have either a view of the Pacific Ocean or open onto the garden. Breakfast features homemade breads, coffee cakes, ham and cheese strata, or baked deviled eggs and cheese. Ken and Janet invite you to enjoy a glass of sherry by the living room fireplace.

Sea View Inn
P.O. BOX 4138, CAMINO REAL, CARMEL, CALIFORNIA 93921

Tel: **(408) 624-8778**
Host(s): **Marshall and Diane Hydorn**
Location: **2 miles from Highway 1**
No. of Rooms: **8**

No. of Private Baths: **6**
Maximum No. of Guests Sharing Bath: **4**
Double/pb: **$50–$62**

Single/pb: **$50–$62**
Double/sb: **$43**
Single/sb: **$43**
Months of Operation: **All year**
Reduced Rates: **No**
Breakfast: **Continental**

Credit Cards: **MC, VISA**
Air-Conditioning: **No**
Pets: **No**
Children: **Welcome, over 12**
Smoking: **No**
Social Drinking: **Permitted**

Located between 11th and 12th streets, three blocks from the ocean, this is one of Carmel's few remaining stately old homes. Marshall and Diane have furnished the guest rooms with lovely antiques and special touches. Complimentary light sherry and pretzels are served in the living room by the fireplace. You're always made to feel special because of the personal attention your hosts extend.

Ocean-Forest Hideaway
P.O. BOX 1193, PEBBLE BEACH, CALIFORNIA 93953

Tel: **(408) 372-7425**
Host(s): **William George**
Location: **3 miles from Highway 1**
No. of Rooms: **3**
No. of Private Baths: **1**
Maximum No. of Guests Sharing Bath: **4**
Double/pb: **$60**
Single/pb: **$60**
Double/sb: **$50**
Single/sb: **$50**

Suites: **$60**
Months of Operation: **All year**
Reduced Rates: **10%, Sunday to Thursday**
Breakfast: **Continental**
Air-Conditioning: **Unnecessary**
Pets: **No**
Children: **Welcome, over 9**
Smoking: **Permitted**
Social Drinking: **Permitted**

It's two minutes to scenic beaches on the famous 17-Mile Drive adjacent to golf courses in the exclusive Pebble Beach forest. On the way to Carmel, just five minutes away, you'll see historic castles overlooking the ocean. A path through the woods brings you to the private entry of the hideaway suite with private bath. The other guest rooms have king-size beds, and you will be pampered with cozy comforters, flowers, and wine. Breakfast is served overlooking the woods where deer and squirrels play.

California Adventure
11801 SHARON DRIVE, SAN JOSE, CALIFORNIA 95129

Tel: (408) 996-1231
Host(s): Jill and Patrick O'Neill
Location: 45 miles south of San Francisco
No. of Rooms: 3
No. of Private Baths: 1
Maximum No. of Guests Sharing Bath: 3
Double/pb: $40
Single/pb: $40
Double/sb: $25
Single/sb: $25
Suites: $50
Months of Operation: All year
Reduced Rates: No
Breakfast: Continental
Air-Conditioning: Yes
Pets: Sometimes
Children: Welcome (crib)
Smoking: Permitted
Social Drinking: Permitted
Airport Pickup: Yes

A garden with a barbecue and swimming pool is at your back door when you visit the O'Neills. They are close to beaches, vineyards, exciting theater, and mountain trails. Jill and Patrick will give good advice about inexpensive outings, area sights, and will help you hire a baby-sitter if needed.

Chateau Victorian
118 FIRST STREET, SANTA CRUZ, CALIFORNIA 95060

Tel: (408) 458-9458
Host(s): Franz Benjamin
Location: 1½ miles from junction of highways 1 and 17
No. of Rooms: 7
No. of Private Baths: 7
Double/pb: $55–$95
Months of Operation: All year
Reduced Rates: No
Breakfast: Continental
Credit Cards: MC, VISA
Air-Conditioning: Unnecessary
Pets: No
Children: No
Smoking: No
Social Drinking: Permitted
Foreign Languages: German

This 100-year-old home has been restored to its former opulence. Five of the bedrooms have working fireplaces, and all the rooms are tastefully decorated. After a hearty breakfast, you can walk a block to the beach, the Municipal Wharf, or the world famous casino and boardwalk. Complimentary wine and cheese are served in the late afternoon as a prelude to dining in one of the area's superb restaurants.

SACRAMENTO AREA

Murphy's Inn
318 NEAL STREET, GRASS VALLEY, CALIFORNIA 95945

Tel: (916) 273-6873
Host(s): **Marc Murphy**
Location: **60 miles northeast of Sacramento**
No. of Rooms: 7
No. of Private Baths: 6
Maximum No. of Guests Sharing Bath: **4**
Double/pb: **$50–$70**
Double/sb: **$50**
Months of Operation: **All year**

Reduced Rates: **10%, Sunday to Thursday; 25%, 5 days or more**
Breakfast: **Full**
Credit Cards: **AMEX, MC, VISA**
Air-Conditioning: **Yes**
Pets: **No**
Children: **Welcome**
Smoking: **No**
Social Drinking: **Permitted**
Airport Pickup: **Yes**

This 100-year-old Victorian inn, on magnificent grounds, is framed by a majestic sequoia tree. The house's beauty is enhanced by the spacious veranda and hanging ivy baskets. The guest rooms are meticulously clean and graced with antiques, lace curtains, and brass beds. Marc invites you to join the other guests in the sitting room. Centrally located in the historic district, it is minutes away from Nevada City and within walking distance of restaurants and unique shops. It is only one and a half hours to Lake Tahoe.

Jean's Riverside Bed & Breakfast
P.O. BOX 2334, OROVILLE, CALIFORNIA 95965

Tel: (916) 533-1413
Host(s): **Jean Pratt**
Location: **1½ miles from Highway 70**
No. of Rooms: 4
No. of Private Baths: 2
Double/pb: **$40**
Single/pb: **$30**
Months of Operation: **All year**
Reduced Rates: **No**

Breakfast: **Continental**
Air-Conditioning: **Yes**
Pets: **Sometimes**
Children: **Welcome**
Smoking: **Permitted**
Social Drinking: **Permitted**
Airport Pickup: Yes
Foreign Languages: **French**

Located on the banks of the Feather River, there are views of the dam and Table Mountain. Swimming, boating, fishing, gold-panning, and canoeing are pleasant pastimes in the area. Jean will happily direct you to Feather Falls (fourth highest in the U.S.), Oroville Lake with its 160 miles of shoreline, and the most authentic Chinese temple in this country.

Jean's Riverside Bed & Breakfast

Bear Flag Inn
2814 I STREET, SACRAMENTO, CALIFORNIA 95816

Tel: **(916) 448-5417**
Host(s): **Robert West and Jennifer Dowley**
Location: **80 miles east of San Francisco**
No. of Rooms: **2**
No. of Private Baths: **2**
Double/pb: **$50**
Single/pb: **$40**
Months of Operation: **All year**
Reduced Rates: **$10, weekdays for California civil servants**

Breakfast: **Continental**
Credit Cards: **MC, VISA**
Air-Conditioning: **Yes**
Pets: **No**
Children: **Welcome**
Smoking: **Yes**
Social Drinking: **Permitted**
Airport Pickup: **Yes**
Foreign Languages: **German**

Located in a residential neighborhood of downtown Sacramento, two blocks from Sutters Fort, within walking distance of fine restaurants, and five minutes by car to the State Capitol, this handsome California "Arts and Crafts-Style" bungalow has been beautifully decorated with period pieces. You are welcome to make yourself comfortable in the large living room with fireplace and piano. Breakfast includes croissants, French coffee, and grapefruit from the garden.

The Briggs House
2209 CAPITOL AVENUE, SACRAMENTO, CALIFORNIA 95816

Tel: (916) 441-3214
Host(s): **Sue Garmston, Barbara Stoltz, Kathy Yeates, Paula Rawles**
Location: **1 mile from Highway 80**
No. of Rooms: **6**
No. of Private Baths: **3**
Maximum No. of Guests Sharing Bath: **2**
Double/pb: **$55–$70**
Single/pb: **$55–$70**
Double/sb: **$45–$55**
Single/sb: **$45–$55**

Guest Cottage: **$75–$90 sleeps 4**
Months of Operation: **All year**
Reduced Rates: **15%, week stay; weekdays, reduced**
Breakfast: **Full**
Credit Cards: **AMEX, MC, VISA**
Air-Conditioning: **Yes**
Pets: **No**
Children: **Cottage only**
Smoking: **Permitted**
Social Drinking: **Permitted**

Just a few blocks from the State Capitol, this is an elegantly restored Victorian house surrounded by stately trees. Antiques add to the splendor of the rich wood paneling, inlaid floor, Oriental rugs, and lace curtains. You'll be pampered with flowers in your room, and English china and fine silver for your gourmet breakfast. You can relax in the spa or sauna after a busy day of sightseeing. Evening treats include wine, fruit, nuts, and unhurried conversation in the living room.

SAN DIEGO AND ORANGE COUNTY AREA

Digs West
8191 CROWLEY CIRCLE, BUENA PARK, CALIFORNIA 90621

Tel: **(714) 739-1669**
Coordinator: **Jean Horn**
States/Regions Covered: **Anaheim, Bellflower, Costa Mesa, Cypress, Fullerton, Hermosa Beach, Santa Ana**

Rates (Single/Double):

	Single	Double
Modest:	**$25**	**$30**
Average:	**$30–$40**	**$36–$50**
Luxury:	**$50**	**$55–$80**

Credit Cards: **No**
Minimum Stay: **No**

Jean offers comfortable accommodations in the areas of San Diego, Los Angeles, and Orange County, (near Disneyland). Sightseeing, guided tours, and car rentals can be arranged.

Seaview Reservations Bed & Breakfast
P.O. BOX 1355, LAGUNA BEACH, CALIFORNIA 92652

Tel: **(714) 494-8878**	Rates (Single/Double):
Coordinator: **Nancy Fine and Marcia Mordkin**	Average: **$35** **$70**
	Luxury: **$40** **$80**
States/Regions Covered: **Laguna Beach, Newport Beach, Orange County, San Diego, San Francisco Bay Area**	Credit Cards: **MC, VISA**

Nancy and Marcia have accommodations in private homes, small inns, and cottages. Homes are available on the oceanfront, near canyons, or walk-to-the-beach locations. Arts and crafts, music festivals, and the University of California at Irvine are a few of the interesting things in the area. This is a membership organization, with a five-dollar fee, paid only once, to join.

Carolyn's B&B Homes
P.O. BOX 84776, SAN DIEGO, CALIFORNIA 92138

Tel: **(619) 435-5009 or 481-7662**	Rates (Single/Double):
Coordinator: **Carolyn Waskiewicz**	Modest: **$20** **$35**
States/Regions Covered: **San Diego: La Jolla, Lakeside, Del Mar, Carolsbad, Jamul, Coronado**	Average: **$30–$35** **$40–$50**
	Luxury: **$40–$65** **$55–$95**
	Credit Cards: **No**

Carolyn represents a wide variety of private homes in the San Diego area. Accommodations vary from simple to luxurious, including an oceanfront home in La Jolla; an historical mansion close to Balboa Park; a farmhouse with stained glass windows and beamed ceilings; a Victorian mansion on the ocean, where presidents and kings have been entertained, and so much more. Send five dollars for her directory of listings, and make your reservations directly with the host of your choice.

Julian Gold Rush Hotel
P.O. BOX 856, 2032 MAIN STREET, JULIAN, CALIFORNIA 92036

Tel: **(619) 765-0201**	No. of Rooms: **15**
Host(s): **Steve and Gig Ballinger**	No. of Private Baths: **3**
Location: **60 miles northeast of San Diego**	Maximum No. of Guests Sharing Bath: **4**

Double/pb: $48–$58
Single/pb: $48–$58
Double/sb: $38–$52
Single/sb: $21–$26
Guest Cottage: $55–$70 sleeps 2
Months of Operation: All year
Reduced Rates: 20%, seniors; families

Breakfast: Full
Air-Conditioning: No
Pets: No
Children: Welcome, Monday to Friday
Smoking: Permitted
Social Drinking: Permitted

This century-old landmark is listed in the National Register of Historic Places, and it is furnished with American antiques lovingly restored by your hosts. The lobby has a wood-burning stove, books and games, and an original, oak player piano. The historic town of Julian has been preserved to look much as it did 100 years ago and it has gold mine tours. Gig and Steve serve a delicious breakfast, and tea and coffee are always available.

Stay-a-Nite
1287-85 VIRGINIA WAY, LA JOLLA, CALIFORNIA 92037

Tel: (619) 459-5888
Host(s): Noel and Paul Stuart
Location: 12 miles north of San Diego
No. of Rooms: 6
No. of Private Baths: 1
Maximum No. of Guests Sharing
  Bath: 3
Double/pb: $48
Single/pb: $45
Double/sb: $45
Single/sb: $42

Months of Operation: All year
Reduced Rates: 10%, weekly
Breakfast: Continental
Air-Conditioning: No
Pets: No
Children: Welcome
Smoking: No
Social Drinking: Permitted
Foreign Languages: Spanish, French,
  Italian

Located in the heart of La Jolla village, it is within a short walk of shops, restaurants, and the ocean. Guests are welcome to use the Jacuzzi, and the music and recreation room. Your hosts prepare a buffet breakfast and offer sherry and nuts in the afternoon. They will be happy to help with tour information. Nearby sights include Sea World, San Diego Zoo, and the University of California.

Jean's Retreat
2308 CALLE LAS PALMAS, SAN CLEMENTE, CALIFORNIA 92672

Tel: (714) 492-1216 or 492-4121
Host(s): Jean Spain
Location: 60 miles south of Los
  Angeles

No. of Rooms: 2
No. of Private Baths: 2
Double/pb: $45
Single/pb: $35

Months of Operation: **All year**
Reduced Rates: **No**
Breakfast: **Continental**
Air-Conditioning: **Unnecessary**

Pets: **No**
Children: **Welcome, over 12**
Smoking: **No**
Social Drinking: **Permitted**

Jean's contemporary house, located in a quiet, exclusive area, is decorated in a comfortable blend of modern and antique pieces. The roses, exotic plantings, and vegetable garden attest to her green thumb. The house is two blocks from the beach, 10 minutes away from San Juan Capistrano, and 45 minutes from Disneyland. At home, there's a fireplace, spa, and large redwood deck for relaxing. Coffee, fruit, and snacks are always available.

Abigail
6310 RAYDEL COURT, SAN DIEGO, CALIFORNIA 92120

Tel: **(619) 583-4738**
Host(s): **Felix and Pearl Ammar**
Location: **200 feet from Freeway 8**
No. of Rooms: **1 suite**
No. of Private Baths: **1**
Suites: **$46**
Months of Operation: **All year**
Reduced Rates: **No**

Breakfast: **Full**
Air-Conditioning: **No**
Pets: **No**
Children: **No**
Smoking: **No**
Social Drinking: **Permitted**
Foreign Languages: **French, German, Greek, Italian**

Felix and Pearl live on the first floor, and they have created a haven for two on the second floor, offering privacy in the exclusive Del Cerro section. There is a separate entrance to the self-contained suite, which includes a kitchen where all the fixings for breakfast are provided; you can prepare what you wish, when you wish. San Diego Zoo, Balboa Park, Sea World, plus the Pacific Ocean and San Diego State College are all close by.

Britt House
406 MAPLE STREET, SAN DIEGO, CALIFORNIA 92103

Tel: **(619) 234-2926**
Host(s): **Daun Martin**
Location: **1 mile from highways 5, 8, 94, 163**
No. of Rooms: **9**
Maximum No. of Guests Sharing Bath: **5**
Double/pb: **n/a**
Single/pb: **n/a**

Double/sb: **$63–$95**
Single/sb: **$63–$95**
Guests Cottage: **$83 sleeps 2**
Months of Operation: **All year**
Reduced Rates: **No**
Breakfast: **Full**
Credit Cards: **MC, VISA**
Air-Conditioning: **No**
Pets: **No**

Children: **Cottage only**
Smoking: **Permitted**
Social Drinking: **Permitted**

Britt House

Fresh flowers and original drawings are part of this historic Victorian house. A winding oak stairway bends past the two-story stained glass windows. A book-filled parlor and grand piano are available for your pleasure. It's close to Balboa Park, the Globe Theater, and the San Diego Zoo, and you can walk to several fine restaurants. Breakfast features homemade delicacies and fresh ground coffee. Daun serves afternoon tea, and there are cookies and fruit thoughtfully placed in each guest room.

The Cottage
3829 ALBATROSS STREET, SAN DIEGO, CALIFORNIA 92103

Tel: **(619) 299-1564**
Host(s): **Robert and Carol Emerick**
Location: **1 mile from Route 5**
Guest Cottage: **$40–$50 sleeps 3**
Months of Operation: **All year**
Reduced Rates: **No**
Breakfast: **Continental**

Credit Cards: **MC, VISA**
Air-Conditioning: **No**
Pets: **No**
Children: **Welcome**
Smoking: **Permitted**
Social Drinking: **Permitted**

Located in the Hillcrest section, where undeveloped canyons and old houses dot the landscape, this private hideaway offers a cottage with a king-size bed in the bedroom, a single bed in the living room, full bath, and fully equipped kitchen. Decorated with turn-of-the-century furniture, the wood-burning stove and oak pump organ evoke memories of long ago. It's two miles to the zoo, less to Balboa Park, and it is within easy walking distance of restaurants, shops, and theater.

Serendipity
6779 PARKSIDE AVENUE, SAN DIEGO, CALIFORNIA 92139

Tel: **(619) 479-7851**
Host(s): **Garrison Lee**
Location: **13 miles north of Tijuana, Mexico**
No. of Rooms: **2**
No. of Private Baths: **2**
Double/pb: **$65**
Single/pb: **$65**
Months of Operation: **All year**
Reduced Rates: **Familes**

Breakfast: **Full**
Air-Conditioning: **Yes**
Pets: **No**
Children: **Welcome, over 10**
Smoking: **No**
Social Drinking: **Permitted**
Airport Pickup: **Yes**
Foreign Languages: **Dutch, French, German, Greek, Hebrew, Hindi, Italian, Japanese, Spanish**

A new luxury town house with swimming pool, sauna, Jacuzzi, and lushly planted patio, it is richly furnished with rare antiques, original artwork, four-poster beds, and Oriental rugs. A gourmet breakfast is served in the country kitchen or on the patio. Garrison will arrange for discount tickets to the famous San Diego sights and freebies for some restaurants. And, to top it all off, there's always a glass of brandy, cordial, tea, or coffee before bedtime.

The Old Oak Table
809 CLEMENSEN AVENUE, SANTA ANA, CALIFORNIA 92701

Tel: **(714) 639-7798**
Host(s): **Norman and Kathi Nicolson**
Location: **1 mile from Route I-5**
No. of Rooms: **2**
Maximum No. of Guests Sharing Bath: **3**
Double/sb: **$30**
Single/sb: **$25**
Guest Cottage: **n/a**

Months of Operation: **All year**
Reduced Rates: **No**
Breakfast: **Continental**
Air-Conditioning: **No**
Pets: **No**
Children: **Welcome**
Smoking: **No**
Social Drinking: **Permitted**
Foreign Languages: **French**

On a quiet tree-lined cul-de-sac, this is the place to relax after visiting the nearby beaches, shops, Disneyland, and Knott's Berry Farm. The patio backs up to a lovely park and is perfect for sunning and swimming. Norman and Kathi offer complimentary wine, fruit, and afternoon tea.

Friends-We-Haven't-Met

10071 STARBRIGHT CIRCLE, WESTMINSTER, CALIFORNIA 92683

Tel: **(714) 531-4269**
Host(s): **Bob and Sandy Runkle**
Location: **25 miles south of Los Angeles**
No. of Rooms: **2**
Maximum No. of Guests Sharing Bath: **6**
Double/sb: **$32**
Single/sb: **$26**
Months of Operation: **All year**

Reduced Rates: **10%, seniors**
Breakfast: **Continental**
Other Meals: **Available**
Air-Conditioning: **No**
Pets: **Sometimes**
Children: **Welcome**
Smoking: **Permitted**
Social Drinking: **Permitted**
Airport Pickup: **Yes**
Foreign Languages: **Spanish**

This large, comfortable home has a spacious backyard with a barbecue and lounge chairs. Bob and Sandy are warm and friendly people who enjoy having guests. Afternoon and evening snacks are always offered. Your hosts will be pleased to help shape your itinerary. The beach, Knotts Berry Farm, and Disneyland are nearby.

SAN FRANCISCO AREA

Bed & Breakfast International—San Francisco

151 ARDMORE ROAD, KENSINGTON, CALIFORNIA 94707

Tel: **(415) 527-8836 or 525-4569**
Coordinator: **Jean Brown**
States/Regions Covered:
  California—Berkeley, Palo Alto, San Francisco, Los Angeles, Lake Tahoe; Nevada—Las Vegas; Hawaii; N.Y.C.

Rates (Single/Double):
  Modest: **$25**
  Average: **$40**
  Luxury: **$85**
Credit Cards: **No**

Jean was the first to bring the concept of a bed and breakfast reservation service to America. Her accommodations range from a city apartment to a villa above an ocean beach with a private pool and tennis court. She has found over 100 hosts in the Los Angeles area for the 1984 Olympics. The price for two will range from $60 to $125 per day, depending upon the proximity to the Olympic sites.

American Family Inn
P.O. BOX 349, SAN FRANCISCO, CALIFORNIA 94101

Tel: (415) 931-3083
Coordinator: **Susan and Richard Kreibich**
States/Regions Covered: **Gold Country, Carmel, Monterey, Marin County, San Francisco, Wine Country**

Rates (Single/Double):
Modest: **$35**   **$45**
Average: **$40–$45** **$50–$55**
Luxury: **$50–$55** **$60–$70**
Creid Cards: **AMEX, MC, VISA**

The San Francisco locations are near all the famous sights, such as Fisherman's Wharf and Chinatown. Many are historic Victorian houses. Some homes offer hot tubs and sun decks, and a few are on yachts.

Thirty-Nine Cypress
BOX 176, POINT REYES STATION, CALIFORNIA 94956

Tel: (415) 663-1709
Host(s): **Julia Bartlett**
Location: **45 miles north of San Francisco**
No. of Rooms: **3**
Maximum No. of Guests Sharing Bath: **6**
Double/sb: **$47**
Single/sb: **$42**

Months of Operation: **All year**
Reduced Rates: **3-day stays**
Breakfast: **Full**
Air-Conditioning: **Unnecessary**
Pets: **No**
Children: **Welcome**
Smoking: **No**
Social Drinking: **Permitted**

Ten miles from the Pacific, surrounded by hills, this lovely home is furnished with antiques, original art, and Oriental rugs. Point Reyes National Seashore is three miles away. Julia knows the area intimately and can always suggest a hike or day trip suited to the weather, energy level, and tastes of her guests. From January through April, one of the world's most beautiful spots for watching the migrating gray whale is only 25 miles away. Each guest room opens on to a private patio on a bluff overlooking grazing cattle and wild birds.

Casa Arguello

225 ARGUELLO BOULEVARD, SAN FRANCISCO, CALIFORNIA 94118

Tel: **(415) 752-9482**	Suites: **$70**
Host(s): **Emma Baires**	Months of Operation: **All year**
No. of Rooms: **5**	Reduced Rates: **No**
No. of Private Baths: **2**	Breakfast: **Continental**
Maximum No. of Guests Sharing Bath: **6**	Air-Conditioning: **No**
	Pets: **No**
Double/pb: **$45**	Children: **Welcome, over 7**
Single/pb: **$40**	Smoking: **Permitted**
Double/sb: **$35**	Social Drinking: **Permitted**
Single/sb: **$30**	Foreign Languages: **Spanish**

This spacious duplex has an elegant living room, dining room, and cheerful bedrooms which overlook neighboring gardens. Tastefully decorated with modern and antique furnishings, it is convenient to Golden Gate Park, Golden Gate Bridge, Union Square, and fine shops and restaurants. Mrs. Baires allows her kitchen to be used for light snacks.

Casita Blanca

330 EDGEHILL WAY, SAN FRANCISCO, CALIFORNIA 94127

Tel: **(415) 564-9339**	Breakfast: **Continental**
Host(s): **Joan Bard**	Air-Conditioning: **Unnecessary**
No. of Rooms: **1 cottage**	Pets: **No**
No. of Private Baths: **1**	Children: **No**
Guest Cottage: **$50 sleeps 2**	Smoking: **Permitted**
Months of Operation: **All year**	Social Drinking: **Permitted**
Reduced Rates: **No**	

Perched on a hill, nestled in the trees, and overlooking the city and bay, this unique cottage is separate from the main house, affording you the luxury of privacy. Every detail has been attended to, down to condiments in the kitchen. Limited to two people at a time, there is a three-day minimum stay. Joan will be happy to direct you to all the non-tourist spots that make this city so exciting.

Inn on Castro
321 CASTRO STREET, SAN FRANCISCO, CALIFORNIA 94114

Tel: **(415) 861-0321**
Host(s): **Joel Roman**
No. of Rooms: **5**
Maximum No. of Guests Sharing
 Bath: **3**
Double/sb: **$75**
Single/sb: **$70**
Months of Operation: **All year**
Reduced Rates: **No**

Breakfast: **Continental**
Credit Cards: **AMEX, MC, VISA**
Air-Conditioning: **Unnecessary**
Pets: **No**
Children: **Welcome**
Smoking: **Permitted**
Social Drinking: **Permitted**
Foreign Languages: **French, Italian,
 Spanish**

Located off the corner of Market and 17th streets, the inn is a beautiful remodeled Victorian, luxuriously decorated with contemporary furnishings, original art, and exotic plants and flowers. It is ideally located on a hill with a view of the city and the bay. Restaurants, entertainment, and shops are within walking distance and the metro is steps away. Joel will arrange for a car rental, tours, theater tickets, or reservations at fine restaurants.

Le Petit Manoir
468 NOE STREET, SAN FRANCISCO, CALIFORNIA 94114

Tel: **(415) 864-7232**
Host(s): **Paul Bernard**
No. of Rooms: **3**
Maximum No. of Guests Sharing
 Bath: **4**
Double/sb: **$55**
Single/sb: **$45**
Months of Operation: **All year**

Reduced Rates: **No**
Breakfast: **Full**
Air-Conditioning: **No**
Pets: **No**
Children: **Welcome, over 12**
Smoking: **Permitted**
Social Drinking: **Permitted**
Foreign Languages: **French**

Paul enjoys nothing better than pleasing his guests. His experience with all phases of running a restaurant is evident in the breakfasts he prepares and serves on elegant china and crystal, either in the formal dining room of this 1902 Edwardian house, or on the glass-enclosed deck by the hot tub. Paul's omelets are inspired! He may even surprise you with eggs Benedict, accompanied by homemade hollandaise sauce, while you are drinking freshly squeezed orange juice.

The Red Victorian
1665 HAIGHT STREET, SAN FRANCISCO, CALIFORNIA 94117

Tel: **(415) 864-1978**
Host(s): **Sami Sunchild, Jan Cueva, Bob Stowell**
Location: **In the Haight-Ashbury District**
No. of Rooms: **16**
No. of Private Baths: **1**
Maximum No. of Guests Sharing Bath: **5**
Double/pb: **$59**
Single/pb: **$54**
Double/sb: **$34–$54**
Single/sb: **$29–$49**

Suites: **$64**
Months of Operation: **All year**
Reduced Rates: **Available**
Breakfast: **Continental**
Credit Cards: **MC, VISA**
Air-Conditioning: **No**
Pets: **Sometimes**
Children: **Welcome**
Smoking: **Permitted**
Social Drinking: **Permitted**
Foreign Languages: **French, German, Spanish**

In the heart of the city's Left Bank neighborhood is this informal combination of salon-art gallery gathering place and B&B. It is located just east of the Golden Gate Park, where you can visit museums and a Japanese tea garden. Breakfast is served in the Pink Parlor. You may meditate, inspired by Sami's paintings, in the Meditation Room. This is a friendly place, run by creative people, and you are certain to enjoy the ambience.

Glen Echo
508 KILKARE ROAD, SONOL, CALIFORNIA 94586

Tel: **(415) 862-2046**
Host(s): **Don and Jan Scheer**
Location: **45 miles southeast of San Francisco**
No. of Rooms: **2**
Maximum No. of Guests Sharing Bath: **4**
Double/sb: **$20**
Single/sb: **$15**
Months of Operation: **All year**

Reduced Rates: **10%, seniors**
Breakfast: **Continental**
Air-Conditioning: **No**
Pets: **No**
Children: **Welcome**
Smoking: **No**
Social Drinking: **No**
Airport Pickup: **Yes**
Foreign Languages: **French**

This comfortable home is located in farm country, and is surrounded by woods, with a creek flowing in front—a fine place to relax. Jan is a vegetarian so whole grains and natural foods are breakfast ingredients. California almonds and fresh fruit are always available. Don is an engineer and enjoys sailing when he's not busy remodeling the house. It is a good home-base for side trips to San Francisco, Carmel, Yosemite, Lake Tahoe, and Wine Country.

SAN JOAQUIN VALLEY

Valley View Citrus Ranch
14801 AVENUE 428, OROSI, CALIFORNIA 93647

Tel: **(209) 528-2275**
Host(s): **Tom and Ruth Flippen**
Location: **40 miles southeast of Fresno**
No. of Rooms: **4**
No. of Private Baths: **3**
Maximum No. of Guests Sharing Bath: **4 (washbasin in each bedroom)**
Double/pb: **$35**
Single/pb: **$32**
Double/sb: **$35**

Single/sb: **$32**
Months of Operation: **All year**
Reduced Rates: **No**
Breakfast: **Full**
Air-Conditioning: **Yes**
Pets: **Sometimes**
Children: **Welcome**
Smoking: **Permitted**
Social Drinking: **Permitted**
Foreign Languages: **Spanish**

Located in the San Joaquin Valley (The Fruit Basket of the World), this modern ranch home is set in the foothills of the Sierra Nevadas. The 70-foot-long porch provides some beautiful views. Tom and Ruth will be happy to plan your itinerary, which might include a visit to Sequoia National Park, Kings Canyon, or Crystal

Caves, or you can play tennis on their clay court. Breakfast specialties are Belgian waffles served in the delightful gazebo. Complimentary beverages are always available.

SANTA BARBARA AREA

Educators' Vacation Alternatives
317 PIEDMONT ROAD, SANTA BARBARA, CALIFORNIA 93105

Tel: (805) 687-2947
Coordinator: LaVerne Long
States/Regions Covered: U.S., Canada, New Zealand

Rates (Single/Double):
Modest:	$12–$17	$18
Average:	$25	$30–$35
Luxury:	$85	$90

Credit Cards: No

EVA is an acronym for Educators' Vacation Alternatives, which caters exclusively to active or retired professional educators. There are hundreds of hosts in the U.S. as well as home exchanges. The directory is available for $5.50, plus one-dollar postage (U.S.), two-dollar postage (overseas). A spring and fall supplement updates the directory so that you can make your arrangements directly.

Megan's Friends B 'n B
1611 9TH STREET, LOS OSOS, CALIFORNIA 93402

Tel: (805) 528-6645
Coordinator: Megan Backer
States/Regions Covered: Carmel, Cayucos, Los Osos, Monterey, Pine Canyon, Pleasanton, San Luis Obispo, Shell Beach, Solvang

Rates (Single/Double):
Modest:	$25	$35
Average:	$30	$35–$40
Luxury:	$40	$60

Credit Cards: No

Megan has a circle of friends offering personal hospitality to visitors. The homes range from a contemporary showplace on an ocean bluff to a cozy cottage in the country. A $10 annual membership fee is required, for which you receive a detailed list of homes for your selection. Smoking indoors is not allowed. Attractions in the area include Hearst Castle, Cal Poly University, Montana de Oro State Park, missions, wineries, water sports, charming restaurants, and shops.

Rose Victorian Inn

789 VALLEY ROAD, ARROYO GRANDE, CALIFORNIA 93420

Tel: **(805) 481-5566**
Host(s): **Ross and Diana Cox**
Location: **200 miles north of Los Angeles**
No. of Rooms: **6**
No. of Private Baths: **1**
Maximum No. of Guests Sharing Bath: **6**
Double/pb: **$80**
Double/sb: **$60–$75**
Suites: **$125 (private baths)**
Months of Operation: **All year**

Reduced Rates: **October 1 to April 30; Sunday to Thursday, $20 less per room**
Breakfast: **Full**
Other Meals: **Available (restaurant on premises)**
Credit Cards: **AMEX, MC, VISA**
Air-Conditioning: **No**
Pets: **No**
Children: **Welcome, over 16**
Smoking: **No**
Social Drinking: **Permitted**
Airport Pickup: **Yes**

This majestic mansion (circa 1885) is painted four shades of rose and the gardens abound in rose bushes of every hue. An arbor leads to the gazebo which is surrounded by Koi ponds. Each room is decorated with authentic, ornate Victorian pieces. The parlor has an onyx fireplace, pump organ, and marvelous view. Breakfast is served in the family dining room and features such delicacies as eggs Benedict, a variety of stuffed croissants, cheese strata or eggs Florentine. It is close to the Oceano Sand Dunes, Hearst Castle, Solvang Danish Village, wineries, and the Pacific.

The Castles

1826 CHORRO STREET, SAN LUIS OBISPO, CALIFORNIA 93401

Tel: (805) 543-2818
Host(s): **Sharon Castle**
Location: **1 mile from Highway 101**
No. of Rooms: **2**
No. of Private Baths: **2**
Double/pb: **$35**
Single/pb: **$35**
Children, 12 and under: **$5**
Guest Cottage: **$45 sleeps 2**

Months of Operation: **All year**
Reduced Rates: **Weekly, 7th night free**
Breakfast: **Full**
Air-Conditioning: **No**
Pets: **Sometimes**
Children: **Yes**
Smoking: **No**
Social Drinking: **Permitted**
Airport Pickup: **Yes**

Separate entrances, handmade curtains, and antique decor make up this homey and private place to be. Picnic lunches and a decanter of wine are available. Guests are served a breakfast of home-baked cakes, fruit, and specialty beverages on the garden patio or in their private quarters. Wineries, hot springs, the beach, and Hearst Castle are nearby.

Blue Quail Inn

1908 BATH STREET, SANTA BARBARA, CALIFORNIA 93101

Tel: (805) 687-2300
Host(s): **Jeanise Suding**
Location: **100 miles north of Los Angeles**
No. of Rooms: **8**
Maximum No. of Guests Sharing Bath: **4**

Double/sb: **$40–$50**
Single/sb: **$40–$50**
Suites: **$36–$70**
Guest Cottage: **$63–$75 sleeps 2 to 3**
Months of Operation: **All year**
Reduced Rates: **30%, weekly; 10%, Sunday to Thursday**

Breakfast: **Continental**
Other Meals: **Available**
Credit Cards: **MC, VISA**
Air-Conditioning: **No**
Pets: **No**

Children: **Welcome, over 12**
Smoking: **Permitted**
Social Drinking: **Permitted**
Airport Pickup: **Yes**

The main house is a California-style bungalow and is adjacent to four quaint cottages. Each guest room is uniquely decorated with antiques and country charm. Jeanise is most cordial and offers complimentary spiced apple cider each evening. You're welcome to borrow her bikes to tour the beach, Santa Barbara Mission, and other historical landmarks.

The Cottage
840 MISSION CANYON ROAD, SANTA BARBARA, CALIFORNIA 93105

Tel: **(805) 682-4997**
Host(s): **Ray and Sylvia Byers**
Location: **2 miles north of downtown Santa Barbara**
Guest Cottage: **$40–$50 sleeps 3**
Months of Operation: **All year**
Reduced Rates: **No**
Breakfast: **Continental**

Air-Conditioning: **Unnecessary**
Pets: **No**
Children: **Sometimes**
Smoking: **No**
Social Drinking: **Permitted**
Airport Pickup: **Yes**
Foreign Languages: **German**

Seclusion and privacy are yours in this self-contained cottage that is set among ancient oaks behind Ray and Sylvia's home. There's a bedroom with a double bed, living room with TV, shower, and compact kitchen stocked with ingredients for your self-catered breakfast. It's an easy drive to the historic downtown area, museums, the beach, and university.

Ocean View House
P.O. BOX 20065, SANTA BARBARA, CALIFORNIA 93102

Tel: **(805) 966-6659**
Host(s): **Bill and Carolyn Canfield**
Location: **3 miles from Civic Center**
No. of Rooms: **2**
No. of Private Baths: **1**
Maximum No. of Guests Sharing Bath: **4**
Double/pb: **$40**

Single/pb: **$35**
Suites: **$55 for 4**
Months of Operation: **All year**
Reduced Rates: **No**
Breakfast: **Continental**
Other Meals: **Available**
Air-Conditioning: **Unnecessary**
Pets: **Sometimes**

Children: **Welcome**   Social Drinking: **Permitted**
Smoking: **No**   Airport Pickup: **Yes**

This California ranch house features a guest room furnished with a queen-size bed and antiques. The adjoining paneled den, with double-bed divan and color TV, is available together with the guest room as a suite. While you relax and sip wine on the patio, you can look out at the sailboats on the ocean. Children will be delighted with the playhouse. It's a short walk to the beach and local shops. Breakfast specialties are apple cake and beer bread served on lovely Lenox china.

Country House Inn
91 MAIN STREET, P.O. BOX 179, TEMPLETON, CALIFORNIA 93465

Tel: **(805) 434-1598**
Host(s): **Barbara and Nick**
Location: **22 miles north of San Luis Obispo**
No. of Rooms: **7**
Maximum No. of Guests Sharing Bath: **6**
Double/sb: **$55**
Single/sb: **$45**
Months of Operation: **All year**

Reduced Rates: **10%, December to January**
Breakfast: **Continental**
Air-Conditioning: **No**
Pets: **No**
Children: **Welcome**
Smoking: **No**
Social Drinking: **Permitted**
Airport Pickup: **Yes**

Step back in time to the warmth of a home built in 1886, a designated historic site. The spacious bedrooms are furnished with queen- and king-size beds and antiques. While you enjoy breakfast, watch the hummingbirds at the dining room window. Walk in the rose-bordered gardens or play the player piano by the fireside. Hearst Castle is about 30 miles away as are a dozen wineries with tasting rooms. Walk to dinner at one of the town's restaurants, and read about its history on the plaques of the old buildings.

COLORADO

Steamboat Springs
• Ault• •Estes Park

Green Mtn. Falls
Central City• • • Denver

Manitou Springs•• Colorado Springs

• Ouray
•Silverton
•Dolores

Bed & Breakfast—Rocky Mountains
P.O. BOX 804, COLORADO SPRINGS, COLORADO 80901

Tel: (303) 630-3433
Coordinator: **Kate Peterson**
States/Regions Covered: **Colorado,**
   Montana, New Mexico, Wyoming

Rates (Single/Double):
   Modest: **$17**   **$25**
   Average: **$25**   **$35**
   Luxury: **$35**   **$45–$95**
Credit Cards: **No**

Kate's roster covers the whole gamut, from modest homes to elegant mansions, log cabins to working cattle ranches, ski chalets with beamed ceilings and hot tubs to homes near lakes and rivers. Send one dollar with a self-addressed envelope (and 37 cents postage) for the descriptive directory. You can then make your arrangements directly.

Bed and Breakfast Colorado
P.O. BOX 20596, DENVER, COLORADO 80220

Tel: **(303) 333-3340**
Coordinator: **Rick Madden**
States/Regions Covered: **Colorado (statewide)**

Rates (Single/Double):
Average: **$20**   **$40**
Luxury: **$40**   **$60**
Credit Cards: **MC, VISA**

Your home away from home could be a bedroom in an historic mansion overlooking a ski village, an apartment in the heart of Denver, or a small cottage all to yourself. Just mention your interests, hobbies, and other requirements, and Rick will do his best to comply. Send two dollars for the descriptive directory of homes, make your selection, and Rick will make the reservations for you.

The Adams House
115 B. STREET, P.O. BOX 512, AULT, COLORADO 80610

Tel: **(303) 834-1587**
Host(s): **Sue and Jim Adams**
Location: **11 miles north of Greeley**
No. of Rooms: **1**
No. of Private Baths: **1**
Double/pb: **$24**
Single/pb: **$16**
Months of Operation: **All year**

Reduced Rates: **No**
Breakfast: **Continental**
Air-Conditioning: **Unnecessary**
Pets: **No**
Children: **Welcome**
Smoking: **No**
Social Drinking: **No**

Sue and Jim offer a restful atmosphere in their 1907 frame house. Summer breakfasts, which feature homemade muffins and garden goodies, are served beneath the yellow umbrella on the patio. A waterfall and pool with rock garden will open your eyes if the coffee doesn't. A city park with tennis courts is just a block away. For cultural activities, the University of Northern Colorado is 11 miles away and Colorado State College is 15 miles from the house. The Cheyenne Rodeo is nearby and a lot of fun too.

Redstone Mountain Chalet
15659 STAR ROUTE 133, CARBONDALE, COLORADO 81623

Tel: **(303) 963-3837**
Host(s): **Tom and Marlene Williams**
Location: **200 miles southwest of**

Denver, 30 miles from I-70 (Glenwood Springs)
No. of Rooms: **2**

No. of Private Baths: **2**
Double/pb: **$30**
Single/pb: **$25**
Months of Operation: **January 2 to April 14, May 16 to December 23 (closed Thanksgiving)**
Reduced Rates: **10%, weekly; families**

Breakfast: **Continental**
Air-Conditioning: **Unnecessary**
Pets: **No**
Children: **Welcome**
Smoking: **Permitted**
Social Drinking: **Permitted**
Airport Pickup: **Yes**

This Swiss chalet is nestled among the trees on a sunny slope in the middle of the White River National Forest, along the bank of the Crystal River. Skiing, hiking, jeeping, fishing, and every other imaginable sport are available. Tom is a ski-school director and Marlene enjoys the home arts. Refreshments are offered to suit the mood of the day.

Hacienda del Sol
9600 SORRELL ROAD, CASTLE ROCK, COLORADO 80104

Tel: **(303) 770-8535**
Host(s): **Verne and Andy Anderson**
Location: **1.5 miles from I-25**
No. of Rooms: **2**
Maximum No. of Guests Sharing Bath: **3**
Double/sb: **$50**
Single/sb: **$40**
Months of Operation: **All year**

Reduced Rates: **10%, seniors**
Breakfast: **Full**
Other Meals: **Available**
Air-Conditioning: **No**
Pets: **No**
Children: **Welcome**
Smoking: **Permitted**
Social Drinking: **Permitted**

This southwest adobe-style home, surrounded by ponderosa pines, will provide you with a restful environment for complete relaxation. Located in the country, it's only 30 minutes to downtown Denver and less than an hour from Colorado Springs. If you enjoy walking or jogging, you can pursue your interest here with gusto.

Two Ten Casey
BOX 154, 210 CASEY AVENUE, CENTRAL CITY, COLORADO 80427

Tel: **(303) 582-5906**
Host(s): **Esther Campbell**
Location: **35 miles northwest of Denver**
No. of Rooms: **1**
No. of Private Baths: **1**

Double/pb: **$30**
Single/pb: **$25**
Months of Operation: **All year**
Reduced Rates: **No**
Breakfast: **Continental**
Air-Conditioning: **No**

Pets: **No**	Smoking: **Permitted**
Children: **Welcome, over 5**	Social Drinking: **Permitted**

The bay windows of this comfortable clapboard cottage overlook Gregory Gulch, where gold was discovered in 1859. Esther, a retired nurse, will be happy to point out the historical sights. She is an experienced hiker and will lead you along the old trails. Area attractions include ski slopes, museums, shops, and restaurants.

Griffin's Hospitality House
4222 NORTH CHESTNUT, COLORADO SPRINGS, COLORADO 80907

Tel: **(303) 599-3035**	Months of Operation: **Closed last week of July and first week of August**
Host(s): **John and Diane Griffin**	
Location: **5 miles north of Colorado Springs**	
No. of Rooms: **3**	Reduced Rates: **10%, families after 3 days**
No. of Private Baths: **1**	Breakfast: **Full**
Maximum No. of Guests Sharing Bath: **4**	Air-Conditioning: **No**
	Pets: **No**
Double/pb: **$35**	Children: **Welcome (crib)**
Single/pb: **$25**	Smoking: **Permitted**
Double/sb: **$30**	Social Drinking: **Permitted**
	Airport Pickup: **Yes**

The welcome mat is always out at Diane and John's house. It's close to Pike's Peak, the Air Force Academy, and the Garden of the Gods. You can use the picnic table, TV, washing machine, and dryer. You will enjoy a fine view of Pike's Peak while eating the bountiful breakfast. In the evening, you are invited to relax in the living room with wine and good conversation.

Four Seasons
1300 MONROE 502, DENVER, COLORADO 80206

Tel: **(303) 393-8294**	Reduced Rates: **No**
Host(s): **Patricia Parks**	Breakfast: **Continental**
Location: **4 miles from I-70**	Air-Conditioning: **Yes**
No. of Rooms: **1**	Pets: **Sometimes**
No. of Private Baths: **1**	Children: **Welcome, over 12**
Double/pb: **$40**	Smoking: **Permitted**
Single/pb: **$30**	Social Drinking: **Permitted**
Months of Operation: **All year**	Airport Pickup: **Yes**

The guest room is done in white wicker with a French provincial theme. Patricia is a walking tour guide for historic Denver and will show you Molly Brown's house and the governor's mansion. It's close to the park, zoo, Botanical Gardens, the mint, museums, and restaurants. In warm weather you'll enjoy having your breakfast on the balcony with a view of snowcapped mountains.

Simon Draw Guest House
13980 COUNTY ROAD 29, DOLORES, COLORADO 81323

Tel: **(303) 565-2153**	Breakfast: **Continental**
Host(s): **Richard and Evelyn Wagner**	Credit Cards: **MC, VISA**
Location: **4½ miles from Highway 160**	Air-Conditioning: **No**
Guest Cottage: **$30 sleeps 4**	Pets: **Yes**
Months of Operation: **April through November**	Children: **Welcome (crib)**
	Smoking: **Permitted**
Reduced Rates: **15%, weekly**	Social Drinking: **Permitted**

This two-story cottage is complete with kitchen, living room, bedroom, and bath. It is in the woods on the edge of a small canyon with a stream at the bottom. It contains a double bed and a twin-size couch in the living room. It is a charming home away from home while visiting Mesa Verde National Park.

Wanek's Lodge at Estes
P.O. BOX 898, 560 PONDEROSA DRIVE, ESTES PARK, COLORADO 80517

Tel: **(303) 586-5851**	Reduced Rates: **No**
Host(s): **Jim and Pat Wanek**	Breakfast: **Continental—$3.50**
Location: **31 miles northwest of Denver**	Other Meals: **Available**
	Air-Conditioning: **Unnecessary**
No. of Rooms: **6**	Pets: **No**
Maximum No. of Guests Sharing Bath: **6**	Children: **Welcome**
	Smoking: **Permitted**
Double/sb: **$34**	Social Drinking: **Permitted**
Single/sb: **$28**	Airport Pickup: **Yes**
Months of Operation: **All year**	

Pat and Jim invite you to share their modern mountain inn, with its wood beams, stone fireplace, old-fashioned hospitality, and gorgeous scenery. The emphasis is on excellent food, lovingly prepared. The Rocky Mountain National Park is minutes away, and boating on Lake Estes is fun. Former educators, the Waneks are people-oriented and you'll feel like friends in no time.

Outlook Lodge
P.O. BOX 5, GREEN MOUNTAIN FALLS, COLORADO 80819

Tel: **(303) 684-2303**
Host(s): **The Ahearn Family**
Location: **15 miles west of Colorado Springs**
No. of Rooms: **11**
No. of Private Baths: **4**
Maximum No. of Guests Sharing Bath: **6**
Double/pb: **$35**
Single/pb: **$28**
Double/sb: **$27**
Single/sb: **$23**

Months of Operation: **Memorial Day to Labor Day**
Reduced Rates: **Families**
Breakfast: **Continental**
Credit Cards: **MC, VISA**
Air-Conditioning: **Unnecessary**
Pets: **Yes**
Children: **Welcome (crib)**
Smoking: **Permitted**
Social Drinking: **Permitted**
Foreign Languages: **German**

This restored Victorian parsonage (1889) is set at the foot of Pike's Peak and is surrounded by pines on property fronted by a creek. The original furnishings, stained glass, and rocking chair veranda all add to the feeling of going to Grandma's. The gracious Ahearns invite you to use the kitchen for making snacks and blender drinks and to use the refrigerator, barbecue, and picnic table. Located just a block away from a lake, pool, tennis court, stables, shops, and restaurants, it is also within easy driving distance of the Garden of the Gods, the Air Force Academy, Royal Gorge, and Cripple Creek.

The Nippersink
106 SPENCER AVENUE, MANITOU SPRINGS, COLORADO 80829

Tel: **(303) 685-9211**
Host(s): **Larry and Memory Schorr**
Location: **On Highway 24**
No. of Rooms: **3**
Maximum No. of Guests Sharing Bath: **5**
Double/sb: **$30**
Single/sb: **$25**

Months of Operation: **All year**
Reduced Rates: **No**
Breakfast: **Continental**
Air-Conditioning: **Unnecessary**
Pets: **No**
Children: **Welcome, over 12**
Smoking: **Permitted**
Social Drinking: **Permitted**

Located at the base of Pikes Peak, this 1885 Victorian house has been restored, and now offers restful and spacious accommoda-

tions with turn-of-the-century charm. You will enjoy the many attractions of Colorado Springs, the Air Force Academy, and the Broadmoor. There are many charming shops in the area. You're invited to observe your host's hobbies—Larry's photography; Memory's 14-room dollhouse and miniature collection. Complimentary evening sherry is served in the parlor.

Back Narrows Inn
1550 GRAND AVENUE, BOX 156, NORWOOD, COLORADO 81423

Tel: **(303) 327-4417**
Host(s): **Joyce and Terre Bucknam**
Location: **125 miles southeast of Grand Junction**
No. of Rooms: **10**
No. of Private Baths: **3**
Maximum No. of Guests Sharing Bath: **5**
Double/pb: **$26**
Single/pb: **$21**
Double/sb: **$20**

Single/sb: **$16**
Months of Operation: **All year**
Reduced Rates: **No**
Breakfast: **Continental**
Other Meals: **Available**
Credit Cards: **MC, VISA**
Air-Conditioning: **No**
Pets: **Yes**
Children: **Welcome**
Smoking: **Permitted**
Social Drinking: **Permitted**

At the edge of the San Juan Mountains, the inn, built in 1880, retains a flavor of the past, with its antique furnishings. The lobby invites relaxation, conversation, darts, and other games.

It's 33 miles to historic Telluride town and ski area for winter fun. Summer diversions are fishing, gold-panning, and music and film festivals.

Baker's Manor Guest House
317 SECOND STREET, OURAY, COLORADO 81427

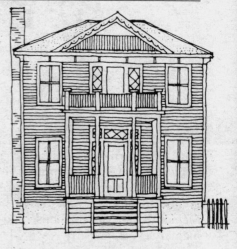

Tel: **(303) 325-4574**
Host(s): **John and Nancy Nixon**
Location: **37 miles south of Montrose**
No. of Rooms: **6**
Maximum No. of Guests Sharing
  Bath: **12**
Double/sb: **$20**
Single/sb: **$18**
Months of Operation: **June through September**
Reduced Rates: **Families; long stays**
Breakfast: **Continental**
Air-Conditioning: **Unnecessary**
Pets: **No**
Children: **Welcome (crib)**
Smoking: **Permitted**
Social Drinking: **Permitted**

This immaculate 100-year-old home was built in the mining days. Ouray is often called the Switzerland of America since it is 8,000 feet high in the San Juan Mountains. There is a natural hot springs municipal pool and Box Canyon Falls. Popular pastimes are jeeping, backpacking, fishing, and mountain climbing. Delightful restaurants and shops are close by.

The House of Yesteryear
516 OAK STREET, P.O. BOX 440, OURAY, COLORADO 81427

Tel: **(303) 325-4277**
Host(s): **Raymond O'Brien**
Location: **4 blocks from Highway 550**
No. of Rooms: **8**
No. of Private Baths: **1½**
Maximum No. of Guests Sharing
  Bath: **5**
Double/pb: **$32**
Double/sb: **$28**
Single/sb: **$26**

Months of Operation: **June 6 to September 9**
Reduced Rates: **10%, June; families**
Breakfast: **Continental—$1.00**
Air-Conditioning: **Unnecessary**
Pets: **No**
Children: **Welcome (crib)**
Smoking: **Permitted**
Social Drinking: **Permitted**

Perched on a hill overlooking spectacular scenery, this spotless home is filled with many museum-quality antiques. Each room is individual in decor; an eclectic mix of old and new. Mount Abrams and Bear Creek Falls are nearby. Take a daytime drive on the Million Dollar Highway—the views are breathtaking.

The Alma House
220 EAST 10TH STREET, SILVERTON, COLORADO 81433

Tel: (303) 387-5336
Host(s): **Don and Jolene Stott**
Location: **50 miles north of Durango, 1 mile from Highway 550**
No. of Rooms: **10**
Maximum No. of Guests Sharing Bath: **5**
Double/sb: **$30**
Single/sb: **$30**
Months of Operation: **June 15 to Labor Day**

Reduced Rates: **No**
Breakfast: **No (coffee or tea only)**
Credit Cards: **MC, VISA**
Air-Conditioning: **No**
Pets: **No**
Children: **Welcome**
Smoking: **No**
Social Drinking: **Permitted**

This 1898 stone-and-frame building has been lovingly restored and comfortably updated. Each spacious room has a deluxe queen-size bed, luxurious linens, antique dressers, and special touches. The plumbing in the bathrooms is up-to-date but the brass and walnut fixtures are faithful to a day gone by. Don and Jolene have a large video tape library for your evening entertainment. Ride the Durango–Silverton Narrow Gauge Railroad to the Mesa Verde National Park. Silverton retains the flavor of the old western town it is. The Bent Elbow Saloon, just next door, is fun.

House on the Hill
P.O. BOX 770598, STEAMBOAT, COLORADO 85477

Tel: (303) 879-1650
Host(s): **Barbara Rennels**
Location: **120 miles northwest of Denver**
No. of Rooms: **3**
Maximum No. of Guests Sharing Bath: **3**
Double/sb: **$50–$60**
Single/sb: **$40–$50**
Months of Operation: **Closed in May**

Reduced Rates: **$10 less, June to October; 10%, seniors; $10, families**
Breakfast: **Continental**
Credit Cards: **MC, VISA**
Air-Conditioning: **No**
Pets: **Sometimes**
Children: **Welcome, over 12**
Smoking: **Permitted**
Social Drinking: **Permitted**
Airport Pickup: **Yes**

This handsome house (circa 1906) offers the warmth and comfort of home to skiers and vacationers. It is centrally located in town, overlooks Soda Creek, and is a five-minute walk to fine restaurants and entertainment. Creatively furnished, it has an air of casual elegance. The natural hot springs in town are a great place to soothe aching muscles in this sports-oriented community. Barbara offers use of her kitchen for light snacks, as well as the use of the picnic table, TV, washing machine, dryer, and hot tub.

KEY TO LISTINGS

Location: As specified, unless B&B is right in town, or its location is clear from address as stated.

No. of Rooms: Refers to the number of guest bedrooms.

Double: Rate for two people in one room.

Single: Rate for one person in a room.

Suite: Can either be two bedrooms with an adjoining bath, or a living room and bedroom with private bath.

Guest Cottage: A separate building that usually has a mini-kitchen and private bath.

pb: Private bath.

sb: Shared bath.

Breakfast: Included, unless otherwise noted.

Air-Conditioning: If "no" or "unnecessary" is stated, it means the climate rarely warrants it.

Children: If "crib" is noted after the word "welcome," this indicates that the host also has a high-chair, baby-sitters are available, and the B&B can accommodate children under the age of three.

Smoking: If permitted, this means it is allowed *somewhere* inside the house.

Social Drinking: Some hosts provide a glass of wine or sherry; others provide setups for bring-your-own.

Please enclose a self-addressed, stamped, business-size envelope when contacting Reservation Services.

Remember the difference in time zones when calling for a reservation.

CONNECTICUT

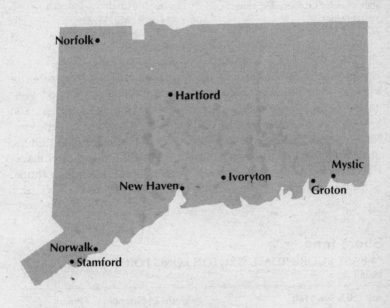

Norfolk•

• Hartford

New Haven• • Ivoryton

Mystic
•
Groton

Norwalk•
• Stamford

Covered Bridge Bed & Breakfast
WEST CORNWALL, CONNECTICUT 06796

Tel: **(203) 672-6052**
Coordinator: **Rae Eastman**
States/Regions Covered:
  **Connecticut—Canaan, Cornwall,
  Lakeville, Kent, Sharon;
  Massachusetts—Sheffield,
  Stockbridge, Williamstown**

Rates (Single/Double):
  Modest: **$30**   **$35**
  Average: **$40**   **$50**
Credit Cards: **No**

If you enjoy historic homes, picture postcard New England scenery, unsurpassed fall foliage, music festivals, theater, antiquing, auto racing, skiing, white-water rafting, or hiking, call Rae. Her host homes are located in the northwest corner of Connecticut, and border New York and western Massachusetts.

Nutmeg Bed & Breakfast
56 FOX CHASE LANE, WEST HARTFORD, CONNECTICUT 06107

Tel: **(203) 236-6698**
Coordinator: **Maxine Kates, Phyllis Nova**
States/Regions Covered: **Connecticut (statewide)**

Rates (Single/Double):
Modest:	**$25**	**$25–$35**
Average:	**$35**	**$35–$50**
Luxury:	**$50**	**$50–$65**

Credit Cards: **MC, VISA**
Minimum Stay: **2 days/holiday weekends**

Experience the Connecticut countryside under the auspices of Maxine and Phyllis, who have selected ideal B&Bs for your comfort and pleasure, spanning every conceivable ambience. You are certain to feel at home as soon as your host greets you. Maxine and Phyllis will guide you to the best the state offers, including cross-country and downhill skiing, brilliant fall foliage, the scenic coastline, the theaters, universities, and antique shops. Send two dollars for their descriptive listing of homes.

Shore Inne
54 EAST SHORE ROAD, GROTON LONG POINT, CONNECTICUT 06340

Tel: **(203) 536-1180**
Host(s): **Helen Ellison**
Location: **3½ miles west of Mystic**
No. of Rooms: **7**
No. of Private Baths: **3**
Maximum No. of Guests Sharing Bath: **2**
Double/pb: **$45**
Single/pb: **$42**
Double/sb: **$38**
Single/sb: **$35**

Months of Operation: **April to November**
Reduced Rates: **20%, April, May, November; 7%, weekly**
Breakfast: **Continental**
Credit Cards: **MC, VISA**
Air-Conditioning: **No**
Pets: **No**
Children: **Welcome**
Smoking: **Permitted**
Social Drinking: **Permitted**

Capturing the charm of the Connecticut coast, the inn's gracious rooms command water views. It is within a few miles of Mystic Seaport, the Marine Life Aquarium, Fort Griswold, and the U.S. Submarine Base and Memorial. Swimming, fishing, biking, and tennis are a few steps from the door. Boats can be anchored immediately off shore, and harbor and day cruises are available. Helen encourages you to enjoy the TV, library, and sun-rooms.

Shore Inne

Ivoryton Inn
MAIN STREET, IVORYTON, CONNECTICUT 06442

Tel: **(203) 767-0422**
Host(s): **Jean and Doug Neumann**
Location: **30 miles south of Hartford**
No. of Rooms: **28**
No. of Private Baths: **28**
Double/pb: **$55**
Single/pb: **$50**
Months of Operation: **All year**
Reduced Rates: **Available**

Breakfast: **Available**
Credit Cards: **AMEX, MC, VISA**
Air-Conditioning: **Yes**
Pets: **No**
Childen: **Welcome**
Smoking: **Permitted**
Social Drinking: **Permitted**
Airport Pickup: **Yes**

The inn takes its name from the days back in 1800 when the ivory trade prospered here. It has a tap room with bar and fireplace, and a living room for reading and relaxing. You may select from a full menu at breakfast (not included in the rates) and may decide to have it served in bed. Many outstanding restaurants, the Ivoryton Playhouse, and historic Essex waterfront are all close by. Minutes away are the Goodspeed Opera House, Gillette Castle, and Mystic Seaport.

Charley's Harbour Guest House
EDGEMONT STREET, MYSTIC, CONNECTICUT 06355

Tel: **(203) 572-9253**
Host(s): **Charles Lecouras, Jr.**
Location: **6 miles east of New London**
No. of Rooms: **4**
No. of Private Baths: **4**
Double/pb: **$60**
Single/pb: **$40**
Guest Cottage: **$100 sleeps 6**
Months of Operation: **All year**

Reduced Rates: **Labor Day to June 1,
$25 (single), $40 (double), $70
(cottage)**
Breakfast: **No**
Air-Conditioning: **Yes**
Pets: **Welcome**
Children: **Welcome**
Smoking: **Permitted**
Social Drinking: **Permitted**
Airport Pickup: **Yes**
Foreign Languages: **Greek**

Charles's house faces 200 feet of private waterfront property where you can view the ships being launched on the Mystic River. He has a private boat dock and will arrange for boat or canoe rentals. Those who travel without cars will appreciate how everything is within walking distance, including the railroad depot, shops, restaurants, and the Mystic Seaport. You are welcome to use the kitchen to prepare your own breakfast.

Comolli's Bed & Breakfast House
36 BRUGGEMAN PLACE, MYSTIC, CONNECTICUT 06355

Tel: **(203) 536-8723**
Host(s): **Dorothy M. Comolli**
Location: **Between routes 1 & 27**
No. of Rooms: **2**
Maximum No. of Guests Sharing
Bath: **3**
Double/sb: **$50**
Single/sb: **$45**

Months of Operation: **All year**
Reduced Rates: **No**
Breakfast: **Continental**
Air-Conditioning: **No**
Pets: **No**
Children: **No**
Smoking: **Permitted**
Social Drinking: **Permitted**
Airport Pickup: **Yes**

Located on a hilltop overlooking the Mystic River, Dorothy's immaculate home is a short walk to the seaport. In summer, a courtesy bus takes you to all the other area attractions. Limited to three adult guests at a time, this assures personal attention and a friendly atmosphere. Always cordial, Dorothy serves light snacks in the evening.

1833 House
33 GREENMANVILLE AVENUE, MYSTIC, CONNECTICUT 06355

Tel: (203) 572-0633
Host(s): **Joan Smith**
Location: **10 miles east of New London**
No. of Rooms: **5**
No. of Private Baths: **2**
Maximum No. of Guests Sharing Bath: **3**
Double/pb: **$42–$46**
Single/pb: **$35**
Double/sb: **$40–$44**
Single/sb: **$24**

Suites: **$48**
Months of Operation: **All year**
Reduced Rates: **November 1 to April 1**
Breakfast: **Continental**
Air-Conditioning: **No**
Pets: **Welcome**
Children: **Welcome (crib)**
Smoking: **Permitted**
Social Drinking: **Permitted**
Airport Pickup: **Yes**

This house is right at the entrance of the world-famous Seaport Museum of Mystic. From Joan's backyard and some of the bedrooms, you can glimpse the tall ships. At the 1833, you will find the atmosphere of old New England in everything. During your stay, you will want to visit the Seaport, the Aquarium, and Old Mystic Village. From June through September the courtesy bus will take you from one exhibit to another. Joan will be happy to watch the family pet while you take in the sights.

The Pentway House
ONE BROADWAY, MYSTIC, CONNECTICUT 06355

Tel: (203) 536-1716 (after 3:30 P.M.)
Host(s): **Paula Norberg**
Location: **1 mile from I-95**
No. of Rooms: **5**
No. of Private Baths: **2**
Maximum No. of Guests Sharing Bath: **4**
Double/pb: **$50**
Single/pb: **$50**
Double/sb: **$45**
Single/sb: **$45**

Suites: **$85 (2-bedroom family unit)**
Months of Operation: **All year**
Reduced Rates: **25%, October 15 to May 15**
Breakfast: **Continental**
Air-Conditioning: **Yes**
Pets: **No**
Children: **Welcome**
Smoking: **Permitted**
Social Drinking: **Permitted**
Airport Pickup: **Yes**

Enjoy the nautical charm of Mystic and relax at this comfortable home located a few blocks from the seaport. You are welcome to use the cable TV or cool off in the huge swimming pool, with a diving board and water slide, in the backyard. The bedrooms are newly furnished in dark pine. Paula's an experienced motel manager so you can expect all the necessary comforts teamed with special hospitality.

The Taber
ROUTE 1, 29 WILLIAMS AVENUE, MYSTIC, CONNECTICUT 06355

Tel: **(203) 536-4904**
Host(s): **Margaret Taber**
Location: **1 mile from I-95**
No. of Rooms: **6**
No. of Private Baths: **2**
Maximum No. of Guests Sharing
  Bath: **4**
Double/pb: **$52**
Single/pb: **$48**
Double/sb: **$48**
Single/sb: **$38**

Guest Cottage: **$90 sleeps 5**
Months of Operation: **All year**
Reduced Rates: **November 1 to May 1**
Breakfast: **Continental**
Credit Cards: **MC, VISA**
Air-Conditioning: **Yes**
Pets: **No**
Children: **Welcome (crib)**
Smoking: **Permitted**
Social Drinking: **Permitted**

Conveniently located two blocks from Amtrak and one block from the beach, this immaculate home was built in 1829 and has been completely restored and refurbished. In addition to the guest rooms, Margaret has built an AAA-rated motel, as well as efficiencies. Rates for these are quoted upon request. Enjoy Mystic Village where various crafts are explained and demonstrated in the quaint shops.

The Mountain View Inn
ROUTE 272, NORFOLK, CONNECTICUT 06058

Tel: **(203) 542-5595**
Host(s): **Lynn and Chuck Amey**
Location: **40 miles west of Hartford**
No. of Rooms: **11**
No. of Private Baths: **5**
Maximum No. of Guests Sharing
  Bath: **6**
Double/pb: **$57**
Single/pb: **$48**
Double/sb: **$52**
Single/sb: **$45**
Suites: **$75**

Months of Operation: **All year**
Reduced Rates: **20%, January to
  March**
Breakfast: **Continental**
Other Meals: **Available**
Credit Cards: **AMEX, MC, VISA**
Air-Conditioning: **No**
Pets: **Sometimes**
Children: **Welcome**
Smoking: **Permitted**
Social Drinking: **Permitted**

Located in a picture-perfect and noncommercial New England town, this charming residence is decorated with Victorian antiques. It is personal and intimate, with several sitting rooms on the first floor, an unusual antique bar, and an outdoor veranda. Chuck is the chef and runs an outstanding restaurant on the premises, featuring unusual cuisine and delicious soups, breads, and pastries. A buffet breakfast is served on the enclosed porch. Dining is by candlelight.

Captain Stannard House
138 SOUTH MAIN STREET, WESTBROOK, CONNECTICUT 06498

Tel: **(203) 399-7565**
Host(s): **Al and Betty Barnett**
Location: **25 miles southeast of New London**
No. of Rooms: **6**
No. of Private Baths: **6**
Double/pb: **$55**
Single/pb: **$55**
Months of Operation: **All year**

Reduced Rates: **No**
Breakfast: **Continental**
Credit Cards: **MC, VISA**
Air-Conditioning: **Yes**
Pets: **No**
Children: **No**
Smoking: **Permitted**
Social Drinking: **Permitted**

This Georgian federal house with its fan windows is the former home of a sea captain. Recapture the charm of yesteryear when you register in the country store atmosphere. Play croquet or horseshoes, relax with a book, or browse through the on-premises antique shop. The village and the beach are close by. It is convenient to Mystic Seaport, Goodspeed Opera House, river cruises, fine restaurants, and charming shops.

DELAWARE

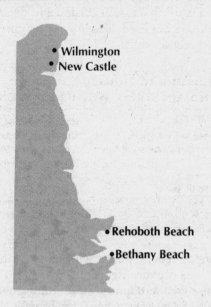

• Wilmington
• New Castle

• Rehoboth Beach

•Bethany Beach

Bed & Breakfast of Delaware
1804 BREEN LANE, WILMINGTON, DELAWARE 19810

Tel: (302) 475-0340
Coordinator: **Barbara Rogers**
States/Regions Covered:
 Delaware—Statewide;
 Maryland—Elkton;
 Pennsylvania—Chadds Ford

Rates (Single/Double):
  Modest: $20-$25 $30-$35
  Average: $25-$30 $35-$40
  Luxury: $30-$35 $45-$50
Credit Cards: **No**

Barbara's host homes are within easy reach of Philadelphia, the Pennsylvania Amish country, Annapolis, Chesapeake Bay, as well as the many historic and beautiful tourist regions within Delaware. They are convenient to historic and artistic communities, and all the accommodations have private baths.

The Sand Box & Sea-Vista Villas
BOX 62, BETHANY BEACH, DELAWARE 19930

Tel: **(302) 539-3354 or (202) 223-0322**
Host(s): **Dale M. Duvall**
Location: **1/2 mile from Route 1**
No. of Rooms: **3**
No. of Private Baths: **3**
Double/pb: **$45–$50**
Single/pb: **$40**
Months of Operation: **April 1 to November 23**

Reduced Rates: **No**
Breakfast: **Full**
Air-Conditioning: **Yes**
Pets: **Sometimes**
Children: **No**
Smoking: **Permitted**
Social Drinking: **Permitted**

Your charming, cosmopolitan, and most cordial host has two villas in a lovely wooded setting near Rehoboth Beach and Ocean City, Maryland. Guests will find the tennis court, swimming pool, terrace, and superb beach fine therapy after an urban winter. The Sandbox has two double bedrooms with baths, a deluxe kitchen, and a fireplace for chilly times. The Sea Vista features a double bedroom and bath. Dale offers Happy Hour on the house.

William Penn Guest House
206 DELAWARE STREET, NEW CASTLE, DELAWARE 19720

Tel: **(302) 328-7736**
Host(s): **Mr. and Mrs. Richard Burwell**
Location: **1 mile from Route 13**
No. of Rooms: **4**
Maximum No. of Guests Sharing Bath: **4**
Double/sb: **$30**
Single/sb: **$25**
Months of Operation: **All year**

Reduced Rates: **No**
Breakfast: **No**
Air-Conditioning: **Yes**
Pets: **No**
Children: **Welcome**
Smoking: **Permitted**
Social Drinking: **Permitted**
Foreign Languages: **Italian**

If you're a history buff, perhaps a stay in a 1682 house named for William Penn is what you've been seeking. Located in the heart of New Castle's historic district, the accommodations here are most comfortable. A lovely park for strolling and for the children to play in borders the Delaware shore, just two blocks away.

Beach House Bedroom
BOX 138, REHOBOTH BEACH, DELAWARE 19971

Tel: **(302) 227-0937**
Host(s): **Sally DeBelles**
Location: **125 miles east of Washington, D.C.**
No. of Rooms: **2**
No. of Private Baths: **1**
Maximum No. of Guests Sharing Bath: **4**
Double/pb: **$40**
Single/pb: **$40**
Double/sb: **$35**
Single/sb: **$35**
Months of Operation: **May to September**
Reduced Rates: **10%, June and September**
Breakfast: **Continental**
Air-Conditioning: **Yes**
Pets: **No**
Children: **No**
Smoking: **Permitted**
Social Drinking: Permitted

This is a modern, tree-shaded beach cottage, with a screened-in porch made for relaxing. The beach is two blocks away, and tennis and sailing are nearby. The atmosphere is casual. It's just a bike ride away from great restaurants, shops, and the boardwalk. Minimum stay is two days; three days for holiday weekends.

DISTRICT OF COLUMBIA

D.C.

Maryland

Virginia

The Bed & Breakfast League, Ltd.
2855 29TH STREET, N.W., WASHINGTON, D.C. 20008

Tel: (202) 232-8718
Coordinator: **Diana Chapin MacLeish**
States/Regions Covered: **Washington, D.C.; U.S.A; Canada; Virgin Islands; United Kingdom; France**

Rates (Single/Double):
Average: **$30**   **$38**
Luxury: **$50**   **$75**
Credit Cards: **AMEX, MC, VISA**

The Bed & Breakfast League is an international reservation service. Membership in the league is required for travel *outside of the Washington, D.C. area only*. The annual fee of $25 entitles you to a toll-free reservation number and the host directory, which describes all available accommodations in 40 states, Canada, the U.S. Virgin Islands, the United Kingdom, and France.

Sweet Dreams & Toast
P.O. BOX 4835-0035, WASHINGTON, D.C. 20008

Tel: (202) 483-9191
Coordinator: **Ellie Chastain**
States/Regions Covered: **Washington, D.C.; Maryland—Annapolis, Bethesda, Chevy Chase, Silver Spring; Virginia—Alexandria, Arlington, McLean**

Rates (Single/Double):
Average: **$25–$35**   **$35–$50**
Luxury: **$40**   **$60**
Credit Cards: **MC, VISA**

The capital of the United States is awe inspiring. You will want to spend several days to take it all in. This is your opportunity to watch history in the making and to visit the glorious monuments erected to memorialize those who shaped America's history.

Ellie's hosts will direct you to restaurants and special shops that are off the beaten tourist track, where you will get the best value for your dollars.

Bed 'n' Breakfast Ltd. of Washington, D.C.
P.O. BOX 12011, WASHINGTON, D.C. 20005

Tel: **(202) 328-3510**
Coordinator: **Mila Brooks, Anna Earle**
States/Regions Covered: **Washington, D.C.**

Rates (Single/Double):

Modest:	**$15**	**$30**
Average:	**$25–$30**	**$41**
Luxury:	**$35–$40**	**$50–$55**

Credit Cards: **No**

This service boasts a network of homes in the city's historic districts. Anna and Mila have been on the Washington scene a long time, and they know that the best places need not cost the most. Several of their accommodations are located in gracious Georgetown and on Dupont Circle. There is a delightful selection of homes on Logan Circle and in the lovely upper Northwest section of town. All of the homes are convenient to public transportation.

Kalorama Guest House
1854 MINTWOOD PLACE, N.W., WASHINGTON, D.C. 20009

Tel: **(202) 667-6369**
Host(s): **Roberta Pieczenik, James Mench**
No. of Rooms: **6**
Maximum No. of Guests Sharing Bath: **6**
Double/sb: **$35–$45**
Single/sb: **$30–$40**
Guest Cottage: **$50 sleeps 4**
Months of Operation: **All year**
Reduced Rates: **7th night free**
Breakfast: **Continental**
Credit Cards: **AMEX, MC, VISA**
Air-Conditioning: **Yes**
Pets: **No**
Children: **Yes**
Smoking: **Permitted**
Social Drinking: **Permitted**

Located in the fashionable embassy district, this Victorian town house maintains the ambience of its era. Guests enjoy breakfast in the dining room each morning and go to the upstairs parlor for sherry in the afternoon. The guest rooms are inviting and gracious, with brass headboards, plush comforters, Oriental carpets, and wing chairs. Jim is an actor; Roberta is a criminologist and they both are dedicated to making your stay comfortable.

The Manse
1307 RHODE ISLAND AVENUE, N.W., WASHINGTON, D.C. 20005

Tel: **(202) 232-9150**
Host(s): **Mila Brooks**
No. of Rooms: **4**
Maximum No. of Guests Sharing
  Bath: **3**
Double/sb: **$41**
Single/sb: **$26–30**
Months of Operation: **All year**
Reduced Rates: **No**
Breakfast: **Continental**
Air-Conditioning: **Yes**
Pets: **Welcome**
Children: **Welcome**
Smoking: **Permitted**
Social Drinking: **Permitted**
Foreign Languages: **Spanish**

Mila is the former deputy director of the Peace Corps in Chile. Her home is a 19th-century Victorian that features bay windows, crystal chandeliers, working fireplaces, antiques, and the handicrafts she collected on her travels. Tourist attractions and government offices are close by. It's a few blocks to the metro and 10 blocks to Ronnie and Nancy's house.

FLORIDA

Fernandina Beach • • Amelia Island
• Pensacola • Jacksonville
Lynn Haven • • St. Augustine
Cedar Key •
Orlando • • Winter Park
Dade City •
Tarpon Springs • • Lakeland
Clearwater • • Tampa
St. Petersburg • • Bradenton
• Fort Myers
Naples •
• Miami Beach
Big Pine Key •
• Key West

1735 House
584 SOUTH FLETCHER, AMELIA ISLAND, FLORIDA 32034

Tel: **(904) 261-5878**
Host(s): **David and Susan Caples**
Location: **35 miles northeast of
   Jacksonville**
No. of Rooms: **5**
No. of Private Baths: **5**
Double/pb: **$55**
Single/pb: **$45**
Guest Cottage: **$85–$115 sleeps
   up to 6**

Months of Operation: **All year**
Reduced Rates: **5%, seniors; families**
Breakfast: **Continental**
Credit Cards: **AMEX, MC, VISA**
Air-Conditioning: **Yes**
Pets: **No**
Children: **Welcome**
Smoking: **Permitted**
Social Drinking: **Permitted**
Airport Pickup: **Yes**

This quaint country inn is situated on the beach of beautiful Amelia Island. The house is furnished with wicker and rattan, and the bedrooms have interesting antiques. David and Susan allow you to use the kitchen for light snacks, and complimentary bags are supplied so you can take home your seashell collection. There's surf-casting right on the beach and deep-sea fishing or boat charters can be arranged. Don't miss the private tour of the renowned Greyfield Inn.

The Barnacle
ROUTE 1, BOX 780 A, LONG BEACH ROAD, BIG PINE KEY, FLORIDA 33043

Tel: **(305) 872-3298**	Reduced Rates: **No**
Host(s): **Woody and Joan Cornell**	Breakfast: **Full**
Location: **33 miles east of Key West**	Air-Conditioning: **Yes**
No. of Rooms: **1**	Pets: **No**
No. of Private Baths: **2**	Children: **No**
Double/pb: **$40**	Smoking: **Permitted**
Guest Cottage: **$50 sleeps 2**	Social Drinking: **Permitted**
Months of Operation: **All year**	Foreign Languages: **French**

For the ultimate in privacy, the self-contained cottage is a tropical tree house with stained glass windows. The guest room in the main house has a view of the ocean and overlooks the atrium, hot tub, and lush plants. The emphasis here is on the sun and the sea, with warm hospitality offered in abundance. There's scuba diving and fishing right off "your own" beach; Bahia Honda State Park is two miles away and Key West has lots of activity.

Bed & Breakfast on the Ocean

P.O. BOX 378, LONG BEACH ROAD, BIG PINE KEY, FLORIDA
33043

Tel: (305) 872-2878
Host(s): Jon and Kathleen Threlkeld
Location: 15 miles southwest of
 Marathon
No. of Rooms: 3
No. of Private Baths: 1
Maximum No. of Guests Sharing
 Bath: 4
Double/pb: $40
Single/pb: $35
Double/sb: $40

Single/sb: $35
Months of Operation: All year
Reduced Rates: No
Breakfast: Continental
Air-Conditioning: No
Pets: No
Children: Welcome, over 12
Smoking: Permitted
Social Drinking: Permitted
Airport Pickup: Yes

This spectacular Spanish-style home is located directly on the
ocean. Shelling and beachcombing are popular local pastimes.
Close to Bahia Honda State Park and Key West, the house's
stained glass windows, plants, and lovely gardens all add to the
charm. The guest rooms are comfortably cooled with large Ba-
hama fans. Jon likes scuba diving and snorkeling; Kathleen likes
gardening and good books. Both enjoy sharing their travel experiences with their guests.

Banyan House

624 FONTANA LANE, BRADENTON, FLORIDA 33529

Tel: (813) 746-8633
Host(s): Sally DeBelles
Location: 30 miles south of St.
 Petersburg
No. of Rooms: 1
No. of Private Baths: 1
Double/pb: $35
Single/pb: $35
Guest Cottage: $55 sleeps 2
Months of Operation: November to
 May

Reduced Rates: 10%, May,
 November, December; 15%, weekly;
 seniors; families
Breakfast: Continental
Air-Conditioning: Yes
Pets: Sometimes
Children: No
Smoking: Permitted
Social Drinking: Permitted

Sun yourself on the whitest sand, swim in the Gulf of Mexico,
play tennis or golf, then return to Sally's home. The separate
guest house shares a terrace with the main house, while the
bedroom and private bath are in the main house. The guest house

has light cooking facilities. The Ringling Museum, Sarasota, Busch Gardens, and Tampa are nearby.

Island Hotel
MAIN STREET, CEDAR KEY, FLORIDA 32625

Tel: **(904) 543-5111**
Host(s): **Marcia Rogers**
Location: **24 miles from Rte. 24**
No. of Rooms: **10**
No. of Private Baths: **3**
Maximum No. of Guests Sharing
  Bath: **4**
Double/pb: **$50**
Single/pb: **$50**
Double/sb: **$35**
Single/sb: **$35**

Months of Operation: **All year**
Reduced Rates: **No**
Breakfast: **Full**
Other Meals: **Available**
Air-Conditioning: **Some**
Pets: **Sometimes**
Children: **Welcome**
Smoking: **Permitted**
Social Drinking: **Permitted**
Airport Pickup: **Yes**
Foreign Languages: **French**

The exterior of this historic landmark (circa 1850) is covered with tabley, made from crushed oyster shell and limestone. The atmosphere, with the slowly turning ceiling fans, potbelly stove, and Chistopher the resident parrot, will bring Casablanca to mind. French doors lead to the dining veranda, and classical music fills the air. Antiques, fresh flowers, oak rockers, and a hammock add to the ambience. The four-star gourmet dining room on the premises will certainly impress you. Marcia is cordial, cosmopolitan, and will do everything she can to assure you a memorable stay in this sleepy fishing village.

Bed & Breakfast of Tampa Bay
3234 TERN WAY, FEATHERSOUND, CLEARWATER, FLORIDA 33520

Tel: **(813) 576-5825**
Host(s): **Vivian and David Grimm**
Location: **7 miles west of Tampa**
No. of Rooms: **3**
No. of Private Baths: **1**
Maximum No. of Guests Sharing
  Bath: **4**
Double/pb: **$30**
Single/pb: **$20**
Double/sb: **$25**

Single/sb: **$15**
Months of Operation: **All year**
Reduced Rates: **No**
Breakfast: **Full**
Air-Conditioning: **Yes**
Pets: **Sometimes**
Children: **Welcome**
Smoking: **Permitted**
Social Drinking: **No**
Airport Pickup: **Yes**

The lovely gardens of this fine stucco home have an Oriental style, and the interior is graced with fine Oriental and European art. Whenever Vivian and David travel, they bring home souvenirs to enhance their decor. Busch Gardens, St. Petersburg Fine Arts Museum, and Tarpon Springs are 15 miles away; Disney World, Circus World, and Sea World are 65 miles away. If you want to stay close to home, the Grimms will lend you their bikes. You're welcome to use the pool, play the piano, or use the kitchen for light snacks.

The Pines
DARBY ROAD, RT. 2 BOX 309F, DADE CITY, FLORIDA 33525

Tel: **(904) 588-2791**
Host(s): **Barbara and Bill Moyse**
Location: **¾ mile from I-75**
No. of Rooms: **2**
No. of Private Baths: **1**
Maximum No. of Guests Sharing
  Bath: **2**
Double/pb: **$18**
Single/pb: **$15**
Double/sb: **$18**

Single/sb: **$15**
Months of Operation: **All year**
Reduced Rates: **No**
Breakfast: **Continental**
Other Meals: **Available**
Air-Conditioning: **Yes**
Pets: **No**
Children: **No**
Smoking: **No**
Social Drinking: **No**

Barbara and Bill's Georgian red brick home is situated on 10 acres of pine and oak trees in an area of rolling hills and orange groves. You will be made to feel right at home and may use the kitchen for your light snacks. It's close to St. Leo College and only 30 minutes to the University of South Florida and fine shops.

The Bailey House—1895
28 SOUTH 7TH STREET, P.O. BOX 805, FERNANDINA BEACH, FLORIDA 32034

Tel: **(904) 261-5390**
Host(s): **Tom and Diane Hay**
Location: **32 miles northeast of Jacksonville (on Amelia Island)**
No. of Rooms: **4**
No. of Private Baths: **4**
Double/pb: **$65–$85**
Single/pb: **$55–$75**
Months of Operation: **All year**
Reduced Rates: **Weekly**

Breakfast: **Continental**
Other Meals: **No**
Credit Cards: **AMEX**
Air-Conditioning: **Yes**
Pets: **No**
Children: **Welcome, over 10**
Smoking: **No**
Social Drinking: **Permitted**
Airport Pickup: **Yes**
Foreign Languages: **French**

Individually cited on the National Register, this house stands in the heart of the 30-block historic district. It is an outstanding example of the Queen Anne style, and was completed in 1895. Furnished with a vast collection of carefully chosen period antiques, its carved furniture, brass beds, pump organs, fringed lamps, footed tubs, and marble-topped tables will win your admiration. Conveniently located, it's less than 10 minutes to the golf course, lighted tennis courts, and fine beaches.

Wind Song Garden
5570-4 WOODROSE COURT, FORT MYERS, FLORIDA 33907

Tel: **(813) 936-6378**
Host(s): **Embe Burdick**
Location: **150 miles northwest of Miami**
No. of Rooms: **1**
No. of Private Baths: **1**
Double/pb: **$35**
Single/pb: **$30**
Months of Operation: **All year**

Reduced Rates: **No**
Breakfast: **Continental**
Air-Conditioning: **Yes**
Pets: **No**
Children: **No**
Smoking: **No**
Social Drinking: **Permitted**
Airport Pickup: **Yes**

This modern cedar-shake and brick town house has a private courtyard and balcony for your enjoyment. The spacious combination bedroom-and-sitting room is most comfortable. Embe's varied interests are in the arts, crafts, and music. It's close to Sanibel and Captiva islands, fine shopping, good restaurants, and the University of Florida. You are welcome to use the barbecue and pool.

The Biding Place
2625 HANDLEY BOULEVARD, LAKELAND, FLORIDA 33803

Tel: **(813) 686-0493**
Host(s): **Ramona Guffey**
Location: **40 miles east of Tampa**
No. of Rooms: **1**
No. of Private Baths: **1**
Double/pb: **$35**
Single/pb: **$35**
Months of Operation: **All year**

Reduced Rates: **No**
Breakfast: **Continental**
Air-Conditioning: **Yes**
Pets: **No**
Children: **No**
Smoking: **No**
Social Drinking: **Permitted**
Airport Pickup: **No**

This charming brick cottage has a warm and welcoming atmosphere. Ramona has tastefully furnished it with an eclectic blend of antique, wicker, and traditional pieces. Her color scheme is sunny yellow with white and green accents. Conveniently located, it is 40 miles to Busch Gardens or Epcot, and only 10 miles to Cypress Gardens. In season, you can pick your breakfast fruit right off the grapefruit or orange tree.

Gulf Coast Inn
324 BELL CIRCLE, LYNN HAVEN, FLORIDA 32444

Tel: (904) 265-5275	Reduced Rates: 10%, September to March; 10%, seniors
Host(s): Louis Escuela	
Location: 4 miles north of Panama City	Breakfast: Full
	Air-Conditioning: Yes
No. of Rooms: 2	Pets: No
Maximum No. of Guests Sharing Bath: 4	Children: Welcome, over 3
	Smoking: No
Double/sb: $38	Social Drinking: Permitted
Single/sb: $34	Airport Pickup: Yes
Months of Operation: All year	Foreign Languages: Spanish

This large executive home is really in Panama City, close to the beach and the Gulf of Mexico. Swimming, fishing, and waterskiing are always available. You can rent a bike and pedal to the two large amusement parks or to St. Andrews State Park. Louis prepares a fine breakfast and wants you to make yourself at home at all times.

Bed & Breakfast of the Florida Keys
5 MAN-O-WAR DRIVE, P.O. BOX 1373, MARATHON, FLORIDA 33050

Tel: (305) 743-4118	Rates (Single/Double):	
Coordinator: Joan E. Hopp	Modest: $20	$25
States/Regions Covered: Big Pine Key, Islamorada, Key Largo, Key West, Marathon, Cudjoe Key, Tavernier	Average: $25	$35
	Luxury: $30	$50
	Credit Cards: No	

Joan arranges placement in private homes, apartments, or condominiums with hospitable hosts who will share their knowledge of the best places to eat, where to find boat rentals, where to scuba dive or snorkel, and where the best seashells can be found. Sightseeing is fabulous in the keys, where the year-round temperature is 72°.

Hopp-Inn Guest Home
5 MAN-O-WAR DRIVE, MARATHON, FLORIDA 33050

Tel: (305) 743-4118
Host(s): **Joan and Joseph Hopp**
Location: **100 miles west of Miami**
No. of Rooms: **3**
No. of Private Baths: **3**
Double/pb: **$35**
Single/pb: **$25**
Guest Cottage: **$75–$90 sleeps 4 to 6**
Months of Operation: **September 13 to July 31**
Reduced Rates: **10%, May, June, September 15 to November 15**

Breakfast: **Full**
Other Meals: **Available**
Air-Conditioning: **Yes**
Pets: **No**
Children: **Welcome (crib)**
Smoking: **Permitted**
Social Drinking: **Permitted**
Airport Pickup: **Yes**
Foreign Languages: **German**

This oceanfront, white stucco Florida Keys house is in a tropical setting. The temperature is 72° year-round, and there is scuba diving, snorkeling, and the best fishing nearby. In fact, if you catch the fish, Joan and Joseph will supply the rest for dinner. The house is attractively decorated and the atmosphere is casual and comfortable.

Bed & Breakfast Co.
1205 MARIPOSA AVENUE #233, MIAMI, FLORIDA 33146

Tel: (305) 661-3270
Coordinator: **Marcella Schaible**
States/Regions Covered: **Delray, Ft. Lauderdale, Hollywood, Jupiter, Lakeland, Miami Beach, Palm Beach, The Keys**

Rates (Single/Double):
　Modest: **$20–28　$28–$32**
　Average: **$28–$40　$40–$45**
　Luxury: **$38–$54 ▪ $54–$65**
Credit Cards: **No**

With her vast selection of accommodations, Marcella is able to match your preferences. A beach house on the ocean, an unbelievable tree house, private quarters on a yacht, a gracious room with a pool outside your door, as well as modest, share-a-bath homes can be your home away from home. Discount admission tickets to many attractions are provided to her guests.

Feller House
2473 LONGBOAT DRIVE, NAPLES, FLORIDA 33942

Tel: **(813) 774-0182**
Host(s): **Wayne and Pat Feller**
Location: **100 miles west of Miami**
No. of Rooms: **1**
No. of Private Baths: **1**
Double/pb: **$30**
Single/pb: **$23**
Months of Operation: **October to April**

Reduced Rates: **No**
Breakfast: **Full**
Air-Conditioning: **Yes**
Pets: **No**
Children: **Welcome, over 5**
Smoking: **Permitted**
Social Drinking: **Permitted**
Airport Pickup: **Yes**
Foreign Languages: **German**

This ranch-style home is decorated with paintings, a few antiques, and a grand piano. Your hosts will gladly serve cocktails on the outside patio. A breakfast includes homemade bread and muffins. Guests may use the swimming pool and nearby tennis courts. Feller House is close to Everglades National Park, the Gulf of Mexico, and the beach.

Avonelle's Bed & Breakfast
4755 ANDERSON ROAD, ORLANDO, FLORIDA 32806

Tel: **(305) 275-8733**
Host(s): **Jan Ross**
Location: **4 miles north of downtown Orlando**
No. of Rooms: **2**
No. of Private Baths: **2**
Double/pb: **$35**
Single/pb: **$30**
Months of Operation: **All year**

Reduced Rates: **No**
Breakfast: **Continental**
Air-Conditioning: **Yes**
Pets: **No**
Children: **Welcome**
Smoking: **No**
Social Drinking: **Permitted**
Airport Pickup: **Yes**

Surrounded by giant oaks and citrus trees, Jan's home combines beauty with rustic charm. It is minutes away from Disney World, Epcot, and all central Florida attractions. Arrangements can be made to sail the Gulf of Mexico with Captain Ken Ross aboard his 35-foot trimaran.

Bed & Breakfast of Orlando
8205 BANYAN BOULEVARD, ORLANDO, FLORIDA 32819

Tel: **(305) 352-9157**
Host(s): **Bobbie Jean Havlish**

Location: **2 miles from I-4**
No. of Rooms: **3**

Maximum No. of Guests Sharing Bath: **6**	Breakfast: **Full**
	Air-Conditioning: **Yes**
Double/sb: **$45–$50**	Pets: **No**
Single/sb: **$40–$45**	Children: **Welcome**
Months of Operation: **All year**	Smoking: **Permitted**
Reduced Rates: **$25–$35, May to August**	Social Drinking: **Permitted**
	Airport Pickup: **Yes**

Located in Sand Lake Hills, close to the country clubs of Bay Hills and Orange Tree, is Bobbie's lovely home. Weather permitting, she serves breakfast in the screened-in Florida room overlooking the orange groves. It is all very quiet and peaceful, yet convenient to Epcot, Disney World, Sea World, and the Orange County Convention Center.

Sunshine Inn
508 DECATUR AVENUE, PENSACOLA, FLORIDA 32507

Tel: **(904) 455-6781**	Breakfast: **Full**
Host(s): **The Jablonskis**	Air-Conditioning: **Yes**
Location: **8 miles from I-10**	Pets: **No**
No. of Rooms: **2**	Children: **Welcome, over 10**
Maximum No. of Guests Sharing Bath: **4**	Smoking: **Permitted**
	Social Drinking: **Permitted**
Double/sb: **$28**	Airport Pickup: **Yes**
Months of Operation: **All year**	Foreign Languages: **German**
Reduced Rates: **No**	

Sun yourself on the whitest sand, swim in the Gulf of Mexico, and return to the Sunshine Inn for a dip in the pool. Or, walk a block to the bayou for fishing. Feel free to relax in the living room and seek touring advice from your knowledgeable hostess, Renate.

Kenwood Inn
38 MARINE STREET, ST. AUGUSTINE, FLORIDA 32084

Tel: **(904) 824-2116**	Double/pb: **$40–$60**
Host(s): **Elsie Hedetniemi, Robert Carr**	Single/pb: **$40–$60**
Location: **40 miles south of Jacksonville**	Double/sb: **$30**
	Single/sb: **$30**
No. of Rooms: **11**	Months of Operation: **All year**
No. of Private Baths: **8**	Reduced Rates: **7th day free**
Maximum No. of Guests Sharing Bath: **6**	Breakfast: **Continental**
	Credit Cards: **MC, VISA**

Air-Conditioning: **Yes**	Smoking: **Permitted**
Pets: **No**	Social Drinking: **Permitted**
Children: **Welcome, over 12**	Airport Pickup: **Yes**

If you are to discover a Victorian building in Florida, how appropriate that it should be in the historic section of St. Augustine, the oldest city in the U.S. This New England-style inn is a rarity in the South; this one has old-fashioned beds with color-coordinated touches right down to the sheets and linens. Breakfast may be taken in your room, in the courtyard surrounded by trees, or by the swimming pool. Tour trains, the waterfront shops, restaurants, and museums are within walking distance.

Bayboro House
1719 BEACH DRIVE S.E., ST. PETERSBURG, FLORIDA 33701

Tel: **(813) 823-4955**	Reduced Rates: **$25–$35, May 1 to**
Host(s): **Gordon and Antonia Powers**	**November 1**
Location: **1/2 mile from I-275**	Breakfast: **Continental**
No. of Rooms: **3**	Air-Conditioning: **Yes**
No. of Private Baths: **3**	Pets: **No**
Double/pb: **$40–$55**	Children: **Welcome, over 10**
Single/pb: **$35–$50**	Smoking: **No**
Months of Operation: **All year**	Social Drinking: **Permitted**

A unique three-story Queen Anne with airy, high-ceilinged rooms and a wraparound veranda in view of Tampa Bay, it is graced with antique furniture plus tropical plants and flowers. It is the ideal spot for sunning, beachcombing, and fishing. You can relax in the hammock or visit unusual shops, fine restaurants, the Sunken Gardens, Salvador Dali museum, or the dog track. Complimentary champagne is served on the veranda when the moon is full; that's just one of the special touches offered by Antonia and Gordon.

A & A Bed & Breakfast of Florida, Inc.
P.O. BOX 1316, WINTER PARK, FLORIDA 32790

Tel: (305) 628-3233
Coordinator: **Brunhilde (Bruni)**
  Fenner
States/Regions Covered: **Orlando**
  area—Disney World, Epcot, Cape
  Kennedy, Sea World, Altamante
  Springs, Winter Park

Rates (Single/Double):
  Modest: **$20**   **$30**
  Average: **$25**   **$35**
  Luxury: **$40**   **$50**
Credit Cards: **No**
Minimum Stay: **2 days**

You should allow several days to really savor all this area has to offer. Bruni's hosts will suggest hints on getting the most out of the major attractions, wonderful un-touristy restaurants, and tips on where to shop for unique gifts to take home. All of her homes have a certain "touch of class" to make you delighted with your visit.

Tallahassee Bed & Breakfast
3023 WINDY HILL LANE, TALLAHASSEE, FLORIDA 32308

Tel: **(904) 385-3768 or 421-5220**
Coordinator: **Martha Thomas**
States/Regions Covered: **Tallahassee**

Rates (Single/Double):
  Modest: **$25**   **$30**
Credit Cards: **MC, VISA**

Tallahassee is the capital of Florida, located in the beautiful Panhandle area near the Gulf of Mexico. The area has much to offer scenically, historically, and culturally. Martha's hosts look forward to having guests and will direct you to places that are tailored to your interests.

The Barnacle

GEORGIA

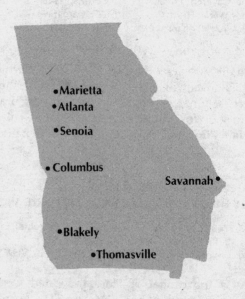

Bed & Breakfast—Atlanta
1221 FAIRVIEW ROAD, N.E., ATLANTA, GEORGIA 30306

Tel: **(404) 872-6338**
Coordinator: **Jane Carney, Madalyne Eplan, Paula Gris**
States/Regions Covered: **Atlanta**

Rates (Single/Double):

Modest:	**$24**	**$28**
Average:	**$28**	**$36**
Luxury:	**$36–$56**	**$40–$60**

Credit Cards: **No**

Visit one of America's most gracious cities, with the advantage of being a houseguest. Jane, Madalyne, and Paula consider transportation and language needs as well as other personal preferences in making your reservation. Locations are offered in the city's most desirable homes, and most offer a private bath. There is a four-dollar surcharge for a one-night stay.

Quail Country Bed & Breakfast, Ltd.
1104 OLD MONTICELLO ROAD, THOMASVILLE, GEORGIA 31792

Tel: **(912) 226-7218 or 226-6882**
Coordinator: **Mercer Watt, Kathy Lanigan**
States/Regions Covered:
  Georgia—Thomas County, Thomasville

Rates (Single/Double):
  Modest: **$25**   **$35**
  Average: **$35**   **$50**
  Luxury: **$50**   **$100**
Credit Cards: **MC, VISA**

Mercer and Kathy have a wide selection of homes, several with swimming pools, in lovely residential areas. There's lots to see and do, including touring historic restorations and plantations. Enjoy the Pebble Hill Plantation museum, historic Glen Arven Country Club, and the April Rose Festival.

Friendly House
946 HIGHLAND VIEW N.E., ATLANTA, GEORGIA 30306

Tel: **(404) 874-0519**
Host(s): **Hilary Jones**
Location: **1½ miles from Peachtree Street**
No. of Rooms: **1**
No. of Private Baths: **1**
Double/pb: **$35**
Single/pb: **$20**
Months of Operation: **All year**

Reduced Rates: **Over 2 nights**
Breakfast: **Continental**
Air-Conditioning: **Yes**
Pets: **No**
Children: **Welcome, over 6**
Smoking: **Permitted**
Social Drinking: **Permitted**
Foreign Languages: **French**

You will enjoy the tranquility of sitting on the porch, surrounded by lovely old trees, after seeing the many city sights. The house, of brick and redwood construction, contains some beautiful antiques and memorabilia Hilary has collected during her many travels abroad. A writer of children's books, she has a myriad of interests, especially people.

Jo's Guest Home
3544 TOLL HOUSE LANE, S.W., ATLANTA, GEORGIA 30331

Tel: **(404) 344-5123**
Host(s): **Mrs. J. L. Foggie**
Location: **2 miles from I-285**
No. of Rooms: **2**

Maximum No. of Guests Sharing Bath: **4**
Double/sb: **$50**
Single/sb: **$30**

Months of Operation: **January to June, September to December**
Reduced Rates: **10%, seniors; 5 or more days**
Breakfast: **Full**
Other Meals: **Available**

Air-Conditioning: **Yes**
Pets: **No**
Children: **Welcome**
Smoking: **Permitted**
Social Drinking: **No**
Airport Pickup: **Yes**

This immaculate and well cared for brick ranch is located on a cul-de-sac in one of Atlanta's finest areas. It's only minutes to the theater, music, dance, sports events, colleges and universities, and shopping malls. When you return from touring, relax on the patio and enjoy the beautiful landscaping, and let Jo spoil you with her gracious hospitality and delicious meals.

Sequoia
727 N. MAIN STREET, BLAKELY, GEORGIA 31723

Tel: **(912) 723-4207**
Host(s): **Joanna Sherman-Dean**
Location: **75 miles from I-75**
No. of Rooms: **2**
Maximum No. of Guests Sharing Bath: **4**
Double/sb: **$35**
Single/sb: **$25**

Months of Operation: **All year**
Reduced Rates: **No**
Breakfast: **Full**
Air-Conditioning: **Yes**
Pets: **No**
Children: **Welcome, over 6**
Smoking: **Permitted**
Social Drinking: **Permitted**

Joanna's two-story Georgian colonial is located in the agricultural belt of south Georgia. Several lakes are nearby, offering water sports and fishing. It is only five miles to the Kolomoki State Park with its museum of Indian artifacts. It is also close to Providence Canyon, as well as to historic restoration villages and plantations. You are welcome to use her kitchen for light snacks.

Mountain View Estate
ROUTE 2, BOX 283, CLEVELAND, GEORGIA 30528

Tel: **(404) 865-4551 (evenings)**
Host(s): **Helen Adams**
Location: **9 miles south of Helen**
No. of Rooms: **2**
No. of Private Baths: **2**
Double/pb: **$25**
Single/pb: **$20**
Suites: **$35 for 2**

Months of Operation: **March 1 to November 30**
Reduced Rates: **Spring**
Breakfast: **Full**
Air-Conditioning: **Yes**
Pets: **No**
Children: **No**
Smoking: **Permitted**
Social Drinking: **No**

Cleveland is known as the Gateway to the Mountains, and it is only nine miles from Helen, the renowned Alpine Village. Helen's ranch-style farmhouse, on six wooded acres, has a deck overlooking the Horse Mountain range. There's a delightful stream for swimming on the property. Alpine Village has a variety of specialty shops and noted ethnic restaurants.

The DeLoffre House
812 BROADWAY, COLUMBUS, GEORGIA 31901

Tel: **(404) 324-1144**
Host(s): **Shirley and Paul Romo**
Location: **Near routes 185 and 280**
No. of Rooms: **4**
No. of Private Baths: **4**
Maximum No. of Guests Sharing
  Bath: **0**
Double/pb: **$53–$57**
Single/pb: **$45–$47**

Months of Operation: **All year**
Reduced Rates: **7th day free**
Breakfast: **Continental**
Credit Cards: **AMEX, MC, VISA**
Air-Conditioning: **Yes**
Pets: **No**
Children: **Welcome, over 11**
Smoking: **Permitted**
Social Drinking: **Permitted**

This 1863 Italianate town house, located in the historic district, is elegantly furnished with Victorian and Empire antiques. The spacious bedrooms have original fireplaces. Each bedroom is supplied with a bowl of fruit, a decanter of sherry, good books, a private phone, and color TV, to make you as comfortable as possible. The opera, theater, museums, and Roosevelt's Little White House are all nearby.

Arden Hall Inn
FOREST OF ARDEN, 1052 ARDEN DRIVE, S.W., MARIETTA, GEORGIA 30060

Tel: **(404) 422-0780**
Host(s): **Dr. and Mrs. Wilkes Henry
  Davis, Jr.**
Location: **18 miles northwest of
  Atlanta**
No. of Rooms: **2**
No. of Private Baths: **2**
Double/pb: **$50**
Single/pb: **$45**
Months of Operation: **All year**

Reduced Rates: **$5 less for 2 nights**
Breakfast: **Full**
Air-Conditioning: **Yes**
Pets: **No**
Children: **No**
Smoking: **No**
Social Drinking: **Permitted**
Airport Pickup: **Yes**
Foreign Languages: **French, German**

This gracious turn-of-the-century home is tastefully furnished with antiques, a grand piano, Oriental rugs, and cherished collected items from all over the world. Wilkes is an ophthalmologist and soloist with the Atlanta Symphony. Dotty is a master chef, professional photographer, and caterer. Don't miss the cruise on the Chattahoochee River and the Calloway Gardens.

The Larsons' House
3740 KENSINGTON DRIVE N.E., MARIETTA, GEORGIA 30066

Tel: **(404) 926-2231**	Months of Operation: **All year**
Host(s): **Doris and Chuck Larson**	Reduced Rates: **No**
Location: **30 miles north of Atlanta**	Breakfast: **Continental**
No. of Rooms: **1**	Air-Conditioning: **Yes**
Maximum No. of Guests Sharing Bath: **2**	Pets: **No**
	Children: **No**
Double/sb: **$35**	Smoking: **No**
Single/sb: **$30**	Social Drinking: **Permitted**

This contemporary ranch-style home is located in the residential section of Canterbury Tales. It has a patio and pool for relaxing, and is across the street from the country club which has golf and tennis facilities. Chuck and Doris will advise on the best things to see and do locally as well as in Atlanta, just 45 minutes away.

Bed & Breakfast Inn
117 GORDON STREET WEST AT CHATHAM SQUARE, SAVANNAH, GEORGIA 31401

Tel: **(912) 238-0518**	Suites: **$44–$48**
Host(s): **Robert T. McAlister**	Months of Operation: **All year**
Location: **½ mile from I-16**	Reduced Rates: **No**
No. of Rooms: **8**	Breakfast: **Continental**
No. of Private Baths: **4**	Credit Cards: **AMEX, MC, VISA**
Maximum No. of Guests Sharing Bath: **4**	Air-Conditioning: **Yes**
	Pets: **No**
Double/pb: **$48**	Children: **Welcome (crib)**
Single/pb: **$44**	Smoking: **Permitted**
Double/sb: **$28**	Social Drinking: **Permitted**
Single/sb: **$24**	

Located in the heart of the historic district, this regal town house, built in 1853, has been beautifully restored. There are both upstairs bedrooms and three-garden apartments, with private entrances, complete kitchens, sofa sleepers for extra guests, overlooking a wonderful garden. Savannah is the epitome of elegance, and the beauty of the floral displays, fountains, and varied architecture is a delight. Don't forget to take a ride in an antique horse-drawn buggy over the cobblestone streets. Bob will be happy to advise you of the best restaurants in the area.

Four Seventeen—The Haslam-Fort House
417 EAST CHARLTON STREET, SAVANNAH, GEORGIA 31401

Tel: **(912) 233-6380**
Host(s): **Alan Fort**
Location: **12 miles from I-95**
No. of Rooms: **1 suite**
No. of Private Baths: **1**
Suites: **$75 (for 2); $125 (for 4)**
Months of Operation: **All year**
Reduced Rates: **July 1 to August 31, $68 for 2, $98 for 4**
Breakfast: **Full**
Air-Conditioning: **Yes**
Pets: **Welcome**
Children: **Welcome (crib)**
Smoking: **Permitted**
Social Drinking: **Permitted**
Foreign Languages: **German, Norwegian, Spanish**

Located in the famed historic district, the ground floor of this lovely town house has a private entrance with easy access for the handicapped, a delightful private garden, two bedrooms, a living room with fireplace, a private bath, and a country kitchen where all the fixings for a do-it-yourself breakfast are on hand. Alan will be happy to direct you to all the special attractions of the area.

The Stoddard-Cooper House
19 W. PERRY STREET, SAVANNAH, GEORGIA 31401

Tel: **(912) 233-6809**
Host(s): **Barbara Hershey**
Location: **12 miles from I-95**
No. of Rooms: **1 suite**
No. of Private Baths: **1**
Suites: **$75 (for 2); $95 (for 3); $125 (for 4)**
Months of Operation: **All year**
Reduced Rates: **July 1 to September 30**
Breakfast: **Continental**
Air-Conditioning: **Yes**
Pets: **No**
Children: **Welcome (crib)**
Smoking: **Permitted**
Social Drinking: **Permitted**

Come stay in the secluded, garden-level suite of this carefully restored historic home (circa 1854), right on Chippewa Square in the heart of the historic district. There are two bedrooms, a wood-burning fireplace in the living room, and a modern kitchen with all the supplies you need for breakfast. The suite is beautifully appointed with antiques.

The Culpepper House
P.O. BOX 462, MORGAN AT BROAD, SENOIA, GEORGIA 30276

Tel: **(404) 599-8182**
Host(s): **Mary A. Brown**
Location: **37 miles south of Atlanta**
No. of Rooms: **4**
No. of Private Baths: **1**
Maximum No. of Guests Sharing
  Bath: **5**
Double/pb: **$45**
Double/sb: **$35**
Single/sb: **$30**
Suites: **$50**

Months of Operation: **All year**
Reduced Rates: **15%, weekly**
Breakfast: **Continental**
Credit Cards: **No**
Air-Conditioning: **Yes**
Pets: **No**
Children: **Welcome, over 12**
Smoking: **Permitted**
Social Drinking: **Permitted**
Airport Pickup: **Yes**

This Queen Anne Victorian was built in 1871. Gingerbread trim, stained glass, sliding doors, bay windows, and provincial furnishings recreate that turn-of-the-century feeling. Snacks and setups are offered. Your hostess will gladly direct you to surrounding antique and craft shops, old homes, state parks, and gardens.

HAWAII

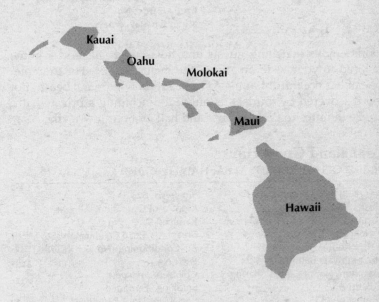

Bed & Breakfast—Hawaii
P.O. BOX 449, KAPAA, HAWAII 96746

Tel: **(808) 822-1582**
Coordinator: **Evie Warner, Al Davis**
States/Regions Covered: **All of the Hawaiian Islands**

Rates (Single/Double):

Modest:	**$15**	**$20–$25**
Average:	**$20**	**$30–$37.50**
Luxury:	**$50**	**$50–$70**

Credit Cards: **No**

Hawaii is a group of diverse islands, offering traditional warmth and hospitality to the visitor through this membership organization. For a five-dollar membership fee, you will receive a descriptive directory of accommodations on all five islands. Some are separate units; others are a part of the main house. Most have private baths.

Pacific—Hawaii Bed & Breakfast
19 KAI NANI PLACE, KAILUA, OAHU, HAWAII 96734

Tel: (808) 262-6026 or 254-5115
Coordinator: **Doris E. Epp**
States/Regions Covered: **All of the Hawaiian islands**

Rates (Single/Double):
Modest:	$18	$20–$25
Average:	$25	$30–$40
Luxury:	$30 and up	$50–$100

Credit Cards: **No**
Minimum Stay: **3 days**

Doris enjoys matching guests and hosts, and will find a home tailored to your taste on any of the major islands. For example, one of her oceanfront homes on a beautiful white sand beach, not yet discovered by tourists, is only $20, including a private bath. It's 20 minutes to Pearl Harbor and half an hour to Waikiki.

Alohaland Guest House
98-1003 OLIWA STREET, ALEA, HAWAII 96701

Tel: (808) 487-0482
Host(s): **Mrs. Abaya**
Location: **10 miles from downtown Honolulu**
No. of Rooms: **4**
No. of Private Baths: **1**
Maximum No. of Guests Sharing Bath: **4**
Double/pb: **$35**
Single/pb: **$35**
Double/sb: **$30**

Single/sb: **$25**
Months of Operation: **All year**
Reduced Rates: **No**
Breakfast: **$2.50 Continental**
Air-Conditioning: **No**
Pets: **No**
Children: **Welcome**
Smoking: **Permitted**
Social Drinking: **Permitted**
Airport Pickup: **Yes**

Mrs. Abaya's home is in a residential area, convenient to all points of interest via public transportation. The inviting beaches of Hawaii, plus the sights and nightlife in Honolulu can be enjoyed to the fullest. A three-day minimum stay is requested in this relaxed and informal getaway.

IDAHO

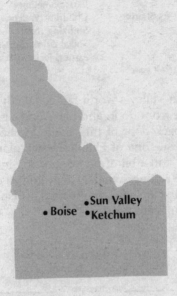

Phoenix Bed & Breakfast
117 S. SECOND AVENUE, SANDPOINT, IDAHO 83864

Tel: (208) 263-4018
Coordinator: **Sanjohn Dimit**
States/Regions Covered: **Northern Idaho—Coeur d'Alene, Lake Pend Or'Eille, Lewiston, Schweitzer Ski Basin**

Rates (Single/Double):
Modest:	$30–$35	$33–$35
Average:	$28–$45	$28–$45
Luxury:	$45	$45

Credit Cards: **No**

Sanjohn has numerous host homes located close to recreational activities, scenic wonders, cultural events, and historic sites. Many are near the Canadian border and some feature hot tubs or saunas in addition to comfortable beds and satisfying breakfasts. There's more to do in Idaho than watching the potatoes grow, and your host will make helpful suggestions to suit your interest.

Sun Tree Hollow
BOX 927, KETCHUM, IDAHO 83340

Tel: **(208) 726-3075**
Host(s): **Elaine and Gary Gronley**
Location: **2 miles south of Sun Valley**
No. of Rooms: **2**
Maximum No. of Guests Sharing
  Bath: **4**
Double/sb: **$25**
Single/sb: **$25**
Months of Operation: **All year**

Reduced Rates: **No**
Breakfast: **Continental**
Air-Conditioning: **Unnecessary**
Pets: **Sometimes**
Children: **Welcome, over 7**
Smoking: **No**
Social Drinking: **No**
Airport Pickup: **Yes**

The ski lift of Sun Valley's world famous Baldy Mountain is five minutes from the front door, and Big Wood's great fishing is 200 yards from the back door of this lovely log house. You may be lucky enough to see one of Elaine's watercolors in progress, or share some wine and a bit of philosophizing in the redwood hot tub. White-water rafting, windsurfing, golf, tennis, gallery hopping, and antiquing are a few of the local pleasures. Nightlife and gourmet restaurants are nearby.

KEY TO LISTINGS

Location: As specified, unless B&B is right in town, or its location is clear from address as stated.
No. of Rooms: Refers to the number of guest bedrooms.
Double: Rate for two people in one room.
Single: Rate for one person in a room.
Suite: Can either be two bedrooms with an adjoining bath, or a living room and bedroom with private bath.
Guest Cottage: A separate building that usually has a mini-kitchen and private bath.
pb: Private bath.
sb: Shared bath.
Breakfast: Included, unless otherwise noted.
Air-Conditioning: If "no" or "unnecessary" is stated, it means the climate rarely warrants it.
Children: If "crib" is noted after the word "welcome," this indicates that the host also has a high-chair, baby-sitters are available, and the B&B can accommodate children under the age of three.
Smoking: If permitted, this means it is allowed *somewhere* inside the house.
Social Drinking: Some hosts provide a glass of wine or sherry; others provide setups for bring-your-own.

Please enclose a self-addressed, stamped, business-size envelope when contacting Reservation Services.

Remember the difference in time zones when calling for a reservation.

ILLINOIS

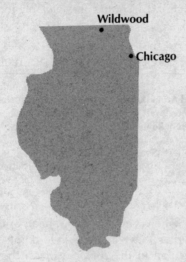

Wildwood

•Chicago

B&B—Chicago
P.O. BOX 14537, CHICAGO, ILLINOIS 60657

Tel: (312) 472-2294	Modest: **$25**	**$30**
Coordinator: **Betsy Sumner**	Average: **$30**	**$35**
States/Regions Covered: **Chicago**	Credit Cards: **No**	
Rates (Single/Double):		

Chicago is 150 years old, and its rich history is the pride of the residents. Betsy's hosts want to share their Windy City with you, and they will suggest many interesting tours, shops, and restaurants off the usual tourist trail. Of course, don't miss the world's tallest building, the Sears Tower.

Bed & Breakfast—Chicago
P.O. BOX 14088, CHICAGO, ILLINOIS 60614

Tel: (312) 951-0085	Rates (Single/Double):	
Coordinator: **Mary Shaw**	Modest: **$25–$30**	**$30–$35**
States/Regions Covered: **Chicago,**	Average: **$30–$50**	**$35–$70**
Door Country, Lake Geneva, Lake	Luxury: **$50–$110**	**$70–$120**
Michigan Shore	Credit Cards: **MC, VISA**	

You will find comfortable accommodations in the city, the suburbs, and some vacation areas close to Chicago. Most of Mary's listings are moderately priced. The luxury rates often include extra amenities such as a suite, fireplace, full breakfast, and access to health club. Discounts are available for weekly stays.

The Keplers
33460 N. LAKE SHORE DRIVE, WILDWOOD, ILLINOIS 60030

Tel: **(312) 223-5680**
Host(s): **Theresa and Arthur Kepler**
Location: **40 miles northwest of Chicago, 3 miles from Route I-94**
No. of Rooms: **2**
Maximum No. of Guests Sharing Bath: **4**
Double/sb: **$26**
Single/sb: **$20**

Months of Operation: **All year**
Reduced Rates: **No**
Breakfast: **Continental**
Air-Conditioning: **No**
Pets: **No**
Children: **No**
Smoking: **Permitted**
Social Drinking: **Permitted**
Airport Pickup: **Yes**

On Gages Lake, where you can swim, boat, and fish through the summer, the Keplers have a ranch-style home and private dock. Spend the afternoon in the rowboat or on the paddleboat, and then relax on the patio, complete with grill. Enjoy a quiet evening by the fire or drive to Lake Geneva, Great America, or Chicago. In winter, there is ice skating on the lake and skiers can drive 25 miles to the slopes. A full breakfast is available for $2.50 each.

INDIANA

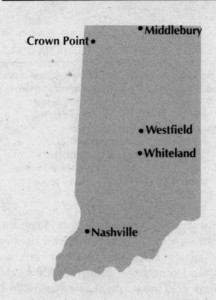

Crown Point •

• Middlebury

• Westfield

• Whiteland

• Nashville

Patchwork Quilt Bed and Breakfast
11748 C.R.#2, MIDDLEBURY, INDIANA 46540

Tel: **(219) 825-2417**
Host(s): **Arletta Lovejoy**
Location: **18 miles east of South Bend**
No. of Rooms: **8**
No. of Baths: **2**
Maximum No. of Guests Sharing
 Bath: **4**
Double/pb: **$45**
Single/pb: **$35**
Double/sb: **$45**
Single/sb: **$35**

Guest Cottage: **$120 sleeps 6**
Months of Operation: **All year**
Reduced Rates: **No**
Breakfast: **Full**
Other Meals: **Available**
Air-Conditioning: **Yes**
Pets: **No**
Children: **No**
Smoking: **No**
Social Drinking: **No**

The house of this 260-acre working farm is furnished with collectibles and antiques. Guests are greeted with cheese, fruit, and
seasonal drinks. Homemade meals are prepared with farm-fresh

ingredients. Breakfast and dinner are served in the oak dining room with adjoining open kitchen. Each guest room has its own patchwork quilt. Your hosts offer tours of the Amish farm country, including stops at orchards, weavers, mills, and craft shops.

Sunset House
RURAL ROUTE 3, BOX 127, NASHVILLE, INDIANA 47448

Tel: **(812) 988-6118**	Reduced Rates: **$5 less, Monday**
Host(s): **Mary Margaret Baird**	**through Thursday; seniors.**
Location: **2½ miles north of Nashville**	Breakfast: **Continental**
No. of Rooms: **3**	Air-Conditioning: **Yes**
No. of Private Baths: **3**	Pets: **Sometimes**
Double/pb: **$45**	Children: **Welcome**
Single/pb: **$45**	Smoking: **Permitted**
Suites: **$55**	Social Drinking: **Permitted**
Months of Operation: **March to**	Airport Pickup: **Yes**
December	

Mary's home is a magnificent contemporary house, with a marvelous deck and patio for relaxing. The guest rooms have separate entrances and all are furnished in fine cherry wood. The master suite has a handsome stone fireplace. Although there are many things to keep you busy, the Little Nashville Opry is a major attraction each Saturday, with country and western stars entertaining.

Camel Lot, Ltd.
4512 WEST 131 STREET, WESTFIELD, INDIANA 46074

Tel: **(317) 873-4370**	Reduced Rates: **No**
Host(s): **Moselle Schaffer**	Breakfast: **Continental**
Location: **21 miles north of**	Air-Conditioning: **Yes**
Indianapolis	Pets: **Sometimes**
No. of Rooms: **1 Suite**	Children: **Welcome**
No. of Private Baths: **1**	Smoking: **Permitted**
Suites: **$40–$60**	Social Drinking: **Permitted**
Months of Operation: **All year**	

Be a guest in Moselle's three-room suite complete with a four-poster bed, private bath, and study, in a private wing of the house. On this exotic animal breeding farm the camels, llamas, and zebras are kept out back. Photography buffs and animal lovers will want to roam the 50 acres of this unusual farm. After breakfast on the terrace that overlooks Siberian tigers Deuchka and Ivan, you can enjoy a full day of exotic sightseeing.

Mar-G's Manor
201 MYERS STREET, WHITELAND, INDIANA 46184

Tel: **(317) 535-9911**
Host(s): **Vivian R. Wood**
Location: **20 miles south of Indianapolis**
No. of Rooms: **3**
Maximum No. of Guests Sharing Bath: **4**
Double/sb: **$40**
Single/sb: **$40**
Months of Operation: **All year**

Reduced Rates: **$30, 3 days or more; 10%, seniors; 10%, families**
Breakfast: **Continental**
Air-Conditioning: **No**
Pets: **No**
Children: **Welcome (crib)**
Smoking: **No**
Social Drinking: **No**
Airport Pickup: **No**

Make yourself at home in this white frame house. Vivian has some lovely antiques and collectibles that add a special ambience to this comfortable home. Her homemade jams, jellies, and pies are delicious. It is less than half an hour drive to the famous Indianapolis 500 Racetrack, the Market Square Arena, and Bush Stadium.

Sunset House

IOWA

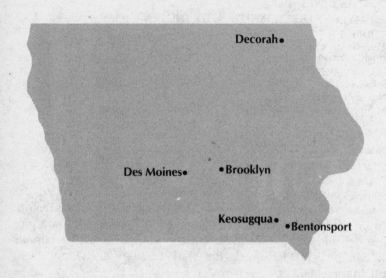

Decorah●

Des Moines● ●Brooklyn

Keosugqua● ●Bentonsport

Bed & Breakfast In Iowa
7104 FRANKLIN AVENUE, DES MOINES, IOWA 50322

Tel: (515) 277-9018
Coordinator: **Iona Ansorge**
States/Regions Covered: **Iowa**
  (statewide)

Rates (Single/Double):
  Modest: **$15–$20** **$20–$30**
  Average: **$25–$35** **$35–$45**
  Luxury: **$35–$50** **$50**
Credit Cards: **MC, VISA**
Minimum Stay: **No**

Iona has a vast variety of accommodations, ranging from working farms where you can participate in agricultural activities, National Registry homes, mansions overlooking the Mississippi River, and huge ranches overlooking the lakes, bluffs, and cliffs of northeast Iowa. The Iowa State Fair and over 200 statewide festivals will suit all interests, including cultural, historic, sports, and crafts.

Hotel Brooklyn
154 FRONT STREET, BROOKLYN, IOWA 52211

Tel: (515) 522-9229
Host(s): **Kay Lawson**
Location: **1½ miles from I-80**
No. of Rooms: 9
No. of Private Baths: 2
Maximum No. of Guests Sharing
  Bath: 5
Double/pb: $26
Single/pb: $18
Double/sb: $20
Single/sb: $15

Months of Operation: **All year**
Reduced Rates: **Groups**
Breakfast: No
Air-Conditioning: **Yes**
Pets: No
Children: **Welcome**
Smoking: **Permitted**
Social Drinking: **Permitted**
Airport Pickup: **Yes**
Foreign Languages: **German**

The hotel, of solid brick with arched window hoods, bracketed eaves, and a three-story tower, was built in 1875. The imposing staircase, marble fireplace, fine woodwork, and hand-painted murals have secured it a spot in the National Register of Historic Places. Operated by the Lawson family for 40 years, the guest rooms are lovely and have been updated to include TV sets.

Fifth Avenue Guest House
204 FIFTH AVENUE, DECORAH, IOWA 52101

Tel: (319) 382-8110
Host(s): **Dan and Dave Kust**
Location: **65 miles southeast of
  Rochester, Minnesota**
No. of Rooms: 4
Maximum No. of Guests Sharing
  Bath: 4
Double/sb: $20
Single/sb: $20

Months of Operation: **All year**
Reduced Rates: No
Breakfast: **Continental**
Air-Conditioning: No
Pets: No
Children: **Welcome**
Smoking: **Permitted**
Social Drinking: **Permitted**
Airport Pickup: **Yes**

This beautifully refurbished home is conveniently located near the campus of Luther College and across the street from a small park. It's close to the Norwegian-American Museum and lovely shops. There's skiing in winter; summer fun can be found on the upper Iowa River, which flows parallel to Fifth Avenue and offers a view of the bluff-lined landscape. Breakfast is highlighted by fresh cinnamon rolls that are enormous, light, and moist. You can relax near the wood-burning stove and enjoy a complimentary glass of wine.

Mason House Inn
FRONT STREET, BENTONSPORT, KEOSAUQUA, IOWA 52565

Tel: (319) 592-3133
Host(s): **Herbert K. and Burretta Redhead**
Location: **7 miles from Keosauqua, Iowa**
No. of Rooms: **10**
Maximum No. of Guests Sharing Bath: **3**
Double/sb: **$30**
Single/sb: **$25–$35**
Suites: **$40**

Guest Cottage: **$75 sleeps 4**
Months of Operation: **All year**
Reduced Rates: **No**
Breakfast: **Full**
Other Meals: **Available**
Air-Conditioning: **Yes**
Pets: **Sometimes**
Children: **No**
Smoking: **Permitted**
Social Drinking: **Permitted**

This Georgian brick inn has offered lodging since 1896. Many of the original furnishings have been preserved, accented with wood and glass pieces. There's coffee, tea, and fruit to snack on; special dishes are prepared for breakfast, and a variety of dinner choices are available. Your hosts, museum curators for 25 years, will be happy to advise on the historic homes, antique shops, and recreational activities in Bentonsport.

KEY TO LISTINGS

Location: As specified, unless B&B is right in town, or its location is clear from address as stated.
No. of Rooms: Refers to the number of guest bedrooms.
Double: Rate for two people in one room.
Single: Rate for one person in a room.
Suite: Can either be two bedrooms with an adjoining bath, or a living room and bedroom with private bath.
Guest Cottage: A separate building that usually has a mini-kitchen and private bath.
pb: Private bath.
sb: Shared bath.
Breakfast: Included, unless otherwise noted.
Air-Conditioning: If "no" or "unnecessary" is stated, it means the climate rarely warrants it.
Children: If "crib" is noted after the word "welcome," this indicates that the host also has a high-chair, baby-sitters are available, and the B&B can accommodate children under the age of three.
Smoking: If permitted, this means it is allowed *somewhere* inside the house.
Social Drinking: Some hosts provide a glass of wine or sherry; others provide setups for bring-your-own.

Please enclose a self-addressed, stamped, business-size envelope when contacting Reservation Services.

Remember the difference in time zones when calling for a reservation.

KANSAS

Manhattan•   Kansas City•

Wakefield •

Kansas City Bed & Breakfast
P.O. BOX 14781, LENEXA, KANSAS 66215

Tel: (913) 268-4214

Coordinator: **Diane C. Kuhn**

States/Regions Covered:

Kansas—Lake Quivira, Leawood, Lenexa, Merriam, Overland Park, Modoc, Prairie Village, Shawnee; Missouri—Belton, Liberty, Parkville

Rates (Single/Double):

Modest:	**$20**	**$30**
Average:	**$30**	**$40**
Luxury:	**$48**	**$50**

Credit Cards: **No**

As the song says, "Everything's up-to-date in Kansas City." You will enjoy visiting such places as Crown Center, Country Club Plaza, Arrowhead Stadium, Royals Stadium, Kemper Arena, and the Missouri Repertory Theatre. A directory fully describing all of the host homes costs $1; please send a self-addressed envelope with 37¢ postage. Advise Diane of your selection and she will do the rest.

Kimble Cliff
ROUTE 1, BOX 139, MANHATTAN, KANSAS 66502

Tel: **(913) 539-3816**	Reduced Rates: **No**
Host(s): **Betty and Neil Anderson**	Breakfast: **Full**
Location: **15 miles from I-70**	Air-Conditioning: **Yes**
No. of Rooms: **2**	Pets: **Sometimes**
Maximum No. of Guests Sharing	Children: **Welcome (crib)**
Bath: **4**	Smoking: **No**
Double/sb: **$30**	Social Drinking: **No**
Single/sb: **$20**	Airport Pickup: **Yes**
Months of Operation: **All year**	

Built of hand-hewn limestone in 1894, this historic home has been tastefully decorated by Neil and Betty, with lovely antiques, lots of plants, and woven baskets. It's five miles away from Kansas State University, the Goodnow Museum, the American Institute of Baking, the Flint Hills, and various recreational activities. Neil is a professor of veterinary medicine, and Betty has a thriving craft business. Cordial people, the coffee pot is always on.

Bed 'n' Breakfast on-Our-Farm
ROUTE ONE, BOX 132, WAKEFIELD, KANSAS 67487

Tel: **(913) 461-5596**	Suites: **$30 (for 4)**
Host(s): **Rod and Pearl Thurlow**	Months of Operation: **All year**
Location: **20 miles northeast of**	Reduced Rates: **No**
Junction City	Breakfast: **Full**
No. of Rooms: **3**	Air-Conditioning: **Yes**
Maximum No. of Guests Sharing	Pets: **Yes**
Bath: **4**	Children: **Welcome**
Double/sb: **$25**	Smoking: **Permitted**
Single/sb: **$18**	Social Drinking: **Permitted**

This is a working farm, with 1,000 fruit trees, wheat fields, hay, cattle, and chickens, all of which children are sure to enjoy. Your hosts have 20 years of entertaining experience at their simple, 100-year-old farmhouse. Guests enjoy the home-cooked breakfasts and exploring the 160 acres. Nearby, there is plenty to do at Wakefield Lake. Antiquing, tennis, museums, and restaurants are a short drive from the farm.

KENTUCKY

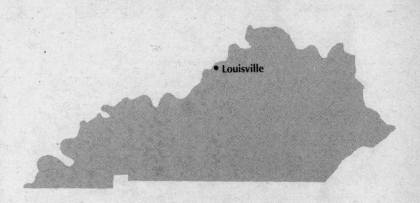

• Louisville

Kentucky Homes B&B
1431 ST. JAMES COURT, LOUISVILLE, KENTUCKY 40208

Tel: (502) 635-7341
Coordinator: Jo DuBose Boone, Lillian
  B. Marshall
States/Regions Covered: **Bardstown,
  Bowling Green, Frankfort,
  Hodgenville, Lexington, Louisville,
  Mayfield, Morehead, Pikeville,
  Shakertown, Sonora**

Rates (Single/Double):
  Modest: **$22**   **$32**
  Average: **$28**   **$38**
  Luxury: **$34**   **$44 and up**
Credit Cards: **No**

Lillian and Jo cordially invite you to be their guest in friendly
Kentucky at one of dozens of host homes. Fish in spectacular
lakes, visit Mammoth Cave, drop in on Shakertown at Pleasant
Hill, or reserve early and assure yourself of a spot at the next
running of the Kentucky Derby (held the first Saturday in May).
Stay in a gorgeous turn-of-the-century town house or a lakeside
cottage; try an efficiency or a luxurious two-bedroom condo at a
lakefront resort with golf course and pool. In many cases, weekly
rates are available.

LOUISIANA

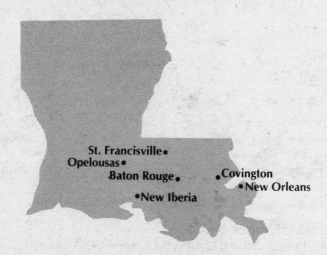

St. Francisville•
Opelousas•
•Baton Rouge•
•Covington
•New Orleans
•New Iberia

Southern Comfort Bed & Breakfast
2856 HUNDRED OAKS, BATON ROUGE, LOUISIANA 70808

Tel: **(504) 346-1928 or 926-9784**
Coordinator: **Susan S. Morris, Helen Heath**
States/Regions Covered:
Louisiana—Alexandria, Baton Rouge, Clinton, Jennings, Lafayette, Lake Charles, Thibodaux; Mississippi—McComb, Natchez, Picayune, Vicksburg

Rates (Single/Double):

	Single	Double
Modest:	$20–$35	$30–$40
Average:	$35–$50	$40–$60
Luxury:	$55–$95	$65–$125

Credit Cards: **No**

Susan and Helen offer a sampler of the Old and New South, and they're branching into southwest New Mexico as well. Their host homes are located in the historic Civil War area, wilderness areas, Acadian country, as well as in townhouses. The region is known for its superb deep-sea fishing. The 1984 World's Fair in New Orleans will increase demand on accommodations, so reserve early.

The Jed
4036 PALM STREET, BATON ROUGE, LOUISIANA 70808

Tel: **(504) 344-5761**
Host(s): **Jane Evans Dutton**
Location: **1½ miles from I-110**
No. of Rooms: **2**
No. of Private Baths: **1**
Maximum No. of Guests Sharing Bath: **2**
Double/pb: **$30**
Single/pb: **$30**
Double/sb: **$25**

Single/sb: **$25**
Months of Operation: **All year**
Reduced Rates: **No**
Breakfast: **Continental**
Air-Conditioning: **Yes**
Pets: **No**
Children: **No**
Smoking: **No**
Social Drinking: **No**

The house is located on a quiet dead-end street, and parking in the driveway is no problem. It is only 75 miles to the New Orleans World's Fair but if you decide to skip the hoopla, Jane will plan an interesting itinerary suited to your taste, right in historic Baton Rouge.

Plantation Bell Guest House
204 WEST 24th AVENUE, COVINGTON, LOUISIANA 70433

Tel: **(504) 892-1952**
Host(s): **Lila Rapier**
Location: **35 miles north of New Orleans**
No. of Rooms: **3**
No. of Private Baths: **3**
Double/pb: **$30–$35**
Single/pb: **$25–$30**

Months of Operation: **All year**
Reduced Rates: **weekly**
Breakfast: **Full**
Air-Conditioning: **Yes**
Pets: **Sometimes**
Children: **Welcome**
Smoking: **Permitted**
Social Drinking: **Permitted**

This late Victorian house has an old-fashioned porch with rocking chairs overlooking a quiet street. Inside, the ceilings are 13 feet high, and the old-time fans add to the nostalgic motif. The guest rooms are decorated with cheerful wallpapers and are very comfortable. Local possibilities include canoeing, cycling, and shopping in Covington.

Mintmere Plantation
1400 EAST MAIN STREET, NEW IBERIA, LOUISIANA 70560

Tel: **(318) 364-6210**	Reduced Rates: **No**
Host(s): **Virginia Jones**	Breakfast: **Full**
Location: **150 miles northwest of New Orleans**	Air-Conditioning: **Yes**
	Pets: **No**
No. of Rooms: **5 suites**	Children: **Welcome, over 12**
No. of Private Baths: **4**	Smoking: **Permitted**
Suites: **$100 (for 2); $150 (for 4)**	Social Drinking: **Permitted**
Months of Operation: **All year**	Foreign Languages: **French**

This magnificent Greek Revival raised cottage was built in 1857. It is furnished with Louisiana antiques and overlooks historic Bayou Teche. The area is on the National Register of Historic Places. Don't miss Konrico, the oldest operating rice mill and country store in the country.

Bed & Breakfast, Inc.
1236 DECATUR STREET, NEW ORLEANS, LOUISIANA 70116

Tel: **(504) 525-4640**	Rates (Single/Double):
Coordinator: **Hazell Boyce**	Modest: **$15–$25 $25–$35**
States/Regions Covered: **New Orleans**	Average: **$30–$55 $40–$65**
	Luxury: **$60 and up $70 and up**
	Credit Cards: **No**

New Orleans is called the City that Care Forgot. You are certain to be carefree, visiting the French Quarter, taking Mississippi riverboat rides, going to the Superdome, taking plantation tours, and enjoying the Mardi Gras, the 1984 World's Fair, as well as dining in fine restaurants or attending jazz concerts. Hazell's hosts will help you get the most out of your stay.

New Orleans Bed & Breakfast
P.O. BOX 8163, NEW ORLEANS, LOUISIANA 70182

Tel: **(504) 949-6705 (toll-free outside Louisiana: 1-800-541-9852)**
Coordinator: **Sarah-Margaret Brown**
States/Regions Covered:
Louisiana—Baton Rouge, Covington, Cottonport, Lafayette, Lake Charles, New Iberia, New Orleans, Shreveport, Vinton;
Mississippi—Biloxi, Ocean Springs, Waveland.

Rates (Single/Double):
Modest: **$10–$15 $20–25**
Average: **$25–$40 $25–$45**
Luxury: **$45–$100 $55–$125**
Credit Cards: **No**

Sarah-Margaret has a wide selection of accommodations available in fine areas, close enough to public transit to bring you downtown or to the popular French Quarter in minutes. If you have ever longed to sample the restaurants, visit Bourbon Street, St. Louis Cathedral, and Pirate's Alley, or to witness the world famous Mardi Gras, then by all means make your plans now. The 1984 World's Fair is here too.

The Estorge House
427 NORTH MARKET STREET, OPELOUSAS, LOUISIANA 70570

Tel: **(318) 948-4592**
Host(s): **Margaret Eagle**
Location: **100 miles northwest of New Orleans**
No. of Rooms: **2 suites**
No. of Private Baths: **2**
Maximum No. of Guests Sharing Bath: **n/a**
Suites: **$100**

Months of Operation: **All year**
Reduced Rates: **No**
Breakfast: **Full**
Air-Conditioning: **Yes**
Pets: **No**
Children: **Welcome, over 12**
Smoking: **Permitted**
Social Drinking: **Permitted**

This house, built in 1827, in the Neoclassic style, is furnished with beautiful period pieces. Opelousas is an historic town which served as the capital of Louisiana during the Civil War. Many historic sites and fine antebellum homes can be seen in the area. Margaret is a tour guide and is very adept at many handcrafts. Her thorough knowledge of her hometown will make your visit quite special.

Cottage Plantation
ROUTE 5, BOX 425, ST. FRANCISVILLE, LOUISIANA 70775

Tel: **(504) 635-3674**
Host(s): **Mr. & Mrs. J. E. Brown**
Location: **6 miles north of St. Francisville**
No. of Rooms: **5**
No. of Private Baths: **5**
Double/pb: **$60**
Single/pb: **$40**
Months of Operation: **All year (closed Christmas)**

Reduced Rates: **No**
Breakfast: **Full**
Air-Conditioning: **Yes**
Pets: **No**
Children: **Welcome**
Smoking: **Permitted**
Social Drinking: **Permitted**

This sprawling antebellum home is a working plantation listed on the National Register of Historic Places. Andrew Jackson once slept here, and today you can see much of the same furnishings he did. A full southern-style breakfast is offered. Guests are welcome to tour the 15 original buildings built over a century ago. Nearby attractions include Audubon Memorial Park and the historic sites of St. Francisville.

Estorge House

MAINE

West Forks•

Kingfield•
Bangor• •Eastbrook
Searsport• Castine
Litchfield• Camden• •Bar Harbor
Wiscasset• Southwest Harbor
South Harpswell• •Pemaquid
•Bath
•Portland
•Kennebunkport
•Ogunquit
•York Beach

Bed & Breakfast Down East, Ltd.

BOX 547, MACOMBER MILL ROAD, EASTBROOK, MAINE 04634

Tel: (207)565-3517
Coordinator: **Sally B. Godfrey**
States/Regions Covered: **Maine**
  (statewide)

Rates (Single/Double):
  Modest: **$20**   **$30**
  Average: **$25**   **$35**
  Luxury: **$35**   **$55**
Credit Cards: **MC, VISA**

There are delightful accommodations waiting for you, from Kittery Point at the New Hampshire border to "way down east" in Lubec, the easternmost town in the United States, and just a stone's throw from Roosevelt's Campobello Island in New Brunswick, Canada. You are certain to enjoy Bar Harbor, Acadia National Park, the rugged coastline, and inland forest and streams. All of Sally's hosts will make you feel welcome.

The Country Cupboard Guesthouse
ROUTE 27, NORTH MAIN STREET, RD1 BOX 1270, KINGFIELD, MAINE 04947

Tel: (207) 265-2193
Host(s): **Sharon and Bud Jordan**
Location: **100 miles northwest of Portland**
No. of Rooms: **7**
Maximum No. of Guests Sharing Bath: **8**
Double/sb: **$53–$63**
Single/sb: **$26.50–$31.50**
Months of Operation: **May 15 to April 15**

Reduced Rates: **Sunday–Wednesday**
Breakfast: **Full**
Other Meals: **Dinner included Thursday, Friday, Saturday**
Credit Cards: **MC, VISA**
Air-Conditioning: **Yes**
Pets: **Sometimes**
Childen: **Welcome**
Smoking: **Permitted**
Social Drinking: **Permitted**

This cozy clapboard farmhouse is only 18 miles from Sugarloaf Mountain. All the bedrooms are carpeted and comfortably furnished with color-coordinated linens. Sharon and Bud will be pleased to suggest fun things to do in all seasons. There's great fishing, hiking, and marvelous skiing. The fall foliage is spectacular. In summer, the Jordans' swimming pool is the place to gather and meet new friends.

Crab Apple Acres Inn
ROUTE 201, WEST FORKS, MAINE 04985

Tel: (207) 663-2218
Host(s): **Chuck and Sharyn Peabody**
Location: **140 miles south of Quebec City, Canada**
No. of Rooms: **7**
Maximum No. of Guests Sharing Bath: **7**
Double/sb: **$30**
Single/sb: **$15**
Months of Operation: **All year**

Reduced Rates: **No**
Breakfast: **Full—$4**
Other Meals: **Available**
Credit Cards: **MC**
Air-Conditioning: **Unnecessary**
Pets: **No**
Children: **Welcome (crib)**
Smoking: **Permitted**
Social Drinking: **Permitted**

This fine old farmhouse, built in 1835, overlooks the Kennebec River; its hosts welcome you with congenial, country hospitality. The house has polished, wide-board pine floors, a wood cookstove, and colorful quilts on the beds. Your hosts are licensed, professional white-water outfitters, and Chuck guides raft trips on the Kennebec and Dead rivers. The coffee pot is always on!

ALONG THE COAST

Birch Haven
RFD#1 BOX 190L, BAR HARBOR, MAINE 04609

Tel: **(207) 288-3571**
Host(s): **Dale and Virginia Kohr**
Location: **15 miles south of Ellsworth**
No. of Rooms: **2**
Maximum No. of Guests Sharing
Bath: **2**
Double/sb: **$45**
Single/sb: **$45**
Months of Operation: **All year**

Reduced Rates: **20%, September to June**
Breakfast: **Full**
Other Meals: **Available**
Credit Cards: **No**
Air-Conditioning: **No**
Pets: **Yes**
Children: **Welcome**
Smoking: **Permitted**
Social Drinking: **Permitted**

Birch Haven is set on five acres in the heart of Mount Desert Island. Guests are invited to use the exercise room or the badminton court, or go cross-country skiing on the many trails. Your host, a retired chef, specializes in gourmet breakfasts of quiche, eggs Benedict, and blueberry pancakes. Acadia National Park and Woodland Lake are three miles away.

Granes Fairhaven Inn
NORTH BATH ROAD, BATH, MAINE 04530

Tel: **(207) 443-4391**
Host(s): **Jane Wyllie, Gretchen Williams**
Location: **3 miles north of Bath**
No. of Rooms: **9**
No. of Private Baths: **1**
Maximum No. of Guests Sharing
Bath: **5**
Double/pb: **$45–$50**
Single/pb: **$45**

Double/sb: **$30–$40**
Single/sb: **$22–$28**
Months of Operation: **All year**
Reduced Rates: **Weekly; 4-night stays**
Breakfast: **Full**
Air-Conditioning: **No**
Pets: **Yes**
Children: **Welcome**
Smoking: **Permitted**
Social Drinking: **Permitted**

The Fairhaven is a rambling colonial inn on 27 acres, overlooking the Kennebec River. The original family quarters date back to 1790. Now the 20-room inn includes a library, a "bring your own" tavern, and is furnished with lots of antiques, wood, and glass. Breakfast specials include orange French toast and homemade sausage. Golf, tennis, the beach, and ski slopes are nearby.

Wooden Goose Inn
RTE. 1, BOX 195, CAPE NEDDICK, MAINE 03902

Tel: (207) 363-5673
Host(s): **Jerry D. Rippetoe, Anthony V. Sienicki**
Location: **70 miles north of Boston**
No. of Rooms: **5**
No. of Private Baths: **1**
Maximum No. of Guests Sharing Bath: **4**
Double/pb: **$55**
Double/sb: **$55**

Single/sb: **$30**
Suites: **$80 (for 3)**
Months of Operation: **All year**
Reduced Rates: **No**
Breakfast: **Full**
Air-Conditioning: **No**
Pets: **No**
Children: **Welcome, over 11**
Smoking: **Permitted**
Social Drinking: **Permitted**

This 19th-century farmhouse was built by a sea captain. It is decorated with porcelain, crystal, and Oriental rugs. Guests are served afternoon tea with croissants and paté, and the coffee pot is always on. Breakfast might feature either eggs Benedict or Florentine, and sausage. Portsmouth, Ogunquit, and the University of New Hampshire are nearby.

Hawthorn Inn
9 HIGH STREET, CAMDEN, MAINE 04843

Tel: (207) 236-8842
Host(s): **Douglas Morrison**
Location: **150 miles north of Boston**
No. of Rooms: **7**
No. of Private Baths: **2**
Maximum No. of Guests Sharing Bath: **3**
Double/pb: **$65**
Double/sb: **$50–$55**
Months of Operation: **All year**

Reduced Rates: **$10 less daily, November to May 24; 15%, weekly**
Breakfast: **Continental**
Air-Conditioning: **No**
Pets: **No**
Children: **Welcome**
Smoking: **Permitted**
Social Drinking: **Permitted**
Airport Pickup: **Yes**

The airy rooms of this Victorian inn are an elegant mixture of the old and the new. Guests are welcome to wine or coffee while relaxing on the deck or getting warm by the fire. Breakfast is served in a sunny dining room and all rooms overlook either Mt. Battle or Camden Harbor. A score of winter sports can be enjoyed in the area, and shops and restaurants are only a short walk away.

Wind Ridge
BOX 547, MACOMBER MILL ROAD, EASTBROOK, MAINE 04634

Tel: **(207) 565-3517**
Host(s): **Syd and Sally Godfrey**
Location: **17 miles northeast of Ellsworth**
No. of Rooms: **1**
Maximum No. of Guests Sharing Bath: **2**
Double/sb: **$30**
Single/sb: **$30**
Guest Cottage: **$45 sleeps 2**

Months of Operation: **All year**
Reduced Rates: **10%, January 1 to April 30; 10%, seniors**
Breakfast: **Full**
Credit Cards: **MC, VISA**
Air-Conditioning: **Unnecessary**
Pets: **No**
Children: **Welcome, over 3**
Smoking: **No**
Social Drinking: **Permitted**

This large, comfortable cedar log home, located high on a ridge, overlooks the Bar Harbor Mountains and surrounding countryside. It is comfortably furnished and contains some lovely antiques. It is just an hour's drive to Acadia National Park and convenient to the seaside charm of Bar Harbor. Syd is a metal sculptor with a studio at home, and Sally knows exactly how to make you feel welcome since she runs a bed and breakfast reservation service. If you bring your own cocktail-time beverage, cheese and crackers will be served. Coffee and tea are always on tap.

The Captain Lord Mansion
PLEASANT STREET, BOX 527, KENNEBUNKPORT, MAINE 04046

Tel: **(207) 967-3141**
Host(s): **Bev Davis, Rick Litchfield**
Location: **30 miles south of Portland**
No. of Rooms: **16**
No. of Private Baths: **16**
Maximum No. of Guests Sharing Bath: **n/a**
Double/pb: **$69–$89**
Single/pb: **$69–$89**
Months of Operation: **All year**

Reduced Rates: **September 1 to May 24**
Breakfast: **Continental**
Air-Conditioning: **Unnecessary**
Pets: **No**
Children: **No**
Smoking: **No**
Social Drinking: **Permitted**
Airport Pickup: **Yes**

Bev and Rick have lovingly restored their home to its 1812 elegance. It is listed in the National Historic Register. The guest rooms are filled with antiques, thick carpets, plus handmade quilts and pillows. Eleven rooms have working fireplaces. Breakfast is delightful and is served in the country kitchen. The beach, galleries, and restaurants are close by.

English Meadows Inn and Whaler Antiques
RFD 1, ROUTE 35, KENNEBUNKPORT, MAINE 04046

Tel: (207) 967-5766
Host(s): Helen and Eugene Kelly
Location: Near Exit 3 off I-95
No. of Rooms: 14
No. of Private Baths: 1
Maximum No. of Guests Sharing Bath: 4
Double/pb: $57
Double/sb: $57
Single/sb: $33

Months of Operation: April to November
Reduced Rates: $28–$50, April 1 to June 15
Breakfast: Full
Air-Conditioning: Unnecessary
Pets: No
Children: Welcome, over 12
Smoking: Permitted
Social Drinking: Permitted

Whether you are staying in the main house, with its brass beds, hooked rugs, early vintage quilts, and prints, or in the paneled carriage house, with its gathering room and fireplace, you are sure to feel comfortable. The six acres of meadows, flowering fruit trees, and pine groves will appeal to anyone who appreciates the outdoors. Dock Square, with its restaurants and galleries, is less than a mile away and the beaches are only a short bike ride.

Old Fort Inn
P.O. BOX 759H, OLD FORT AVENUE, KENNEBUNKPORT, MAINE 04046

Tel: (207) 967-5353
Host(s): Sheila and David Aldrich
Location: Near Exit 3, Maine Turnpike
No. of Rooms: 12
No. of Private Baths: 12
Double/pb: $59–$75
Single/pb: $59–$75
Suites: $90
Months of Operation: May to October

Reduced Rates: 20%, May 1 to June 15; 4-day midweek package
Breakfast: Continental
Credit Cards: AMEX, MC, VISA
Air-Conditioning: Unnecessary
Pets: No
Children: Welcome, over 7
Smoking: Permitted
Social Drinking: Permitted

Built in 1880, the inn has yesterday's charm and today's conveniences. The guest rooms are in a brick-and-stone carriage house, and are beautifully decorated with early pine and oak furniture. Each has a fully equipped kitchen unit, TV, and maid service. There's a large pool, tennis court, and shuffleboard on premises, and it is an easy walk to the ocean.

Old Tavern Inn
POST ROAD, P.O. BOX 445, LITCHFIELD, MAINE 04350

Tel: **(207) 268-4965**
Host(s): **Virginia Albert**
Location: **12 miles southwest of Augusta**
No. of Rooms: **6**
Maximum No. of Guests Sharing Bath: **4**
Double/sb: **$30**
Single/sb: **$25**

Months of Operation: **All year**
Reduced Rates: **Families**
Breakfast: **Full**
Air-Conditioning: **No**
Pets: **Sometimes**
Children: **Welcome**
Smoking: **Permitted**
Social Drinking: **Permitted**

Virginia's home was built as a tavern in 1808, and the hitching posts that flank it go back to the time when stagecoach horses were tethered there. Furnished with traditional pieces, comfortable antiques, and plants, it is warm and cozy. There's a heated in-ground pool and a pond for fishing; it's an easy walk to Tacoma Lake for boating and fishing.

Bed 'n Breakfast at Penury Hall
BOX 68, MAIN STREET, SOUTHWEST HARBOR, MT. DESERT ISLAND, MAINE 04679

Tel: **(207) 244-7102**
Host(s): **Gretchen and Toby Strong**
Location: **15 miles west of Bar Harbor on Route 102**
No. of Rooms: **3**
Maximum No. of Guests Sharing Bath: **5**
Double/sb: **$35–$40**
Single/sb: **$25–$30**

Months of Operation: **All year**
Reduced Rates: **October 1 to June 1**
Breakfast: **Full**
Air-Conditioning: **Unnecessary**
Pets: **No**
Children: **Welcome, over 16**
Smoking: **Permitted**
Social Drinking: **Permitted**
Airport Pickup: **Yes**

This gray frame house has a red door and a crisp, welcoming air about it. Built in 1830, it is comfortably furnished with traditional pieces, antiques, and original art. Gretchen and Toby are cosmopolitan and cordial. Their motto is: "Each guest is an honorary member of the family," and you will be made to feel completely at home. Knowledgeable about the area's highlights, they'll direct you to special shops and restaurants and all the best things to see and do.

The Harbor Lights
P.O. BOX 593, SOUTHWEST HARBOR, MT. DESERT ISLAND, MAINE 04679

Tel: **(207) 244-3835**
Host(s): **Hilda Leighton**
Location: **15 miles west of Bar Harbor**
No. of Rooms: **9**
No. of Private Baths: **7**
Maximum No. of Guests Sharing Bath: **4**
Double/pb: **$30**
Single/pb: **$30**
Double/sb: **$27**
Single/sb: **$27**

Months of Operation: **All year**
Reduced Rates: **After Labor Day to July 1, $18–$20**
Breakfast: **No**
Credit Cards: **MC, VISA**
Air-Conditioning: **Unnecessary**
Pets: **Sometimes**
Children: **Welcome (crib)**
Smoking: **Permitted**
Social Drinking: **Permitted**
Airport Pickup: **Yes**

This area is a fabulous combination of mountains, ocean, caves, forests, quaint villages, and stately homes. Acadia National Park is here, and it rivals Yellowstone in popular acclaim. This is a spacious, comfortable home with a wide porch and a living room with fireplace and TV. It is close to many fine restaurants. Don't miss the lobster pier for the best buy in a delicious meal.

Hearthside Inn
7 HIGH STREET, BAR HARBOR, MT. DESERT ISLAND, MAINE 04609

Tel: **(207) 288-4533**
Host(s): **Dan and Ginger Desrosiers, Lois Gregg**
Location: **½ block off Route 3**
No. of Rooms: **10**
No. of Private Baths: **7**
Maximum No. of Guests Sharing Bath: **4**

Double/pb: **$52–$60**
Single/pb: **$46–$54**
Double/sb: **$44–$48**
Single/sb: **$40–$44**
Suites: **$100 (for 4)**
Months of Operation: **June 1 to October 15**
Reduced Rates: **No**

Breakfast: **Continental**
Credit Cards: **MC, VISA**
Air-Conditioning: **Unnecessary**
Pets: **No**

Children: **Welcome, over 12**
Smoking: **Permitted**
Social Drinking: **Permitted**

On a quiet street, just a short walk to town, is this gracious home, furnished in the manner of a country cottage. You are invited to share the special ambience of a living room with a cozy fireplace and brimming with books, or the music room with its grand piano and game table. Either a balcony or fireplace graces each bedroom. Complimentary wine, cheese, coffee, and iced tea are offered.

Hartwell House
116 SHORE ROAD, OGUNQUIT, MAINE 03907

Tel: **(207) 646-7210**
Host(s): **Tony and Bonnie Raine**
Location: **75 miles north of Boston**
No. of Rooms: **9**
No. of Private Baths: **9**
Double/pb: **$95**
Single/pb: **$95**
Months of Operation: **All year**
Reduced Rates: **No**

Breakfast: **Full**
Credit Cards: **MC, VISA**
Air-Conditioning: **Yes**
Pets: **No**
Children: **Welcome, over 14**
Smoking: **Permitted**
Social Drinking: **Permitted**
Foreign Languages: **French**

Tony and Bonnie offer the serenity of Maine country life, although they're only minutes from the bustle of this thriving summer resort. Each guest room is tastefully furnished with early American and English antiques. Most have private balconies overlooking the lawn with its sculptured flower gardens. Breakfast often features such exotic dishes as lobster pie. There's a pool and tennis court right on the premises.

High Tor
FRAZIER PASTURE ROAD, OGUNQUIT, MAINE 03907

Tel: **(207) 646-8232**
Host(s): **Julie O'Brien, Cleda Farris
    Wiley**
Location: **75 miles north of Boston**
No. of Rooms: **2**
No. of Private Baths: **2**
Double/pb: **$50**

Single/pb: **$50**
Months of Operation: **June 15 to
    September 15**
Reduced Rates: **No**
Breakfast: **No**
Air-Conditioning: **Unnecessary**
Pets: **No**

Children: **No**
Smoking: **No**
Social Drinking: **Permitted**

This gracious home overlooks Marginal Way, a coastal footpath, and is midway between town and Perkins Cove. Located in an exclusive residential area, the quiet is only broken by the sound of the surf. The wood interior, beamed ceiling, fieldstone fireplace, and lovely antiques add to the cozy atmosphere. The guest rooms (each with an ocean view) have queen-size beds and down comforters, plus a guest refrigerator where you can keep your breakfast makings. Coffee is provided in each room. You'll enjoy the theater, museums, and auctions as well as the outdoors activities.

Little River Inn
ROUTE 130, PEMAQUID, MAINE 04558

Tel: **(207) 677-3678**
Host(s): **Jeffrey and Judith Burke**
Location: **9½ miles south of Damariscotta, 9½ miles from Route 1**
No. of Rooms: **6**
No. of Private Baths: **2**
Maximum No. of Guests Sharing Bath: **4**
Double/pb: **$40**
Single/pb: **$35**
Double/sb: **$35**

Single/sb: **$30**
Months of Operation: **All year**
Reduced Rates: **No**
Breakfast: **Full**
Credit Cards: **MC, VISA**
Air-Conditioning: **Unnecessary**
Pets: **Sometimes**
Children: **Welcome**
Smoking: **Permitted**
Social Drinking: **Permitted**
Foreign Languages: **Spanish**

This charming home is located in an historic area on the bank of the river and above the waterfalls. Jeffrey has painstakingly refurbished each room to reflect its original charm. Judy's breakfast quiche is the best ever and her talent for setting a lovely table will be obvious. It's close to the beach, Fort William Henry, and archeological digs.

McGilvery House
BOX 588, SEARSPORT, MAINE 04974

Tel: **(207) 548-6289**
Host(s): **Stephen Stier, Sue Omness**

Location: **30 miles southwest of Bangor**

No. of Rooms: **5**
No. of Private Baths: **3**
Maximum No. of Guests Sharing
  Bath: **4**
Double/pb: **$40**
Single/pb: **$30**
Double/sb: **$35**
Single/sb: **$25**
Months of Operation: **All year**

Reduced Rates: **10%, seniors**
Breakfast: **Continental**
Air-Conditioning: **Unnecessary**
Pets: **Sometimes**
Children: **Welcome, over 10**
Smoking: **No**
Social Drinking: **Permitted**
Airport Pickup: **Yes**

This elegant 19th-century mansion was once the home of a prosperous sea captain. The veranda offers a commanding view of the harbor. The house is filled with unusual antiques, marble fireplaces, and an old reed organ. A breakfast of homemade cakes and jams is served by your host. The local marine museum, antique shops, and Fort Knox are just a few of the local pleasures.

The Maine Stay
RD2, BOX 355, SOUTH HARPSWELL, MAINE 04079

Tel: **(207) 729-1373**
Host(s): **Paul and Barbara Hansen**
Location: **6 miles south of Brunswick**
No. of Rooms: **2**
Maximum No. of Guests Sharing
  Bath: **4**
Double/sb: **$35**
Single/sb: **$20**
Months of Operation: **May 1 to
  October 31**

Reduced Rates: **After 2 nights**
Breakfast: **Full**
Air-Conditioning: **Unnecessary**
Pets: **Sometimes**
Children: **Welcome**
Smoking: **Permitted**
Social Drinking: **Permitted**
Airport Pickup: **Yes**

Paul and Barbara have a sprawling 19th-century home on two acres dotted with berry bushes and mushrooms, and just a short walk to the ocean. Inside, the curved staircase leads up to the guest rooms, art studios, and darkroom. There are cultural events at Bowdoin College in Brunswick, and the symphony in Portland. Advance reservations are requested.

The Artemus Ward House
WATERFORD, MAINE 04088

Tel: **(207) 583-4106**
Host(s): **Lynn Baker**
Location: **50 miles northwest of
  Portland**

No. of Rooms: **4**
No. of Private Baths: **2**
Maximum No. of Guests Sharing
  Bath: **4**

Double/pb: **$40**
Single/pb: **$35**
Double/sb: **$35**
Single/sb: **$32**
Months of Operation: **May 15 to January 15**
Reduced Rates: **10%, weekly**

Breakfast: **Full**
Other Meals: **Available**
Air-Conditioning: **Unnecessary**
Pets: **No**
Children: **Welcome**
Smoking: **Permitted**
Social Drinking: **Permitted**

This white clapboard farmhouse is set on five acres. Guests will enjoy the lakefront beach and equestrian center. Inside, the decor is antique, and there is a special tearoom done in a blue and white motif. Nearby sights include the picturesque village and the White Mountains, offering sports in all seasons.

Roberts House Bed & Breakfast

MAIN STREET AND PLEASANT STREET, P.O. BOX 143, WISCASSET, MAINE 04578

Tel: **(207) 882-5055**
Host(s): **Alice and Ed Roberts**
Location: **40 miles north of Portland**
No. of Rooms: **3**
Maximum No. of Guests Sharing Bath: **3**
Double/sb: **$35–$45**
Single/sb: **$28–$38**
Months of Operation: **All year**

Reduced Rates: **No**
Breakfast: **Full**
Air-Conditioning: **Unnecessary**
Pets: **No**
Children: **Welcome**
Smoking: **Permitted**
Social Drinking: **Permitted**
Foreign Languages: **French, German**

Beautifully furnished in a tasteful blend of contemporary comfort and lovely antiques, this 18th-century home is a wonderful base for day trips. Alice and Ed request a two-night minimum stay so that you can truly take advantage of seeing Bath, Brunswick, Boothbay Harbor, and Pemaquid. Don't miss the spectacular Portland Museum of Modern Art. Wiscasset may be Maine's prettiest village and abounds in classic homes, lovely gardens, antique shops, and fine restaurants. There's fine boating and fishing in the Sheepscott River.

The Jo-Mar Guest House on-the-Ocean

41 FREEMAN STREET, BOX 838, YORK BEACH, MAINE 03910

Tel: **(207) 363-4826**
Host(s): **Mary Della Puietra, Joan Curtis**
Location: **5 miles from I-95**

No. of Rooms: **6**
Maximum No. of Guests Sharing Bath: **5**
Double/sb: **$28.50–$37**

Single/sb: **$25**
Guest Cottage: **$275 per week sleeps
2–3**
Months of Operation: **May 15 to
October 15**
Reduced Rates: **Weekly; May 15 to
June 25; October 1 to 15**

Breakfast: **Continental**
Air-Conditioning: **Unnecessary**
Pets: **No**
Children: **Welcome**
Smoking: **Permitted**
Social Drinking: **Permitted**
Foreign Languages: **Italian**

This comfortable home is located on a bluff overlooking Short Sands Beach. Most of the rooms have ocean views and are attractively furnished with antique pieces. The backyard has a barbecue and picnic table, and you can view the mighty Atlantic from a comfortable lawn chair. You are welcome to store your snacks in the refrigerator and to visit in the cozy living room. The amusement park, galleries, and craft shops are just minutes away. It is convenient to Ogonquit's great restaurants and renowned summer theater. Mary and Joan enjoy having visitors and will do everything they can to make your stay pleasant.

MARYLAND

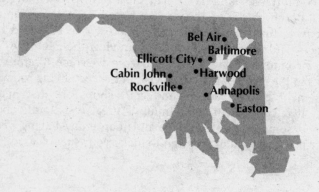

Sharp-Adams
33 WEST STREET, ANNAPOLIS, MARYLAND 21401

Tel: (301) 269-6232 or 261-2233
Coordinator: **B. J. Adams and Cecily Sharp-Whitehill**
States/Regions Covered:
Maryland—Annapolis, Baltimore, Eastern Shore; Washington, D.C.

Rates (Single/Double):
Average: **$28–40 $38–$48**
Luxury: **$40 and up $48 and up**
Credit Cards: **AMEX, MC, VISA**

Maryland lies between the Atlantic Ocean and the Allegheny Mountains. Chesapeake Bay offers marvelous fishing and boating, and Washington, D.C. is convenient to many of the B&Bs. Don't miss the U.S. Naval Academy at Annapolis. Maryland celebrates its 350th anniversary in 1984, which promises to be quite interesting for visitors.

The Unicorn House
327 EAST 29TH STREET, BALTIMORE, MARYLAND 21218

Tel: (301) 889-4066
Host(s): **Thomas Migliaccio**
No. of Rooms: **2**
No. of Private Baths: **1**
Maximum No. of Guests Sharing
  Bath: **4**
Double/pb: **$40**
Single/pb: **$25**
Double/sb: **$40**

Single/sb: **$25**
Months of Operation: **All year**
Reduced Rates: **No**
Breakfast: **Full**
Air-Conditioning: **Yes**
Pets: **No**
Children: **No**
Smoking: **Permitted**
Social Drinking: **Permitted**

Built in 1927, this brick and stone row house is located in the Waverly–Charles Village district near Johns Hopkins University. Furnished in art-deco from the Jazz Age, it has a relax-and-put-your-feet-up ambience. Tom is interested in fashion, theater, writing, and yoga, and he is by nature an organizer. He'll welcome you with coffee and pastry, and give you a complimentary copy of *Baltimore* magazine.

Heritage Hill
304 VALE ROAD, BEL AIR, MARYLAND 21014

Tel: (301) 879-7595
Host(s): **June and Frank Wanek**
Location: **30 miles northeast of Baltimore**
No. of Rooms: **2 suites**
No. of Private Baths: **2**
Suites: **$30–$35**
Months of Operation: **All year**

Reduced Rates: **Extended stays**
Breakfast: **Full**
Air-Conditioning: **Yes**
Pets: **No**
Children: **Welcome**
Smoking: **No**
Social Drinking: **Permitted**
Airport Pickup: **Yes**

This 200-year-old handsome white colonial house is located in an historic area. Each suite consists of a living room with a sleep-sofa, a bedroom with twin beds, a fully equipped kitchen, and a bath. Both have private entrances and lovely views of the surrounding countryside and nearby horse farms. They are attractively furnished with antique wardrobes, poster beds, and restored mission pieces. June and Frank stock the kitchen with everything you'll need for breakfast.

The Winslow Home
8217 CARAWAY STREET, CABIN JOHN, MARYLAND 20818

Tel: (301) 229-4654
Host(s): Jane Winslow
Location: 9 miles from Washington, D.C.
No. of Rooms: 2
Maximum No. of Guests Sharing Bath: 4
Double/sb: $35
Single/sb: $25
Months of Operation: All year

Reduced Rates: 5 days or more; seniors; families
Breakfast: Full
Air-Conditioning: Yes
Pets: Welcome
Children: Welcome
Smoking: No
Social Drinking: No
Airport Pickup: Yes

You may enjoy the best of two worlds while staying at Jane's. This comfortable home is located in a lovely residential section of Bethesda, and it is just 20 minutes from downtown Washington, D.C. Imagine the advantage of touring the capital with some extra pocket money saved on high hotel costs. You are welcome to use the kitchen, laundry facilities, and piano.

Robin's Nest I
7298 MEADOW WOOD WAY, CLARKSVILLE, MARYLAND 21029

Tel: (301) 490-7842 or 454-3622
Host(s): Milt and Francesca Nelson
Location: 35 miles north of Washington, D.C.
No. of Rooms: 2
No. of Private Baths: 2
Double/pb: $45
Single/pb: $30
Months of Operation: June, July, August; weekends and holidays

Reduced Rates: 10%, seniors
Breakfast: Full
Other Meals: Available
Air-Conditioning: Yes
Pets: No
Children: Welcome
Smoking: No
Social Drinking: Permitted
Airport Pickup: Yes
Foreign Languages: Spanish, Japanese

In a thickly wooded area midway between Baltimore and Washington, D.C., this new ranch-style home has all the comforts you could wish for. Milt is a plant lover and works for the University of Maryland; Francesca teaches elementary school. You are welcome to use the kitchen for light snacks. The picnic table, barbecue, and laundry facilities are also available. If you forget your tennis racket, your hosts will lend you theirs. That's hospitality!

Hynson Tourist Home
804 DOVER ROAD, EASTON, MARYLAND 21601

Tel: (301) 822-2777
Host(s): **Nellie Hynson**
Location: **35 miles north of Annapolis**
No. of Rooms: **6**
Maximum No. of Guests Sharing
  Bath: **5**
Double/sb: **$30**
Single/sb: **$15–$17**
Months of Operation: **All year**

Reduced Rates: **December to
  February, $15–$25**
Breakfast: **No**
Air-Conditioning: **No**
Pets: **Welcome**
Children: **Welcome**
Smoking: **Permitted**
Social Drinking: **No**

With the great attractions and conveniences this area affords, many visitors are making it a base from which to visit Washington, D.C., and tour the surrounding region. Located on the eastern shore of Maryland, recreational activities are plentiful. The oldest Quaker meeting house in the U.S. is in town; William Penn worshipped here. St. Michaels, the historic waterfront town featuring fine seafood and an interesting museum, is nearby. Nellie has been welcoming guests for 25 years and many keep coming back because of her warm hospitality.

Hayland Farm
5000 SHEPPARD LANE, ELLICOTT CITY, MARYLAND 21043

Tel: (301) 531-5593 or (301) 596-9119
Host(s): **Louis and Dorothy Mobley**
Location: **20 miles northeast of
  Baltimore**
No. of Rooms: **2**
Maximum No. of Guests Sharing
  Bath: **2**
Double/sb: **$35**
Single/sb: **$25**

Months of Operation: **All year**
Reduced Rates: **No**
Breakfast: **Full**
Air-Conditioning: **No**
Pets: **No**
Children: **Welcome (crib)**
Smoking: **Permitted**
Social Drinking: **Permitted**

When you breathe the country-fresh air, it may surprise you that Baltimore and Washington, D.C. are only a short drive from the house. At Hayland Farm you will find gracious living in a large manor house that is furnished in a handsome yet comfortable style. Louis and Dorothy are retired and have traveled extensively. They enjoy sharing conversations with their guests. In warm weather, the 20′ by 50′ swimming pool is a most enjoyable treat.

The Stockmans
P.O. BOX 125, TAYLOR LANDING ROAD, GIRDLETREE, MARYLAND 21829

Tel: **(301) 632-3299**
Host(s): **John and Joan Stockman**
Location: **6 miles south of Snow Hill**
No. of Rooms: **2**
Maximum No. of Guests Sharing Bath: **4**
Double/sb: **$28**
Single/sb: **$26**
Months of Operation: **March to December**

Reduced Rates: **$22 and $20, November 1 to April 30**
Breakfast: **Continental**
Air-Conditioning: **Yes**
Pets: **No**
Children: **Welcome, over 4**
Smoking: **No**
Social Drinking: **Permitted**

This large Victorian country house is comfortably furnished with a wonderful blend of antiques and charm. Fishing, crabbing, and swimming are nearby as well as interesting historic sites. The coffee pot is usually full and you are welcome to enjoy a cup while relaxing on the front porch.

Oakwood
4566 SOLOMONS ISLAND ROAD, HARWOOD, MARYLAND 20776

Tel: **(301) 261-5338**
Host(s): **Dennis and Joan Brezina**
Location: **30 miles southeast of Washington, D.C.**
No. of Rooms: **3**
Maximum No. of Guests Sharing Bath: **4**
Double/sb: **$45**
Single/sb: **$40**

Months of Operation: **All year**
Reduced Rates: **20%, weekly; 20%, families**
Breakfast: **Full**
Air-Conditioning: **Yes**
Pets: **No**
Children: **Welcome, over 12**
Smoking: **Permitted**
Social Drinking: **Permitted**

The elegant motif of this antebellum manor house features six fireplaces, 11-foot ceilings, and handmade rugs. Guests are welcome to relax on the veranda or stroll in the terraced gardens. Your hosts serve an English-style breakfast in the open-hearthed kitchen. They are happy to advise on day trips to Washington, D.C., or visits to nearby Chesapeake Bay and Annapolis.

Swift's B&B
13819 LOREE LANE, ROCKVILLE, MARYLAND 20853

Tel: **(301) 460-4648**
Host(s): **Marietta and Jerry Swift**
Location: **13 miles north of Washington, D.C.**
No. of Rooms: **5**
No. of Private Baths: **1**
Maximum No. of Guests Sharing Bath: **2**
Double/pb: **$39**
Single/pb: **$29**
Double/sb: **$39**
Single/sb: **$29**

Months of Operation: **All year**
Reduced Rates: **No**
Breakfast: **Full**
Air-Conditioning: **Yes**
Pets: **No**
Children: **Welcome (crib)**
Smoking: **Permitted**
Social Drinking: **Permitted**
Airport Pickup: **Yes**
Foreign Languages: **French, German, Hungarian**

Jerry and Marietta offer old world hospitality just miles from the White House. Having worked and traveled extensively in Europe, they know the importance of neighborliness, especially to foreign visitors. You will be welcomed with flowers in true continental tradition. Maps, guidance, and personal tours are available in English, or in your own language. Beautiful linen and china bring graciousness to hearty breakfasts that feature homemade breads from European recipes.

MASSACHUSETTS

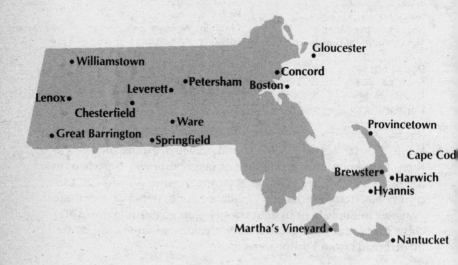

- Williamstown
- Gloucester
- Concord
- Leverett
- Petersham
- Boston
- Lenox
- Chesterfield
- Ware
- Provincetown
- Great Barrington
- Springfield
- Cape Cod
- Brewster
- Harwich
- Hyannis
- Martha's Vineyard
- Nantucket

Pineapple Hospitality
384 RODNEY FRENCH BOULEVARD, NEW BEDFORD, MASSACHUSETTS 02744

Tel: **(617) 990-1696**
Coordinator: **Joan A. Brownhill**
States/Regions Covered: **All six New England states**

Rates (Single/Double):
Modest: $23–$27 $30–$35
Average: $27–$36 $35–$55
Luxury: $45–$72 $55–$72
Credit Cards: **No**

The pineapple has been the symbol of rare hospitality since early colonial days, and the host homes on Joan's roster personify this spirit. They are located in cities and in the countryside, at beach resorts and lakeside communities, in historic districts and near hundreds of schools and colleges; you are bound to find just the spot to call home. Please send a self-addressed envelope with 37 cents postage affixed and three dollars for the descriptive directory.

Bed & Breakfast Associates—Bay Colony
P.O. BOX 166, BABSON PARK, BOSTON, MASSACHUSETTS 02157

Tel: **(617) 872-6990**
Coodinator: **Arline Kardasis, Phyllis Levenson, Marilyn Mitchell**
States/Regions Covered: **Eastern Massachusetts, Maine, New Hampshire, Vermont**

Rates (Single/Double):
Modest: **$25**   **$35**
Average: **$35**   **$45**
Luxury: **$45**   **$60**
Credit Cards: **MC, VISA**
Minimum Stay: **2 days**

A wide variety of host homes are available in the city, in the country, and at the shore. They range from pre–Revolutionary horse farms to contemporary condominiums. Many are convenient to the major colleges and universities. Send two dollars for the descriptive directory, then contact Arline, Phyllis, and Marilyn, and they'll do the rest.

BOSTON AREA

City Cousins
111 LAKE VIEW AVENUE, CAMBRIDGE, MASSACHUSETTS 02138

Tel: **(617) 369-8416**
Coordinator: **Patty Joffee, Peggy Ross, Libby Ingalls**
States/Regions Covered: **Arlington, Boston, Brookline, Cambridge, Concord, Gloucester, Ipswich, Magnolia, Marblehead, Medford, Somerville, Wellesley, Weston**

Rates (Single/Double):
Modest: **$25**   **$35**
Average: **$30**   **$45**
Luxury: **$40**   **$60**
Credit Cards: **No**

Patty, Peggy, and Libby maintain a registry of unique host homes throughout the greater Boston area. There are home owners and apartment dwellers with an extra room or two, and there are "hostless" homes where you may enjoy complete privacy. Many are located on exclusive Beacon Hill, in Back Bay, or near Harvard Square; many are convenient to public transportation.

Greater Boston Hospitality
P.O. BOX 1142, BROOKLINE, MASSACHUSETTS 02146

Tel: (617) 734-0807
Coordinator: **Lauren A. Simonelli**
States/Regions Covered: **Boston, Brookline, Cambridge, Newton, Needham, Wellesley**

Rates (Single/Double):

Modest:	$25	$30
Average:	$30	$35
Luxury:	$35	$50

Credit Cards: **No**

Lauren's homes are convenient to many of the 75 colleges and universities in the greater Boston area. What a boon it is for people applying to school, and to parents visiting undergrads, to have a home-away-from-home nearby.

New England Bed & Breakfast
1045 CENTRE STREET, NEWTON, MASSACHUSETTS 02159

Tel: **(617) 244-2112 (evenings) or 498-9810**
Coordinator: **John Gardiner**
States/Regions Covered: **Massachusetts—Boston, Brookline, Cambridge; Maine; New Hampshire; Vermont**

Rates (Single/Double):

Modest:	$21	$31
Average:	$24–$28	$39–$45
Luxury:	$36	$49

Credit Cards: **No**
Minimum Stay: **No**

While John has many homes in several New England states, he features moderate-priced host homes in the greater Boston area convenient to public transportation. There is a stunning carriage house in the posh section of Brookline. In another, a retired State Department official delights in picking guests up at the airport and giving tours of Harvard Square as part of her hospitality.

The Carriage House
11 HYSLOP ROAD EXTENSION, BROOKLINE, MASSACHUSETTS 02146

Tel: **(617) 566-2668**
Host(s): **Susan and Jay Lerman**
Location: **2 miles west of Boston**
No. of Rooms: **2**
No. of Private Baths: **1**
Maximum No. of Guests Sharing Bath: **4**
Double/pb: **$50**
Single/pb: **$40**
Double/sb: **$50**

Single/sb: **$40**
Months of Operation: **All year**
Reduced Rates: **No**
Breakfast: **Continental**
Air-Conditioning: **Yes**
Pets: **No**
Children: **Welcome, over 16**
Smoking: **Permitted**
Social Drinking: **Permitted**

This brick Georgian carriage house was part of a former estate in the exclusive Fisher Hill section of town. The rooms are furnished with lovely antiques and Oriental rugs, plus there are thoughtful touches like mints and fresh flowers. It is close to the Museum of Fine Arts, gourmet restaurants, and elegant shops. Susan and Jay are experts on the Cambridge/Boston area and will happily help you arrange an interesting visit.

Williams Guest House
136 BASS AVENUE, GLOUCESTER, MASSACHUSETTS 01930

Tel: (617) 283-4931
Host(s): **Betty Williams**
Location: **30 miles north of Boston**
No. of Rooms: **7**
No. of Private Baths: **5**
Maximum No. of Guests Sharing Bath: **4**
Double/pb: **$40–$45**
Single/pb: **$40–$45**
Double/sb: **$30–$35**
Single/sb: **$30–$35**

Guest Cottage: **$350 (week) sleeps 4**
Months of Operation: **May 1 to November 1**
Reduced Rates: **May 1 to June 27; Labor Day to November 1**
Breakfast: **Continental**
Air-Conditioning: **Unnecessary**
Pets: **No**
Children: **Welcome in cottage**
Smoking: **Permitted**
Social Drinking: **Permitted**

Located five miles from Rockport and one and a half miles from Rocky Neck, Gloucester is a quaint fishing village on the North Shore. Betty's colonial Revival house borders the finest beach, Good Harbor. The guest rooms are furnished with your comfort in mind, and her homemade breakfast muffins are delicious. Betty will be happy to suggest many interesting things to do, such as boat tours, sport fishing, whale-watching trips, sightseeing cruises around Cape Ann, the Hammond Castle Museum, and the shops and galleries of the artist colony.

CAPE COD

Bed & Breakfast—Cape Cod
BOX 341, W. HYANNISPORT, MASSACHUSETTS 02672

Tel: (617) 775-2772
Coordinator: **Elaine Borowick, Kay Traywick**
States/Regions Covered: **Cape Cod**

Rates (Single/Double):

	Single	Double
Modest:	$24	$32
Average:	$24	$40
Luxury:	$40	$60

Credit Cards: **MC, VISA**

It is just a little over an hour's drive from sophisticated Boston to the relaxed quaint charm of the Cape. Year-round, you can choose from a roster of homes, compiled by Elaine and Kay. The house you stay in may be a vine-covered cottage, a Victorian estate, a sea captain's home, or an oceanfront house with a private beach. Your hosts will direct you to the restaurants and shops off the tourist trail.

House Guests—Cape Cod
85 HOKUM ROCK ROAD, DENNIS, MASSACHUSETTS 02638

Tel: (617) 398-0787
Coordinator: **Allison D. Caswell**
States/Regions Covered: **Cape Cod, Martha's Vineyard, Nantucket**

Rates (Single/Double):
Modest:	**$20**	**$30**
Average:	**$22–$24**	**$36–$40**
Luxury:	**$30–$35**	**$44–$52**

Credit Cards: **No**
Minimum Stay: **August only—2 days**

Allison's accommodations range from a simple single bedroom with shared bath to historic homes furnished with antiques. Some are on the ocean; others are in wooded country areas. There are even a few self-contained guest cottages on private estates. The area is beautiful in all seasons.

Old Cape House
108 OLD MAIN STREET, BASS RIVER, MASSACHUSETTS 02664

Tel: (617) 398-1068
Host(s): **George and Linda Arthur**
Location: **5 miles east of Hyannis**
No. of Rooms: **5**
No. of Private Baths: **1**
Maximum No. of Guests Sharing Bath: **3**
Double/pb: **$40**
Double/sb: **$30**
Single/sb: **$25**
Months of Operation: **May through October**

Reduced Rates: **7th night free; 12%, September 16 to June 14**
Breakfast: **Continental**
Other Meals: **No**
Credit Cards: **No**
Air-Conditioning: **No**
Pets: **No**
Children: **Welcome, over 9**
Smoking: **No**
Social Drinking: **Permitted**
Foreign Languages: **French, Italian**

This fine home was built in 1815 and is convenient to fine beaches, restaurants, and scenic attractions of Cape Cod. You will enjoy home-baked items at breakfast, plus the use of a spacious porch and garden. All the rooms are charmingly decorated in New England style. It's a great place to stay in the fall for visits to antique shops and craft fairs. Linda is from London, and George also lived in Europe for many years, so they know exactly how to bring the bed and breakfast tradition here.

Old Sea Pines Inn
2553 MAIN STREET, BREWSTER, MASSACHUSETTS 02631

Tel: **(617) 896-6114**
Host(s): **Michele and Steve Rowan**
Location: **16 miles east of Hyannis**
No. of Rooms: **13**
No. of Private Baths: **8**
Maximum No. of Guests Sharing Bath: **3**
Double/pb: **$35–$45**
Double/sb: **$28**
Months of Operation: **All year**

Reduced Rates: **No**
Breakfast: **Continental**
Credit Cards: **MC, VISA**
Air-Conditioning: **Yes**
Pets: **No**
Children: **Welcome, over 10**
Smoking: **Permitted**
Social Drinking: **Permitted**
Foreign Languages: **German, Italian**

Originally a women's finishing school, this sprawling inn has kept many of its turn-of-the-century features, such as brass and iron beds, plus antique and wicker furniture. Your hosts invite you to share wine and cheese next to the fire. A breakfast of homemade treats is served on the porch or in the sunny dining room. Located on over three acres, the inn is close to beaches, bike paths, shops, and restaurants.

Mostly Hall Bed & Breakfast Inn
27 MAIN STREET, FALMOUTH, MASSACHUSETTS 02540

Tel: (617) 548-3786
Host(s): **Jim and Ginny Austin**
Location: **27 miles south of Boston**
No. of Rooms: **6**
No. of Private Baths: **5**
Maximum No. of Guests Sharing
   Bath: **2**
Double/pb: **$50–$55**
Single/pb: **$45–50**
Double/sb: **$33–$43**

Single/sb: **$29–$39**
Months of Operation: **All year**
Reduced Rates: **Winter, spring, fall**
Breakfast: **Full**
Air-Conditioning: **No**
Pets: **No**
Children: **Welcome, over 16**
Smoking: **Permitted**
Social Drinking: **Permitted**
Airport Pickup: **Yes**

Located in the historic district on the village green, and convenient to the ferry, this 1849 house is a faithful copy of a Mississippi River mansion. It's on a beautiful lawn with a charming gazebo, and is tastefully decorated with poster beds in classic country style, accented with antiques. The bountiful breakfast often features popovers with creamed eggs or stuffed French toast. Jim and Ginny serve complimentary lemonade in summer, and tea or sherry in winter.

Somerset House
378 COMMERCIAL STREET, PROVINCETOWN, MASSACHUSETTS 02657

Tel: (617) 487-0383
Host(s): **Jon Gerrity**
Location: **124 miles east of Boston**
No. of Rooms: **13**
No. of Private Baths: **10**
Maximum No. of Guests Sharing
   Bath: **6**
Double/pb: **$42–$52**
Single/pb: **$36–$48**
Double/sb: **$34–$38**
Single/sb: **$28–$32**
Guest Cottage: **$400 weekly for 2**
Months of Operation: **April 1 to
   November 30**

Reduced Rates: **10%, two weeks;
   33%, spring, fall**
Breakfast: **No**
Credit Cards: **MC, VISA**
Air-Conditioning: **No**
Pets: **No**
Children: **Welcome**
Smoking: **Permitted**
Social Drinking: **Permitted**
Foreign Languages: **Spanish, French,
   German**

This historic inn dates back to 1850. The guest rooms are large, high-ceilinged, and comfortably decorated with Victorian and contemporary pieces. The inn is located in the center of town,

and your host will be glad to advise on nearby restaurants. It's 100 feet to the beach. Other possibilities include tennis, whale-watching trips, sailing, biking, and the Provincetown Playhouse.

Haven Guest House
278 MAIN STREET, P.O. BOX 1022, VINEYARD HAVEN, MARTHA'S VINEYARD, MASSACHUSETTS 02568

Tel: **(617) 693-3333**
Host(s): **Karl and Lynn Buder**
Location: **70 miles south of Boston**
No. of Rooms: **9**
No. of Private Baths: **9**
Double/pb: **$65–$75**
Single/pb: **$65–$75**
Months of Operation: **All year**
Reduced Rates: **May 13 to June 16 and September 6 to October 16,**

$52–$55; prior to May 13 and after October 16, $40
Breakfast: **Continental**
Credit Cards: **AMEX, MC, VISA**
Air-Conditioning: **No**
Pets: **No**
Children: **Welcome, over 6**
Smoking: **Permitted**
Social Drinking: **Permitted**

This rambling, two-chimney home was built in 1918. It is situated in a quiet, residential neighborhood, and it is completely surrounded by woodlands, despite its proximity to the ocean. Karl and Lynn will direct you to all the special attractions. The atmosphere is that of visiting old friends in a truly lovely setting.

Sjöholm Inn Bed & Breakfast
17 CHASE ROAD, WEST FALMOUTH, MASSACHUSETTS 02574

Tel: **(617) 540-5706**
Host(s): **Karen and Alan Cassidy**

Location: **5 miles north of Woods Hole,** 1/2 **mile from Route 28A**

175

No. of Rooms: **19**
No. of Private Baths: **4**
Maximum No. of Guests Sharing
  Bath: **4**
Double/pb: **$49**
Single/pb: **$31**
Double/sb: **$33–$43**
Single/sb: **$24–$29**
Guest Cottage: **$380 sleeps 4**
Months of Operation: **All year**

Reduced Rates: **30%, September to
  May; 15%–25%, weekly**
Breakfast: **Full**
Air-Conditioning: **No**
Pets: **Sometimes**
Children: **Welcome**
Smoking: **Permitted**
Social Drinking: **Permitted**
Foreign Languages: **French**

This white, rambling, early Cape Cod homestead (circa 1890) is furnished with a comfortable blend of styles and lots of plants. Located in a quiet, country setting, it is close to all the activities the Cape is known for. Karen and Alan take a particular interest in their guests to assure that each is given individual attention.

Lion's Head Inn

**P.O. BOX 444, 186 BELMONT ROAD, WEST HARWICH,
MASSACHUSETTS 02671**

Tel: **(617) 432-7766**
Host(s): **Laurie and Djordje Soc**
Location: **8 miles from Mid Cape
  Highway**
No. of Rooms: **4**
No. of Private Baths: **2**
Maximum No. of Guests Sharing
  Bath: **4**
Double/pb: **$48–$50**

Single/pb: **$48–$50**
Double/sb: **$38–$40**
Single/sb: **$38–$40**
Guest Cottage: **$300–$350 sleeps
  3 to 5**
Months of Operation: **April 1 to
  December 31**
Reduced Rates: **No**
Breakfast: **Full**

Air-Conditioning: **No**
Pets: **No**
Children: **Welcome**
Smoking: **Permitted**

Social Drinking: **Permitted**
Airport Pickup: **Yes**
Foreign Languages: **French, Italian**

The original pine floors, root cellar, and captain's stairs are part of this inn's traditional flavor. Laurie and Djordje will be happy to point out the best things to see and do on the Cape; after a busy day, a complimentary glass of wine will await you. After dinner at one of the fine restaurants close by, you are welcome to visit or play chess or backgammon in the living room.

The Manor House
57 MAINE AVENUE, WEST YARMOUTH, MASSACHUSETTS 02673

Tel: **(617) 771-9211**
Host(s): **Sherry Braun**
Location: **1 mile east of Hyannis**
No. of Rooms: **6**
No. of Private Baths: **6**
Double/pb: **$38–$42**
Single/pb: **$38–$42**
Months of Operation: **May 15 to October 8**

Reduced Rates: **$28–$35, May 15 to June 15, September 15 to October 4**
Breakfast: **Continental**
Air-Conditioning: **Unnecessary**
Pets: **No**
Children: **Welcome**
Smoking: **Permitted**
Social Drinking: **Permitted**

This large, white Dutch colonial is two blocks from the beach and overlooks the bay. It is tastefully decorated with lovely antiques, handmade quilts, plants, and dried flower arrangements. It is close to golf, tennis, antique shops, fine restaurants, and the ferry dock. Sherry is a science teacher and textbook editor interested in crafts and baking.

The Marlborough
320 WOODS HOLE ROAD, WOODS HOLE,
MASSACHUSETTS 02543

Tel: **(617) 548-6218**
Host(s): **Patricia Morris**
Location: **2½ miles from Route 28**
No. of Rooms: **7**
No. of Private Baths: **2**
Maximum No. of Guests Sharing Bath: **7**
Double/pb: **$40–$55**

Single/pb: **$40–$45**
Double/sb: **$40–$55**
Single/sb: **$40–$55**
Months of Operation: **All year**
Reduced Rates: **20%, Labor Day to Memorial Day**
Breakfast: **Full**
Air-Conditioning: **Unnecessary**

Pets: **Sometimes**
Children: **Welcome**
Smoking: **Permitted**

Social Drinking: **Permitted**
Foreign Languages: **French**

This faithful reproduction of a Full Cape house is decorated with antiques, designer quilts, and handcrafted spreads. It is situated on a shaded half acre that includes a paddle tennis court, swimming pool, a hammock, croquet, and picnicking facilities. There is a private beach nearby with a three-mile bike path running past it. It's a mile from the ferries to Martha's Vineyard and Nantucket. Patricia graciously serves a pre-dinner treat of cheese and sherry, and her gourmet breakfast is a celebration. The Oceanographic and Marine Biological laboratories are in town.

NANTUCKET ISLAND

Carlisle House
**26 NORTH WATER STREET, NANTUCKET,
MASSACHUSETTS 02554**

Tel: **(617) 228-0720**
Host(s): **Peter Conway**
Location: **30 miles south of Cape Cod**
No. of Rooms: **15**
No. of Private Baths: **5**
Maximum No. of Guests Sharing
  Bath: **6**
Double/pb: **$75–$85**
Single/pb: **$75–$85**
Double/sb: **$53–$60**
Single/sb: **$30**

Months of Operation: **April 1 to
  December 31**
Reduced Rates: **15%–20%,
  October 1 to May 25**
Breakfast: **Continental**
Air-Conditioning: **No**
Pets: **No**
Children: **Welcome, over 10**
Smoking: **Permitted**
Social Drinking: **Permitted**

This 1765 home is graced with a veranda, fireplace, canopied or brass beds, wicker furniture, and plants. It offers travelers a warm, personal place to spend vacation days. Weather permitting, breakfast is served on the sun porch. Peter will be happy to tell you of restaurants and local happenings. He'll also lend you inner tubes to enjoy at the beach.

The Carriage House
4 RAY'S COURT, NANTUCKET, MASSACHUSETTS 02554

Tel: **(617) 228-0326**	Reduced Rates: **No**
Host(s): **Jeanne and Bill McHugh**	Breakfast: **Continental**
No. of Rooms: **7**	Air-Conditioning: **No**
No. of Private Baths: **7**	Pets: **No**
Double/pb: **$50–$85**	Children: **Welcome, over 5**
Single/pb: **$40–$70**	Smoking: **Permitted**
Months of Operation: **All year**	Social Drinking: **Permitted**

Located in the center of town, this landmark was built in 1865. It is a charming example of early Victorian architecture, restored and transformed into an inviting home. Guests enjoy the quiet serenity of a country lane and immediately warm to their cordial hosts, Jeanne and Bill. The home-baked muffins are delicious at breakfast. Helpful suggestions are made to provide you with the opportunity of exploring the island to the fullest.

Cliff Lodge
9 CLIFF ROAD, NANTUCKET, MASSACHUSETTS 02554

Tel: **(617) 228-0893**	Suites: **$400 per week (for 4)**
Host(s): **Kay and Andy Lynch**	Months of Operation: **April 15 to November 1**
Location: **30 miles from Hyannis**	
No. of Rooms: **12**	Reduced Rates: **April 15 to June 15; September 15 to October 31**
No. of Private Baths: **6**	
Maximum No. of Guests Sharing Bath: **8**	Breakfast: **No**
Double/pb: **$55**	Air-Conditioning: **Unnecessary**
Single/pb: **$35**	Pets: **No**
Double/sb: **$35–$40**	Children: **Welcome**
Single/sb: **$20–$25**	Smoking: **Permitted**
	Social Drinking: **Permitted**

Located in a superb spot away from the traffic and noise stands this gracious old captain's home built in 1771. The attractively furnished bedrooms are immaculate. Kay and Andy will make you feel like family and enjoy having you visit in their antique-filled living room or relax on the lush lawn. It's convenient to the beaches, tennis courts, and great restaurants.

The Periwinkle Guest House
7 & 9 NORTH WATER STREET, NANTUCKET, MASSACHUSETTS 02554

Tel: **(617) 228-9267**
Host(s): **Sara Shlosser-O'Reilly**
No. of Rooms: **18**
No. of Private Baths: **6**
Maximum No. of Guests Sharing
  Bath: **6**
Double/pb: **$85**
Single/pb: **$85**
Double/sb: **$63–$65**
Single/sb: **$30–$35**
Suites: **$130**

Months of Operation: **All year**
Reduced Rates: **Mid-October to mid-June (except for holidays)**
Breakfast: **Continental**
Credit Cards: **AMEX, MC, VISA**
Air-Conditioning: **No**
Pets: **No**
Children: **Welcome (crib)**
Smoking: **Permitted**
Social Drinking: **Permitted**

The Periwinkle is just around the corner from the Whaling Museum, and only a two-minute walk from the center of town. Built in 1850, it's been refurbished with period antiques, hand-made quilts, and lots of flowers and plants. Sara wants you to feel perfectly at home, so you are free to use the kitchen for light snacks or lunch. The coffee and tea pots are always on.

CENTRAL/WESTERN MASSACHUSETTS

Berkshire Bed & Breakfast
141 NEWTON ROAD, SPRINGFIELD, MASSACHUSETTS 01118

Tel: **(413) 783-5111**
Coordinator: **Mary and Tim Allen**
States/Regions Covered:
  Massachusetts—Lenox, Pittsfield, Sheffield, Williamstown, Great Barrington; New York—Canaan, Lebanon Springs, Berlin

Rates (Single/Double):
Modest:	**$20–$35**	**$25–$35**
Average:	**$25–$35**	**$40–$55**
Luxury:	**$60–$85**	**$60–$85**

Credit Cards: **MC, VISA**

Most of Tim and Mary's host homes are off the beaten track, offering the visitor pastoral, historical, and cultural attractions. Many are close to Albany, New York, the area near the Tanglewood Music Festival, Williams College, or Jiminey Peak for skiing. The homes vary from a 1750 colonial farmhouse to a large manor house with pool and tennis court. A two-day minimum stay is required in the summer.

Pioneer Valley Bed & Breakfast
141 NEWTON ROAD, SPRINGFIELD, MASSACHUSETTS 01118

Tel: **(413) 783-5111**
Coordinator: **Mary and Tim Allen**
States/Regions Covered: **Amherst, Northampton, Springfield, Longmeadow**

Rates (Single/Double):
Modest:	**$20–$30**	**$25–$35**
Average:	**$25–$35**	**$30–$40**
Luxury:	**$35–$55**	**$45–$55**

Credit Cards: **MC, VISA**

Many of the host homes are located close to Smith College, Mt. Holyoke, the University of Massachusetts, and Amherst. Accommodations vary from a farmhouse offering fresh goats' milk, to a restored 1800 colonial, to an historic mansion. The Basketball Hall of Fame, the Eastern States Exposition, and the fall foliage are highlights of the area.

Sturbridge Bed & Breakfast
141 NEWTON ROAD, SPRINGFIELD, MASSACHUSETTS 01118

Tel: **(413) 783-5111**
Coordinator: **Mary and Tim Allen**
States/Regions Covered:
Belchertown, Brimfield, Charleton, Sturbridge, Worcester

Rates (Single/Double):
Modest:	**$25–$35**	**$25–$35**
Average:	**$35–$45**	**$35–$45**
Luxury:	**$45–$55**	**$45–$55**

Credit Cards: **MC, VISA**

Colonial Old Sturbridge Village is New England's answer to Williamsburg, Virginia. On weekends, local craftsmen will teach their crafts to interested visitors. The Brimfield Flea Market is a mecca for antique collectors. Host homes vary from a traditional house near the village green to a chalet nestled in the forest. Many are convenient to Clark University and Holy Cross.

The Turning Point Inn
R.D. 2, BOX 140, ROUTE 23 AND LAKE BUEL ROAD, GREAT BARRINGTON, MASSACHUSETTS 01230

Tel: **(413) 528-4777**
Host(s): **Irving and Shirley Yost**
Location: **130 miles north of New York City**
No. of Rooms: **7**

No. of Private Baths: **1**
Maximum No. of Guests Sharing
Bath: **4**
Double/pb: **$65**
Single/pb: **$55**

Double/sb: **$50**
Single/sb: **$35**
Months of Operation: **All year**
Reduced Rates: **10%, Monday to
  Thursday; 10%, November,
  December, March, April**

Breakfast: **Full**
Air-Conditioning: **No**
Pets: **No**
Children: **Welcome (crib)**
Smoking: **No**
Social Drinking: **Permitted**

Irv and Shirley offer old-style comfort in an atmosphere of informality and warmth. Situated in the Berkshire Mountains, the house is 15 minutes from the music of Tanglewood and within walking distance of Butternut Ski Basin. The inn is 200 years old and has been lovingly restored and refurbished with antiques and fine reproductions. A naturally delicious homemade breakfast of eggs, whole grain pancakes, cereals, and fresh fruits is served. There is a two-day minimum stay required on summer weekends.

Oldwall Farm
RUSSELL ROAD, PETERSHAM, MASSACHUSETTS 01366

Tel: **(617) 724-3391**
Host(s): **Carole Thompson**
Location: **70 miles west of Boston**
No. of Rooms: **4**
No. of Private Baths: **3**
Maximum No. of Guests Sharing
  Bath: **2**
Double/pb: **$50**
Single/pb: **$25**
Double/sb: **$50**

Single/sb: **$25**
Months of Operation: **All year**
Reduced Rates: **10%, seniors; 10%,
  4 nights or more**
Breakfast: **Full**
Air-Conditioning: **No**
Pets: **Sometimes**
Children: **Welcome, school-age**
Smoking: **No**
Social Drinking: **Permitted**

This 200-year-old farmhouse has been restored and decorated with period pieces. The original kitchen fireplace with beehive oven warms your body and spirit on cool evenings. While having a delicious breakfast of homemade sausage with eggs from the farm flock, you will enjoy the lovely view of the pasture and beaver pond. Carole is a stress management consultant who breeds and trains Arabian horses. It is close to the Quabbin Reservoir, so you can fish, observe the eagles, or walk the nature trails. It's 25 miles to Smith, Mt. Holyoke, Amherst, and the University of Massachusetts.

The Wildwood Inn
121 CHURCH STREET, WARE, MASSACHUSETTS 01082

Tel: **(413) 967-7798**
Host(s): **Margaret, Geoffrey, Heathe, and Lori Lobenstine**
Location: **70 miles west of Boston**
No. of Rooms: **5**
No. of Private Baths: **0**
Maximum No. of Guests Sharing Bath: **3**
Double/sb: **$25–$45**
Single/sb: **$25–$45**

Months of Operation: **All year**
Reduced Rates: **10%, weekly; 10%, weekdays; November to April for seniors**
Breakfast: **Continental**
Air-Conditioning: **Yes**
Pets: **No**
Children: **Welcome, over 6**
Smoking: **Permitted**
Social Drinking: **Permitted**

Everything about this old-fashioned Victorian home with its rambling two acres is designed to help you unwind. There's a swing on the porch, a hammock under the firs, a blazing fire in the winter, a Norman Rockwell-esque brook-fed swimming hole in the summer. Your warm hosts have furnished their guest rooms with heirloom quilts, family treasures, and rockers, all of which work to spell home. Homemade bread and Margaret's own peach butter are included with continental breakfast, while "country yummies" are offered for one dollar extra. Sturbridge Village, Old Deerfield, and Amherst offer recreational activities that are all close by. You can stroll to the tennis court or borrow the canoe.

The Wildwood Inn

MICHIGAN

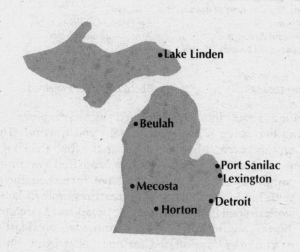

- Lake Linden
- Beulah
- Port Sanilac
- Lexington
- Mecosta
- Detroit
- Horton

Windermere Inn

747 CRYSTAL DRIVE, BEULAH, MICHIGAN 49617

Tel: **(616) 882-7264**
Host(s): **Loralee and Bill Ludwig**
Location: **200 miles north of Detroit**
No. of Rooms: **4**
No. of Private Baths: **4**
Double/pb: **$55**
Single/pb: **$55**
Months of Operation: **All year**
Reduced Rates: **10%, March to November**

Breakfast: **Continental**
Credit Cards: **MC, VISA**
Air-Conditioning: **Unnecessary**
Pets: **No**
Children: **No**
Smoking: **Permitted**
Social Drinking: **Permitted**

Set among century-old pine trees, this many gabled white farm-house is delightfully decorated in a rural style, with lots of antiques. Loralee and Bill put fresh fruit and flowers in each room daily, and coffee and snacks are always available. There's a fine view of Crystal Lake, and you're close to Sleeping Bear National Lakeshore and Interlocken Arts Academy. Recreational activities are plentiful in all seasons.

Wellman General Store Guest Apartment
P.O. BOX 58, 205 MAIN STREET, HORTON, MICHIGAN 49246

Tel: (517) 563-2231
Host(s): **Karen D. Gauntlett**
Location: **10 miles southwest of
 Jackson**
No. of Rooms: **1 suite**
No. of Private Baths: **1**
Suites: **$45 (for 2)**
Months of Operation: **All year**
Reduced Rates: **No**

Breakfast: **Full**
Other Meals: **Available**
Air-Conditioning: **Unnecessary**
Pets: **Sometimes**
Children: **Welcome**
Smoking: **Permitted**
Social Drinking: **Permitted**
Airport Pickup: **Yes**

Karen's B&B is a designer apartment that was previously a turn-of-the-century general store. There's a large, carpeted living room/sleeping area containing a double bed, color TV, leather card table, and phone where the dry goods and groceries used to be kept. Settle down by the fire and enjoy the original art or take a place in the sun in the garden or patio. The adjacent mill pond is great for swimming and fishing, and cross-country skiing is everywhere in winter. Karen is a well-traveled person and a former professional cook. Her gourmet four-course dinner is served with complimentary wines. Detroit is one and a half hours away and Chicago is three hours from the house.

Governor's Inn
7277 SIMONS STREET, P.O. BOX 471, LEXINGTON, MICHIGAN 48455

Tel: (313) 359-5770
Host(s): **Jane and Bob MacDonald**
Location: **20 miles north of Port
 Huron**
No. of Rooms: **3**
No. of Private Baths: **1**
Maximum No. of Guests Sharing
 Bath: **4**
Double/pb: **$40**
Single/pb: **$40**
Double/sb: **$30**

Single/sb: **$30**
Months of Operation: **April to
 October 31**
Reduced Rates: **$150 week**
Breakfast: **Continental**
Air-Conditioning: **No**
Pets: **No**
Children: **Welcome, over 12**
Smoking: **Permitted**
Social Drinking: **Permitted**

A handsome residence built in 1859, it is located near the shore of Lake Huron. It has been refurbished in its original "summer home" style. Wicker furniture, rag rugs, iron beds, and green plants accent the light, airy decor. You can stroll to the nearby beach, browse through interesting shops, fish from the breakwater, or play golf or tennis. Jane and Bob, both educators, look forward to sharing their quaint village surroundings with you.

Blue Lake Lodge
9765 BLUE LAKE LODGE LANE, P.O. BOX 1, MECOSTA, MICHIGAN 49332

Tel: **(616) 972-8391**
Host(s): **Frank and Elaine Huisgen**
Location: **65 miles northeast of Grand Rapids**
No. of Rooms: **6**
Maximum No. of Guests Sharing Bath: **6**
Double/sb: **$25**
Single/sb: **$25**

Months of Operation: **All year**
Reduced Rates: **Seniors; weekly rates**
Credit Cards: **MC, VISA**
Air-Conditioning: **Unnecessary**
Pets: **Sometimes**
Children: **Welcome**
Smoking: **Permitted**
Social Drinking: **Permitted**

This is a large, informal home built in 1913 and located on the shore of a beautiful lake. All lakeside activities, such as swimming, boating, fishing, and snowmobiling, are available. It's close to restaurants, but cooking grills, guest refrigerators, and picnic tables will help you cut down on dining costs.

Raymond House Inn
101 SOUTH RIDGE STREET, PORT SANILAC, MICHIGAN 48469

Tel: **(313) 622-8800**
Host(s): **Shirley Denison**
Location: **30 miles north of Port Huron**
No. or Rooms: **6**
No. of Private Baths: **4**
Maximum No. of Guests Sharing Bath: **4**
Double/pb: **$40**
Single/pb: **$40**

Double/sb: **$30**
Single/sb: **$30**
Months of operation: **May–September**
Breakfast: **Continental**
Air-Conditioning: **No**
Pets: **No**
Children: **Welcome, over 12**
Smoking: **Permitted**
Social Drinking: **Permitted**

Shirly will put your right at ease in her antique-filled inn that provides the conveniences of today but the ambience of 1895. Each bedroom is furnished with period furniture, brightly colored spreads, and lace curtains. There's an old-fashioned parlor, and a dining room where you are served a delightful breakfast. Sport fisherman and sailboat enthusiasts will enjoy this area; cultural activities, quilting bees, and the annual summer festival are longtime traditions here.

MINNESOTA

Bed & Breakfast Registry—North America
P.O. BOX 80174, ST. PAUL, MINNESOTA 55108

Tel: **(612) 646-4238**
Coordinator: **Mary Winget**
States/Regions Covered: **Statewide and national**

Rates (Single/Double):
Modest: **$16**   **$18**
Average: **$17–$30**   **$19–$40**
Luxury: **$40 and up** **$40 and up**
Credit Cards: **MC, VISA**

Minnesota abounds in over 15,000 lakes, so it is no wonder that canoers and fishermen love to visit. But there's something for everyone, from the cultural resources of St. Paul and Minneapolis to the glorious prairie farmland. Mary has branched out her network of hospitable host homes, and she can now find accommodations for you throughout the U.S.

Gabrielson's B&B
RURAL ROUTE 1, DASSEL, MINNESOTA 55325

Tel: **(612) 275-3609**
Host(s): **Elaine and Don Gabrielson**
Location: **60 miles west of Minneapolis**
No. of Rooms: **1**
No. of Private Baths: **1**
Double/pb: **$30**
Single/pb: **$18**

Months of Operation: **All year**
Reduced Rates: **No**
Breakfast: **Continental**
Air-Conditioning: **Yes**
Pets: **No**
Children: **Welcome, over 10**
Smoking: **Permitted**
Social Drinking: **Permitted**

Perched on a hilltop, this 1910 white clapboard farmhouse, decorated in early American style, overlooks a private lake. You are welcome to use the paddleboat for getting to the little island where you can picnic. Or, try your hand at archery, trap shooting, or pond fishing. Elaine and Don are busy raising corn and beans but they'll happily arrange a farm tour of Meeker county. Wine, cheese, and rolls are stocked in the guest refrigerator.

Thorwood Bed & Breakfast
FOURTH AND PINE, HASTINGS, MINNESOTA 55033

Tel: **(612) 437-3297**
Host(s): **Dick and Pam Thorsen**
Location: **19 miles southeast of St. Paul**
No. of Rooms: **3**
No. of Private Baths: **1**
Maximum No. of Guests Sharing Bath: **4**
Double/pb: **$45**
Single/pb: **$39**
Double/sb: **$38**
Single/sb: **$32**
Guest Cottage: **n/a**
Months of Operation: **All year**
Reduced Rates: **No**
Breakfast: **Continental**
Air-Conditioning: **No**
Pets: **Welcome**
Children: **Welcome**
Smoking: **Permitted**
Social Drinking: **Permitted**
Foreign Languages: **Norwegian**

You will enjoy comfort and warm hospitality in this elegant 1880 French Second Empire home, which boasts such details as frescoed ceilings and marble fireplaces. The town is located on the Mississippi and the town's bluff views are beautiful. Dick and Pam serve a generous breakfast, put wine and goodies in your room, and if you are a midnight snacker, they'll not send you to bed hungry. The area abounds in history, fine restaurants, specialty shops, nature trails, and cordial people.

Evelo's Bed & Breakfast
2301 BYRANT AVENUE SOUTH, MINNEAPOLIS, MINNESOTA 55405

Tel: (612) 374-9656
Host(s): David and Sheryl Evelo
Location: 10 blocks from downtown
No. of Rooms: 3
Maximum No. of Guests Sharing
  Baths: 6
Double/sb: $30–$40
Single/sb: $20
Guest Cottage: $40 (for 3)

Months of Operation: All year
Reduced Rates: Weekly
Breakfast: Full
Air-Conditioning: No
Pets: No
Children: Welcome
Smoking: No
Social Drinking: Permitted

Located in the historic Lowry Hill East neighborhood, this 87-year-old Victorian has one of the best-preserved interiors in the area and is furnished with fine period pieces. David and Sheryl are both schoolteachers. Breakfast often features quiche or egg casseroles. The house is within walking distance of the Guthrie Theater and the Walker Art Center.

Kings Oakdale
6933 232 AVENUE N.E., STACY, MINNESOTA 55079

Tel: (612) 462-5598
Host(s): Donna and Charles Solem
Location: 38 miles from St. Paul
No. of Rooms: 3
No. of Private Baths: 2
Double/pb: $28
Single/pb: $28
Double/sb: $20
Single/sb: $18
Suites: $28

Months of Operation: All year
Reduced Rates: No
Breakfast: Continental
Air-Conditioning: Yes
Pets: Sometimes
Children: No
Smoking: Permitted
Social Drinking: Permitted
Foreign Languages: French

This comfortable home is situated on four landscaped acres on the banks of Typo Creek. The picnic tables, volleyball net, and horseshoe game are sure signs of a hospitable country place. It is a perfect retreat for people on business trips to the Twin Cities. The Wisconsin border and the scenic St. Croix River, where boat trips are offered, are minutes from the house. Charles and Donna will direct you to the most reasonable restaurants in town. For late snacks, refrigerators in the bedrooms are provided.

KEY TO LISTINGS

Location: As specified, unless B&B is right in town, or its location is clear from address as stated.

No. of Rooms: Refers to the number of guest bedrooms.

Double: Rate for two people in one room.

Single: Rate for one person in a room.

Suite: Can either be two bedrooms with an adjoining bath, or a living room and bedroom with private bath.

Guest Cottage: A separate building that usually has a mini-kitchen and private bath.

pb: Private bath.

sb: Shared bath.

Breakfast: Included, unless otherwise noted.

Air-Conditioning: If "no" or "unnecessary" is stated, it means the climate rarely warrants it.

Children: If "crib" is noted after the word "welcome," this indicates that the host also has a high-chair, baby-sitters are available, and the B&B can accommodate children under the age of three.

Smoking: If permitted, this means it is allowed *somewhere* inside the house.

Social Drinking: Some hosts provide a glass of wine or sherry; others provide setups for bring-your-own.

Please enclose a self-addressed, stamped, business-size envelope when contacting Reservation Services.

Remember the difference in time zones when calling for a reservation.

MISSISSIPPI

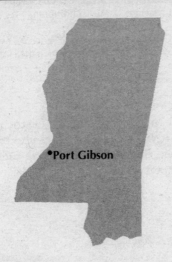

•Port Gibson

Oak Square
1207 CHURCH STREET, PORT GIBSON, MISSISSIPPI 39150

Tel: **(601) 437-4350 or 437-5771**
Host(s): **Mr. and Mrs. William D. Lum**
Location: **60 miles southwest of Jackson**
No. of rooms: **7**
No. of Private Baths: **7**
Double/pb: **$55–$65**
Single/pb: **$50–$60**
Guest Cottage: **Available**

Months of Operation: **All year**
Reduced Rates: **No**
Breakfast: **Full**
Credit Cards: **AMEX, MC, VISA**
Air-Conditioning: **Yes**
Pets: **No**
Children: **Welcome, over 10**
Smoking: **Permitted**
Social Drinking: **Permitted**

This is the largest and most palatial antebellum mansion (circa 1850) in Port Gibson, and it is listed on the National Historic Register. The guest rooms are all furnished with exquisite antiques, and most have canopied beds. Guests will enjoy the courtyard, gazebo, and beautiful grounds. A chairlift for upstairs rooms is available. You will enjoy the delightful southern breakfast and tour of the house. Your gracious hosts offer complimentary wine, tea, or coffee, and will enlighten you as to the many historic attractions in the area.

Square Ten Inn
242 DEPOT STREET, P.O. BOX 371, WOODVILLE, MISSISSIPPI

Tel: **(601) 888-3993**
Host(s): **Elizabeth M. Treppendahl**
Location: **35 miles south of Natchez**
No. of Rooms: **3**
No. of Private Baths: **3**
Double/pb: **$34**
Suites: **$39.50**
Months of operaiton: **All year**

Reduced Rates: **25%, 5 day stay**
Breakfast: **Continental**
Air-Conditioning: **Yes**
Pets: **No**
Children: **Welcome, over 6**
Smoking: **Permitted**
Social Drinking: **Permitted**

This one-story town house was built in 1830 and is located close to Courthouse Square, a National Historic District. Elizabeth has artistically furnished it with lovely antiques and brass beds. You are welcome to relax in the comfortable living room or secluded courtyard. Complimentary wine, coffee or tea is served.

MISSOURI

St. Joseph
Lathrop
Kansas City
Arrow Rock
Hannibal
St. Louis
Washington
Carthage
Rogersville
Branson

Bed & Breakfast St. Louis
16 GREEN ACRES, ST. LOUIS, MISSOURI 63137

Tel: **(314) 868-2335**	Rates (Single/Double):
Coordinator: **Evelyn Ressler**	Modest: **$20** **$30**
States/Regions Covered: **Missouri**	Average: **$30** **$35–$40**
(statewide)	Credit Cards: **No**

"Show me. I'm from Missouri" works in reverse for visitors, because Missourians will want to show *you* what makes their area so special. You can't miss the Gateway Arch, and shouldn't miss a tour of the Anheuser–Busch Brewery, the Museum of Transport, Six Flags Amusement Park, Busch Stadium, and the symphony, theater, and historic sites. Send for Evelyn's descriptive directory and select your host home. There's no charge for the booklet and she'll reserve your choice spot.

Ozark Mountain Country B&B Service
BOX 295, BRANSON, MISSOURI 65616

Tel: **(417) 334-5077 or 334-4720**
Coordinator: **Linda Johnson, Kay Cameron**
States/Regions Covered:
  Missouri—Branson, Cape Fair, Forsyth, Galena, Hollister,
  Kimberling City, Rockaway Beach, Rogersville, Walnut Shade;
  Arkansas—Eureka Springs
Rates (Single/Double):
  Average: **$20–$33 $25–$38**
Credit Cards: **No**

This region is known for the Lake of the Ozarks, arts and handicrafts, restored historic buildings, mountain music shows, Silver Dollar City (an 1800 theme town), and the unspoiled countryside. Linda and Kay will send you a complimentary copy of their descriptive listing of homes, so you can select the host of your choice; they'll take care of making your reservation.

Borgman's Bed & Breakfast
ARROW ROCK, MISSOURI 65320

Tel: **(816) 837-3350**
Host(s): **Helen and Kathy Borgman**
Location: **100 miles east of Kansas City**
No. of Rooms: **4**
Maximum No. of Guests Sharing Bath: **4**
Double/sb: **$30–$35**
Single/sb: **$30**
Months of Operation: **All year**
Reduced Rates: **10%, three nights; 10%, seniors, Monday to Friday**
Breakfast: **Continental**
Other Meals: **Dinner (winter only)**
Air-Conditioning: **Yes**
Pets: **Sometimes**
Children: **Welcome**
Smoking: **No**
Social Drinking: **Permitted**

This 1860 home is spacious and comfortable, and it is furnished with cherished family pieces. Helen is a seamstress, artisan, and baker. Wait till you taste her cinnamon rolls. Daughter Kathy is a town tour guide, so you will get first-hand information on the historic sites. A fine repertory theater, the Lyceum, is open in summer. Dine at the Old Tavern, which has been serving fine meals since 1834. Craft shops, antique stalls, and the old country store are fun places to browse in.

Morgan's Woodhaven
RR 70, BOX 833, CAMDENTON, MISSOURI 65020

Tel: (314) 346-3944
Host(s): **Gladys Morgan**
Location: **¼ mile from U.S. 54**
No. of Rooms: **1**
No. of Private Baths: **1**
Double/pb: **$30**
Single/pb: **$20**
Months of Operation: **May 1 to October 31**

Reduced Rates: **No**
Breakfast: **Continental**
Air-Conditioning: **Yes**
Pets: **No**
Children: **No**
Smoking: **No**
Social Drinking: **Permitted**

This contemporary ranch-style home, beautifully furnished, is located two miles from all the recreational activities to be found on and around the Lake of the Ozarks. The guest room has a sliding glass door which provides a private entrance and opens onto the deck which overlooks the woods. Gladys wants you to feel at home and welcomes you to use her kitchen should you tire of all the excellent restaurants in the area.

Hill House
1157 SOUTH MAIN STREET, CARTHAGE, MISSOURI 64836

Tel: **(417) 358-6145**
Host(s): **Dean and Ella Mae Scoville**
Location: **140 miles south of Kansas City**
No. of Rooms: **2**
No. of Private Baths: **2**
Double/pb: **$40**
Single/pb: **$25**

Months of Operation: **All year**
Reduced Rates: **No**
Breakfast: **Full**
Air-Conditioning: **No**
Pets: **No**
Children: **Welcome**
Smoking: **No**
Social Drinking: **No**

Located in the historic district, a stay at this brick Victorian mansion includes the grand tour of all the rooms. The house has stained glass, sliding-pocket doors, 10 fireplaces, and rare period furnishings. Your hosts will prepare dietetic foods to order and the coffee pot is always on. Breakfast includes homemade muffins and jams. Carthage Square, a mining museum, and Harry Truman's birthplace are nearby.

The Victorian Guest House
3 STILLWELL PLACE, HANNIBAL, MISSOURI 63401

Tel: (314) 221-3093
Host(s): Katherine and Beth McKinney
Location: 117 miles north of St. Louis
No. of Rooms: 3
Maximum No. of Guests Sharing
   Bath: 5
Double/sb: $30
Single/sb: $25
Months of Operation: All year

Reduced Rates: 10%, seniors
Breakfast: Continental
Air-Conditioning: Yes
Pets: Sometimes
Children: Welcome, over 6
Smoking: Permitted
Social Drinking: Permitted
Airport Pickup: Yes

Located in a residential area, this gracious Victorian brick home is
attractively furnished and is eight blocks from the historic Mark
Twain area. Katherine's connection with the Missouri Tourist
Information office will enable her to give you added assistance
with touring ideas. A full breakfast is served September through
May.

Anchor Hill Lodge
ANCHOR HILL RANCH, ROUTE 1, ROGERSVILLE, MISSOURI 65742

Tel: (417) 753-2930
Host(s): Dr. and Mrs. T. E. Atkinson
Location: 20 miles southeast of
   Springfield
No. of Rooms: 2
No. of Private Baths: 2
Double/pb: $35
Single/pb: $25
Months of Operation: All year

Reduced Rates: No
Breakfast: Continental
Air-Conditioning: No
Pets: No
Children: Welcome (crib)
Smoking: Permitted
Social Drinking: Permitted
Airport Pickup: Yes

If your horse hasn't taken a vacation in a while, he's most
welcome to accompany you to this rural ranch in the foothills of
the Ozark Mountains. For five dollars he will have a box stall and
all he can eat, while you enjoy the comfort of an old-fashioned
country home. Your hosts breed and ride Arabian horses and
there are miles of trails for you to enjoy. In addition, there's lots
to do and see, including an exotic animal farm, theater, museums, water sports, hiking, and craft fairs. You'll enjoy the relax-

ing hot tub experience on premises, as well as the beautiful views.

McNally House Bed & Breakfast
1105 SOUTH 15TH STREET, ST. JOSEPH, MISSOURI 64503

Tel: **(816) 232-0623**	Months of Operation: **All year**
Host(s): **Reva Allen, Charles St. Clair**	Reduced Rates: **10%, seniors**
Location: **50 miles north of Kansas City**	Breakfast: **Continental**
	Air-Conditioning: **Yes**
No. of Rooms: **1**	Pets: **No**
Maximum No. of Guests Sharing Bath: **3**	Children: **Welcome**
	Smoking: **No**
Double/sb: **$25**	Social Drinking: **Permitted**
Single/sb: **$20**	

There are lots of plants, leaded stained glass windows, and a grand piano set in the bay window of this 75-year-old clapboard house. It boasts two porches and a variety of gardens. Located in the historic area, you can visit the Pony Express Stables, Patee House, Jesse James Home, and the Doll Museum. Reva is a professor of social work at Missouri Western, and Charles is a community development specialist. They both enjoy travel and travelers.

The Schwegmann House B&B Inn
438 WEST FRONT STREET, WASHINGTON, MISSOURI 63090

Tel: **(314) 239-5025**	Single/sb: **$35**
Host(s): **George Bocklage, Barbara Lee, Cathy French**	Months of Operation: **All year**
	Reduced Rates: **No**
Location: **50 miles west of St. Louis**	Breakfast: **Continental**
No. of Rooms: **9**	Credit Cards: **MC, VISA**
No. of Private Baths: **7**	Air-Conditioning: **Yes**
Maximum No. of Guests Sharing Bath: **4**	Pets: **No**
	Children: **Welcome, over 7**
Double/pb: **$50**	Smoking: **Permitted**
Single/pb: **$50**	Social Drinking: **Permitted**
Double/sb: **$35**	Foreign Languages: **French**

A three-story 1861 Georgian brick house nominated for inclusion on the National Historic Register, it is located on the Missouri

River. It is tastefully furnished with antiques; handmade quilts complement the decor of each guest room. It is close to Daniel Boone's home, Meramec Caverns, Missouri's Rhineland wineries, unique shops, and fine restaurants. Relax in the graceful parlor by the fireside or stroll the formal gardens that overlook the river. George, Barbara, and Cathy serve a bountiful breakfast including fresh ground coffee, imported cheeses, homemade bread, and grape juice from Missouri's vineyards.

KEY TO LISTINGS

Location: As specified, unless B&B is right in town, or its location is clear from address as stated.

No. of Rooms: Refers to the number of guest bedrooms.

Double: Rate for two people in one room.

Single: Rate for one person in a room.

Suite: Can either be two bedrooms with an adjoining bath, or a living room and bedroom with private bath.

Guest Cottage: A separate building that usually has a mini-kitchen and private bath.

pb: Private bath.

sb: Shared bath.

Breakfast: Included, unless otherwise noted.

Air-Conditioning: If "no" or "unnecessary" is stated, it means the climate rarely warrants it.

Children: If "crib" is noted after the word "welcome," this indicates that the host also has a high-chair, baby-sitters are available, and the B&B can accommodate children under the age of three.

Smoking: If permitted, this means it is allowed *somewhere* inside the house.

Social Drinking: Some hosts provide a glass of wine or sherry; others provide setups for bring-your-own.

Please enclose a self-addressed, stamped, business-size envelope when contacting Reservation Services.

Remember the difference in time zones when calling for a reservation.

MONTANA

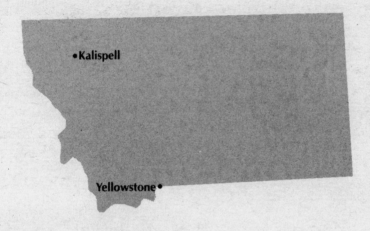

• Kalispell

Yellowstone •

Western Bed & Breakfast Hosts
P.O. BOX 322, KALISPELL, MONTANA 59901

Tel: (406) 257-4476
Coordinator: Sylva Jones
States/Regions Covered: **Montana**
  (statewide)

Rates (Single/Double):
  Modest: **$18**   **$22**
  Average: **$22**   **$38**
Credit Cards: **No**

Silva brings you the opportunity of experiencing the vast and beautiful region between Calgary, Canada, in the north, and Yellowstone National Park in the south. This area includes Glacier National Park, the National Bison Range, and Bob Marshall Wilderness. The whole region is popular for hiking, hunting, fishing, skiing, and gorgeous mountain scenery.

NEBRASKA

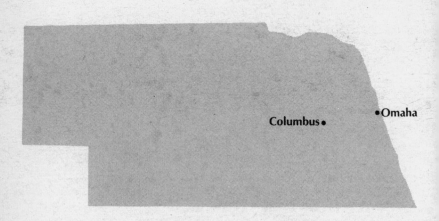

Columbus •   •Omaha

Bed & Breakfast of Nebraska
1464 28TH AVENUE, COLUMBUS, NEBRASKA 68601

Tel: **(402) 564-7591**
Coordinator: **Marlene Van Lent**
States/Regions Covered: **Statewide**

Rates (Single/Double):
  Modest: **$15**   **$20**
  Average: **$20–$25**   **$30–$45**
Credit Cards: **No**

Marlene has delightful homes in cities, towns, villages, and on farms and ranches. Many are located close to I-80, making it convenient for cross-country travelers. Visit the vacation area of Chadron, the wagon trails of Scotts Bluff, the Bill Cody Museum in North Platte, the Indian culture of Fort Robinson, the De Soto Bend Wildlife Refuge, and the world renowned Boys Town in Omaha. Many areas feature fine fishing and hunting, and the Missouri River has many tourist attractions. You are assured of warm welcomes wherever you stop.

NEVADA

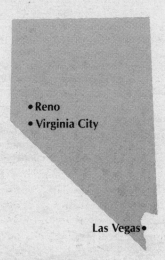

- Reno
- Virginia City

Las Vegas•

Chrisi's Bed & Breakfast
519 LODGEPOLE, INCLINE VILLAGE, LAKE TAHOE, NEVADA 89450

Tel: **(702) 831-0135**
Host(s): **Sharon and Bud Studdard**
Location: **1 block from Highway 28**
No. of Rooms: **4**
No. of Private Baths: **1**
Maximum No. of Guests Sharing Bath: **5**
Double/pb: **$60**
Single/pb: **$55**
Double/sb: **$50**

Single/sb: **$45**
Months of Operation: **All year**
Reduced Rates: **2 day-stay**
Breakfast: **Full**
Air-Conditioning: **Unnecessary**
Pets: **No**
Children: **Welcome**
Smoking: **Permitted**
Social Drinking: **Permitted**
Airport Pickup: **Yes**

Staying with Sharon and Bud, you will enjoy a panoramic view of Lake Tahoe and have the convenience of being close to great restaurants and the gaming casinos. In summer, the private beach features boating and swimming; in winter, the nearby slopes cater to skiers of every aptitude. The countryside is so lovely, if you have never hiked you will want to do so here. Wine and cheese are served each afternoon. Flowers in the guest room, plus fruit and cookies at the bedside, add to the cozy comfort of being a welcome and pampered guest.

Haus Bavaria
P.O. BOX 3308, 593 NORTH DYER CIRCLE, INCLINE VILLAGE, LAKE TAHOE, NEVADA 89450

Tel: **(702) 831-6122**
Host(s): **Wolfgang and Anna Zimmermann**
Location: **45 miles southwest of Reno**
No. of Rooms: **5**
No. of Private Baths: **5**
Double/pb: **$45**
Single/pb: **$35**
Months of Operation: **All year**

Reduced Rates: **10%, weekly**
Breakfast: **Full**
Air-Conditioning: **Unnecessary**
Pets: **No**
Children: **Welcome, over 10**
Smoking: **Permitted**
Social Drinking: **Permitted**
Foreign Languages: **German**

This immaculate residence is framed by the mountains and convenient to the splendid lake. It's hard to believe you're not in the Swiss Alps! The guest rooms are lovely and each opens on to a balcony. Continental hosts, Wolfgang and Anna set a beautiful breakfast table with bountiful platters of cold cuts, imported cheeses, sliced fruits, boiled eggs, cake, rolls, and endless cups of delicious coffee or tea. It's close to the gambling casinos and shows, all water sports and, in winter, the challenging slopes of Incline, Mount Rose, and Heavenly Valley. Best of all is returning to visit in the comfortable family room.

Las Vegas B&B
CONTACT: BED AND BREAKFAST INTERNATIONAL, 151
ARDMORE ROAD, KENSINGTON, CALIFORNIA 94707

Tel: **(415) 527-2928**
Host(s): **Jean Brown**
Location: **8 miles from I-15**
No. of Rooms: **1 suite**
No. of Private Baths: **1**
Suites: **$40 (for 2); $60 (for 4)**
Guest Cottage: **n/a**
Months of Operation: **All year**

Reduced Rates: **No**
Breakfast: **Full**
Air-Conditioning: **Yes**
Pets: **No**
Children: **Welcome**
Smoking: **Permitted**
Social Drinking: **Permitted**

This contemporary home is located at the foot of Sunrise Mountain. The host is a retired building contractor and the hostess is a gourmet cook. You can expect that breakfast will feature special treats. It is a 10-minute drive to the exciting shows and gambling on the Strip. What a pleasure to be able to leave all the frenzy and return to a quiet, relaxing atmosphere.

Savage Mansion
P.O. BOX 445, 146 SOUTH "D" STREET, VIRGINIA CITY,
NEVADA 89440

Tel: **(702) 847-0574**
Host(s): **Ann Louise Mertz, Irene and
  Bob Kugler**
Location: **14 miles east of Carson City**
No. of Rooms: **6**
No. of Private Baths: **1**
Maximum No. of Guests Sharing
  Bath: **6**
Double/pb: **$60–$80**
Single/pb: **$40**
Double/sb: **$60**
Single/sb: **$40**

Suites: **$100 (for 2)**
Months of Operation: **All year**
Reduced Rates: **No**
Breakfast: **Continental**
Other Meals: **No**
Credit Cards: **MC, VISA**
Air-Conditioning: **Unnecessary**
Pets: **No**
Children: **Welcome**
Smoking: **Permitted**
Social Drinking: **Permitted**

This fine example of gingerbread architecture was once a mine superintendent's home. It is efficiently hosted by Irene, Bob, and Ann Louise; you will receive every attention since they limit their guests to 10 at a time. The entire area has been restored to its 1870 appearance, including the saloons, mansions, and Piper's Opera House where Edwin Booth and Sarah Bernhardt once performed.

NEW HAMPSHIRE

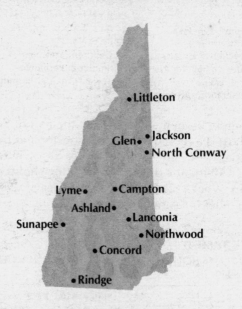

New Hampshire Bed & Breakfast
RFD 3, BOX 53, LACONIA, NEW HAMPSHIRE 03246

Tel: **(603) 279-8348**
Coordinator: **Martha W. Dorais**
States/Regions Covered: **Statewide**

Rates (Single/Double):

	Single	Double
Modest:	**$15**	**$25**
Average:	**$20**	**$30–$35**
Luxury:	**$25–$30**	**$50**

Credit Cards: **No**

New Hampshire is a haven for the sports-minded, having facilities for every type of recreation. Shoppers will find it a bargain haven since there's no sales tax on merchandise. Martha's roster ranges from an 18th-century Cape house where the hostess makes her own cheese, to a mountainside home ovelooking Lake Winnepesaukee with its own pool and tennis court, to a contemporary home convenient to the Manchester factory outlets. Send one dollar for her descriptive directory, make your selection, and she will make the reservation for you.

Cheney House

P.O. BOX 683, 40 HIGHLAND STREET, ASHLAND, NEW HAMPSHIRE 03217

Tel: **(603) 968-7968**
Host(s): **Michael and Daryl Mooney**
Location: **45 miles north of Concord**
No. of Rooms: **3**
Maximum No. of Guests Sharing
  Bath: **6**
Double/sb: **$30–$35**
Single/sb: **$28**
Months of Operation: **Memorial Day to Columbus Day**

Reduced Rates: **No**
Breakfast: **Full**
Air-Conditioning: **No**
Pets: **No**
Children: **Welcome**
Smoking: **Permitted**
Social Drinking: **Permitted**

Michael and Daryl cordially invite you to their Victorian home on a residential street where pasture land and old village homes meet. This is a great base for seeing New Hampshire. It's one mile to the beach on Squam Lake, six miles to Plymouth State College, and in 20 minutes you're at the White Mountain parks, Waterville Valley, and Lake Winnipesaukee. Relax on a porch overlooking stone walls and flower gardens, help feed the chickens, or take in the New Hampshire Symphony.

Mountain-Fare Inn

BOX 553, CAMPTON, NEW HAMPSHIRE 03223

Tel: **(603) 726-4283**
Host(s): **Susan and Dick Preston**
Location: **40 miles north of Concord**
No. of Rooms: **10**
No. of Private Baths: **5**
Maximum No. of Guests Sharing
  Bath: **4**
Double/pb: **$20**
Single/pb: **$20**
Double/sb: **$18**
Single/sb: **$18**

Guest Cottage: **$60 for 4**
Months of Operation: **All year**
Reduced Rates: **10%, Sunday to Thursday**
Breakfast: **Full**
Other Meals: **Sometimes**
Air-Conditioning: **No**
Pets: **Sometimes**
Children: **Welcome**
Smoking: **No**
Social Drinking: **Permitted**

Built in the 1800s, this white clapboard farmhouse is located in the foothills of the White Mountains and just minutes away from Franconia Notch and the Waterville Valley Resort. Susan and Dick are professional skiers and into physical fitness. Their enthusiasm is contagious! Seasonal snacks are generously offered. During the ski season, you are invited to have a family-style dinner for seven dollars per person.

The Bernerhof Inn
P.O. BOX 381, ROUTE 302, GLEN, NEW HAMPSHIRE 03838

Tel: **(603) 383-4414**
Host(s): **Ted and Sharon Wroblewski**
Location: **65 miles west of Portland, Maine**
No. of Rooms: **10**
No. of Private Baths: **2**
Maximum No. of Guests Sharing Bath: **4**
Double/pb: **$55**
Single/pb: **$30**
Double/sb: **$45**
Single/sb: **$23**

Months of Operation: **December 21 to April 30; June to Thanksgiving**
Reduced Rates: **No**
Breakfast: **Full**
Other Meals: **Available**
Credit Cards: **AMEX, MC, VISA**
Air-Conditioning: **Unnecessary**
Pets: **No**
Children: **Welcome (crib)**
Smoking: **No**
Social Drinking: **Permitted**

Gather by the fireplace of this oak-paneled lounge at this Victorian inn with a Tyrolean touch. Hot drinks, cheese fondue, and informal camaraderie make for fun-filled après-ski evenings. It's close to fine skiing in winter and the swimming pool is outside for summer enjoyment. If you stay three days, Ted and Sharon pamper you with a champagne breakfast in bed!

The Beal House Inn
247 WEST MAIN STREET, LITTLETON, NEW HAMPSHIRE 03561

Tel: **(603) 444-2661**
Host(s): **Doug and Brenda Clickenger**
Location: **85 miles north of Concord**
No. of Rooms: **15**
No. of Private Baths: **10**
Maximum No. of Guests Sharing Bath: **5**
Double/pb: **$38–$48**
Single/pb: **$30**
Double/sb: **$30**
Single/sb: **$25**

Suites: **$50–$70**
Months of Operation: **All year**
Reduced Rates: **Groups**
Breakfast: **Available**
Credit Cards: **AMEX, DC, MC, VISA**
Air-Conditioning: **Unnecessary**
Pets: **Sometimes**
Children: **Welcome (crib)**
Smoking: **Permitted**
Social Drinking: **Permitted**
Foreign Languages: **Greek, Spanish**

Doug and Brenda have an antique shop and have furnished their federal-style home with choice pieces. The decor is constantly changing since so many guests buy these pieces and take them home. Breakfast costs $3.75 and features hot popovers served by the fireside. The inn is conveniently accessible to six great ski areas, Franconia Notch, and the famed Old Man of the Mountain.

1895 House
74 PLEASANT STREET, LITTLETON, NEW HAMPSHIRE 03561

Tel: **(603) 444-5200**
Host(s): **Susanne Watkins**
Location: **180 miles northwest of Boston**
No. of Rooms: **6**
No. of Private Baths: **1**
Maximum No. of Guests Sharing Bath: **6**
Double/pb: **$40–$60**
Single/pb: **$40–$60**
Double/sb: **$24–$50**

Single/sb: **$20**
Months of Operation: **All year**
Reduced Rates: **No**
Breakfast: **Continental**
Credit Cards: **AMEX, MC, VISA**
Air-Conditioning: **Unnecessary**
Pets: **Sometimes**
Children: **Welcome, over 10**
Smoking: **Permitted**
Social Drinking: **Permitted**

An exquisite Queen Anne three-story Victorian house, its interior is an excellent example of artistry, craftsmanship, and Susan's exquisite taste. It is centrally located, so you can explore the delights of the White Mountains in all seasons. Summer is for water sports, the fall foliage is fabulous, spring is for antiquing, and winter is for skiing down Cannon Mountain. Breakfast often features zucchini muffins, cinnamon butter, raspberry jam, and freshly ground amaretto coffee.

Cranmore Mountain Lodge
P.O. BOX 1194, KEARSARGE ROAD, NORTH CONWAY, NEW HAMPSHIRE 03860

Tel: **(603) 356-2044**
Host(s): **Dawn and Robert Brauel**
Location: **60 miles west of Portland**
No. of Rooms: **17**
No. of Private Baths: **6**
Maximum No. of Guests Sharing Bath: **4**
Double/pb: **$75**
Single/pb: **$58**
Double/sb: **$60**
Single/sb: **$42**
Suites: **$80**

Months of Operation: **All year**
Reduced Rates: **Midweek; summer, $31–$45, $39–$53**
Breakfast: **Full**
Other Meals: **Dinner (included)**
Credit Cards: **MC, VISA**
Air-Conditioning: **Yes**
Pets: **No**
Children: **Welcome (crib)**
Smoking: **Permitted**
Social Drinking: **Permitted**

In the heart of the White Mountains, this lovely guest house is a mecca for summer delights and winter challenges. The magnificent grounds include a trout pond, Jacuzzi, swimming pool, tennis and basketball courts. It's a winter wonderland for ice-skating and snowmobiling; five major ski areas are within 20 minutes of the house. Dawn and Robert love entertaining people and look forward to welcoming you and your children. Please note that in summer, no dinner is served.

The Resort at Lake Shore Farm
JENNESS POND ROAD, NORTHWOOD, NEW HAMPSHIRE 03261

Tel: **(603) 942-5921**	Months of Operation: **All year**
Host(s): **Ellis and Eloise Ring**	Reduced Rates: **10%, midweek**
Location: **16 miles east of Concord**	Breakfast: **Full**
No. of Rooms: **28**	Other Meals: **Lunch & dinner**
No. of Private Baths: **20**	Air-Conditioning: **Unnecessary**
Maximum No. of Guests Sharing Bath: **4**	Pets: **Sometimes**
	Children: **Welcome (crib)**
Double/pb: **$90**	Smoking: **Permitted**
Single/pb: **$45**	Social Drinking: **Permitted**
Double/sb: **$80**	Airport Pickup: **Yes**
Single/sb: **$40**	

This fine old farmhouse, built in 1848, is surrounded by 150 acres. Guests have been coming since 1926, and each year additions have been made to provide every comfort. Beach, lake, tennis, and fishing are some of the summer recreations on the premises. Winter features snow sports. Your genial hosts Ellis and Eloise serve delicious meals and look forward to entertaining you.

Tokfarm Inn
BOX 229, WOOD AVENUE, RINDGE, NEW HAMPSHIRE 03461

Tel: **(603) 899-6646**	Reduced Rates: **No**
Host(s): **Mrs. W. B. Nottingham**	Breakfast: **Continental**
Location: **45 miles northwest of Boston**	Air-Conditioning: **Unnecessary**
	Pets: **No**
No. of Rooms: **5**	Children: **No**
Maximum No. of Guests Sharing Bath: **4**	Smoking: **No**
	Social Drinking: **Permitted**
Double/sb: **$27–$30**	Airport Pickup: **Yes**
Single/sb: **$15**	Foreign Languages: **Dutch, French, German**
Months of Operation: **April 16 to November 14**	

This 100-year-old farmhouse has a spectacular view of three states from its 1,400-foot hilltop. Mt. Monadnock, the second most climbed peak in the world (Mt. Fuji is first!), is practically in the backyard. Mrs. Nottingham raises Christmas trees, is a world traveler, and loves to ski. She'll recommend plenty of things to keep you busy in all seasons. Don't miss the lovely Cathedral of the Pines.

Times Ten Inn
ROUTE 103B, BOX 572, SUNAPEE, NEW HAMPSHIRE 03782

Tel: **(603) 763-5120**	Months of Operation: **All year**
Host(s): **Audrey and Dick Kelly**	Reduced Rates: **Families**
Location: **90 miles northwest of Boston**	Breakfast: **Full**
	Air-Conditioning: **No**
No. of Rooms: **3**	Pets: **Sometimes**
Maximum No. of Guests Sharing Bath: **6**	Children: **Welcome**
	Smoking: **Permitted**
Double/sb: **$25–$30**	Social Drinking: **Permitted**
Single/sb: **$20–24**	Airport Pickup: **Yes**

An 1820 New England farmhouse, with floor-to-ceiling living room windows overlooking a wildlife preserve. It's 25 miles to Dartmouth College, recreational Lake Sunapee, and skiing. Audrey and Dick offer a huge breakfast of Swedish pancakes, real maple syrup, homemade preserves, bacon, or sausage. Complimentary wine and good conversation are always on tap.

NEW JERSEY

Milford• Hazlet• •Red Bank
Stockton• •Ocean Grove
•Spring Lake
Bay Head•

•Atlantic City

•Sea Isle

•Cape May

Conover's Bay Head Inn
646 MAIN AVENUE, BAY HEAD, NEW JERSEY 08742

Tel: **(201) 892-4664**
Host(s): **Carl and Beverly Conover**
Location: **50 miles south of Newark, 10 miles from Garden State Parkway, Exit 98**
No. of Rooms: **12**
No. of Private Baths: **6**
Maximum No. of Guests Sharing Bath: **4**
Double/pb: **$60–$75**
Single/pb: **$55–$70**

Double/sb: **$43–$50**
Single/sb: **$38–$45**
Months of Operation: **February 15 to December 15**
Reduced Rates: **February 15 to Easter**
Breakfast: **Continental**
Air-Conditioning: **Yes**
Pets: **No**
Children: **Welcome, over 13**
Smoking: **Permitted**
Social Drinking: **Permitted**

This is the 15th season Carl and Beverly have been receiving guests in their lovely refurbished home, but the Bay Head Inn has been treating travelers to a homespun atmosphere since 1900.

Tastefully furnished with antiques, original artwork, old-fashioned photographs, and other special touches, this is a delightful summer and winter retreat. Located a block from the beach, it is also convenient to fine restaurants and shops. A full breakfast is served after October 15.

The Abbey
COLUMBIA AVENUE AND GURNEY STREET, CAPE MAY, NEW JERSEY 08204

Tel: **(609) 884-4506**
Host(s): **Jay and Marianne Schatz**
Location: **95 miles southeast of Philadelphia**
No. of Rooms: **7**
No. of Private Baths: **4**
Maximum No. of Guests Sharing Bath: **6**
Double/pb: **$50–$80**
Single/pb: **$40–$70**
Double/sb: **$65**
Single/sb: **$55**
Months of Operation: **April to November**
Reduced Rates: **10%, weekly**
Breakfast: **Continental**
Credit Cards: **MC, VISA**
Air-Conditioning: **No**
Pets: **No**
Children: **Welcome, over 12**
Smoking: **Permitted**
Social Drinking: **Permitted**

One block from the beach and in the center of the historic district sits this handsome Gothic Revival villa built in 1869 and authentically restored. Furnished with museum quality antiques, the decor is formal but the attitude is warm and casual. Jan and Marianne are former chemists who have passionate interests in antiques and restoration. A full breakfast is served in the spring and fall, often featuring egg casseroles or quiches. Late-afternoon refreshments are always available.

Albert G. Stevens Inn
127 MYRTLE AVENUE, CAPE MAY, NEW JERSEY 08204

Tel: **(609) 884-4717**
Host(s): **Dean Krumrine, Dick Flynn**
Location: **40 miles south of Atlantic City**
No. of Rooms: **6**
No. of Private Baths: **6**
Double/pb: **$45–$50**
Suites: **$65**
Months of Operation: **April through October**
Reduced Rates: **No**
Breakfast: **Full**
Air-Conditioning: **No**
Pets: **No**
Children: **No**
Smoking: **Permitted**
Social Drinking: **Permitted**

This 80-year-old Victorian is located next door to historic Wilbraham Mansion and three blocks from the beach. The antique decor includes mother-of-pearl inlay in the parlor suite, an oak mantel, and exquisite treasures throughout. The wraparound veranda is a wonderful place for sipping your second cup of coffee or for relaxing later in the day. Breakfast often features ham and cheese quiche or waffles with whipped cream.

Barnard-Good House
238 PERRY STREET, CAPE MAY, NEW JERSEY 08204

Tel: **(609) 884-5381**
Host(s): **Nan and Tom Hawkins**
No. of Rooms: **6**
No. of Private Baths: **3**
Maximum No. of Guests Sharing
  Bath: **4**
Double/pb: **$60**
Single/pb: **$55**
Double/sb: **$50**
Single/sb: **$45**
Suites: **$70**

Months of Operation: **April to November**
Reduced Rates: **10%, weekly**
Breakfast: **Continental**
Air-Conditioning: **No**
Pets: **No**
Children: **Welcome, over 12**
Smoking: **Permitted**
Social Drinking: **Permitted**
Airport Pickup: **Yes**

Nan and Tom cordially invite you to their Second Empire Victorian cottage (circa 1869), just two blocks from the "swimming" beach. They love antiques and are continually adding to their cherished collection. They use them generously to create the warm and comfortable atmosphere. Nan's breakfast includes homemade exotic juices, delicious home-baked breads, and unusual preserves, served in the spring and the fall. Iced tea and snacks are served in the evening.

The Brass Bed Inn
719 COLUMBIA AVENUE, CAPE MAY, NEW JERSEY 08204

Tel: **(609) 884-8075**
Host(s): **John and Donna Dunwoody**
No. of Rooms: **8**
No. of Private Baths: **2**
Maximum No. of Guests Sharing
  Bath: **4**
Double/pb: **$60**
Single/pb: **$60**
Double/sb: **$45–$50**
Single/sb: **$45–$50**

Months of Operation: **All year**
Reduced Rates: **September 16 to May 15**
Breakfast: **Full**
Air-Conditioning: **No**
Pets: **No**
Children: **Welcome, over 12**
Smoking: **Permitted**
Social Drinking: **Permitted**
Airport Pickup: **Yes**

This Gothic Revival home was built in 1872. The original furnishings have all been restored, and you are welcome to visit in the handsome parlor and dining room. It is two block to the ocean, shops and restaurants on the mall. John and Donna suggest that you bring your bikes to truly enjoy this historic town; there's a lock-up area to keep them safe.

The Gingerbread House
28 GURNEY STREET, CAPE MAY, NEW JERSEY 08204

Tel: **(609) 884-0211**
Host(s): **Joan and Fred Eschevarria**
No. of Rooms: **6**
No. of Private Baths: **3**
Maximum No. of Guests Sharing
  Bath: **5**
Double/pb: **$65–$72**
Single/pb: **$65–$72**
Double/sb: **$52**
Single/sb: **$45**

Suites: **$72**
Months of Operation: **All year**
Reduced Rates: **September 15 to
  June 15**
Breakfast: **Continental**
Air-Conditioning: **Unnecessary**
Pets: **No**
Children: **Welcome, over 10**
Smoking: **Permitted**
Social Drinking: **Permitted**

Listed on the National Register of Historic Places, this charming seaside cottage features cozy guest rooms. The house is cheerfully decorated with plants, lots of fresh flowers, period furniture, and photographs by Fred Eschevarria. Located a block from the beach and two blocks from the mall, the house has a comfortable living room and breezy porch that are the gathering places for friendly conversation.

The Mainstay Inn

635 COLUMBIA AVENUE, CAPE MAY, NEW JERSEY 08204

Tel: **(609) 884-8690**
Host(s): **Tom and Sue Carroll**
No. of Rooms: **12**
No. of Private Baths: **8**
Maximum No. of Guests Sharing
Bath: **4**
Double/pb: **$50–$72**
Single/pb: **$40–$62**
Double/sb: **$40–$50**
Single/sb: **$30–$40**

Months of Operation: **April 1 to
October 31**
Reduced Rates: **Spring and fall,
weekdays**
Breakfast: **Full**
Air-Conditioning: **No**
Pets: **No**
Children: **Welcome, over 12**
Smoking: **No**
Social Drinking: **Permitted**

Located in the heart of the historic district, this 110-year-old
mansion was originally built as a private gambling club. Except
for a few 20th-century concessions, it still looks much as it did
when the gamblers were there, with 14-foot ceilings, elaborate
chandeliers, and outstanding Victorian antiques. Tom and Sue
serve breakfast either in the formal dining room or on the
veranda; afternoon tea and homemade snacks are a ritual. Breakfast often features ham and apple pie, or corn quiche with baked
ham. Continental breakfast is served in the summer. You're
welcome to rock on the wide veranda, enjoy croquet in the
garden, or retreat to the cupola.

The Open Hearth Guest House
705 COLUMBIA AVENUE, CAPE MAY, NEW JERSEY 08204

Tel: **(609) 884-4933**
Host(s): **Harold and Eileen Kirsch**
No. of Rooms: **5**
Maximum No. of Guests Sharing
  Bath: **5**
Double/sb: **$30–$50**
Single/sb: **$30–$50**
Months of Operation: **January to
  October; December**

Reduced Rates: **No**
Breakfast: **No**
Air-Conditioning: **Yes**
Pets: **No**
Children: **Welcome**
Smoking: **Permitted**
Social Drinking: **Permitted**

Located in the historic district, this comfortable home is close to everything. Eileen and Harold invite you to share their living room and its most unusual fireplace. You can read, watch TV, or just visit. The lovely porch is a relaxing spot too. They have thoughtfully provided an outside shower/dressing room for your après-beach convenience.

The Queen Victoria
102 OCEAN STREET, CAPE MAY, NEW JERSEY 08204

Tel: **(609) 884-8702**
Host(s): **Joan and Dane Wells**
No. of Rooms: **12**
No. of Private Baths: **4**
Maximum No. of Guests Sharing
  Bath: **7**
Double/pb: **$84**
Single/pb: **$79**
Double/sb: **$48–$58**
Single/sb: **$43–$53**
Suites: **$135 (for 4)**

Months of Operation: **All year**
Reduced Rates: **20%, weekdays,
  Columbus Day to Mother's Day**
Breakfast: **Full**
Credit Cards: **MC, VISA**
Air-Conditioning: **Unnecessary**
Pets: **No**
Children: **No**
Smoking: **Permitted**
Social Drinking: **Permitted**

This 100-year-old seaside inn is a celebration of Victorian elegance. Curl up beside the evening fire and perhaps a friendly cat will curl up next to you. Retire amid colorful quilts, antique furnishings, and fresh flowers. Walk to the beach or ride through the charming village on bicycles provided by Joan and Dane. Breakfast and complimentary afternoon tea and snacks are served in the dining room. There is a two-day minimum stay on weekends.

The Seventh Sister Guesthouse
10 JACKSON STREET, CAPE MAY, NEW JERSEY 08204

Tel: **(609) 884-2280**
Host(s): **Bob and Jo-Anne Myers**
No. of Rooms: **6**
Maximum No. of Guests Sharing
  Bath: **4**
Double/sb: **$48**
Single/sb: **$48**
Months of Operation: **All year**

Reduced Rates: **5% weekly,
  September to June**
Breakfast: **Available**
Air-Conditioning: **No**
Pets: **No**
Children: **Welcome, over 7**
Smoking: **Permitted**
Social Drinking: **Permitted**
Foreign Languages: **Spanish**

This delightful seaside cottage was built in 1888 and is beautifully restored. It is registered in the Library of Congress as an historic American building. The guest rooms have ocean views and are appropriately furnished. Bob and Jo-Anne invite you to visit in the living room, spacious yard, or on the breeze-cooled sun porch. The have an unusual wicker collection. The beach is 100 feet away.

The Residence
56 NEVADA DRIVE, HAZLET, NEW JERSEY 07730

Tel: **(201) 264-9778 or 264-2892**
Host(s): **Ralph and Sally Stat**
Location: **40 miles south of New York
  City**
No. of Rooms: **2**
Maximum No. of Guests Sharing
  Bath: **2**
Double/sb: **$35**
Single/sb: **$30**

Months of Operation: **All year**
Reduced Rates: **No**
Breakfast: **Full**
Air-Conditioning: **No**
Pets: **Welcome**
Children: **Welcome**
Smoking: **No**
Social Drinking: **Permitted**
Foreign Languages: **Yiddish**

Ralph and Sally invite you to their light blue split ranch, located in a residential area. It's 18 miles from the seashore at Asbury Park, and close to shopping malls with major department stores, historic Menlo Park where Thomas Edison had his bright idea, and Raritan Bay for boating and fishing. The guest rooms are cozy and comfortable, and you are invited to join the Stats for conversation, TV, and snacks.

The Studio of John F. Peto
BOX 306, 102 CEDAR AVENUE, ISLAND HEIGHTS, NEW JERSEY 08732

Tel: (201) 270-6058
Host(s): Joy Peto Smiley
Location: 56 miles east of Philadelphia
No. of Rooms: 7
No. of Private Baths: 1
Maximum No. of Guests Sharing
  Bath: 3
Double/pb: $60
Single/pb: $55
Double/sb: $50–$55
Single/sb: $35–$40
Suites: $60–$65

Months of Operation: All year
Reduced Rates: Families
Breakfast: Full
Air-Conditioning: No
Pets: No
Children: Welcome, over 11
Smoking: Permitted
Social Drinking: Permitted
Airport Pickup: Yes
Foreign Languages: Italian,
  Portuguese, Spanish

The two-story Queen Anne home of the renowned artist John F. Peto was built in 1889. Recently restored, it retains a Victorian atmosphere, with his paintings, memorabilia, and antiques. The town is on the National Register of Historic Sites. Attractive to joggers and cyclists, there is no commercial traffic. There are three beaches, and fine crabbing and sailing nearby. Joy, Mr. Peto's granddaughter, serves a gourmet breakfast in the up-to-date kitchen. You are always greeted with a warm smile and a beverage appropriate to the season. There's a guest refrigerator in which to store your snacks.

Chestnut Hill on-the-Delaware
63 CHURCH STREET, MILFORD, NEW JERSEY 08848

Tel: (201) 995-9761
Host(s): Linda, Rob, and Michael
  Castagna
Location: 12 miles south of
  Phillipsburg
No. of Rooms: 5
No. of Private Baths: 1
Maximum No. of Guests Sharing
  Bath: 6
Double/sb: $45–$50

Single/sb: $45–$50
Suites: $65
Months of Operation: All year
Reduced Rates: Weekly
Breakfast: Full
Air-Conditioning: 2 rooms
Pets: No
Children: Welcome
Smoking: No
Social Drinking: Permitted

The veranda of this 1878 Neo-Italianate Victorian overlooks the peaceful Delaware River. Linda, Rob, and teenage son Michael have refurbished and restored their home with charm, grace, and beauty. The historic countryside is great for antique hunting, water sports, art shows, and restaurants. Dozens of factory outlets are close by, and it's only minutes to arty New Hope and Bucks County delights.

Cordova

26 WEBB AVENUE, OCEAN GROVE, NEW JERSEY 07756

Tel: **(201) 774-3084**
Host(s): **The Chernik Family**
Location: **30 miles from Newark**
No. of Rooms: **20**
No. of Private Baths: **3**
Maximum No. of Guests Sharing
  Bath: **8**
Double/pb: **$45**
Double/sb: **$21–$32**
Single/sb: **$18–$23**
Guest Cottage: **$300 (week) sleeps 4**
Months of Operation: **Memorial Day
  to Labor Day**

Reduced Rates: **Stay 7 days, pay for 5;
  10%, seniors; 10%, groups; 10%,
  families**
Breakfast: **Continental**
Air-Conditioning: **No**
Pets: **No**
Children: **Welcome (crib)**
Smoking: **Permitted**
Social Drinking: **Permitted**
Foreign Languages: **French, Russian**

This century-old Victorian is located in a lovely beach community. It has a friendly family atmosphere with old world charm. There's a white sandy beach, a wooden boardwalk, and no honky tonk. Many rooms have oak chests, rockers, and washbasins. If you stay a week, the Cherniks invite you to their family barbecue.

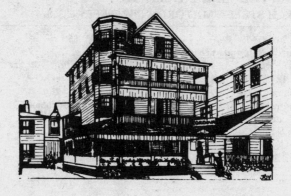

Cape Associates
340 46TH PLACE, SEA ISLE CITY, NEW JERSEY 08243

Tel: **(609) 263-8700 or 263-4461**
Host(s): **Wish Zurawski, Eileen Rodan**
Location: **2 miles from Route 9**
No. of Rooms: **4**
No. of Private Baths: **1**
Maximum No. of Guests Sharing
    Bath: **5**
Double/pb: **$45–$60**
Single/pb: **$35–$45**
Double/sb: **$35–$50**

Single/sb: **$20–$35**
Months of Operation: **All year**
Reduced Rates: **October 1 to May 15**
Breakfast: **Continental**
Air-Conditioning: **Unnecessary**
Pets: **Sometimes**
Children: **Welcome**
Smoking: **Permitted**
Social Drinking: **Permitted**

It's four blocks to the beach from this 1962 brick and wood colonial house. It's casual and comfortable with lots of books, records, and artwork. Close to historic Cape May and Atlantic City, Eileen and Wish will arrange to escort you to the casinos. You are welcome to use the kitchen for light snacks as well as the laundry facilities. Cooled by the bay breezes, the deck is a lovely place to relax.

Bay and Beach View
108 B 32ND STREET, SEA ISLE CITY, NEW JERSEY 08243

Tel: **(215) 623-2426**
Host(s): **Lucretia and Gregory Aiello**
Location: **3 miles from Route 9**
No. of Rooms: **2**
No. of Private Baths: **1**
Maximum No. of Guests Sharing
    Bath: **4**
Double/pb: **$36**
Single/pb: **$36**
Double/sb: **$28**
Single/sb: **$28**

Months of Operation: **May to
    November**
Reduced Rates: **May and November,
    $30–$22; 10%, seniors**
Breakfast: **Continental**
Air-Conditioning: **No**
Pets: **No**
Children: **Welcome**
Smoking: **No**
Social Drinking: **No**

Located in one of the smaller towns along the South Jersey shore, Sea Isle offers fishing, crabbing, beachcombing, sunning, and bathing. It's just 20 miles to Atlantic City, and it is convenient to the famous Wildwood Boardwalk and Victorian Cape May.

Normanday Inn
21 TUTTLE AVENUE, SPRING LAKE, NEW JERSEY 07762

Tel: **(201) 449-7172**
Host(s): **Michael and Susan Ingino**
Location: **80 miles from New York City and Philadelphia**
No. of Rooms: **18**
No. of Private Baths: **12**
Maximum No. of Guests Sharing Bath: **5**
Double/pb: **$50–$76**
Single/pb: **$32–$68**
Double/sb: **$50–$76**

Single/sb: **$32–$68**
Months of Operation: **All year**
Reduced Rates: **15%, weekly; 30%, Labor Day to June 15**
Breakfast: **Full**
Air-Conditioning: **Yes**
Pets: **Sometimes**
Children: **Welcome**
Smoking: **Permitted**
Social Drinking: **Permitted**

This Victorian inn dates back to 1888. White wicker tables and chairs adorn the wraparound porch where guests can enjoy a complimentary glass of wine. Antique clocks, walnut and oak period pieces, and old-fashioned beds carry the 19th century style into the many rooms. A breakfast of blueberry pancakes, home-made Irish oatmeal, or soda bread is served in the sunny dining room. The beach is down the street, and shops, restaurants, golf, tennis, and riding are nearby.

The Woolverton Inn
R.D. 3, BOX 233-A, STOCKTON, NEW JERSEY 08559

Tel: **(609) 397-0802**
Host(s): **Deborah Clark**
Location: **60 miles southeast of Philadelphia**
No. of Rooms: **8**
Maximum No. of Guests Sharing Bath: **4**
Double/sb: **$45–$65**
Single/sb: **$45–$65**
Suites: **$70**

Months of Operation: **All year**
Reduced Rates: **No**
Breakfast: **Continental**
Credit Cards: **AMEX**
Air-Conditioning: **Yes**
Pets: **No**
Children: **Welcome, over 14**
Smoking: **Permitted**
Social Drinking: **Permitted**

Built in 1793, this elegant stone manor house set amidst formal gardens and stately trees is listed on the National Register of Historic Places. It is beautifully furnished with family antiques. You will enjoy home-baked breads and sweets for breakfast and afternoon tea. Explore the many craft and antique shops for which the area is noted, or read by the fire in the spacious living room and library. It's not too far from Princeton University.

KEY TO LISTINGS

Location: As specified, unless B&B is right in town, or its location is clear from address as stated.
No. of Rooms: Refers to the number of guest bedrooms.
Double: Rate for two people in one room.
Single: Rate for one person in a room.
Suite: Can either be two bedrooms with an adjoining bath, or a living room and bedroom with private bath.
Guest Cottage: A separate building that usually has a mini-kitchen and private bath.
pb: Private bath.
sb: Shared bath.
Breakfast: Included, unless otherwise noted.
Air-Conditioning: If "no" or "unnecessary" is stated, it means the climate rarely warrants it.
Children: If "crib" is noted after the word "welcome," this indicates that the host also has a high-chair, baby-sitters are available, and the B&B can accommodate children under the age of three.
Smoking: If permitted, this means it is allowed *somewhere* inside the house.
Social Drinking: Some hosts provide a glass of wine or sherry; others provide setups for bring-your-own.

Please enclose a self-addressed, stamped, business-size envelope when contacting Reservation Services.

Remember the difference in time zones when calling for a reservation.

NEW MEXICO

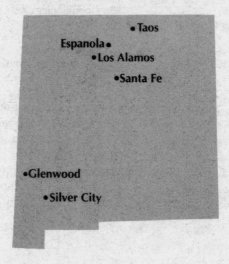

La Puebla House
ROUTE 1, BOX 172 A, ESPANOLA, NEW MEXICO 87532

Tel: **(505) 753-3981**
Host(s): **Elvira Bain, Barbara Thornton**
Location: **4 miles east of Espanola**
No. of Rooms: **4**
Maximum No. of Guests Sharing
  Bath: **6**
Double/sb: **$29**
Single/sb: **$23**
Months of Operation: **All year**

Reduced Rates: **$3 less, March 1 to
  October 31; weekly**
Breakfast: **Continental**
Credit Cards: **MC, VISA**
Air-Conditioning: **No**
Pets: **Sometimes**
Children: **Welcome**
Smoking: **Permitted**
Social Drinking: **Permitted**

The house is situated between the famous landscapes of Santa Cruz and Chimayo. Elvira and Barbara will be happy to direct you to the sights of nearby Santa Fe. Occasionally, Elvira, a gourmet cook, will invite you to be seated at her table for a reasonable price. If you prefer to cook and clean up on your own, the kitchen is available. You are welcome to use the laundry facilities and the women offer snacks to go along with your self-supplied cocktails.

La Casita
ROUTE 10, BOX 137, GLENWOOD, NEW MEXICO 88039

Tel: (505) 539-2124
Host(s): **Dan and Sally Campbell**
Location: **63 miles north of Silver City**
No. of Rooms: **2**
No. of Private Baths: **2**
Double/pb: **$30**
Single/pb: **$20**
Guest Cottage: **$50 sleeps 4**
Months of Operation: **All year**

Reduced Rates: **No**
Breakfast: **Full**
Other Meals: **Available**
Air-Conditioning: **Yes**
Pets: **Sometimes**
Children: **Welcome (crib)**
Smoking: **Permitted**
Social Drinking: **Permitted**
Foreign Languages: **Spanish**

La Casita means the little house. This one is a modern adobe guest house surrounded by cottonwoods and a pond on the Campbells' 15-acre farm. The southern end of the Rockies, with the famous Catwalk, deep canyons, and the cool coniferous forests of the Gila Wilderness Area a mile away. The Gila Cliff Dwellings are within picnicking distance, and the Mexican border is 100 miles away. Sally and Dan provide garden vegetables along with the full kitchen facilities.

Los Alamos Bed & Breakfast
BOX 1212, LOS ALAMOS, NEW MEXICO 87544

Tel: (505) 662-6041
Host(s): **Mary and Roland Pettitt**
Location: **32 miles north of Santa Fe**
No. of Rooms: **2**
No. of Private Baths: **1**
Maximum No. of Guests Sharing
  Bath: **2**
Double/pb: **$30**
Single/pb: **$25**
Single/sb: **$10–$15**
Months of Operation: **All year**

Reduced Rates: **10%, seniors; families; weekly**
Breakfast: **Full**
Other Meals: **Dinner ($5.00)**
Air-Conditioning: **Unnecessary**
Pets: **No**
Children: **Welcome (crib)**
Smoking: **No**
Social Drinking: **Permitted**
Foreign Languages: **Spanish**

This comfortable ranch-style home has a charming, fully equipped apartment with a separate entry adjoining the patio and garden. At an elevation of 7,500 feet, this town is truly a breath of fresh air. It is close to the Los Alamos National Laboratory (where Roland is a geologist) and within minutes of ski slopes, hiking trails, and Indian pueblos. Mary has a lovely garden and enjoys exchanging travel experiences with her guests.

Orange Street Bed & Breakfast
3496 ORANGE STREET, LOS ALAMOS, NEW MEXICO 87544

Tel: (505) 662-2651
Host(s): **Phil and Hester Sargent**
Location: **32 miles north of Santa Fe**
No. of Rooms: **3**
Maximum No. of Guests Sharing
  Bath: **5**
Double/sb: **$28**
Single/sb: **$22**
Months of Operation: **All year**

Reduced Rates: **No**
Breakfast: **Full**
Air-Conditioning: **No**
Pets: **No**
Children: **No**
Smoking: **No**
Social Drinking: **Permitted**
Airport Pickup: **Yes**

At an elevation of 7,300 feet in the Jemez Mountains, the fresh air is exhilarating. Hester is a tennis coach, and Phil plays a good game too. They also ski, hike, and bike, and they will suggest how you can enjoy these pursuits during your stay. The Indian pueblos and old mining towns are just two of the not-to-be-missed sights. A bowl of fruit and homemade dessert are placed in your room daily.

Bed & Breakfast of Santa Fe
218 E. BUENA VISTA STREET, SANTA FE, NEW MEXICO 87501

Tel: (505) 982-3332
Coodinator: **Star and Ed Jones**
States/Regions Covered: **Santa Fe**

Rates (Single/Double):

	Single	Double
Modest:	**$30**	**$35**
Average:	**$40**	**$45**
Luxury:	**$60**	**$60**

Credit Cards: **No**

Santa Fe was settled in 1610 by Spanish explorers, and it is near eight Indian pueblos. Don't miss the cliff dwellings at Bandelier National Monument nor Los Alamos where the atomic bomb was developed. It's one and a half hours to Taos, which boasts the oldest continuously inhabited building in the U.S. The area abounds with many art galleries, and the world-famous Indian painter R. C. Gorman is exhibited here. Star and Ed will surely find a host home suited to your needs.

Bear Mountain Guest Ranch
P.O. BOX 1163, SILVER CITY, NEW MEXICO 88061

Tel: (505) 538-2538
Host(s): **Myra B. McCormick**

Location: **45 miles north of I-10**
No. of Rooms: **10**

No. of Private Baths: **10**
Double/pb: **$58**
Single/pb: **$39**
Suites: **$83 (for 3); $93 (for 4)**
Guest Cottage: **$92 sleeps 8**
Months of Operation: **All year**
Reduced Rates: **10%, seniors**
Breakfast: **Full**
Other Meals: **Lunch and dinner (included)**

Air-Conditioning: **Unnecessary**
Pets: **Welcome**
Children: **Welcome**
Smoking: **Permitted**
Social Drinking: **Permitted**
Airport Pickup: **Yes**
Foreign Languages: **French, Spanish, Tagalog**

At an elevation of 6,250 feet, on 160 acres, the ranch adjoins the Gila National Forest. Home-baked breads, natural foods, and family-style meals are featured. The rate quoted for the guest cottage is without meals. If you prefer Myra's cooking to your own, add $12 per person. Myra leads groups of guests into the area's four life zones in search of southwestern birds, tropical-looking wild plants, archeological sites, and scenery. You will enjoy investigating the Gila Cliff Dwellings, Glenwood Catwalk, hot springs, the Gila Wilderness, and the Gila River Bird Habitat.

Mountain Light Bed & Breakfast
P.O. BOX 241, TAOS, NEW MEXICO 87571

Tel: **(505) 776-8474**
Host(s): **Gail Russell**
Location: **12 miles north of Taos**
No. of Rooms: **2**
No. of Private Baths: **1**
Maximum No. of Guests Sharing Bath: **4**
Double/pb: **$40**
Single/pb: **$30**
Double/sb: **$35**

Single/sb: **$20**
Months of Operation: **All year**
Reduced Rates: **15%, 5-day stay**
Breakfast: **Continental**
Air-Conditioning: **No**
Pets: **Sometimes**
Children: **Welcome**
Smoking: **Permitted**
Social Drinking: **Permitted**

This large, traditional adobe home is perched on the edge of a mesa and commands a spectacular view. Gail is a professional photographer and the house is her home, studio, and gallery. Her photographs have appeared in many national magazines. There are cozy fireplaces and a wood-burning stove. It is close to the D. H. Lawrence Ranch, the Millicent Rogers Museum, Ski Valley, and the Rio Grande. This is where the buffalo roam and good trout fishing is nearby. The coffee pot is always on.

NEW YORK

• Three Mile Bay

• Lake Placid

• Bolton Landing
Lake George • • Granville
Camden • • Glens Falls
Buffalo • Syracuse • • Cazenovia • Greenwich
Colden • Geneva •
Oneonta • Albany • • Rensselaer
Ithaca • Stamford • • Ghent
Corning •
Kingston •
Barryville •
• Cold Spring
Johnson • • Garrison • Shelter Island
Warwick • • Croton-
Yonkers • • on-Hudson • Southampton
New York City
Long Island

THE CATSKILLS

The All Breeze Farm
STAR ROUTE 234, BARRYVILLE, NEW YORK 12719

Tel: **(914) 557-8232**
Host(s): **Paul and Sue Clark**
Location: **18 miles northwest of Port Jervis**
No. of Rooms: **4**
No. of Private Baths: **4**
Double/pb: **$25**
Single/pb: **$15**
Months of Operation: **March to December**

Reduced Rates: **No**
Breakfast: **Full**
Other Meals: **Available**
Air-Conditioning: **No**
Pets: **Yes**
Children: **Welcome**
Smoking: **Permitted**
Social Drinking: **Permitted**

The All Breeze is a 100-year-old working farm. Your hosts invite you to farm-fresh meals in the main house, including homemade coffee cakes and desserts. Sullivan County is known for trout fishing, hunting, and the Delaware River rapids. Children will want to take a hay ride, feed the animals, and explore the woods around the farm.

Elaine's Guest House
P.O. BOX 27, JOHNSON, NEW YORK 10933

Tel: **(914) 355-8811**
Host(s): **Elaine Scott**
Location: **10 miles from I-84**
No. of Rooms: **2**
No. of Private Baths: **1**
Maximum No. of Guests Sharing
  Bath: **2**
Double/pb: **$20**
Single/pb: **$10**
Double/sb: **$20**

Single/sb: **$10**
Months of Operation: **All year**
Reduced Rates: **No**
Breakfast: **Full**
Air-Conditioning: **No**
Pets: **No**
Children: **Welcome**
Smoking: **No**
Social Drinking: **Permitted**

Located ten minutes from Middletown, between Westown and Slate Hill, Elaine's home features warm hospitality and comfort. It is furnished with choice items from her on-premises antique and collectibles shop. She will be pleased to direct you to the area's points of special interest and will suggest good places to dine, suited to your budget.

A Secret Garden
6071-10 MALDEN TURNPIKE, SAUGERTIES, NEW YORK 12477

Tel: **(914) 246-3338**
Host(s): **Michael and Suzanne Kolb**
Location: **38 miles south of Albany**
No. of Rooms: **2**
No. of Private Baths: **2**
Double/pb: **$25**
Single/pb: **$18**
Suites: **$50 for four; $48 for three**

Months of Operation: **All year**
Reduced Rates: **10%, seniors**
Breakfast: **Continental**
Air-Conditioning: **No**
Pets: **No**
Children: **Welcome, over 6**
Smoking: **Permitted**
Social Drinking: **Permitted**

This country house was built in 1820; additions were built during the Civil War, and Michael has used his artistic ability for restoration and remodeling. Suzanne's expertise with antiques and her good taste have made it comfortable and attractive. Located minutes from historic Kingston and the renowned art colony of Woodstock, you'll find plenty to keep you busy. You're invited to have complimentary wine and cheese before you go out to dinner at one of the area's fine restaurants.

The Eggery Inn
COUNTY ROAD 16, TANNERSVILLE, NEW YORK 12485

Tel: (518) 589-5363
Host(s): Julie and Abe Abramczyk
Location: 125 miles north of New York City
No. of Rooms: 10
No. of Private Baths: 7
Maximum No. of Guests Sharing Bath: 6
Double/pb: $45
Single/pb: $40
Double/sb: $38
Single/sb: $33

Months of Operation: June 1 to March 31
Reduced Rates: No
Breakfast: Full
Other Meals: Available
Credit Cards: MC, VISA
Air-Conditioning: Unnecessary
Pets: No
Children: Welcome
Smoking: Permitted
Social Drinking: Permitted
Foreign Languages: Yiddish

The guest rooms are comfortably furnished with simple pine and maple pieces enhanced by heirloom bedspreads. The old-fashioned print wallpaper and the carpet underfoot add to the cozy feeling. Each shared bath accommodation has a sink in the bedroom. During a hearty breakfast, you will enjoy the beautiful, unobstructed view of the Hunter Mountain ski slopes. Julie and Abe do their best to make you feel welcome.

Tranquality Guest Home
P. O. BOX 347, WEST STREET EXTENSION, WARWICK, NEW YORK 10990

Tel: (914) 986-4364
Host(s): Virginia Beckert, Frances Scalza
Location: 60 miles northwest of New York City
No. of Rooms: 2
No. of Private Baths: 1
Maximum No. of Guests Sharing Bath: 2
Double/pb: $40
Single/pb: $20
Double/sb: $36

Single/sb: $18
Months of Operation: All year
Reduced Rates: 10%, weekly; 10%, seniors
Breakfast: Continental
Other Meals: Available
Air-Conditioning: Yes
Pets: No
Children: No
Smoking: No
Social Drinking: Permitted

This century-old farmhouse with its comfortable full porch features the best of the old and the new. You can enjoy the cable TV, extensive library, and music room. Take a stroll on the spacious lawns or into Warwick for international restaurants and fine antique shops. It is close to tennis, golf, and the Appalachian Trail. Virginia and Frances offer complimentary wine and cheese along with good conversation.

Willow Brook Farm
P. O. BOX 375, WARWICK TURNPIKE, WARWICK, NEW YORK 10990

Tel: **(201) 853-7728**
Host(s): **Frances Jacobsen**
Location: **2 miles from Route 94**
No. of Rooms: **25**
Maximum No. of Guests Sharing
Bath: **6**
Double/sb: **$40**
Single/sb: **$20**
Months of Operation: **All year**

Reduced Rates: **10%, seniors**
Breakfast: **Full**
Other Meals: **Available**
Air-Conditioning: **No**
Pets: **No**
Children: **Welcome**
Smoking: **Permitted**
Social Drinking: **Permitted**

Situated in a lovely setting, the Willow Brook is a fine place to enjoy recreational activities in all seasons. The fishing pond is big enough for summer rowboating and is well lit in winter for nighttime skating. Located on the New York/New Jersey state line, it's minutes to the Appalachian Trail, Vernon Valley Action Park, and Great Gorge. It is also an easy drive to Sterling Forest, Mt. Peter, Waywayanda State Park, and Hidden Valley. Frances is a most cordial hostess and will make you feel right at home.

HUDSON VALLEY/ALBANY AREA

Bed & Breakfast, U.S.A., Ltd.
P.O. BOX 528, CROTON-ON-HUDSON, NEW YORK 10521

Tel: **(914) 271-6228**
Coordinator: **Barbara Notarius**
States/Regions Covered: **Hudson Valley, Westchester county, and upstate New York**

Rates (Single/Double):
Modest:	**$25**	**$25–30**
Average:	**$30**	**$30–40**
Luxury:	**$50**	**$50**

Credit Cards: **No**

Barbara's extensive network of host homes are convenient to colleges, corporate headquarters, historic sites, recreational activities, and cultural events. Some have easy access to New York City, and others are rustic country places; the ambience ranges from a simple cabin to an elegant mansion, with many choices in between. The $25 annual membership fee includes unlimited reservations and the informative newsletter. If you choose not to be a member, there is a $15 processing fee for each booking.

Battenkill Bed and Breakfast
R.D. 1, CAMBRIDGE, NEW YORK, 12816

Tel: **(518) 677-8868**	Months of Operation: **All year**
Host(s): **Veronica and Walter Piekarz**	Reduced Rates: **No**
Location: **30 miles east of Saratoga, New York**	Breakfast: **Continental**
	Other Meals: **Available**
No. of Rooms: **2**	Air-Conditioning: **No**
Maximum No. of Guests Sharing Bath: **4**	Pets: **No**
	Children: **No**
Double/sb: **$30**	Smoking: **Permitted**
Single/sb: **$20**	Social Drinking: **Permitted**

The post-and-beam structure of this Yankee barn contemporary can be spotted throughout its interior. Guests will enjoy the gourmet meals served by their hosts who are interested in music and a back-to-basics kind of life. Bromley Mountain, Saratoga Performing Arts Center, and Manchester, Vermont, are nearby.

Olde Post Inn
43 MAIN STREET, COLD SPRING, NEW YORK 10516

Tel: **(914) 265-2510**	Months of Operation: **All year**
Host(s): **Carole Zeller, George Argila**	Reduced Rates: **No**
Location: **50 miles north of New York City**	Breakfast: **Continental**
	Credit Cards: **MC, VISA**
No. of Rooms: **4**	Air-Conditioning: **Yes**
Maximum No. of Guests Sharing Bath: **8**	Pets: **No**
	Children: **Welcome, over 5**
Double/sb: **$50**	Smoking: **Permitted**
Single/sb: **$50**	Social Drinking: **Permitted**

Built in 1820 as a post office and customhouse, the inn is listed on the National Historic Register. The wide-plank floors, exposed beam ceilings, and original moldings have been retained. It is comfortably decorated in country style. George is a musician who graduated from Juilliard, and Carole enjoys hostessing and crafts.

One Market Street
COLD SPRING ON HUDSON, NEW YORK 10516

Tel: (914) 265-3912
Host(s): **Philip and Esther Baumgarten**
Location: **50 miles north of New York City**
No. of Rooms: **1 suite**
No. of Private Baths: **1**
Suites: **$55**
Months of Operation: **All year**

Reduced Rates: **$45, Monday to Thursday**
Breakfast: **Continental**
Credit Cards: **VISA**
Air-Conditioning: **Yes**
Pets: **No**
Children: **Welcome, over 10**
Smoking: **Permitted**
Social Drinking: **Permitted**

This beautiful Federal-style building dates back to the 1800s and looks out on the Hudson, surrounding mountains, and the foliage of the valley. The suite's kitchenette is stocked with rolls, juice, tea, and coffee for a make-it-at-your-leisure breakfast. Don't miss nearby West Point, Vassar College, and the Vanderbilt Mansion. Philip and Esther will direct you to the fine restaurants and antique shops in their historic town.

Barbara's Bed & Breakfast
49 VAN WYCK STREET, CROTON-ON-HUDSON, NEW YORK 10520

Tel: (914) 271-6228
Host(s): **Barbara and George Klein**
Location: **30 miles north of New York City**
No. of Rooms: **2**
No. of Private Baths: **1**
Maximum No. of Guests Sharing Bath: **4**
Double/pb: **$50**
Single/pb: **$50**

Months of Operation: **All year**
Reduced Rates: **$40, winter; $210, weekly; families**
Breakfast: **Full**
Air-Conditioning: **Yes**
Pets: **No**
Children: **Welcome**
Smoking: **No**
Social Drinking: **Permitted**
Foreign Languages: **Russian**

A handsome 95-year-old Victorian mansion, it is eclectically furnished with antiques, Oriental rugs, and unusual decorator touches. Lush landscaping punctuates the pool area and the lovely view from the rear garden is of the Hudson River and Catskill Mountains. It is close to the Sleepy Hollow restoration, Cold Spring, and West Point. Barbara is interested in art and history; George is a computer consultant interested in woodworking. Breakfast often includes such delicacies as raspberry pancakes, baked eggs, and homemade challah.

Golden Eagle Inn
GARRISON'S LANDING, GARRISON, NEW YORK 10524

Tel: **(914) 424-3067**
Host(s): **George and Stephanie Templeton**
Location: **50 miles north of New York City**
No. of Rooms: **5**
No. of Private Baths: **4**
Maximum No. of Guests Sharing Bath: **4**
Double/pb: **$55–$70**
Single/pb: **$55–$70**
Double/sb: **$50–$60**
Single/sb: **$50–$60**

Months of Operation: **April 1 to January 15**
Reduced Rates: **No**
Breakfast: **Continental**
Other Meals: **Lunch available weekends**
Credit Cards: **AMEX, MC, VISA**
Air-Conditioning: **Yes**
Pets: **No**
Children: **Welcome, over 12 on weekdays**
Smoking: **Permitted**
Social Drinking: **Permitted**

In the highlands on the banks of the Hudson River, this gracious brick mansion (circa 1848) is listed on the National Register of Historic Places. It's close to West Point and Boscobel, as well as to Hyde Park and the Sleepy Hollow restorations. All the rooms are decorated with antiques and original artwork. The Templetons will direct you to some of the best restaurants in the area.

Captain Schoonmaker Bed & Breakfast
R.D. 2, BOX 37, HIGH FALLS, NEW YORK 12440

Tel: **(914) 687-7946**
Host(s): **Sam and Julia Krieg**
Location: **80 miles north of New York City**
No. of Rooms: **6**
Maximum No. of Guests Sharing Bath: **4**
Double/sb: **$45–$55**
Single/sb: **$35**

Months of Operation: **All year**
Reduced Rates: **No**
Breakfast: **Full**
Air-Conditioning: **No**
Pets: **No**
Children: **Welcome, over 4**
Smoking: **Permitted**
Social Drinking: **Permitted**

This stone house, built in 1760, is furnished with a charming early American feeling. You can fish in the trout stream or duck under the waterfalls for a refreshing swim. Visit historic Hyde Park to see the Roosevelt and Vanderbilt mansions, or just relax and read with a spot of tea or sherry in the sunny solarium. The breakfast breads, pastries, and preserves are outstanding.

House on the Hill
P.O. BOX 86, OLD ROUTE 213, HIGH FALLS, NEW YORK 12440

Tel: **(914) 687-9627**
Host(s): **Shelley and Sharon Glassman**
Location: **10 miles south of Kingston**
No. of Rooms: **3 suites**
No. of Private Baths: **1**
Maximum No. of Guests Sharing
  Bath: **4**
Suites: **$60–$65**

Months of Operation: **All year**
Reduced Rates: **No**
Breakfast: **Full**
Air-Conditioning: **Unnecessary**
Pets: **No**
Children: **Welcome**
Smoking: **Permitted**
Social Drinking: **Permitted**

A bowl of fruit, a bouquet of flowers, and handmade quilts give the suites in this spacious colonial their special charm. Breakfast is served by the fireside in the living room, or on the glass porch facing the pond. There are woods to explore, lawns for the children to play on, and ice-skating on the pond in winter. Tennis, golf, and fine skiing are all nearby. Lake Mohonk and historic Kingston are minutes away. Complimentary wine and cheese are served, and Shelley and Sharon will direct you to the two four-star restaurants within walking distance of their home.

Brookside Manor
MAIN STREET, LEBANON SPRINGS, NEW YORK 12114

Tel: **(518) 794-9620**
Host(s): **Leslie and Arnold Gallo**
Location: **8 miles west of Pittsfield, Massachusetts**
No. of Rooms: **5**
Maximum No. of Guests Sharing Bath: **4**
Double/sb: **$65–$80**
Single/sb: **$55–$65**
Months of Operation: **All year**

Reduced Rates: **10%, March to April; 15%, weekly; $10, Sunday to Thursday**
Breakfast: **Full**
Air-Conditioning: **Unnecessary**
Pets: **Sometimes**
Children: **Welcome**
Smoking: **Permitted**
Social Drinking: **Permitted**

This 1860 Victorian Georgian mansion is situated on 60 acres in an historic area. It has been newly renovated and decorated to emphasize its original beauty. It is convenient to skiing at Jiminy Peak and Brodie Mountain. It is also close to the Tanglewood Music Festival in the Berkshires, Shaker Village, and many antique shops and restaurants. There is a pool on premises and tennis is nearby.

Shadybrook Farm
OLD POST ROAD, MARLBORO, NEW YORK 12542

Tel: **(914) 236-4123 or 236-4125**
Host(s): **Margaret Schramm, Judy Rivera**
Location: **70 miles north of New York City**
No. of Rooms: **5**
Maximum No. of Guests Sharing Bath: **4**
Double/sb: **$35**
Single/sb: **$25**

Months of Operation: **All year**
Reduced Rates: **No**
Breakfast: **Full**
Air-Conditioning: **No**
Pets: **No**
Children: **No**
Smoking: **Permitted**
Social Drinking: **Permitted**
Foreign Languages: **French**

Over a dozen wineries are within minutes of this gracious home situated on 10 beautiful acres. There's a brook with a waterfall, plus paths and lanes to stroll; warm hospitality is a constant feature. Enjoy a hearty breakfast before touring West Point, Hyde Park, the 17th-century stone houses of New Paltz, and the charming shops and fine restaurants in the area.

Tibbitt's House Inn
100 COLUMBIA TURNPIKE, CLINTON HEIGHTS, RENSSELAER, NEW YORK 12144

Tel: **(518) 472-1348**
Host(s): **Claire and Herb Rufleth**
Location: **2 miles east of Albany**
No. of Rooms: **5**
Maximum No. of Guests Sharing
  Bath: **4**
Double/sb: **$22**
Single/sb: **$20**

Months of Operation: **All year**
Reduced Rates: **$35 less, weekly**
Breakfast: **$2–$4**
Air-Conditioning: **No**
Pets: **No**
Children: **No**
Smoking: **Permitted**
Social Drinking: **No**

This cozy, cheerful clapboard farmhouse is 127 years old and is surrounded by lovely trees and flowers. You will enjoy relaxing on the porch and breathing the fresh air. If you are more ambitious, you may enjoy the bike/hike path along the Hudson River. Claire and Herb look forward to your visit and will direct you to the area sights. It's just across the river from Albany, and it is near Fort Crailo, which was built by the Dutch in 1642 and is the oldest fort preserved in the country. (It is also where "Yankee Doodle" was composed.)

Corner House
110 EAST MARKET STREET, RHINEBECK, NEW YORK 12572

Tel: **(914) 876-4758**
Host(s): **Mary Decker**
Location: **90 miles north of New York City**
No. of Rooms: **2**
Maximum No. of Guests Sharing
  Bath: **4**
Double/sb: **$30–35**
Single/sb: **$20–25**

Months of Operation: **All year**
Reduced Rates: **No**
Breakfast: **Full**
Air-Conditioning: **No**
Pets: **No**
Children: **Welcome**
Smoking: **Permitted**
Social Drinking: **Permitted**
Foreign Languages: **Spanish**

Through all its 180 years, the Corner House has had just two owners. The furnishings range from country Chippendale to all vintages of Victorian. Each morning a hearty breakfast including homemade muffins is served. The sights of Hudson county, its wineries, universities, farms, and ski slopes are all within easy reach. The mansions of the Vanderbilts and Roosevelts are just two of the stops you might make on a historic tour of the area.

Spencertown Guests
BOX 122, SPENCERTOWN, NEW YORK 12165

Tel: **(518) 392-2358 or 392-3583**
Host(s): **Mary and Isabel Zander**
Location: **On Route 203 between Taconic Parkway and Route 22**
No. of Rooms: **4**
Maximum No. of Guests Sharing Bath: **4**
Double/sb: **$25**
Single/sb: **$18**
Months of Operation: **April to November**

Reduced Rates: **20% weekly; 20% off-season**
Breakfast: **Continental**
Air-Conditioning: **No**
Pets: **Sometimes**
Children: **Welcome, over 12**
Smoking: **Permitted**
Social Drinking: **Permitted**

This 18th-century saltbox is surrounded by a white picket fence. It is located in the center of Spencertown, said to be one of the 10 best small towns in America. The living room has a stone fireplace, and the bedrooms are low-ceilinged and have wide-plank floors. The rolling hills of Columbia county are a riot of color in autumn. You will enjoy the country fair, holiday parades, church or firehouse suppers, band concerts, and bazaars. Recreational activities are available in all seasons.

LAKE GEORGE AREA

Hayes's B&B Guest House
P.O. BOX 537, 7161 LAKESHORE DRIVE, BOLTON LANDING, NEW YORK 12814

Tel: **(518) 644-5941**
Host(s): **Dick Hayes, Mrs. Martha Hayes**
Location: **250 miles north of New York City**
No. of Rooms: **3**
No. of Private Baths: **3**
Double/pb: **$37–$42**
Single/pb: **$32**
Suites: **$45**

Months of Operation: **June 1 to March 1**
Reduced Rates: **No**
Breakfast: **Continental**
Air-Conditioning: **Unnecessary**
Pets: **No**
Children: **Welcome, over 12**
Smoking: **Permitted**
Social Drinking: **Permitted**

Close to the shores of Lake George, this elegantly appointed 1920s Cape Cod–style home is located across from the town beach, picnic area, and public docks. A five-minute walk to town brings you to tennis courts, shops, and fine restaurants. The Hayes family will arrange boat tours and a picnic lunch for a nominal fee in summer and fall. Cable TV and HBO are available. It's only 40 minutes to Saratoga and its famous racetrack.

Willow Glen Hill
RD 1, BOX 40, GRANVILLE, N.Y. 12832

Tel: **(518) 642-2079**
Host(s): **Jim and Jo Keats**
Location: **25 miles southwest of Rutland, Vermont**
No. of Rooms: **3**
Maximum No. of Guests Sharing Bath: **5**
Double/sb: **$20**
Single/sb: **$12**

Months of Operation: **All year**
Reduced Rates: **Available**
Breakfast: **Continental**
Air-Conditioning: **Unnecessary**
Pets: **Sometimes**
Children: **Welcome (crib)**
Smoking: **Permitted**
Social Drinking: **Permitted**

This lovely farmhouse is set on top of a hill with a magnificent view of the Green Mountains. It is just 1,500 feet from the Vermont border. In summer, enjoy Lake St. Catherine, Lake George, and Lake Champlain. Drive down Route 30 to the Dorset Playhouse and the Southern Vermont Art Center. Skiers may choose from Pico, Stratton, Killington, Bromley, and West Mountain, all within an hour's drive. Jim and Jo offer coffee, tea, and cold drinks as a pleasant extra.

Corner Birches Guest House
86 MONTCALM STREET, LAKE GEORGE, NEW YORK 12845

Tel: **(518) 668-2837**
Host(s): **Ray and Janice Dunklee**
Location: **Exit 21 on N.Y. Northway Route 87**
No. of Rooms: **4**
Maximum No. of Guests Sharing Bath: **8**
Double/sb: **$20–$24**
Single/sb: **$20**

Months of Operation: **All year**
Reduced Rates: **$2 less October 13 to June 30 (except holiday weekends)**
Breakfast: **Continental**
Air-Conditioning: **Unnecessary**
Pets: **Welcome**
Children: **Welcome**
Smoking: **Permitted**
Social Drinking: **Permitted**

This green-shuttered white house has a comfortable front porch for relaxed rocking. It is located a short stroll from the shores of Lake George. The attractively furnished bedrooms are all cross-ventilated to capture the fresh mountain air. Skiers will be pleased to know that Gore and West Mountain are close by. You are invited to visit in the living room with Ray and Janice, who welcome everyone from children to senior citizens.

East Lake George House

MAILING ADDRESS: 492 GLEN STREET, GLENS FALLS, NEW YORK 12801

Tel: **(518) 656-9452 (summer)**; **792-9296 (winter)**	Suites: **$85 (for 4)**
Host(s): **Joyce and Harold Kirkpatrick**	Months of Operation: **July and August**
Location: **10 miles north of Glens Falls, 8 miles from I-87**	Reduced Rates: **No**
No. of Rooms: **7**	Breakfast: **Full**
No. of Private Baths: **4**	Credit Cards: **MC, VISA**
Maximum No. of Guests Sharing Bath: **4**	Air-Conditioning: **Unnecessary**
Double/pb: **$50**	Pets: **No**
Single/pb: **$50**	Children: **Welcome (crib)**
Double/sb: **$50**	Smoking: **Permitted**
Single/sb: **$50**	Social Drinking: **Permitted**
	Foreign Languages: **French**

The view across the water to the mountains on the eastern shore is well worth the trip to this 19th-century country inn. Relax on the screened-in porch overlooking the lawn, and swim in the clear waters of Lake George. George and Harold invite you to use the sailboat and canoes. Lake George Village, the opera festival, Glens Falls, and the Saratoga Performing Arts Center are some of the nearby diversions.

LONG ISLAND

A Reasonable Alternative

117 SPRING STREET, PORT JEFFERSON, NEW YORK 11777

Tel: **(516) 928-4034**	Rates (Single/Double):	
Coordinator: **Kathleen B. Dexter**	Modest: **$20**	**$28**
States/Regions Covered: **Long Island**	Average: **$28**	**$32**
	Luxury: **$40**	**$48–$80**
	Credit Cards: **MC, VISA**	

Bounded by Long Island Sound and the Atlantic Ocean, from the New York City border to Montauk 100 miles to the east, the cream of host homes has been culled by Kathleen for you. There's much to see and do, including museums, historic homes, theater, horse racing, and the famous beaches, including Jones Beach, Fire Island, Shelter Island, and the exclusive Hamptons. (The Hamptons require a two-day minimum stay in July and August.)

Hampton on-the-Water
33 RAMPASTURE ROAD, HAMPTON BAYS, NEW YORK 11946

Tel: **(516) 728-3560**
Host(s): **Ute Lambur**
Location: **90 miles east of New York City**
No. of Rooms: **2**
No. of Private Baths: **2**
Double/pb: **$45–$65**
Single/pb: **$40–$60**
Months of Operation: **May 15 to January 3**
Reduced Rates: **40%, October to January 3; weekly; monthly**

Breakfast: **Full**
Other Meals: **Available**
Air-Conditioning: **Unnecessary**
Pets: **No**
Children: **No**
Smoking: **Permitted**
Social Drinking: **Permitted**
Foreign Languages: **French, German, Spanish**

A spanking white ranch-style home right on the water of Shinnecock Bay awaits your visit. There's a terrace and large garden for relaxing when you aren't busy clamming, fishing, or swimming. Ute will permit you to use her windsurfer, small motorboat, or bicycles when the mood strikes you. It's only seven miles from the exclusive shops of Southampton. Minimum stay is three days in July and August; two days the rest of the time. Ute also has a fabulous spot in Acapulco, Mexico, available from January 15 until April 15.

Duvall Bed and Breakfast
237 CATHEDRAL AVENUE, HEMPSTEAD, NEW YORK 11550

Tel: **(516) 292-9219**
Host(s): **Wendy and Richard Duvall**
Location: **20 miles east of New York City**
No. of Rooms: **2**
No. of Private Baths: **2**
Double/pb: **$45**
Single/pb: **$35**

Months of Operation: **All year**
Reduced Rates: **10%, weekly**
Breakfast: **Continental**
Other Meals: **Available**
Air-Conditioning: **Yes**
Pets: **Sometimes**
Children: **Welcome (crib)**
Smoking: **No**

Social Drinking: **Permitted**   Foreign Languages: **Spanish, German**
Airport Pickup: **Yes**

Guests feel right at home in this Dutch colonial with four-poster beds and antique reproductions. Coffee, soft drinks, or wine is served on arrival and breakfast ranges from pancakes to muffins and homemade breads. Jones Beach, Fire Island, Westbury Gardens, and Bethpage Village are nearby. Guests are welcome to use the patio, garden, barbecue, and bicycles.

NEW YORK CITY AREA

The B&B Group (New Yorkers at Home)
301 EAST 60TH STREET, NEW YORK, N.Y. 10022

Tel: **(212) 838-7015**
Coordinator: Farla Zammit
States/Regions Covered: **New York City, the Hampton Beaches**

Rates (Single/Double):
Modest: **$30**   **$45**
Average: **$35–$40**   **$50–$55**
Luxury: **$50**   **$65–$75**
Credit Cards: **No**
Minimum Stay: **2 days**

Accommodations appropriate to your purpose and purse are available, from the chic East Side to the arty West Side, to Greenwich Village, SoHo, Chelsea, and the Wall Street area. They range from luxury high-rise apartments to historic brownstone mansions, and are hosted by a variety of people, including artists, actors, doctors, engineers, and writers. All are enthusiastic about the Big Apple and eager to share it with you.

Bed & Breakfast in the Big Apple (Urban Ventures)
P.O. BOX 426, NEW YORK, NEW YORK 10024

Tel: **(212) 662-1234**
Coordinator: **Frances Dworan, Mary McAulay**
States/Regions Covered: **New York City**

Rates (Single/Double):
Modest: **$22–$32**   **$30–$40**
Average: **$38–$50**   **$44–$52**
Luxury: **$45 and up $60 and up**
Credit Cards: **MC, VISA**
Minimum Stay: **2 days**

The biggest bargains since the Indians sold Manhattan for $24 are offered by this registry. Mary and Fran have bedrooms and complete apartments located throughout the best areas of New

York City, including landmarked historic districts. They will be happy to help with theater tickets, restaurant information, current museum exhibits, as well as special tours.

The Tilted Barn
41 DEERFIELD AVENUE, EASTCHESTER, NEW YORK 10707

Tel: **(914) 779-5061**
Host(s): **Sud and Lydia Sudler**
Location: **20 miles north of New York City**
No. of Rooms: **3**
Maximum No. of Guests Sharing Bath: **6**
Double/sb: **$40**
Single/sb: **$40**
Months of Operation: **All year**

Reduced Rates: **No**
Breakfast: **Full**
Other Meals: **Available**
Air-Conditioning: **No**
Pets: **No**
Children: **Welcome, school-age**
Smoking: **Permitted**
Social Drinking: **Permitted**
Airport Pickup: **Yes**

Only two miles from the Hutchinson River Parkway, this updated Victorian house was originally built in 1895. It is attractively furnished with family heirlooms. Lydia is a wonderful hostess. Weather permitting, you can enjoy breakfast on the screened-in porch. She'll also share her kitchen for light snacks, and offer you use of the barbecue, washer, and dryer to help you cut down on expenses. Sud is an antique car buff. It's just minutes away from Sarah Lawrence College, horseback riding, and tennis, and you are welcome guests at the swim club.

A Bit o' the Apple—New York City
Contact: TRAILS END, RD 2 BOX 355A, GREENTOWN, PENNSYLVANIA 18426

Tel: **(717) 857-0856**
Host(s): **Nancy Kramer**
Location: **In Manhattan**
No. of Rooms: **1 Suite**
No. of Private Baths: **1**
Suites: **$50 for 2; $65 for 3**
Months of Operation: **All year**

Reduced Rates: **No**
Breakfast: **Continental**
Air-Conditioning: **Yes**
Pets: **No**
Children: **No**
Smoking: **Permitted**
Social Drinking: **Permitted**

This pied-à-terre in a luxury high-rise building on the Battery is within walking distance of the World Trade Center, the Wall Street Stock Exchanges, Trinity Church, the Statue of Liberty ferry, and the South Street Seaport. The accommodations consist of a one-bedroom, self-contained apartment with twin beds, a hide-a-bed sofa in the living room, fully-equipped kitchen, and commodious bath. It is tastefully furnished in a traditional style with fine furniture, antiques, and lots of plants. Your hosts, native New Yorkers, have the adjacent apartment and will happily suggest special restaurants and shops off the tourist trail that will make your visit affordable and memorable.

Sixteen Firs
352 ST. PAULS AVENUE, STATEN ISLAND, NEW YORK 10304

Tel: **(212) 727-9188**
Host(s): **Drs. Karl and Shirley Leone**
Location: **5 miles west of Manhattan**
No. of Rooms: **3**
Maximum No. of Guests Sharing
 Bath: **4**
Double/sb: **$30–$35**
Single/sb: **$30–$35**
Months of Operation: **All year**

Reduced Rates: **No**
Breakfast: **Continental**
Air-Conditioning: **Yes**
Pets: **No**
Children: **Welcome**
Smoking: **Permitted**
Social Drinking: **Permitted**
Airport Pickup: **Yes**

This gracious Victorian is located in a residential borough. It's a 25-minute ferry ride across fabulous New York Harbor to the Wall Street area of Manhattan. Karl and Shirley are native New Yorkers and will help you plan a low-cost visit to the Big Apple. There's a guest refrigerator and coffee is always available.

I-Love-New York Bed & Breakfast
190-11 HILLSIDE AVENUE, HOLLISWOOD, NEW YORK 11423

Tel: **(212) 776-6434**
Host(s): **Helena and Fred Sommer**
Location: **15 miles east of Manhattan
 on Route 25**
No. of Rooms: **2**
No. of Private Baths: **1**
Maximum No. of Guests Sharing
 Bath: **2**
Double/pb: **$30**
Single/pb: **$25**
Double/sb: **$25**

Months of Operation: **All year**
Reduced Rates: **No**
Breakfast: **Full**
Other Meals: **Available**
Air-Conditioning: **Yes**
Pets: **No**
Children: **Welcome**
Smoking: **Permitted**
Social Drinking: **Permitted**
Airport Pickup: **Yes**
Foreign Languages: **Lithuanian, Polish**

This gracious, white, center-hall colonial is located in Queens, a borough of New York City. This is a lovely residential section, convenient to excellent buses or subways to whisk you to the Big Apple in a half hour. LaGuardia and Kennedy airports are 10 minutes away. It's also close to Shea Stadium, famous racetracks, and several beaches. Helena and Fred have traveled widely and have many interesting collectibles accenting their comfortable furnishings. You will be made to feel very welcome.

Beehive Bed & Breakfast
82 VERMONT TERRACE, TUCKAHOE, NEW YORK 10707

Tel: **(914) 779-6411**	Months of Operation: **All year**
Host(s): **Gloria and Norman Bantz**	Reduced Rates: **15%, weekly; 10%, families**
Location: **10 miles north of New York City**	
	Breakfast: **Full**
No. of Rooms: **5**	Other Meals: **Available**
No. of Private Baths: **1**	Air-Conditioning: **Yes**
Maximum No. of Guests Sharing Bath: **6**	Pets: **No**
	Children: **Welcome (crib)**
Double/pb: **$44**	Smoking: **No**
Single/pb: **$40**	Social Drinking: **Permitted**
Double/sb: **$40**	Airport Pickup: **Yes**
Single/sb: **$32**	

This large brick federal-style home is located in a lovely residential section of Westchester County, yet it's less than 30 minutes away from Manhattan. The rooms are immaculate, and your hosts are quite hospitable. You may use the kitchen for light snacks and the laundry facilities; complimentary wine, cheese, and beverages are always offered. Gloria and Norman are hobby beekeepers so you know the homemade honey bread is the real thing. They'll lend you bikes so you can work off the effects of the hearty breakfast, by following the 25 miles of cycling and jogging paths along the Bronx River, which passes in front of the door.

UPSTATE NEW YORK

Bed & Breakfast of Central New York
1846 BELLEVUE AVENUE, SYRACUSE, NEW YORK 13204

Tel: **(315) 472-5050**	States/Regions Covered: **Camillus, Dewitt, Fayetteville, Ithaca, Marcellus, Oswego, Syracuse, Thousand Islands**
Coordinator: **Mary Lou Karrat, Linda Packard**	

Rates (Single/Double):
 Average: **$28**   **$36**
 Luxury: **$50**   **$70**

Credit Cards: **No**

Mary Lou and Linda have a network of host homes convenient to Syracuse University, Lemoyne College, and Cornell University, as well as the recreational area of the Finger Lakes. Beautiful country in all seasons, there are many historic sites to see and cultural activities to enjoy.

North Country B&B Reservation Service
THE BARN, BOX 286, LAKE PLACID, NEW YORK 12946

Tel: **(518) 523-3739**
Coordinator: **Lyn Witte**
States/Regions Covered:
 Chestertown, Cranberry Lake, Keene, Lake George, Lake Placid, Old Forge, Port Henry, Saranac Lake, Severance, Westport, Wilmington

Rates (Single/Double):
 Modest: **$10**   **$20**
 Average: **$20**   **$49**
 Luxury: **$30**   **$100**
Credit cards: **No**

Lyn has dozens of hosts waiting to show you Adirondack mountain hospitality. Your choice may be convenient to Champlain Valley, Revolutionary War forts, John Brown's farm, or Camp Sagamore. Fourty-three mountains are over 4,000 feet high, providing skiing and sports for all season.

Erie Bridge Inn
FLORENCE HILL ROAD, CAMDEN, NEW YORK 13316

Tel: **(315) 245-1555**
Host(s): **The Maleys**
Location: **20 miles west of Rome**
No. of Rooms: **7**
No. of Private Baths: **4**
Maximum No. of Guests Sharing
 Bath: **6**
Double/pb: **$39**
Single/pb: **$39**
Double/sb: **$39**
Single/sb: **$39**

Months of Operation: **May 1 to November 15**
Reduced Rates: **10%, seniors**
Breakfast: **Full**
Credit Cards: **MC, VISA**
Air-Conditioning: **No**
Pets: **No**
Children: **Welcome**
Smoking: **Permitted**
Social Drinking: **Permitted**
Airport Pickup: **Yes**

This is a casual, comfortable home that has a swimming pool and a hot tub for your seasonal enjoyment. It is close to Rome Canal Village, Fort Stanwich, and the Charles Town Outlet Mall. Homemade breads, jams, and omelets are breakfast specialties.

Bristol Bed & Breakfast
4861 ROUTE 64, BRISTOL VALLEY ROAD, CANANDAIGUA, NEW YORK 14424

Tel: **(716) 229-2003**
Host(s): **Patricia Merit-Rodger**
Location: **7 miles from routes 5 and 20**
No. of Rooms: **5**
No. of Private Baths: **2**
Maximum No. of Guests Sharing Bath: **4**
Double/pb: **$50**
Single/pb: **$48**
Double/sb: **$47**
Single/sb: **$38**

Months of Operation: **All year**
Reduced Rates: **15%, seniors; summer season**
Breakfast: **Full**
Other Meals: **Available**
Air-Conditioning: **Yes**
Pets: **Welcome**
Children: **Welcome**
Smoking: **Permitted**
Social Drinking: **Permitted**
Airport Pickup: **Yes**
Foreign Languages: **French, German**

This gracious Federal-style home was built in 1790. The rooms are decorated with paintings and crafts of local artists, and the bedrooms have the original fireplaces. In winter, Bristol Valley is a skiers' wonderland. In other seasons, you can use the lighted tennis court, the hot tub, skate, or borrow Pat's bikes for a tour of the beautiful surroundings. Charming shops, restaurants, and cultural activities are nearby.

The Eastwood House
45 SOUTH MAIN STREET, CASTILE, NEW YORK 14427

Tel: **(716) 493-2335**
Host(s): **Joan Ballinger**
Location: **63 miles southeast of Buffalo on Route 34**
No. of Rooms: **2**
Maximum No. of Guests Sharing Bath: **4**
Double/sb: **$21**
Single/sb: **$18**

Months of Operation: **All year**
Reduced Rates: **No**
Breakfast: **Continental**
Air-Conditioning: **No**
Pets: **Sometimes**
Children: **Welcome, over 5**
Smoking: **No**
Social Drinking: **Permitted**
Airport Pickup: **Yes**

This comfortable house is a few minutes' drive from Letchworth State Park. Your hostess offers coffee, fresh fruit, and juice on arrival. Hot biscuits, freshly whipped cream, and jam are featured at breakfast each morning. Local sights include the Historical Society and the Indian Museum.

Back of the Beyond
7233 LOWER EAST HILL ROAD, COLDEN, NEW YORK 14033

Tel: **(716) 652-0427**
Host(s): **Bill and Shash Georgi**
Location: **30 miles south of Buffalo**
No. of Rooms: **3**
Maximum No. of Guests Sharing
Bath: **6**
Double/sb: **$40**
Single/sb: **$35**
Guest Cottage: **$80 sleeps 6**

Months of Operation: **All year**
Reduced Rates: **No**
Breakfast: **Full**
Air-Conditioning: **No**
Pets: **Sometimes**
Children: **Welcome**
Smoking: **No**
Social Drinking: **Permitted**

Bill and Shash have a small country estate near a ski area and an hour from Niagara Falls. They maintain an herbtique greenhouse, and grow their vegetables organically. Breakfast reflects all this "healthiness" with delicious herbal omelets, organic juice, plus lots of other surprise goodies. The guest quarters are in a separate three-bedroom chalet, fully equipped down to the fireplace.

The Inn at Brook Willow Farm
R.D. 2, BOX 514, MIDDLEFIELD CENTER ROAD, COOPERSTOWN, NEW YORK 13326

Tel: **(607) 547-9700**
Host(s): **Joan and Jack Grimes**
Location: **65 miles west of Albany**
No. of Rooms: **5**
No. of Private Baths: **3**
Maximum No. of Guests Sharing
Bath: **4**
Double/pb: **$30–$34**
Single/pb: **$30–$34**
Double/sb: **$30–$34**

Single/sb: **$30–$34**
Months of Operation: **All year**
Reduced Rates: **No**
Breakfast: **Full**
Air-Conditioning: **Unnecessary**
Pets: **No**
Children: **Welcome (crib)**
Smoking: **Permitted**
Social Drinking: **Permitted**

Located on 14 acres of meadow and woods, nestled among the pines and willows, this charming Victorian cottage house and restored barn is much as it was at the turn of the century.

Brook Willow

Antiques and collectibles are the decor, and hospitality is the motto. You are welcome to enjoy the pool, play badminton, and use the kitchen for snacks. You may also use the laundry facilities. The world famous Baseball Hall of Fame is here as well as countless historic, cultural, and recreational activities. Please note that Hall of Fame Weekend requires a two-day minimum stay and the rate is $44 per day.

Highland Springs
ALLEN ROAD, EAST CONCORD, NEW YORK 14055

Tel: **(716) 592-4323**
Host(s): **Lew and Judy Markle**
Location: **40 miles south of Buffalo**
No. of Rooms: **3**
No. of Private Baths: **2**
Maximum No. of Guests Sharing
  Bath: **4**
Double/pb: **$40**
Single/pb: **$30**
Double/sb: **$40**

Single/sb: **$30**
Months of Operation: **All year**
Reduced Rates: **No**
Breakfast: **Continental**
Air-Conditioning: **No**
Pets: **No**
Children: **Welcome (crib)**
Smoking: **No**
Social Drinking: **Permitted**

This 70-acre country estate offers a comfortable homey ambience. Alpine and Nordic skiing are close by, and summer pleasures may be enjoyed in the on-premises pond where you can swim and fish. Judy loves to bake with natural ingredients; her vegetarian breakfast is delicious and bountiful. The University of Buffalo is 40 miles away.

The Cobblestones
RD 2, GENEVA, NEW YORK 14456

Tel: **(315) 789-1896**
Host(s): **The Lawrence Graceys**
Location: **On routes 5 and 20**
No. of Rooms: **3**
Maximum No. of Guests Sharing
  Bath: **6**
Double/sb: **$10**
Single/sb: **$5**

Months of Operation: **All year**
Reduced Rates: **No**
Breakfast: **No**
Air-Conditioning: **Unnecessary**
Pets: **Welcome**
Children: **Welcome**
Smoking: **Yes**
Social Drinking: **Permitted**

This exquisite example of Greek Revival cobblestone architecture was built in 1848. The handsome fluted columns crowned by Ionic capitals at the entrance add to its beauty. There are precious antiques and Oriental rugs, which reflect the fine taste of your gracious hosts. Located in the heart of the Finger Lakes area, tours are available at nearby wineries. Hobart and William Smith Colleges are right in town.

Laurel Hill Guest House
2670 POWDERHOUSE ROAD, CORNING, NEW YORK 14830

Tel: **(607) 936-3215**
Host(s): **Dick and Marge Woodbury**
Location: **1.7 miles from Route 17**
No. of Rooms: **2**
Maximum No. of Guests Sharing
  Bath: **4**
Double/sb: **$33**
Single/sb: **$28**
Months of Operation: **All year**

Reduced Rates: **Family rates; 2-day
  stays**
Breakfast: **Continental**
Air-Conditioning: **No**
Pets: **Sometimes**
Children: **Welcome**
Smoking: **Permitted**
Social Drinking: **Permitted**
Airport Pickup: **Yes**

This traditional Cape Cod house is nestled on a wooded hillside. Inside, paneled doors, period moldings, and wooden eaves add to its authenticity. A breakfast of homemade breads and muffins is served beside the kitchen fireplace. Nearby attractions include the Finger Lakes wineries, Corning Glass Center, historic Market Street, and Watkins Glen.

Rosewood Inn
134 EAST FIRST STREET, CORNING, NEW YORK 14830

Tel: **(607) 962-3253**
Host(s): **Winnie and Dick Peer**
Location: **1 block off Route 17**
No. of Rooms: **5**
No. of Private Baths: **3**
Maximum No. of Guests Sharing
  Bath: **4**
Double/pb: **$39**
Single/pb: **$34**
Double/sb: **$34**

Single/sb: **$29**
Months of Operation: **All year**
Reduced Rates: **No**
Breakfast: **Continental**
Air-Conditioning: **No**
Pets: **No**
Children: **Welcome (crib)**
Smoking: **Permitted**
Social Drinking: **Permitted**
Airport Pickup: **Yes**

This two-story stucco English Tudor is decorated with both antiques and originality. Each guest room is named for a famous person and the accessories echo the personality of that individual's era. It's within walking distance of the Corning Glass Museum and the Rockwell Museum of Western Art. Winnie teaches first grade, and Dick is the editor of the daily newspaper. They look forward to your arrival and will greet you with refreshments to make you feel right at home.

Victoria House
222 PINE STREET, CORNING, NEW YORK 14830

Tel: **(607) 962-3413**
Host(s): **Tom and Janet Madigan**
Location: **4 blocks south of Route 17**
No. of Rooms: **4**
Maximum No. of Guests Sharing
  Bath: **4**
Double/sb: **$35**
Single/sb: **$25**

Months of Operation: **All year**
Reduced Rates: **Families**
Breakfast: **Continental**
Air-Conditioning: **No**
Pets: **No**
Children: **Welcome**
Smoking: **Permitted**
Social Drinking: **No**

This turn-of-the-century home has been restored to its former elegance, and is located in a quiet residential area within walking distance of the Corning Glass Center, Rockwell Museum, and the unique shops and restaurants of Market Street. The rooms are furnished with cherished antiques. You are invited to relax in the spacious reception rooms and on the veranda in summer.

Elmshade Guest House
402 SOUTH ALBANY STREET, ITHACA, NEW YORK 14850

Tel: **(607) 273-1707**
Host(s): **Ethel D. Pierce**
Location: **3 blocks from Route 13**
No. of Rooms: **9**
Maximum No. of Guests Sharing
  Bath: **5**
Double/sb: **$36–$40**
Single/sb: **$18–$20**

Months of Operation: **All year**
Reduced Rates: **No**
Breakfast: **No**
Air-Conditioning: **Unnecessary**
Pets: **No**
Children: **Welcome, over 6**
Smoking: **Permitted**
Social Drinking: **Permitted**

Located in a lovely residential area, the house is convenient to shopping and excellent, inexpensive restaurants. The guest rooms are large, bright, comfortable, and immaculate. Ethel delights in having visitors and limits the occupancy to nine at a time so that she can give personal attention to everyone.

Iris Hill Bed and Breakfast
1660 MECKLENBURG ROAD, ITHACA, NEW YORK 14850

Tel: **(607) 273-2157**
Host(s): **Cindy and Tom Roy**
Location: **On Route 79**
No. of Rooms: **5**
No. of Private Baths: **1**
Maximum No. of Guests Sharing
  Bath: **3**
Double/pb: **$35**
Single/pb: **$25**
Double/sb: **$35**
Single/sb: **$25**

Months of Operation: **All year**
Reduced Rates: **10%, seniors**
Breakfast: **Full**
Other Meals: **Box lunch, $2.50**
Air-Conditioning: **No**
Pets: **Yes**
Children: **Welcome (crib)**
Smoking: **No**
Social Drinking: **Permitted**
Airport Pickup: **Yes**

Located on five acres high above Cayuga's waters, this 1840 Greek Revival country house has wide pine floors, stenciled walls, and period antiques. You can watch the deer, rabbits, and birds in the yard, or try your hand at the piano in the parlor. Tom is an educator and competitive biker; Cindy's an investment broker; daughter Kristin will baby-sit while you take in the Finger Lake wineries, races at Watkins Glen, or the cultural activities at Cornell University. The coffee pot is always on and wine is provided in your room.

Libby's Lodgings
32 EVELYN STREET, JOHNSON CITY, NEW YORK 13790

Tel: (607) 729-6839
Host(s): Elizabeth Ashcraft
Location: 1 mile from Binghamton
No. of Rooms: 2
Maximum No. of Guests Sharing
    Bath: 4
Double/sb: $30
Single/sb: $20
Months of Operation: All year

Reduced Rates: No
Breakfast: Continental
Air-Conditioning: Yes
Pets: Sometimes
Children: No
Smoking: Permitted
Social Drinking: Permitted
Airport Pickup: Yes

This comfortable house is located in a quiet neighborhood, with a shaded back porch for relaxing. In the scenic southern tier of the state, it is convenient to malls, restaurants, state parks, historical sites, and Harper College. Libby has decorated with Junktique (little inexpensive treasures) and expects to open a consignment shop soon. Her hand-hooked rugs and carpentry add a special touch. She is ever ready with conversation and a bottomless coffee pot.

Bark Eater Inn
ALSTEAD MILL ROAD, KEENE, NEW YORK 12942

Tel: (518) 576-2221
Host(s): Joe and Pete Wilson, Harley
    McDevitt
Location: 135 miles north of Albany
No. of Rooms: 7
Maximum No. of Guests Sharing
    Bath: 6
Double/sb: $60
Single/sb: $30
Guest Cottage: $394 (day) sleeps 15

Months of Operation: All year
Reduced Rates: 10%, for 5 days;
    $30–$42, April 1 to October 31
Breakfast: Full
Other Meals: Available
Pets: Sometimes
Children: Welcome
Smoking: Permitted
Social Drinking: Permitted
Airport Pickup: Yes

This 150-year-old farmhouse has two fireplaces, a beautiful view of the Adirondack Mountains, and is furnished with antiques. It is close to Whiteface Mountain, Ausable Chasm, and seasonal recreational sports. The cottage has two baths, a kitchen, and is perfect for a group of friends vacationing together.

Stagecoach Inn
OLD MILITARY ROAD, LAKE PLACID, NEW YORK 12946

Tel: (518) 523-9474
Host(s): **Peter and Sherry Moreau**
Location: **235 miles north of New York City**
No. of Rooms: **6**
No. of Private Baths: **2**
Maximum No. of Guests Sharing Bath: **4**
Double/pb: **$35**
Single/pb: **$30**
Double/sb: **$30**

Single/sb: **$25**
Suites: **$50**
Months of Operation: **All year**
Reduced Rates: **No**
Breakfast: **Continental**
Air-Conditioning: **No**
Pets: **Sometimes**
Children: **Welcome**
Smoking: **Permitted**
Social Drinking: **Permitted**

The original wainscoting, high-ceilinged common room, and five fireplaces will make you feel like you've arrived as the inn's original guests did—by stagecoach. Several thousand lakes and ponds for fishing and canoeing are in nearby Adirondack State Park. Other local possibilities include golf, tennis, and the village of Lake Placid.

"Adirondack Hotel" on-the-Lake
ONE LAKE STREET, LONG LAKE, NEW YORK 12847

Tel: (518) 624-4700
Host(s): **Robert and Marijane Lucci**
Location: **55 miles south of Lake Placid**
No. of Rooms: **30**
No. of Private Baths: **12**
Maximum No. of Guests Sharing Bath: **6**
Double/pb: **$30**
Single/pb: **$20**
Double/sb: **$25**

Single/sb: **$20**
Months of Operation: **Memorial Day weekend to December 1**
Reduced Rates: **Families**
Breakfast: **Continental**
Other Meals: **Available**
Air-Conditioning: **No**
Pets: **No**
Children: **Welcome, over 3**
Smoking: **Permitted**
Social Drinking: **Permitted**

It's called a hotel, but to Marijane and Robert, it's home; making you feel at home is their prime ambition. The atmosphere is back-to-basics involvement with their guests, and they do a fine job. There's lots to do, including free tennis, swimming at the protected beach across the way, hiking, and trout fishing in the pond. If you're ambitious, you can canoe all the way to Saranac Lake or the Hudson River, or just relax and enjoy the scenery framed by the high peaks of the Adirondacks.

Crafts' Place
10283 RIDGE ROAD AT GEDDA, MEDINA, NEW YORK 14103

Tel: (716) 735-7243
Host(s): **Peg and Bob Crafts**
Location: **On Route 104**
No. of Rooms: **4**
Maximum No. of Guests Sharing
Bath: **4**
Double/sb: **$25**
Single/sb: **$20**
Suites: **n/a**
Months of Operation: **April 15 to November 15**

Reduced Rates: **Available to seniors and families**
Breakfast: **Full**
Other Meals: **No**
Air-Conditioning: **No**
Pets: **Sometimes**
Children: **Welcome**
Smoking: **Permitted**
Social Drinking: **Permitted**
Foreign Languages: **Spanish**

Located in the historic Lake Ontario–Lake Erie area, this comfortable century-old home with its handsome stone porch is convenient to everything. Local museums, wineries, arts and crafts shows, boating, swimming, and fishing will keep you busy. Buffalo, Rochester, and Niagara Falls are nearby. Bob and Peg, longtime residents of the area, will be happy to help with your plans.

Anne Pauly's Home
BOX 105, DEPOT STREET, MOIRA, NEW YORK 12957

Tel: (518) 529-6278
Host(s): **Anne Pauly**
Location: **Intersection of routes 11 and 95**
No. of Rooms: **5**
Maximum No. of Guests Sharing
Bath: **4**
Double/sb: **$30**
Single/sb: **$25**
Months of Operation: **May to December**

Reduced Rates: **10%, seniors; 10%, families**
Breakfast: **Full**
Other Meals: **Available**
Air-Conditioning: **No**
Pets: **Welcome**
Children: **Welcome (crib)**
Smoking: **Permitted**
Social Drinking: **Permitted**

Anne is a retired math teacher, currently devoted to making her Victorian mansion a haven for guests. Her lovely needlepoint and handmade quilts accent the antique furnishings. The beautiful old woodwork, stonework, and gorgeous veranda of her home are evidence of a quality of workmanship seldom seen today. You are welcome to use her kitchen for light snacks, watch TV, or play the piano. All the attractions of the Adirondack Mountains are 20 minutes away.

Pink House Inn

9125 SOUTH MAIN STREET, P.O. BOX 85, SANDY CREEK, NEW YORK 13145

Tel: **(315) 387-3276**
Host(s): **Evelyn Sadowski**
Location: **46 miles north of Syracuse**
No. of Rooms: **2**
Maximum No. of Guests Sharing
Bath: **3**
Double/sb: **$35**
Single/sb: **$25**
Months of Operation: **All year**

Reduced Rates: **No**
Breakfast: **Continental**
Air-Conditioning: **No**
Pets: **Sometimes**
Children: **Welcome (crib)**
Smoking: **Permitted**
Social Drinking: **Permitted**
Airport Pickup: **Yes**

Evelyn owns an antique shop, and many fine pieces accent her comfortable home. This clapboard house, built in 1872, has an inviting screened-in porch. If you are heading for Canada, this is a fine place to rest up, since the house is located on Route 11. It is only five miles to Lake Ontario. Your hostess truly enjoys people and will do all she can to make your stay pleasant.

Walnut Lawn

3379 BROCKPORT SPENCERPORT ROAD, SPENCERPORT, NEW YORK 14620

Tel: **(716) 352-6053**
Host(s): **Sandy Worbois**
Location: **10 miles west of Rochester**
No. of Rooms: **2**
Maximum No. of Guests Sharing
Bath: **3**
Double/sb: **$30**
Single/sb: **$25**
Months of Operation: **All year**

Reduced Rates: **$125, weekly**
Breakfast: **Continental**
Air-Conditioning: **No**
Pets: **Sometimes**
Children: **Welcome (crib)**
Smoking: **Permitted**
Social Drinking: **Permitted**
Airport Pickup: **Yes**

Located in the lovely Lake Ontario fruit belt, this 1860 farmhouse offers you the beauty of blossoms in the spring and luscious fruit in summer. You're invited to join occasional campfires with sing-alongs and games, and use the barbecue, picnic table, and swimming pool. There are fishing derbies, festivals, golf courses, and Niagara Falls is only 50 miles away.

The Lanigan Farmhouse
BOX 399, RD1, STAMFORD, NEW YORK 12167

Tel: **(607) 652-7455/6263**
Host(s): **June and Richard Lanigan**
Location: **23 miles east of Oneonta**
No. of Rooms: **4**
Maximum No. of Guests Sharing
  Bath: **9**
Double/sb: **$35**
Single/sb: **$30**

Months of Operation: **All year**
Reduced Rates: **No**
Breakfast: **Full**
Air-Conditioning: **No**
Pets: **Yes**
Children: **Welcome**
Smoking: **Permitted**
Social Drinking: **Permitted**

The Lanigan Farmhouse offers the charm of country rural life, and is convenient to cultural activities. Guests are welcome to wine and cheese, and are served a breakfast of homemade breads and jams, ham, and omelets. The well-stocked library is a good place for relaxing. Deer Run ski area, golf courses, hiking, tennis, swimming, and antique shops are all nearby.

Ivy Chimney
143 DIDAMA STREET, SYRACUSE, NEW YORK 13224

Tel: **(315) 446-4199**
Host(s): **Elaine Samuels**
Location: **3 miles from U.S. 90**
No. of Rooms: **2**
Maximum No. of Guests Sharing
  Bath: **2**
Double/sb: **$40**
Single/sb: **$25–$30**
Months of Operation: **All year**

Reduced Rates: **No**
Breakfast: **Continental**
Air-Conditioning: **No**
Pets: **Sometimes**
Children: **No**
Smoking: **No**
Social Drinking: **Permitted**
Airport Pickup: **Yes**

This cozy white colonial (circa 1920) with its wide porch is located on a quiet residential street. The bedrooms are cheerful and furnished with some antiques and collectibles. It is close to the Civic Center, Syracuse University, and recreational sports facilities. Elaine's interests are fine art, theater, and music.

Le Muguet
2553 CHURCH STREET, THREE MILE BAY, NEW YORK 13693

Tel: **(315) 649-5896**
Host(s): **Elisabeth Dibrell**

Location: **18 miles west of Watertown,**
  18 miles from Route 81

No. of Rooms: **3**
No. of Private Baths: **2**
Maximum No. of Guests Sharing
  Bath: **3**
Double/pb: **$20**
Single/pb: **$10**
Double/sb: **$20**
Single/sb: **$10**
Months of Operation: **June 1 to
  September 30**

Reduced Rates: **Weekly, $60 per
  person**
Breakfast: **Continental—$1.75**
Air-Conditioning: **No**
Pets: **Welcome**
Children: **Welcome, over 6**
Smoking: **No**
Social Drinking: **Permitted**
Airport Pickup: **Yes**
Foreign Languages: **French**

This 100-year-old farmhouse is cozily furnished with antiques, plants, and lots of decorator touches. Elisabeth specialized in fine arts and has a good eye for innovative decor. There are many things to do in this lovely area of the scenic Thousand Islands.

Simpsons
16 BIRD STREET, WESTFIELD, NEW YORK 14787

Tel: **(716) 326-2523**
Host(s): **Mrs. James Simpson**
Location: **1 mile from I-90**
No. of Rooms: **1**
Maximum No. of Guests Sharing
  Bath: **2**
Double/sb: **$20**
Single/sb: **$15**
Months of Operation: **All year**

Reduced Rates: **No**
Breakfast: **Full**
Other Meals: **Available**
Air-Conditioning: **No**
Pets: **No**
Children: **Welcome**
Smoking: **Permitted**
Social Drinking: **Permitted**

Westfield is a small, rural village located at the hub of I-90 and routes 17, 20, and 5. Primarily an agricultural community specializing in Concord grapes, there are six wineries nearby that you may tour. The famous Chautauqua Institute is 10 miles away, and Westfield is a mecca for antique collectors. There are 14 antique shops right in town. Mrs. Simpson is most cordial and will allow you to use her kitchen for light snacks.

NORTH CAROLINA

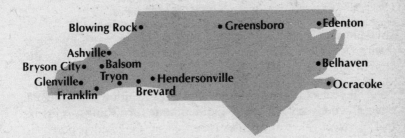

Blowing Rock•
•Greensboro
•Edenton
Ashville•
Bryson City• •Balsom
Glenville• Tryon •Hendersonville
Franklin Brevard
•Belhaven
•Ocracoke

Flint Street Inn
116 FLINT STREET, ASHEVILLE, NORTH CAROLINA 28801

Tel: **(704) 253-6723**
Host(s): **Rick and Lynne Vogel**
Location: **¼ mile from Route 240**
No. of Rooms: **4**
Maximum No. of Guests Sharing
  Bath: **4**
Double/sb: **$40**
Single/sb: **$35**
Months of Operation: **All year**

Reduced Rates: **Weekly**
Breakfast: **Full**
Air-Conditioning: **No**
Pets: **No**
Children: **Welcome, over 12**
Smoking: **Permitted**
Social Drinking: **Permitted**
Airport Pickup: **Yes**

This turn-of-the-century home is listed on the National Register
of Historic Places. Stained glass, pine floors, and a claw-footed
bathtub are part of the Victorian decor. Guests are served wine,
coffee, and soft drinks; at breakfast, homemade biscuits with
honey and jam are featured. The art deco buildings and craft
shops of downtown Asheville are minutes away. The mountains
and Blue Ridge Parkway are nearby.

The Ray House
83 HILLSIDE STREET, ASHEVILLE, NORTH CAROLINA 28801

Tel: **(704) 252-0106**	Months of Operation: **All year**
Host(s): **Will and Alice Curtis**	Reduced Rates: **No**
Location: **5 miles from I-40**	Breakfast: **Continental**
No. of Rooms: **3**	Air-Conditioning: **No**
No. of Private Baths: **1**	Pets: **Sometimes**
Maximum No. of Guests Sharing	Children: **Welcome**
Bath: **5**	Smoking: **Permitted**
Double/pb: **$35**	Social Drinking: **Permitted**
Single/pb: **$35**	Airport Pickup: **Yes**
Double/sb: **$30**	Foreign Languages: **French**
Single/sb: **$25**	

This 80-year-old colonial house features windows of unusual design, woodwork, fireplaces, and antique furnishings. A breakfast of sweet cakes and jellies is served on the shaded porch, in the formal dining room, or in the garden. Guests are invited to browse through the books in the beamed living room. The Blue Ridge Parkway, Great Smoky Mountains, and many craft exhibits and concerts can be enjoyed locally.

Balsam Lodge
BOX 279, RIVER ROAD, BALSAM, NORTH CAROLINA 28707

Tel: **(704) 456-6528**	Single/sb: **$20**
Host(s): **Marie and Gordon Pike**	Months of Operation: **June 1 to**
Location: **35 miles east of Asheville**	**October 31**
No. of Rooms: **8**	Reduced Rates: **10%, weekly**
No. of Private Baths: **4**	Breakfast: **Continental**
Maximum No. of Guests Sharing	Air-Conditioning: **No**
Bath: **7**	Pets: **Sometimes**
Double/pb: **$35**	Children: **Welcome**
Single/pb: **$30**	Smoking: **Permitted**
Double/sb: **$25**	Social Drinking: **Permitted**

Local crafts, fresh flowers, and period pieces fill the rooms of this turn-of-the-century home. The depot, which once served the town of Balsam, is now divided into private accommodations for guests. At the main house, enjoy an evening on a porch rocker; in the morning, your hosts offer homemade muffins and cakes. They are glad to advise on trips to nearby Great Smoky National Park, Blue Ridge Parkway, and the Cherokee Indian Reservation.

River Forest Manor
600 EAST MAIN STREET, BELHAVEN, NORTH CAROLINA 27810

Tel: **(919) 943-2151**
Host(s): **Axson and Melba Smith**
Location: **50 miles east of Greenville**
No. of Rooms: **8**
No. of Private Baths: **7**
Maximum No. of Guests Sharing
  Bath: **2**
Double/pb: **$40–$48**
Single/pb: **$40–$48**
Double/sb: **$36**

Months of Operation: **All year**
Reduced Rates: **No**
Breakfast: **Full**
Other Meals: **Available**
Air-Conditioning: **Yes**
Pets: **No**
Children: **Welcome**
Smoking: **Permitted**
Social Drinking: **Permitted**
Airport Pickup: **Yes**

The decor of this turn-of-the-century mansion features oak mantels, crystal chandeliers, leaded glass, and an old player piano. Guests are welcome to use the tennis courts and hot tub. A reasonably priced smorgasbord of 75 dishes is spread out nightly in the dining room. Fine wines, fireplaces, and elegant guest rooms are sure to relax the traveler. A marina, shops, and museum are steps away.

Gideon Ridge
P.O. BOX 1929, BLOWING ROCK, NORTH CAROLINA 28605

Tel: **(704) 295-3644**
Host(s): **Phil Hall, Nick Lollo, John
  Weisner**
Location: **36 miles north of Hickory**
No. of Rooms: **7**
No. of Private Baths: **5**
Maximum No. of Guests Sharing
  Bath: **4**
Double/pb: **$85–$95**
Single/pb: **$85–$95**
Double/sb: **$75**
Single/sb: **$75**

Months of Operation: **All year**
Reduced Rates: **No**
Breakfast: **Full**
Other Meals: **Dinner included**
Credit Cards: **MC, VISA**
Air-Conditioning: **Unnecessary**
Pets: **No**
Children: **No**
Smoking: **Permitted**
Social Drinking: **Permitted**
Airport Pickup: **Yes**

This European-style country stone house is situated 4,000 feet high in the mountains. Stand near the pinnacle of Blowing Rock and toss an object out into space. The mysterious winds will blow it back to you! Phil, Nick, and John will direct you to horseback riding, hiking and jogging trails, fine shops, and skiing. Don't miss the outdoor drama in Boone during the summer.

Ragged Garden Inn
BOX 1927 SUNSET DRIVE, BLOWING ROCK, NORTH CAROLINA 28605

Tel: **(704) 295-9703**
Host(s): **Joe and Joyce Villani**
Location: **35 miles north of Hickory**
No. of Rooms: **4**
No. of Private Baths: **4**
Double/pb: **$55**
Single/pb: **$55**
Suites: **$75**
Months of Operation: **January to February; April to October; December**

Reduced Rates: **No**
Breakfast: **Continental**
Credit Cards: **AMEX, MC, VISA**
Air-Conditioning: **Unnecessary**
Pets: **No**
Children: **Welcome, over 12**
Smoking: **Permitted**
Social Drinking: **Permitted**
Foreign Languages: **Italian**

You will discover a touch of the past in this grand turn-of-the-century chestnut-bark home set on an acre surrounded by majestic trees and lovely flower gardens. Joe and Joyce have restored and refurbished it with taste and comfort in mind. In addition to the guest rooms, they have an on-premises gourmet dining room, featuring continental cuisine. It's close to interesting sightseeing as well as fine seasonal recreational activities.

Colonial Inn
410 EAST MAIN STREET, BREVARD, NORTH CAROLINA 28712

Tel: **(704) 884-2105**
Host(s): **David Chotiner**
Location: **25 miles west of Hendersonville**
No. of Rooms: **12**
No. of Private Baths: **10**
Maximum No. of Guests Sharing Bath: **4**
Double/pb: **$38**
Single/pb: **$34**
Double/sb: **$38**

Single/sb: **$34**
Months of Operation: **All year**
Reduced Rates: **$10 less, November 16 to April 15**
Breakfast: **Full**
Air-Conditioning: **Yes**
Pets: **No**
Children: **Welcome**
Smoking: **Permitted**
Social Drinking: **No**

This white-columned inn is listed on the National Register of Historic Places and has retained such touches as the original brass hardware, carved fireplace mantels, and antique furnishings to recall old-time southern charm. The bedrooms are comfortable and the setting is serene; clear air and mountain breezes refresh you. Explore the many splendors of this Land of Waterfalls, and return to spend a peaceful evening relaxing with the other guests on the porch or in the sitting room.

Folkestone Lodge
ROUTE 1, BOX 310, BRYSON CITY, NORTH CAROLINA 28713

Tel: **(704) 488-2730**
Host(s): **Irene and Bob Kranich**
Location: **60 miles west of Asheville, 2 miles from Route 19A**
No. of Rooms: **5**
No. of Private Baths: **5**
Double/pb: **$45**
Single/pb: **$32**
Months of Operation: **All year**

Reduced Rates: **No**
Breakfast: **Full**
Credit Cards: **MC, VISA**
Air-Conditioning: **Unnecessary**
Pets: **No**
Children: **Welcome**
Smoking: **Permitted**
Social Drinking: **Permitted**
Foreign Languages: **Spanish**

The lodge is a quaint mountain retreat; small, secluded, and old-fashioned, it is located 10 minutes from Great Smoky Mountain National Park. The park offers hiking, trout fishing, camping, and tubing. The Cherokee Indian Reservation is also close by. Bob and Irene have tastefully furnished the guest rooms; antiques, fresh flowers, high headboards, hand-crocheted bedspreads, and Oriental rugs add to the charm. An unforgettable country breakfast awaits you each morning.

The Lords Proprietors' Inn
300 NORTH BROAD STREET, EDENTON, NORTH CAROLINA 27932

Tel: **(919) 482-3641**
Host(s): **Arch and Jane Edwards**
Location: **75 miles southwest of Norfolk, Virginia on Route 17**
No. of Rooms: **12**
No. of Private Baths: **12**
Double/pb: **$50**
Single/pb: **$41**
Months of Operation: **All year**

Reduced Rates: **No**
Breakfast: **Continental**
Air-Conditioning: **Yes**
Pets: **No**
Children: **Welcome**
Smoking: **Permitted**
Social Drinking: **Permitted**
Airport Pickup: **Yes**

The inn consists of two adjacent Victorian houses, one a large brick dwelling and the other a smaller frame house. Both have stained glass windows and comfortable porches. The elegant bedrooms are furnished by local antique dealers and craftsmen. You can enjoy the decor and perhaps buy what you like! Located on Albemarle Sound, it is near Nags Head, Hope Plantation, and Somerset House.

The Franklin Terrace
67 HARRISON AVENUE, FRANKLIN, NORTH CAROLINA 28734

Tel: **(704) 524-7907**
Host(s): **Mike and Pat Giampola**
Location: **65 miles north of Atlanta, 2 blocks from 441**
No. of Rooms: **7**
No. of Private Baths: **7**
Double/pb: **$38–$42**
Single/pb: **$34–$38**
Guest Cottage: **Available**
Months of Operation: **May to October**

Reduced Rates: **No**
Breakfast: **Continental**
Credit Cards: **MC, VISA**
Air-Conditioning: **Unnecessary**
Pets: **No**
Children: **Welcome**
Smoking: **Permitted**
Social Drinking: **Permitted**

Located close to the Cowee Valley ruby mines and the Standing Indian campground, this 95-year-old home, wrapped on three sides by comfortable porches, is listed on the National Register of Historic Places. Pat and Mike are in the antique business so you can imagine the special furnishings with which they have decorated their home. On the premises is an elegant old-fashioned ice cream parlor that will more than satisfy your sweet tooth.

Mountain High
BIG RIDGE ROAD, GLENVILLE, NORTH CAROLINA 28736

Tel: **(704) 743-3094**
Host(s): **Margaret and George Carter**
Location: **2 miles from Route 107**
No. of Rooms: **3**
No. of Private Baths: **1**
Maximum No. of Guests Sharing Bath: **4**
Single/pb: **$15**
Double/sb: **$15**

Months of Operation: **June to November**
Reduced Rates: **Weekly**
Breakfast: **Full**
Air-Conditioning: **Unnecessary**
Pets: **No**
Children: **No**
Smoking: **No**
Social Drinking: **Permitted**

It is located 4,200 feet high in the Smoky Mountains, only a short distance from the Carolina Highlands. Margaret and George offer warm hospitality to their guests. You are invited to take a horseback ride on the premises or join your hosts in a fox hunt (the hounds are trained not to kill the fox—just to chase him). You are welcome to use the kitchen for light snacks, and you may freshen your wardrobe in the washer and dryer.

Greenwood
P.O. BOX 6948, GREENSBORO, NORTH CAROLINA 27405

Tel: **(919) 656-7908**
Host(s): **Lee and Jo Anne Green**
Location: **1 mile from U.S. 29**
No. of Rooms: **5**
No. of Private Baths: **1**
Maximum No. of Guests Sharing
  Bath: **4**
Double/pb: **$40**
Single/pb: **$30**
Double/sb: **$35**
Single/sb: **$25**

Suites: **$80**
Months of Operation: **All year**
Reduced Rates: **Weekly; monthly;
  seniors**
Breakfast: **Continental**
Credit Cards: **MC, VISA**
Air-Conditioning: **Yes**
Pets: **Sometimes**
Children: **Welcome**
Smoking: **Permitted**
Social Drinking: **Permitted**

In the center of this 15-acre property is a pool and patio. Inside the house, the decor includes wood carvings and art from all over the world. Guests are welcome to relax by the fireside and enjoy wine or soft drinks. Breakfast features fresh fruit, cereals, breads, and jam. Golf, tennis, boating, and hiking are nearby, in Bryan Park.

Havenshire Inn
ROUTE 4, BOX 455, HENDERSONVILLE, NORTH CAROLINA 28739

Tel: **(704) 692-4097**
Host(s): **Cindy Findley, Kay Coppock**
Location: **20 miles from Asheville**
No. of Rooms: **6**
No. of Private Baths: **2**
Maximum No. of Guests Sharing
  Bath: **4**
Double/pb: **$60**
Single/pb: **$45**
Double/sb: **$60**
Single/sb: **$45**
Months of Operation: **April 15 to
  October 31**

Reduced Rates: **After 2 nights, $40
  (single), $50 (double)**
Breakfast: **Continental**
Credit Cards: **MC, VISA**
Air-Conditioning: **Unnecessary**
Pets: **No**
Children: **Welcome, over 10**
Smoking: **Permitted**
Social Drinking: **Permitted**
Airport Pickup: **Yes**
Foreign Languages: **Spanish**

Located on the French Broad River, this restored English home was built in 1880. The house is surrounded by 40 acres of magnificent landscaping and boasts a pond. The Carl Sandburg Home, Biltmore House, Pisgah National Forest, and the Blue Ridge Mountain Parkway are all within a 20-minute drive. Cindy and Kay will direct you to the best restaurants to suit your palate and purse.

Ye Olde Cherokee Inn
MILE POST 8, BEACH ROAD, KILL DEVIL HILLS, NORTH CAROLINA 27948

Tel: **(919) 441-6127**
Host(s): **Robert and Phyllis Combs**
Location: **80 miles south of Norfolk,
  Virginia**
No. of Rooms: **7**
No. of Private Baths: **7**
Double/pb: **$25–$60**
Single/pb: **$25–$60**
Months of Operation: **March 1 to
  December 31**

Reduced Rates: **March and November**
Breakfast: **Continental**
Credit Cards: **AMEX, MC, VISA**
Air-Conditioning: **Yes**
Pets: **No**
Children: **Welcome, over 12**
Smoking: **Permitted**
Social Drinking: **Permitted**

Situated 600 feet from the Atlantic Ocean, this pink beach cottage has big porches for relaxing, with an interior that is cozy and restful. It's close to the Wright Brothers Monument, Jockey Ridge Sand Dunes, and Roanoke Island. Robert and Phyllis are genealogy buffs; in July and August their homemade ice-cream is a treat.

Beach House
BOX 443, OCRACOKE, NORTH CAROLINA 27960

Tel: (919) 928-6471
Host(s): **Tom and Carol Beach**
Location: **on State Highway 12**
No. of Rooms: **3**
Maximum No. of Guests Sharing Bath: **8**
Double/sb: **$35**
Months of Operation: **March 1 to October 31**

Reduced Rates: **No**
Breakfast: **Full**
Air-Conditioning: **Yes**
Pets: **No**
Children: **Welcome**
Smoking: **Permitted**
Social Drinking: **Permitted**
Airport Pickup: **Yes**

This beach cottage has an old-fashioned front porch with ginger-bread details. It offers a fine view of the harbor. Inside, the furnishings are comfortable, some dating back to the 1930s. Your hosts prepare homemade breads, preserves, and eggs for breakfast. They will be happy to advise on the sights of the Cape Hatteras National Seashore.

Mill Farm Inn
P.O. BOX 1251, TRYON, NORTH CAROLINA 28782

Tel: (704) 859-6992 or 859-6242
Host(s): **Chip and Penny Kessler**
Location: **45 miles southeast of Asheville**
No. of Rooms: **8**
No. of Private Baths: **8**
Double/pb: **$48**
Single/pb: **$40**
Suites: **$80–90**
Months of Operation: **March to November**

Reduced Rates: **No**
Breakfast: **Continental**
Air-Conditioning: **Yes**
Pets: **No**
Children: **Welcome**
Smoking: **Permitted**
Social Drinking: **Permitted**
Foreign Languages: **French**

The Pacolet River flows past the edge of this three-and-one-half-acre property in the foothills of the Blue Ridge Mountains. Sitting porches and the living room with fireplace are fine spots to relax. A hearty breakfast of fresh fruit, cereal, specialty breads, and preserves is served daily. Your hosts offer kitchen privileges and will advise on nearby dining.

NORTH DAKOTA

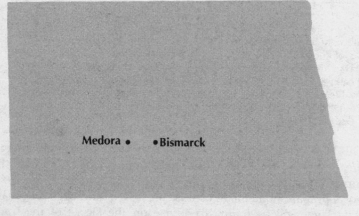

Medora • • Bismarck

The Rough Riders
MEDORA, NORTH DAKOTA 58645

Tel: **(701) 623-4422**
Host(s): **John Conway**
Location: **135 miles west of Bismarck**
No. of Rooms: **9**
No. of Baths: **9**
Double/pb: **$41.50**
Single/pb: **$36**
Months of operation: **Memorial Day–Labor Day**
Reduced Rates: **No**

Breakfast: **Continental**
Other Meals: **Available**
Credit Cards: **AMEX**
Air-Conditioning: **Yes**
Pets: **No**
Children: **Welcome**
Smoking: **Permitted**
Social Drinking: **Permitted**
Airport Pickup: **Yes**

Located at the center of town, the hotel is constructed inside and out of rough lumber. The facade bears the many branding marks of cattle barons, including that of Theodore Roosevelt. The "cowtown" atmosphere has been retained, down to the wooden sidewalk. The center staircase leads to the guest quarters, which are furnished with antiques. Don't miss the Outdoor Memorial Musical, an extravaganza complete with horses, stagecoaches, and a rousing tribute to Teddy Roosevelt. The Museum of Wildlife, the Doll House Museum, and the spectacular beauty of the Badlands will make your visit memorable.

OHIO

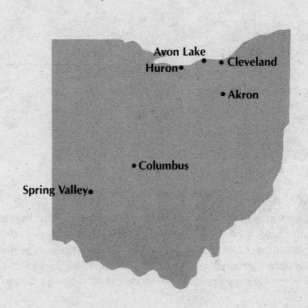

Portage House
601 COPLEY ROAD, STATE ROUTE 162, AKRON, OHIO 44320

Tel: **(216) 535-9236**
Host(s): **Jeanne and Harry Pinnick**
Location: **2 miles from I-77**
No. of Rooms: **5**
No. of Private Baths: **1½**
Maximum No. of Guests Sharing
  Bath: **7**
Double/pb: **$24**
Single/pb: **$18**
Double/sb: **$24**
Single/sb: **$18**

Months of Operation: **All year**
Reduced Rates: **No**
Breakfast: **Full**
Other Meals: **Available**
Air-Conditioning: **No**
Pets: **Yes**
Children: **Welcome (crib)**
Smoking: **Permitted**
Social Drinking: **Permitted**
Foreign Languages: **French**

Nestled in a parklike setting, this gracious Tudor home dates back
to 1917. Seeped in history, there is a stone wall down the street

that was the western boundary of the United States in 1785. Harry is a physics professor at the university, and Jean is a gracious hostess. The coffee pot is always on, refreshments are available, and if bread is being baked, you'll be given some with butter.

Williams House
249 VINEWOOD, AVON LAKE, OHIO 44012

Tel: **(216) 933-5089**	Reduced Rates: **10%, seniors**
Host(s): **Edred and Margaret Williams**	Breakfast: **Full**
Location: **20 miles west of Cleveland**	Air-Conditioning: **No**
No. of Rooms: **1**	Pets: **No**
No. of Private Baths: **1**	Children: **No**
Double/pb: **$30**	Smoking: **Permitted**
Single/pb: **$24**	Social Drinking: **Permitted**
Months of Operation: **All year**	Airport Pickup: **Yes**

Located a mile from the Lake Erie public beach, Edred and Margaret live in a quiet, residential neighborhood. The house is comfortably decorated in a harmonious blend of styles; you will be made to feel right at home. They serve beverages and snacks upon your arrival, and will help you plan a pleasant visit. Breakfast is complete, from juice to cereal to eggs to bacon to coffee or tea.

Private Lodgings
P.O. BOX 18590, CLEVELAND, OHIO 44118

Tel: **(216) 321-3213**	Rate: (Single/Double):	
Coordinator: **Jane McCarroll; Kate Terrell**	Modest: **$20**	**$30**
	Average: **$25**	**$35**
States/Regions Covered: **Cleveland**	Luxury: **$30**	**$65**
	Credit Cards: **No**	

This is a city with world-renowned cultural and biomedical resources, as well as major corporations and recreational areas. Special attention is given to the needs of relocating and visiting professionals, out-patients, and relatives of hospital in-patients, as well as vacationers. Every effort is made to accommodate persons with physical handicaps. Discounted rates are provided for extended stays.

The Tudor House
P.O. BOX 18590, CLEVELAND, OHIO 44118

Tel: **(216) 321-3213**
Host(s): **Jane McCarroll**
Location: **12 miles from Ohio Turnpike**
No. of Rooms: **2**
No. of Private Baths: **2**
Double/pb: **$50**
Single/pb: **$35**

Months of Operation: **All year**
Reduced Rates: **No**
Breakfast: **Full**
Air-Conditioning: **No**
Pets: **No**
Children: **Welcome, over 16**
Smoking: **Permitted**
Social Drinking: **Permitted**

This lovely 1920s Tudor-style house is listed in the National Register of Historic Places. Situated on an acre of landscaped grounds, it is within minutes of Cleveland's major business district as well as the cultural, academic, and biomedical establishments. Fine restaurants and shops are within easy walking distance. The house is attractively furnished with period furniture and antiques. Your hosts are a professional couple who have traveled widely and enjoy sharing their home and conversation with their guests.

Columbus Bed & Breakfast
763 S. THIRD STREET, GERMAN VILLAGE, COLUMBUS, OHIO 43206

Tel: **(614) 443-3680 or 444-8888**
Coordinator: **Fred Holdridge, Howard Burns**
States/Regions Covered: **Columbus**

Rates (Single/Double):
Average: **$26** **$36**
Luxury: **$30** **$40**
Credit Cards: **No**

Historic German Village is a registered National Historic Area. It's close to downtown Columbus but a century away in character. Small brick houses, brick sidewalks and streets, and wrought-iron fences combine to create an Old World atmosphere. Charming shops and restaurants are within walking distance of the hosts' homes.

The Beach House

213 KIWANIS AVENUE, CHASKA BEACH, HURON, OHIO 44839

Tel: **(419) 433-5839**
Host(s): **Donna Lendrum**
Location: **60 miles west of Cleveland**
No. of Rooms: **3**
Maximum No. of Guests Sharing
  Bath: **6**
Double/sb: **$50**
Single/sb: **$50**

Months of Operation: **May through
  September**
Reduced Rates: **No**
Breakfast: **Continental**
Air-Conditioning: **No**
Pets: **No**
Children: **Welcome, over 12**
Smoking: **Permitted**
Social Drinking: **Permitted**

Located on the shore of Lake Erie, this spacious home is tastefully furnished with antiques. The guest rooms are in a separate wing of the house with a private entrance. You will enjoy the private sandy beach, the local fishing pier, the summer theater, or a side trip to Milan with its antique shops and museums. Depending upon the weather, Donna serves breakfast on the porch overlooking the lake or around the cozy kitchen table. A guest refrigerator and picnic table are available.

3B's Bed 'n' Breakfast

103 RACE STREET, SPRING VALLEY, OHIO 45370

Tel: **(513) 862-4241 or 878-9944**
Host(s): **Pat and Herb Boettcher**
Location: **16 miles southeast of
  Dayton**
No. of Rooms: **3**

Maximum No. of Guests Sharing
  Bath: **4**
Double/sb: **$25**
Single/sb: **$20**
Months of Operation: **All year**

Reduced Rates: **30%, families**
Breakfast: **Full**
Other Meals: **Available**
Air-Conditioning: **Yes**
Pets: **Sometimes**

Children: **Welcome, over 4**
Smoking: **Permitted**
Social Drinking: **Permitted**
Airport Pickup: **Yes**

This restored 19th-century farmhouse is a great place to unwind. The rooms are spacious and airy, and they abound with family heirlooms and homemade crafts. The quilts on the beds are handmade. Nearby attractions include historic Lebanon, Kings Island, Dayton's Air Force Museum, and Sugarcreek Ski Hills at Bellbrook. Pat and Herb are retired from the Air Force and look forward to visiting with you.

OKLAHOMA

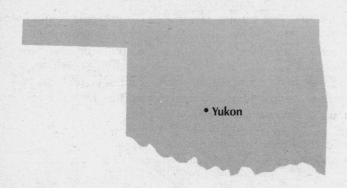

• Yukon

Tulp House
1210 KOUBA DRIVE, YUKON, OKLAHOMA 73099

Tel: **(405) 354-3280**
Host(s): **Margaret and John Tulp**
Location: **12 miles west of Oklahoma City**
No. of Rooms: **1**
No. of Private Baths: **1**
Double/pb: **$30**
Single/pb: **$20**
Months of Operation: **All year**
Reduced Rates: **No**

Breakfast: **Continental**
Credit Cards: **No**
Air-Conditioning: **Yes**
Pets: **No**
Children: **No**
Smoking: **Permitted**
Social Drinking: **Permitted**
Airport Pickup: **Yes**
Foreign Languages: **French, Spanish**

This two-story Dutch colonial is located on a residential street lined with stately old trees. Furnished in early American style, there is a delightful patio and garden out back. The guest bedroom is immaculate and has a comfortable double bed. Breakfast features fresh-ground coffee and homemade bread; you are welcome to use the kitchen for light cooking. Margaret and John are warm, hospitable people who will help you plan a delightful stay. Oklahoma City, with its cultural attractions and great restaurants, is minutes away. You will enjoy the western flavor of the area. Don't miss the Cowboy Hall of Fame, Indian City (site of the Artifacts of the Five Civilized Tribes), and a tour of the Oklahoma State Capitol, with operating oil well and the Pioneer Museum.

OREGON

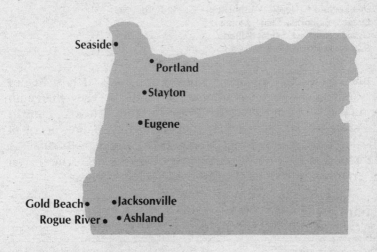

Bed & Breakfast—Oregon
5733 S.W. DICKINSON STREET, PORTLAND, OREGON 97219

Tel: **(503) 245-0642**
Coordinator: **Marcelle Tebo**
States/Regions Covered:
  **Oregon—Bend, La Pine, Lincoln
City, Mt. Hood, Portland, West Linn;
Washington—Hazel Dell, Long
Beach**

Rates (Single/Double):
  Average: **$18–$23**   **$30–$35**
Credit Cards: **No**
Minimum Stay: **Varies**

Marcelle has a variety of accommodations ranging from a condo in Long Beach (minimum stay: three days) to a mobile home in La Pine (minimum stay: one week), with many traditional B&Bs in between. For the sports enthusiast, there is skiing on the Skyline Trail, fishing in the Columbia River for salmon; eight-foot sturgeon have been caught at Bonneville Dam. Don't miss the famous Elephant Herd, as well as the Rose Gardens in Portland.

Northwest Bed and Breakfast
7707 SW LOCUST STREET, PORTLAND, OREGON 97223

Tel: **(503) 246-8366**
Coordinator: **Laine Friedman and Gloria Shaich**
States/Regions Covered: **Washington, Oregon, California, Idaho, Montana, Nevada, Illinois; Canada—Alberta, British Columbia; United Kingdom**

Rates (Single/Double):
   Average: **$14–$25**   **$18–$40**
   Luxury: **$35**   **$50–$55**
Credit Cards: **No**

Laine and Gloria have a network of hundreds of host homes throughout the Pacific Northwest and Canada. They charge an annual membership fee of $15 (individual) or $20 (two or more in the same family). Upon joining, you will receive a directory of all the lodgings, which range from city to suburban to rural. A variety of package tours, complete with car rental if required, can be arranged with stops at suitable B&Bs along the way.

Chanticleer
120 GRESHAM STREET, ASHLAND, OREGON 97520

Tel: **(503) 482-1919**
Host(s): **Jim and Nancy Beaver**
Location: **350 miles north of San Francisco**
No. of Rooms: **6**
No. of Private Baths: **6**
Double/pb: **$59**
Single/pb: **$54**
Months of Operation: **All year**

Reduced Rates: **20%, except singles, November to February**
Breakfast: **Full**
Air-Conditioning: **Yes**
Pets: **No**
Children: **Welcome**
Smoking: **Permitted**
Social Drinking: **Permitted**
Airport Pickup: **Yes**

The Chanticleer overlooks Bear Creek Valley and the Cascade foothills. A large living room with a stone fireplace, a sunny patio, and French country furnishings create a comfortable atmosphere. Guests are welcome to juices, coffee, and sherry. Some of the specialty breakfast items include, Italian roast coffee, blintzes, and cheese-baked eggs. Shops, restaurants, and the site of the Shakespearean Festival are a short walk away. Mount Ashland ski area and the Rogue River are a 30-minute drive from the house.

The Coach House Inn
70 COOLIDGE STREET, ASHLAND, OREGON 97520

Tel: (503) 482-2257
Host(s): Pamela and Jack Evans
No. of Rooms: 3
Maximum No. of Guests Sharing
  Bath: 6
Double/sb: $39
Single/sb: $34
Months of Operation: February 20 to
  October 31

Reduced Rates: No
Breakfast: Continental
Air-Conditioning: No
Pets: No
Children: Welcome, over 12
Smoking: No
Social Drinking: Permitted
Airport Pickup: Yes
Foreign Languages: German

The guest rooms at this Victorian inn are decorated with antiques and offer mountain views. Enjoy soaking in the clawfoot bathtub or a game of croquet on the spacious lawn. Breakfast features fresh fruit cobblers and homemade jams. Guests are welcome to join daily picnic tours of the local creamery and vineyards. The Shakespeare Theatre, historic homes, and antique shops are all nearby.

Neil Creek House
341 MOWETZA DRIVE, ASHLAND, OREGON 97520

Tel: (503) 482-1334
Host(s): Edith and Thomas Heumann
No. of Rooms: 2
No. of Private Baths: 2
Double/pb: $65
Single/pb: $65
Months of Operation: All year
Reduced Rates: 10%, weekly

Breakfast: Full
Air-Conditioning: Yes
Pets: No
Children: No
Smoking: Permitted
Social Drinking: Permitted
Airport Pickup: Yes
Foreign Languages: French, German

This country house is set on five wooded acres with a duck pond for boating. Guests are welcome to relax by the swimming pool or on the deck. Wine, champagne, and coffee are served. Breakfast treats may include homemade jams and syrups, ranch eggs, sausage, bacon, or Danish. The guest rooms overlook the creek or mountains, and are furnished with antiques and 19th-century art. Skiing, sailing, river rafting, and Shakespeare performances are nearby.

Royal Carter House
514 SISKIYOU BOULEVARD, ASHLAND, OREGON 97520

Tel: **(503) 482-5623**	Breakfast: **Full**
Host(s): **Alyce and Roy Levy**	Air-Conditioning: **No**
No. of Rooms: **2**	Pets: **No**
No. of Private Baths: **2**	Children: **Welcome, over 7**
Double/pb: **$45–$55**	Smoking: **No**
Suites: **$55**	Social Drinking: **Permitted**
Months of Operation: **All year**	Airport Pickup: **Yes**
Reduced Rates: **No**	

This beautiful 1909 home is listed on the National Historic Register and located four blocks from Ashland's famous Shakespearian Theatre. It is surrounded by lovely old trees in a parklike setting. It is comfortable and suitably modernized. Alyce has added decorator touches of vintage hats and old periodicals to the antique furnishings. The Levys have traveled extensively abroad and will share stories of their experiences with you.

Shutes Lazy "S" Farm B&B
200 MOWETZA DRIVE, ASHLAND, OREGON 97520

Tel: **(503) 482-5498**	Reduced Rates: **No**
Host(s): **Denny and Rodna Shutes**	Breakfast: **Full**
No. of Rooms: **1**	Air-Conditioning: **Yes**
No. of Private Baths: **1**	Pets: **No**
Double/pb: **$45**	Children: **No**
Single/pb: **$42**	Smoking: **No**
Months of Operation: **All year**	Social Drinking: **Permitted**

Denny and Rodna have a ranch-style home with a long porch— perfect for taking in the fabulous mountain views. You may observe or participate in feeding the goats and lambs. Breakfast is prepared from the organically grown food that they raise on their five-acre farm. Rodna is a retired college instructor of drama, and Denny is a retired college instructor of ecology and conservation. Complimentary beverages are served on arrival and after an evening at the famed Shakespearean Theatre.

Copper Windmill Ranch
33263 DILLARD ROAD, EUGENE, OREGON 97405

Tel: (503) 686-2194
Host(s): **Bill and Lyn Neel**
Location: **6 miles south of Eugene**
No. of Rooms: **2**
No. of Private Baths: **1**
Maximum No. of Guests Sharing Bath: **4**
Double/pb: **$38**
Single/pb: **$25**
Double/sb: **$38**
Single/sb: **$25**
Suites: **$55**

Months of Operation: **All year**
Reduced Rates: **No**
Breakfast: **Full**
Other Meals: **Yes**
Credit Cards: **MC, VISA**
Air-Conditioning: **Unnecessary**
Pets: **No**
Children: **Welcome, over 3**
Smoking: **Permitted**
Social Drinking: **Permitted**
Airport Pickup: **Yes**
Foreign Languages: **Spanish**

You are sure to enjoy your visit on this 80-acre ranch if Bill and Lyn have their way. The house is a replica of the original homestead, including hand-hewn timber beams and an antique cast-iron kitchen stove for cozy breakfasts. There's a small pond with a rowboat for your pleasure, and trips on the McKenzie River can be arranged. Most of the food served is raised on the ranch, and you can collect your own eggs for breakfast. Your horse is invited to come along too. Stall, barn, and pasturing costs eight dollars.

Griswold Guest Homes
5361 BURNETT AVENUE, EUGENE, OREGON 97402

Tel: (503) 689-0680 or 688-9556
Coordinator: **Phyllis Griswold**
States/Regions Covered: **Eugene, Florence, Westlake**

Rates (Single/Double):
  Average: **$20–$75**   **$25–$80**
Credit Cards: **No**

Nestled in Willamette Valley between the mountains and the ocean, Eugene is the Jogging Capital of the U.S. The miles of bicycle and pedestrian trails lead to the University of Oregon or to the fabulous shopping mall. The Performing Arts Center is a main attraction.

Bien Venue Le Cottage
95629 JERRYS FLAT ROAD, GOLD BEACH, OREGON 97444

Tel: **(503) 247-2335**
Host(s): **Forrest and Lucille Pendergast**
Location: **80 miles south of Coos Bay**
No. of Rooms: **1**
No. of Private Baths: **1**
Double/pb: **$35**
Single/pb: **$35**
Guest Cottage: **$45 sleeps 3**
Months of Operation: **All year**

Reduced Rates: **No**
Breakfast: **Continental**
Air-Conditioning: **No**
Pets: **No**
Children: **One child only**
Smoking: **No**
Social Drinking: **Permitted**
Foreign Languages: **French**

This homey cottage is situated on the Rogue River, near the beach and all the river recreational activities. Furnished with memorabilia collected from the hosts' travels to Europe and China, each room has a beautiful view of the river. The guest room in the house has its own entrance, and the cottage is very private. You are welcome to use the barbecue and picnic table; complimentary wine and coffee are available.

Livingston Mansion
4132 LIVINGSTON ROAD, BOX 1476, JACKSONVILLE, OREGON 97530

Tel: **(503) 899-7107**
Host(s): **Wally and Sherry Lossing**
No. of Rooms: **3**
No. of Private Baths: **3**
Double/pb: **$65–$75**
Single/pb: **$65–$75**
Months of Operation: **All year**
Reduced Rates: **No**

Breakfast: **Full**
Credit Cards: **MC, VISA**
Air-Conditioning: **Yes**
Pets: **No**
Children: **Welcome**
Smoking: **Permitted**
Social Drinking: **Permitted**
Airport Pickup: **Yes**

This stately inn dates to the turn of the century. The porch, pool, patio, and the window seats inside are fine spots to relax. Wine, snacks, and sherry are complimentary. Breakfast cookies and eggs prepared in a variety of ways are served each morning. Nearby, you can enjoy skiing, white-water rafting, and performances of Shakespeare.

The Riverside Inn
430 SOUTH HOLLADAY, SEASIDE, OREGON 79138

Tel: (503) 738-8254
Host(s): **Stephen Tuckman, Cindy McKee**
Location: **79 miles west of Portland; ¼ mile from Route 101**
No. of Rooms: **7**
No. of Private Baths: **7**
SIngle/pb: **$23**
Suites: **$29–$43**

Months of Operation: **All year**
Reduced Rates: **October to May**
Breakfast: **Continental**
Credit Cards: **MC, VISA**
Air-Conditioning: **Unnecessary**
Pets: **No**
Children: **Welcome (crib)**
Smoking: **Permitted**
Social Drinking: **Permitted**

Situated on the Necanicum River on the northern Oregon coast, it is an easy walk to the beach and shops. Furnished with a country flavor, each suite has its own entrance and television. Fresh and clean, it is reminiscent of a visit to grandmother's summer cottage. Breakfast is graciously served in the library lounge.

Horncroft
42156 KINGSTON LYONS DRIVE, STAYTON, OREGON 97383

Tel: (503) 769-6287
Host(s): **Dorothea and Kenneth Horn**
Location: **17 miles east of Salem**
No. of Rooms: **3**
No. of Private Baths: **1**
Maximum No. of Guests Sharing Bath: **4**
Double/pb: **$30**
Single/pb: **$20**
Double/sb: **$25**

Single/sb: **$15**
Months of Operation: **All year**
Reduced Rates: **No**
Breakfast: **Full**
Air-Conditioning: **Unnecessary**
Pets: **No**
Children: **Welcome (crib)**
Smoking: **No**
Social Drinking: **Permitted**
Foreign Languages: **German**

This lovely home is situated in the foothills of the Cascade Mountains on the edge of Willamette Valley. In summer, swim in the heated pool or hike on one of the scenic nature paths. The area is dotted with farms, and the valley is abundant in fruits, berries, and vegetables. Willamette and Oregon state universities are nearby. The Mount Jefferson Wilderness hiking area is an hour away.

PENNSYLVANIA

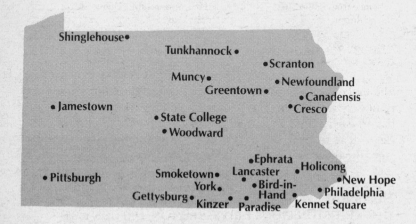

Shinglehouse•

Tunkhannock •

•Scranton

Muncy•　　　•Newfoundland

Greentown •

•Canadensis

• Jamestown

•Cresco

• State College

• Woodward

• Pittsburgh

•Ephrata　•Holicong

Smoketown•　Lancaster

•New Hope

York•　　•Bird-in-

Gettysburg•　　　Hand •　•Philadelphia

Kinzer•　Paradise　Kennet Square

BUCKS COUNTY

Barley Sheaf Farm

BOX 66, HOLICONG, PENNSYLVANIA 18928

Tel: **(215) 794-5104**	Single/sb: **$45–$55**
Host(s): **Ann and Don Mills**	Suites: **$80**
Location: **40 miles north of Philadelphia, 60 miles southeast of New York City**	Months of Operation: **March 1 to December 16**
No. of Rooms: **9**	Reduced Rates: **No**
No. of Private Baths: **6**	Breakfast: **Full**
Maximum No. of Guests Sharing Bath: **6**	Air-Conditioning: **Unnecessary**
Double/pb: **$65**	Pets: **No**
Single/pb: **$65**	Children: **Welcome, over 8**
Double/sb: **$45–$55**	Smoking: **Permitted**
	Social Drinking: **Permitted**
	Foreign Languages: **French**

Situated between New Hope and Doylestown, just around the bend from the antique stalls and quaint shops of Peddlers'

Village, this charming 30-acre farm awaits you. The old stone house is a National Historic Site. The bank barn, swimming pool, pond, and old trees round out a peaceful setting, the serenity of which may be broken by the sound of sheep in the meadow or the honking of Canada geese. Ann and Don will make you feel most welcome.

Pineapple Hill
RD 3, BOX 34C, RIVER ROAD, NEW HOPE, PENNSYLVANIA 18938

Tel: **(215) 862-9608**
Host(s): **Mary and Stephen Darlington**
No. of Rooms: **4**
No. of Private Baths: **0**
Double/sb: **$45**
Single/sb: **$45**
Months of Operation: **All year**
Reduced Rates: **No**

Breakfast: **Continental**
Credit Cards: **AMEX**
Air-Conditioning: **No**
Pets: **No**
Children: **Welcome (crib)**
Smoking: **Permitted**
Social Drinking: **Permitted**
Foreign Languages: **German**

The 18-inch walls, fireplace, and traditional woodwork attest to the 18th-century origin of this charming farmhouse. Steve and Mary have furnished it beautifully with family heirlooms, and spool and brass beds. An elegant afternoon tea is served in the parlor in winter or at poolside in summer. And, when you return from the dozens of activities the area offers, you are welcome to relax in front of the fire, read, play backgammon, and visit.

The Wedgwood Bed & Breakfast Inn
111 WEST BRIDGE STREET, NEW HOPE, PENNSYLVANIA 18938

Tel: **(215) 862-2570**
Host(s): **Nadine Silnutzer, Carl Glassman**
No. of Rooms: **7**
No. of Private Baths: **3**
Maximum No. of Guests Sharing Bath: **4**
Double/pb: **$70**
Single/pb: **$65**
Double/sb: **$55–$60**
Single/sb: **$45–$55**
Suites: **$70–$90**

Months of Operation: **All year**
Reduced Rates: **10%, Sunday to Thursday; weekly; groups; January to March**
Breakfast: **Continental**
Air-Conditioning: **No**
Pets: **Sometimes**
Children: **Welcome**
Smoking: **No**
Social Drinking: **Permitted**
Foreign Languages: **Dutch, Spanish**

Listed on the Historic Register, this gracious 1870 Victorian features a veranda for leisurely relaxing. It is surrounded by manicured lawns. Nadine and Carl take pride in their home, which features guest rooms beautifully furnished with antiques and original artwork and cooled by brass-fitted ceiling fans. You can use their kitchen for light snacks or curl up in the parlor with a book. A complimentary decanter of Amaretto, chocolate mints, plus discounts in many of the local shops are some of the little extras that will make your stay special.

Whitehall Farm
R.D. 2, BOX 250, NEW HOPE, PENNSYLVANIA 18938

Tel: **(215) 598-7945**	Months of Operation: **All year**
Host(s): **Chuck and Marylin Matthews**	Reduced Rates: **Monday to Thursday;**
No. of Rooms: **7**	**10%, seniors**
No. of Private Baths: **3**	Breakfast: **Full**
Maximum No. of Guests Sharing	Credit Cards: **AMEX, MC, VISA**
Bath: **2**	Air-Conditioning: **Yes**
Double/pb: **$65–$75**	Pets: **Sometimes**
Single/pb: **$58–$67**	Children: **Welcome**
Double/sb: **$50–$60**	Smoking: **Permitted**
Single/sb: **$45–$54**	Social Drinking: **Permitted**

This is an elegant, plastered stone manor house (circa 1794) set amid towering trees in lush horse country. Four bedrooms have fireplaces. Marylin and Chuck invite you to use their tennis court and pool, and there's horseback riding (with instruction) if you wish. You're only minutes from Peddlers' Village and the famed Bucks County Playhouse. Afternoon tea is served daily. Marylin is a decorator and the furnishings are both eclectic and comfortable. Chuck is a retired food executive and chef so you know breakfast will be special.

GETTYSBURG AREA

Dorothy Kime's Tourist Home
1214 BALTIMORE PIKE (ROUTE 97), GETTYSBURG, PENNSYLVANIA 17325

Tel: **(717) 334-2723**
Host(s): **Dorothy Kime**
No. of Rooms: **2**
Maximum No. of Guests Sharing
  Bath: **4**
Double/sb: **$15–$20**
Single/sb: **$15**
Months of Operation: **All year**

Reduced Rates: **No**
Breakfast: **Beverages only**
Air-Conditioning: **Yes**
Pets: **Sometimes**
Children: **Welcome, over 9**
Smoking: **Yes**
Social Drinking: **Permitted**

This ranch-style home is five minutes from the historic Gettysburg battlefield. Local attractions include the National Tower, National Museum, and Cemetery. Your hostess offers morning coffee, and guests are welcome to use the refrigerator to store snacks and have a meal outside on the picnic table.

The Homestead
785 BALTIMORE STREET, GETTYSBURG, PENNSYLVANIA 17325

Tel: **(717) 334-2037**
Host(s): **Ruth S. Wisler**
No. of Rooms: **2**
Maximum No. of Guests Sharing
  Bath: **4**
Double/sb: **$17**
Single/sb: **$13**
Months of Operation: **May to
  October**

Reduced Rates: **No**
Breakfast: **No**
Air-Conditioning: **Yes**
Pets: **No**
Children: **Welcome, over 4**
Smoking: **No**
Social Drinking: **No**

The Homestead is a gracious home standing on the historic battlefield, near the National Cemetery. It was originally an orphanage for children made homeless during the Civil War. It is comfortably furnished with family antiques and boasts several Civil War relics. Ruth is a retired English teacher who has a green thumb for raising African violets. She is a most cordial lady and likes nothing better than helping her guests get the most out of their visit to the area. You are welcome to store your perishable snacks in her refrigerator. Gettysburg has four-score and more things to see.

Beck Mill Farm
R.D. 1, BOX 452, BECK MILL ROAD, HANOVER, PENNSYLVANIA 17331

Tel: **(717) 637-8992**
Host(s): **Alan and Teena Smith**
Location: **35 miles south of Harrisburg**
No. of Rooms: **2**
Maximum No. of Guests Sharing
  Bath: **4**
Double/sb: **$32**
Single/sb: **$25**
Months of Operation: **All year**

Reduced Rates: **10%, December 1 to March 31; 10%, seniors**
Breakfast: **Full**
Other Meals: **Available**
Air-Conditioning: **Yes**
Pets: **Sometimes**
Children: **Welcome**
Smoking: **No**
Social Drinking: **Permitted**

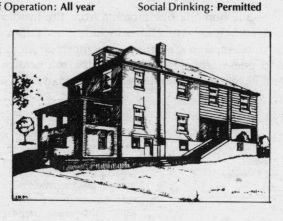

Outside this 60-year-old farmhouse are fruit trees, a swimming pool, and a barn. The interior features chestnut woodwork, early American furnishings, and a player piano in the living room. Guests may have breakfast in their private quarters or the country kitchen. Attractions such as the Hanover and Lana Lobell Standardbred horse farms and Gettysburg National Military Park are nearby.

PENNSYLVANIA DUTCH AREA

Spring House
MUDDY CREEK FORKS, AIRVILLE, PENNSYLVANIA 17302

Tel: **(717) 927-6906**
Host(s): **Ray Constance Hearne**
Location: **18 miles south of York**
No. of Rooms: **3**
Maximum No. of Guests Sharing
  Bath: **4**
Double/sb: **$48**
Single/sb: **$42**
Months of Operation: **March to December**

Reduced Rates: **10%, 5 days**
Breakfast: **Full**
Air-Conditioning: **No**
Pets: **Sometimes**
Children: **Welcome**
Smoking: **No**
Social Drinking: **Permitted**
Foreign Languages: **Spanish**

This unique 200-year-old stone house, situated in a charming, 18th-century valley village, is decorated with whitewashed and stenciled walls, and furnished with a pleasant mixture of antiques, paintings, and handmade pottery. The antique beds have handmade quilts and featherbeds. Ray is never too busy to direct you to the river for water sports, show you where to hike, or explain where the award-winning wine is made. She'll even introduce you to some of her interesting neighbors.

Greystone Motor Lodge
2658 OLD PHILADELPHIA PIKE, BIRD-IN-HAND, PENNSYLVANIA 17505

Tel: **(717) 393-4233**
Host(s): **James and Phyllis Reed**
No. of Rooms: **12**
No. of Private Baths: **12**
Double/pb: **$28**
Single/pb: **$28**
Suites: **$44–$47**
Months of Operation: **All year**
Reduced Rates: **$24–$36, September 1 to October 31, April 1 to June 30; $16–$28, November 1 to March 16**

Breakfast: **No**
Credit Cards: **AMEX, MC, VISA**
Air-Conditioning: **Yes**
Pets: **No**
Children: **Welcome (crib)**
Smoking: **Permitted**
Social Drinking: **Permitted**
Foreign Languages: **Sign-language**

Situated on two acres of lush lawn and trees, the lodge was built in 1883. Back then, this French Victorian mansion and carriage house did not boast of air-conditioning, TV, and suites with kitchens as it does today. Though a great deal of renovation has taken place, the antique features and charm of the mansion are intact. James and Phyllis will be pleased to provide you with all the necessary touring advice.

Groff Tourist Farm Home
R.D. 1, BOX 36, BRACKBILL ROAD, KINZER, PENNSYLVANIA 17535

Tel: **(717) 442-8223**	Single/sb: **$13**
Host(s): **Harold and Mary Groff**	Months of Operation: **All year**
Location: **15 miles east of Lancaster**	Reduced Rates: **No**
No. of Rooms: **5**	Breakfast: **No**
No. of Private Baths: **1**	Air-Conditioning: **No**
Maximum No. of Guests Sharing Bath: **6**	Pets: **No**
	Children: **Welcome**
Double/pb: **$25**	Smoking: **No**
Single/pb: **$20**	Social Drinking: **No**
Double/sb: **$16**	

This old-fashioned stone farmhouse, recently redecorated, has a porch on which to relax; each comfortable bedroom is cross-ventilated, so you can enjoy the crisp country air. When Mary isn't busy keeping her home shipshape, she's off tending her lovely garden. In her spare time, she enjoys visiting with her guests, while stitching the gorgeous quilts her grandmother taught her to make.

Sycamore Haven Farm Guest House
35 SOUTH KINZER ROAD, KINZER, PENNSYLVANIA 17535

Tel: **(717) 442-4901**	Reduced Rates: **No**
Host(s): **Charles and Janet Groff**	Breakfast: **No**
No. of Rooms: **3**	Air-Conditioning: **No**
Maximum No. of Guests Sharing Bath: **8**	Pets: **Sometimes**
	Children: **Welcome**
Double/sb: **$20**	Smoking: **No**
Single/sb: **$15**	Social Drinking: **No**
Months of Operation: **All year**	

This spacious home is a dairy farm where 40 cows get milked each day; you are welcome to watch the process. The children will be kept busy enjoying the swing, kittens, sheep, and games. You may use the Groff kitchen to fix light snacks and the guest refrigerator for storing them.

Groff Farm—"Abend-Ruhe"
2324 LEAMAN ROAD, LANCASTER, PENNSYLVANIA 17602

Tel: **(717) 687-0221**
Host(s): **Herb and Debbie Groff**
Location: **4 miles east of Lancaster**
No. of Rooms: **4**
No. of Private Baths: **2**
Maximum No. of Guests Sharing
   Bath: **4**
Double/pb: **$22**
Single/pb: **$22**
Double/sb: **$17**

Single/sb: **$17**
Months of Operation: **All year**
Reduced Rates: **No**
Breakfast: **Continental**
Credit Cards: **MC**
Air-Conditioning: **Yes**
Pets: **Sometimes**
Children: **Welcome**
Smoking: **No**
Social Drinking: **Permitted**

This roomy 110-year-old brick farmhouse has an inviting wrap-around porch and lovely shade trees. It is comfortably furnished with simple country charm. Herb is a woodsmith with a shop located on the farm, and Debbie is a fulltime hostess interested in handicrafts. Her homemade breads and jams are delicious. Don't miss the famous Strasburg Railroad and Train Museum, just five minutes away.

Meadowview Guest House
2169 NEW HOLLAND PIKE, LANCASTER, PENNSYLVANIA 17601

Tel: **(717) 299-4017**
Host(s): **Edward and Sheila Christie**
No. of Rooms: **4**
No. of Private Baths: **2**
Maximum No. of Guests Sharing
   Bath: **5**
Double/pb: **$22**
Single/pb: **$21**
Double/sb: **$17**
Single/sb: **$16**

Months of Operation: **April to
   November**
Reduced Rates: **$3 off after 3 days**
Breakfast: **No**
Air-Conditioning: **Yes**
Pets: **No**
Children: **Welcome**
Smoking: **Permitted**
Social Drinking: **Permitted**

Situated in the heart of Pennsylvania Dutch country, the house has a pleasant blend of modern and traditional furnishings. Your hosts offer a fully equipped guest kitchen where you can store and prepare your own breakfast. Ed and Sheila supply coffee and tea. The area is known for great farmers' markets, antique shops, craft shops, country auctions, and wonderful restaurants.

Maple Lane Guest House
505 PARADISE LANE, PARADISE, PENNSYLVANIA 17562

Tel: (717) 687-7479
Host(s): **Marion and Edwin Rohrer**
Location: **60 miles west of Philadelphia**
No. of Rooms: **4**
No. of Private Baths: **1**
Maximum No. of Guests Sharing Bath: **4**
Double/pb: **$24**
Single/pb: **$20**

Double/sb: **$20**
Single/sb: **$18**
Months of Operation: **All year**
Reduced Rates: **No**
Breakfast: **No**
Air-Conditioning: **Yes**
Pets: **Sometimes**
Children: **Welcome**
Smoking: **No**
Social Drinking: **Permitted**

From the Maple Lane lawn you can see for 40 miles. Stroll the 200 acres of this working farm, with its stream and woodland. Your hosts welcome you to rooms decorated with homemade quilts, needlework, and antiques. The sights of the Amish country, such as the Farmers' Market, antique shops, flea markets, and restaurants, are nearby.

Neffdale Farm
604 STRASBURG ROAD, PARADISE, PENNSYLVANIA 17562

Tel: (717) 687-7837
Host(s): **Roy and Ellen Neff**
Location: **13 miles southeast of Lancaster**
No. of Rooms: **3**
No. of Private Baths: **1**
Maximum No. of Guests Sharing Bath: **8**
Double/pb: **$22**
Single/pb: **$20**
Double/sb: **$20**

Single/sb: **$18**
Months of Operation: **March to November**
Reduced Rates: **No**
Breakfast: **No**
Air-Conditioning: **Yes**
Pets: **Sometimes**
Children: **Welcome**
Smoking: **No**
Social Drinking: **No**

This 200-year-old farmhouse has large, comfortable rooms overlooking 115 acres of beautiful croplands, woods, meadows, and shady lawns. You are invited to watch the huge farm machinery in action, feed the calves, gather eggs, and visit the pigs and ducks. Roy is a busy dairy farmer and Ellen enjoys quilting and making sure that her guests have an enjoyable visit.

Rayba Acres Farm
183 BLACK HORSE ROAD, PARADISE, PENNSYLVANIA 17562

Tel: **(717) 687-6729**
Host(s): **J. Ray and Reba Ranck**
No. of Rooms: **6**
No. of Private Baths: **2**
Maximum No. of Guests Sharing
  Bath: **6**
Double/pb: **$24**
Single/pb: **$24**
Double/sb: **$18**

Single/sb: **$18**
Months of Operation: **All year**
Reduced Rates: **10%, 5 days**
Breakfast: **No**
Air-Conditioning: **Yes**
Pets: **No**
Children: **Welcome**
Smoking: **No**
Social Drinking: **No**

Five generations of the Ranck family have worked this dairy farm. The kids will enjoy visiting the animals, especially at milking time. The farmhouse is comfortably furnished, and your hosts will make you feel at home by helping to arrange your tour. Local possibilities include the antique shops and the Pennsylvania Dutch shops and farmland.

El Shaddai
**229 MADISON AVENUE, HYDE VILLA, READING,
PENNSYLVANIA 19605**

Tel: **(215) 929-1341 or 373-6639**
Host(s): **Dale and Joan Gaul**
No. of Rooms: **2**
No. of Private Baths: **2**

Double/pb: **$32**
Single/pb: **$22**
Months of Operation: **All year**
Reduced Rates: **Families**

Breakfast: **Continental**
Credit Cards: **MC, Visa**
Air-Conditioning: **Yes**
Pets: **No**

Children: **No**
Smoking: **No**
Social Drinking: **No**
Airport Pickup: **Yes**

El Shaddai is a stone farmhouse over one hundred years old. Guests will enjoy relaxing in the sitting room with cooking hearth and spacious outdoor side porch. Each morning a hearty breakfast featuring homemade jam is prepared by your hostess. Nearby places of interest include the factory outlet in Reading, the historical sites of Berks County, and the Pennsylvania Dutch country.

Smoketown Village Tourist Home
2495 OLD PHILADELPHIA PIKE, ROUTE 340, SMOKETOWN, PENNSYLVANIA 17576

Tel: **(717) 393-5975**
Host(s): **Paul and Margaret Reitz**
Location: **5 miles east of Lancaster**
No. of Rooms: **5**
Maximum No. of Guests Sharing
Bath: **5**
Double/sb: **$13–$15**
Single/sb: **$13**

Months of Operation: **All year**
Reduced Rates: **No**
Breakfast: **No**
Air-Conditioning: **Yes**
Pets: **No**
Children: **Welcome (crib)**
Smoking: **Permitted**
Social Drinking: **Permitted**

A stately brick colonial with white shutters, surrounded by lush lawns, this lovely home is graced with a comfortable porch where you may relax after touring the local sights. You are welcome to store your breakfast makings in the guest refrigerator, use the kitchen to prepare it, and enjoy it on the picnic table while breathing in the clean, country air.

Fairhaven
RD 12, BOX 445, YORK, PENNSYLVANIA 17406

Tel: **(717) 252-3726**
Host(s): **Adelaide and George Price**
Location: **10 miles east of York**
No. of Rooms: **3**
Maximum No. of Guests Sharing
Bath: **6**
Double/sb: **$30**
Single/sb: **$20**
Months of Operation: **All year**

Reduced Rates: **10%, November to
March; 10%, seniors; 15%, families**
Breakfast: **Full**
Air-Conditioning: **No**
Pets: **Sometimes**
Children: **Welcome (crib)**
Smoking: **No**
Social Drinking: **No**

Relax in an old German farmhouse furnished with treasures handed down for generations. A bountiful breakfast, featuring homemade goodies and eggs fresh from the henhouse, is prepared on an antique stove. Take a dip in the pool or visit where history was made in Gettysburg or York. Visit Lancaster for museums and local attractions, Hershey's Chocolate World, and numerous outlet shops.

Memory Lane Bed & Breakfast
1950 MEMORY LANE, YORK, PENNSYLVANIA 17402

Tel: **(717) 755-7409**
Host(s): **Patricia Wilson**
No. of Rooms: **2**
Maximum No. of Guests Sharing
  Bath: **4**
Double/sb: **$35**
Single/sb: **$30**
Months of Operation: **All year**

Reduced Rates: **No**
Breakfast: **Full**
Air-Conditioning: **Yes**
Pets: **Sometimes**
Children: **Welcome**
Smoking: **No**
Social Drinking: **Permitted**
Foreign Languages: **Spanish**

Come to the nation's first capital and enjoy this gray stone English country house surrounded by lovely trees. The newly decorated upstairs bedrooms offer ample space and comfort. Breakfast is always hearty and is served in a nook that overlooks a vista of birds, trees, and pasture. If you wish to cut down on expenses, feel free to use the guest refrigerator, gas barbecue, and picnic table. Patricia has extensive collections of Will Rogers memorabilia and first editions of contemporary writers.

PHILADELPHIA AREA

Bed & Breakfast of Philadelphia
P.O. BOX 101, ORELAND, PENNSYLVANIA 19075

Tel: **(215) 884-1084**
Coordinator: **Janet Mochel**
States/Regions Covered:
  **Pennsylvania—Berwyn, Chadds
Ford, Chester Springs, Doylestown,
New Hope, Philadelphia,
Wallingford, Wayne; New
Jersey—Cherry Hill, Moorestown**

Rates (Single/Double):
  Modest: **$18**   **$25**
  Average: **$25**   **$35**
  Luxury: **$35**   **$45 and up**
Credit Cards: **MC, VISA**

Janet's selection of accommodations varies from a Society Hill town house, a sedate row home near the university, a suburban manor house, a modern ranch, a colonial farmhouse in Bucks County, or a house in the hunt country. Philadelphia is the City of Brotherly Love, and you will be made to feel like "family" in all the B&Bs. Please send three dollars for a descriptive directory.

Bed & Breakfast—Center City
1908 SPRUCE STREET, PHILADELPHIA, PENNSYLVANIA 19103

	Rates (Single/Double):	
Tel: **(215) 735-0881, 735-1137 or 923-5459**		
	Modest: **$25**	**$35**
Coordinator: **Nancy Frenze, Stella Pomerantz**	Average: **$30–$35**	**$40–$45**
	Luxury: **$40–$50**	**$50–$55**
States/Regions Covered: **Philadelphia**	Credit Cards: **No**	

Lodgings range from Dickensian-type houses in lamplit cobblestone courtyards, to restored town houses, to elegant high-rise apartments with spectacular views of the city, and the entire spectrum between. There are unique and charming homes in the best sections of the city including Society Hill, Rittenhouse Square, Antique Row, University City, and Fitler Square. All are within easy reach of theaters, museums, fine restaurants, elegant shops, and galleries.

Bed & Breakfast of Chester County
P.O. BOX 825, KENNETT SQUARE, PENNSYLVANIA 19348

	Rates (Single/Double):	
Tel: **(215) 444-1367**		
Coordinator: **Doris Passante**	Modest: **$18–$20**	**$25–$30**
States/Regions Covered: **Chester County**	Average: **$21–$30**	**$31–$40**
	Luxury: **$31–$40**	**$41–$50**
	Credit Cards: **No**	

Doris has a wide selection of homes located in the beautiful and historic Brandywine Valley, which is known for the River Museum, Brandywine Battlefield, and Valley Forge. The area is convenient to Winterthur as well as the Pennsylvania Dutch Country. Send for her brochure which fully describes each B&B.

Mrs. K's
404 RIDGE AVENUE, KENNETT SQUARE, PENNSYLVANIA 19348

Tel: **(215) 444-5559** or **(302) 478-3000**
Host(s): **Charlotte Kanofsky**
Location: **30 miles south of Philadelphia**
No. of Rooms: **2**
Maximum No. of Guests Sharing Bath: **4**
Double/sb: **$25–$30**
Single/sb: **$18**

Months of Operation: **All year**
Reduced Rates: **No**
Breakfast: **Full**
Air-Conditioning: **Yes**
Pets: **No**
Children: **Welcome, over 6**
Smoking: **No**
Social Drinking: **Permitted**

Arriving guests are greeted with cheese, crackers, and appropriate beverages. Charlotte delights in people and this has made her guest-house business a labor of love. Her lovely home is on a quiet residential street but close to many attractions. This is Andrew Wyeth's territory (Chadds Ford). Longwood Gardens, Brandywine Battlefield, and Brandywine River Museum are all worthwhile stops to make. It's less than a half-hour from Wilmington, Delaware, home of the Hagley and Natural History museums as well as Winterthur. You are welcome to use the kitchen for snacks, and the laundry facilities.

POCONO MOUNTAINS

Bed & Breakfast Pocono Northeast
P.O. BOX 115, BEAR CREEK, PENNSYLVANIA 18602

Tel: **(717) 472-3045**
Coordinator: **Ann Magagna**
States/Regions Covered: **Bartonsville, Bushkill, Honesdale, Milford, Mountainhome, Paupack, Stroudsburg, Tobyhanna, Wilkes-Barre**

Rates (Single/Double):

Modest:	**$12**	**$24**
Average:	**$20**	**$30**
Luxury:	**$35**	**$50**

Credit Cards: **No**

The above is merely a partial listing of the area covered by this registry. A variety of accommodations has been chosen by Ann for visitors coming to the northeastern corner of the state. Whatever your recreational bent, you are certain to find it, in all seasons, in this land of fresh air and mountain beauty. From skiing to water and land sports, antiquing, country fairs, theater, historic sites, fine restaurants, and handcraft shops. Business travelers, vacationers, and visitors to the renowned Geisinger and Robert Packer medical centers will all be made to feel perfectly at home.

Dreamy Acres
P.O. BOX 7, SEESE HILL ROAD, CANADENSIS, PENNSYLVANIA 18325

Tel: **(717) 595-7115**
Host(s): **Esther and Bill Pickett**
Location: **16 miles north of Stroudsburg**
No. of Rooms: **6**
No. of Private Baths: **4**
Maximum No. of Guests Sharing Bath: **4**
Double/pb: **$32–$34**
Single/pb: **$32–$34**
Double/sb: **$28**

Single/sb: **$28**
Guest Cottage: **$38 sleeps 4**
Months of Operation: **All year**
Reduced Rates: **No**
Breakfast: **Continental**
Air-Conditioning: **No**
Pets: **No**
Children: **Welcome, over 4**
Smoking: **Permitted**
Social Drinking: **Permitted**

Situated in the heart of the Pocono Mountains, this comfortably furnished 100-year-old lodge is on over three acres, with a stream and a pond. Year-round recreation includes fishing, tennis, state parks, golf, horseback riding, skiing, and skating. There are many fine restaurants, boutiques, and churches in the area. Esther and Bill have been successfully entertaining guests for over 23 years, and their motto is: "You are a stranger here but once."

Nearbrook
ROUTE 447, CANADENSIS, PENNSYLVANIA 18325

Tel: **(717) 595-3152**
Host(s): **Barbie and Rick Robinson**
No. of Rooms: **4**
Maximum No. of Guests Sharing Bath: **4**
Double/sb: **$25–$30**
Single/sb: **$15**
Months of Operation: **All year**

Reduced Rates: **No**
Breakfast: **Full**
Air-Conditioning: **Unnecessary**
Pets: **Sometimes**
Children: **Welcome**
Smoking: **No**
Social Drinking: **Permitted**
Airport Pickup: **Yes**

Barbie and Dick have a lovely home that stands in a natural setting; their artistic talent is evident in both the landscaping and in the house. Meander through the rock gardens and down a wooded path to a secluded mountain stream. Or, enjoy the beautiful hiking trails and nearby Buck Hill Falls. The Robinsons will help you plan sightseeing to suit your individual preferences.

La Anna Guest House
R.D. 2, BOX 1051, CRESCO, PENNSYLVANIA 18326

Tel: **(717) 676-4225 (after 6:00 PM)**
Host(s): **Kay and Julie Swingle**
Location: **90 miles northwest of New York City**
No. of Rooms: **4**
Maximum No. of Guests Sharing Bath: **4**
Double/sb: **$20**
Single/sb: **$12**

Months of Operation: **All year**
Reduced Rates: **Families**
Breakfast: **Continental**
Air-Conditioning: **No**
Pets: **Welcome**
Children: **Welcome (crib)**
Smoking: **Permitted**
Social Drinking: **Permitted**

This Victorian home has large rooms furnished in antiques; it is nestled on 25 acres of lush, wooded land, and has its own pond. Kay will happily direct you to fine dining spots that are kind to your wallet. You will enjoy scenic walks, waterfalls, mountain vistas, Tobyhanna and Promised Land state parks; there's cross-country skiing right on the property. Lake Wallenpaupack is only 15 minutes away.

The Mountain House
**P.O. BOX 253, MOUNTAIN ROAD, DELAWARE WATER GAP,
PENNSYLVANIA 18327**

Tel: **(717) 424-2254**
Host(s): **Frank and Yolanda Brown**
Location: **½ miles from I-80**
No. of Rooms: **32**
No. of Private Baths: **8**
Maximum No. of Guests Sharing
  Bath: **8**
Double/pb: **$35**
Single/pb: **$25**
Double/sb: **$30**
Single/sb: **$20**
Months of Operation: **All year**

Reduced Rates: **No**
Breakfast: **Continental**
Other Meals: **Available**
Credit Cards: **AMEX, DC, MC, VISA**
Air-Conditioning: **Yes**
Pets: **Sometimes**
Children: **Welcome (crib)**
Smoking: **Permitted**
Social Drinking: **Permitted**
Airport Pickup: **Yes**
Foreign Languages: **German**

This 1870 yellow clapboard inn has a huge screened-in veranda and is filled with rare antiques and lots of wicker. The parlor has a piano and rocking chairs, and the dining room has a fine display of exquisite cut glass. All the attractions of the Poconos are nearby. Delaware River sports are a block away and the house is on the Appalachian Trail. Frank and Yolanda are most cordial and welcome you to use the pool, shuffleboard court, washing machine, and dryer.

Trails End
R.D. 2 BOX 355A, GREENTOWN, PENNSYLVANIA 18426

Tel: **(717) 857-0856**
Host(s): **Betty and Bob Rundback**

No. of Rooms: **2**
No. of Private Baths: **1**

Maximum No. of Guests Sharing
Bath: **2**
Double/pb: **$40**
Single/pb: **$35**
Double/sb: **$35**
Single/sb: **$30**
Months of Operation: **All year**
Reduced Rates: **No**

Breakfast: **Full**
Air-Conditioning: **No**
Pets: **No**
Children: **Welcome, over 12**
Smoking: **Permitted**
Social Drinking: **Permitted**
Airport Pickup: **No**

Drive down a steep, wooded lane to this bi-level country home perched on a knoll. It boasts an unobstructed view of 17-mile Lake Wallenpaupack framed by the dramatic landscape of the mountains. The lake is the center of activity in all seasons. Summer offers swimming, picnicking, fishing, boating, and relaxing on the large deck or nearby island. Tennis, golf, and horse stables are nearby. Winter offers snowmobiling, downhill and cross-country skiing, and ice-fishing. After a day in the country air, you are invited to have a pre-dinner cocktail and complimentary cheese and crackers. When conditions permit, Betty and Bob will take you sailing or waterskiing.

White Cloud
R.D. 1, BOX 215, NEWFOUNDLAND, PENNSYLVANIA 18445

Tel: **(717) 676-3162**
Host(s): **George Wilkinson**
Location: **25 miles from Scranton**
No. of Rooms: **20**
No. of Baths: **6**
Maximum No. of Guests Sharing
Bath: **5**
Double/pb: **$41**
Single/pb: **$32**
Double/sb: **$31**
Single/sb: **$24**

Months of Operation: **All year**
Reduced Rates: **No**
Breakfast: **Continental**
Other Meals: **Available**
Credit Cards: **AMEX, MC, VISA, DC**
Air-Conditioning: **Unnecessary**
Pets: **Sometimes**
Children: **Welcome (crib)**
Smoking: **No**
Social Drinking: **Permitted**
Airport Pickup: **Yes**

This is a quiet country place where the emphasis is on natural, wholesome living. George has made this a haven away from the clatter of modern life. There's a pool and tennis court for your summer pleasure, and the surrounding area offers a spectrum of activities, including skiing in winter and all sports on 17-mile Lake Wallenpaupack. Accommodations are simple but comfortable. The dining room serves delicious meals. Fruits and vegetables are organically grown in season, and the homemade breads and herb teas are outstanding. No meat is served. The library features books on metaphysical and philosophical subjects.

L'Auberge—The Country Inn
BOX 30, SOUTH STERLING, PENNSYLVANIA 18460

Tel: **(717) 676-9400**	Reduced Rates: **10%, seniors**
Host(s): **Erhard Rohrmuller**	Breakfast: **Continental**
Location: **34 miles southeast of Scranton**	Other Meals: **Yes**
No. of Rooms: **4**	Credit Cards: **AMEX, MC, VISA**
Maximum No. of Guests Sharing Bath: **4**	Air-Conditioning: **Yes**
	Pets: **Sometimes**
Double/sb: **$32**	Children: **Welcome**
Single/sb: **$16**	Smoking: **No**
Months of Operation: **All year**	Social Drinking: **Permitted**
	Foreign Languages: **German**

This 100-year-old cedar-shake country inn adds a touch of French-style class to the Poconos. The accent is on French cuisine, exquisitely prepared and served in an intimate setting. It is only eight miles to Lake Wallenpaupack for recreational sports in all seasons. Erhard is the *chef-de-cuisine* as well as an antique buff. You can visit famous Holly Ross pottery for demonstrations of tableware being made.

SCRANTON AREA

The Bodine House
307 SOUTH MAIN STREET, MUNCY, PENNSYLVANIA 17756

Tel: **(717) 546-8949**	Months of Operation: **All year**
Host(s): **David and Marie Louise Smith**	Reduced Rates: **No**
Location: **85 miles north of Harrisburg**	Breakfast: **Full**
No. of Rooms: **3**	Other Meals: **Available**
Maximum No. of Guests Sharing Bath: **4**	Air-Conditioning: **No**
	Pets: **No**
Double/sb: **$25–$30**	Children: **Welcome**
Single/sb: **$20**	Smoking: **Permitted**
	Social Drinking: **Permitted**

This restored town house dates back to 1805. A baby grand piano, four fireplaces, and a candlelit living room add to its old-fash-

ioned appeal. A full country breakfast and wine and cheese are on the house; a light supper is served by arrangement. Local attractions include the Susquehanna River, the Endless Mountains, and the fall foliage.

Anderson Acres
R.D. 1, STEVENS LAKE, TUNKHANNOCK, PENNSYLVANIA 18657

Tel: **(717) 836-5228**
Host(s): **John and Doris Anderson**
Location: **26 miles west of Scranton, 4 miles from Route 6**
No. of Rooms: **2**
No. of Private Baths: **1**
Maximum No. of Guests Sharing Bath: **4**
Double/pb: **$25**
Single/pb: **$20**

Double/sb: **$25**
Single/sb: **$20**
Months of Operation: **All year**
Reduced Rates: **No**
Breakfast: **Continental**
Air-Conditioning: **No**
Pets: **Yes**
Children: **Welcome**
Smoking: **Permitted**
Social Drinking: **Permitted**

This 45-acre hobby farm is located in the Endless Mountains. The farm animals are kept in the barn area and the children will surely want to visit them. In town, five minutes away, there is a theater, roller skating rink, and golf course. The house has a lovely view of Steven's Lake. It's a 40-minute ride to the ski slopes at Elk Mountain.

Powder Mill Farms
BOX 294B, UNION DALE, PENNSYLVANIA 18470

Tel: **(717) 679-2425**
Host(s): **Jeanne and Paul Spillane**
Location: **35 miles north of Scranton**
No. of Rooms: **2**
Maximum No. of Guests Sharing
Bath: **4**
Double/sb: **$30**
Single/sb: **$15**

Months of Operation: **All year**
Reduced Rates: **10%, families**
Breakfast: **Full**
Air-Conditioning: **Yes**
Pets: **Sometimes**
Children: **Welcome**
Smoking: **Permitted**
Social Drinking: **Permitted**

Jeanne and Paul offer warm hospitality and country comfort in a picturesque 1826 home that is filled with cut glass and fine antiques. Nestled in the Endless Mountains, it's only three miles to Elk Mountain for great skiing. This colonial gray home is surrounded by 42 wooded acres, a fishing pond, a bubbling trout stream, and lovely country trails. You are welcome to store your snacks in the guest refrigerator.

SOUTH-CENTRAL PENNSYLVANIA

County Cousins Bed & Breakfast Registry
228 WEST MAIN STREET, WAYNESBORO, PENNSYLVANIA 17268

Tel: **(717) 762-2722**
Coordinator: **Karen Ingraham Bercaw**
States/Regions Covered:
  Pennsylvania—Carlisle, Fairfield, Mercerberg, Red Lyon, Shippensburg, Wrightsville; West Virginia—Gerrardstown, Summit Point

Rates (Single/Double):
Modest:	**$25**	**$30**
Average:	**$30**	**$36**
Luxury:	**$42**	**$50**

Credit Cards: **No**

Karen covers south central Pennsylvania from the Susquehanna River to Bedford. Attractions of the area include historic sites, auctions, recreational activities, and a variety of good restaurants. Church suppers and county fairs offer you the opportunity to make new friends.

WESTERN PENNSYLVANIA

Rest & Repast Bed & Breakfast Service
P.O. BOX 126, PINE GROVE MILLS, PENNSYLVANIA 16868

Tel: **(814) 238-1484**
Coordinator: **Linda Feltman, Brant Peters**
States/Regions Covered: **Penn State College Area**
Rates (Single/Double):
  Average: **$20–$27 $28–$37**
Credit Cards: **No**

You will enjoy touring historic mansions, Penns Cave, Woodward Cave, and several Civil War museums in this lovely area of Pennsylvania State College. A two-day minimum stay is required for the second week in July, the time of the annual Central Pennsylvania Festival of the Arts and the Penn State University Homecoming Football game in autumn; both events draw thousands of people. Rates are increased ten dollars per night during football weekends only.

Pittsburgh Bed & Breakfast
P.O. BOX 25353, PITTSBURGH, PENNSYLVANIA 15242

Tel: **(412) 241-5746**
Coordinator: **Karen Krull**
States/Regions Covered: **Pittsburgh and western Pennsylvania**

Rates (Single/Double):
  Modest: **$18 $25**
  Average: **$28 $35**
  Luxury: **$35 $45**
Credit Cards: **No**

Karen has many comfortable accommodations in the historic Northside, Southside, Shadyside, Squirrel Hill, and Mount Washington areas. Many homes are convenient to the Carnegie-Mellon University, Duquesne, and the University of Pittsburgh. This is a great place to stop off en route to Cleveland (80 miles), Chicago (400 miles), and West Virginia (4 miles).

Das Tannen-Lied (The Singing Pines)
1195 EAST LAKE ROAD, JAMESTOWN, PENNSYLVANIA 16134

Tel: **(412) 932-5029**
Host(s): **Marion Duecker**
Location: **85 miles north of Pittsburgh**
No. of Rooms: **2**
Maximum No. of Guests Sharing
    Bath: **4**
Double/sb: **$30**
Single/sb: **$25**

Months of Operation: **April 2 to
    October 31**
Reduced Rates: **No**
Breakfast: **Full**
Air-Conditioning: **No**
Pets: **No**
Children: **Welcome, over 10**
Smoking: **Permitted**
Social Drinking: **Permitted**

This Victorian home, built in 1872, is set on the shore of Pymatuning Lake, which offers many recreational activities. Or, you may simply sit on the big front porch and watch the boats go by. Marion is a retired home economics teacher and dietitian, and on advance notice she will prepare picnic baskets, lunch, or dinner at reasonable prices. You are welcome to play the piano, browse in her library, and enjoy a cool beverage whenever you wish.

―――――――― KEY TO LISTINGS ――――――――

Location: As specified, unless B&B is right in town, or its location is clear from address as stated.
No. of Rooms: Refers to the number of guest bedrooms.
Double: Rate for two people in one room.
Single: Rate for one person in a room.
Suite: Can either be two bedrooms with an adjoining bath, or a living room and bedroom with private bath.
Guest Cottage: A separate building that usually has a mini-kitchen and private bath.
pb: Private bath.
sb: Shared bath.
Breakfast: Included, unless otherwise noted.
Air-Conditioning: If "no" or "unnecessary" is stated, it means the climate rarely warrants it.
Children: If "crib" is noted after the word "welcome," this indicates that the host also has a high-chair, baby-sitters are available, and the B&B can accommodate children under the age of three.
Smoking: If permitted, this means it is allowed *somewhere* inside the house.
Social Drinking: Some hosts provide a glass of wine or sherry; others provide setups for bring-your-own.

―――――――

Please enclose a self-addressed, stamped, business-size envelope when contacting Reservation Services.

―――――――

Remember the difference in time zones when calling for a reservation.

RHODE ISLAND

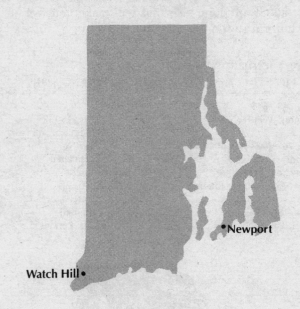

•Newport

Watch Hill•

House of Snee
191 OCEAN ROAD, NARRAGANSETT, RHODE ISLAND 02882

Tel: **(401) 783-9494**
Host(s): **Mildred Snee**
Location: **15 miles southeast of Newport**
No. of Rooms: **2**
Maximum No. of Guests Sharing Bath: **4**
Double/pb: **n/a**
Single/pb: **n/a**
Double/sb: **$35**

Single/sb: **$35**
Months of Operation: **All year**
Reduced Rates: **10%, seniors**
Breakfast: **Full**
Air-Conditioning: **No**
Pets: **No**
Children: **Welcome**
Smoking: **Permitted**
Social Drinking: **Permitted**

This century-old Dutch colonial overlooks the waters of Rhode Island Sound. It's just across the street from the fishing pier where you can buy tackle and anything else you need to hook a big one. It's a mile to the beach and just minutes from the Block Island Ferry. Mildred's kitchen is her kingdom and her breakfast often features delicious specialties such as crepes, johnnycake, and Scotch ham. You are welcome to use the laundry facilities and just about anything else that will make you feel at home. Winery tours are a fun diversion in the area.

Brinley Victorian
23 BRINLEY STREET, NEWPORT, RHODE ISLAND 02840

Tel: **(401) 849-7645**
Host(s): **Amy Weintraub, Edwina Sebest**
Location: **70 miles south of Boston**
No. of Rooms: **17**
No. of Private Baths: **8**
Maximum No. of Guests Sharing Bath: **6**
Double/pb: **$55–$65**
Double/sb: **$45–$55**

Suites: **$75**
Guest Cottage: **$150 sleeps 4**
Months of Operation: **All year**
Reduced Rates: **No**
Breakfast: **Continental**
Air-Conditioning: **No**
Pets: **No**
Children: **Welcome, over 12**
Smoking: **Permitted**
Social Drinking: **Permitted**

Located in the prestigious Kay Street and Bellevue Avenue area, this lovely home offers the charm of the Victorian era, plus contemporary comfort and a convenient central location. It's an easy walk to the mansions, harbor, quaint shops, restaurants, and historic sites. Amy and Edwina prepare a delightful breakfast to start your day and appropriate beverages are always available.

Hartley's Guest House
LARKIN ROAD, WATCH HILL, RHODE ISLAND 02891

Tel: **(401) 348-8253**
Host(s): **Elizabeth Flynn Reilly**
Location: **Route 95 to Westerly**
No. of Rooms: **10**
No. of Private Baths: **2**
Maximum No. of Guests Sharing
  Bath: **4**
Double/pb: **$45–$50**
Single/pb: **$30–$35**
Double/sb: **$40–$45**

Single/sb: **$20–$25**
Months of Operation: **All year**
Reduced Rates: **Available**
Breakfast: **Continental ($1.50)**
Air-Conditioning: **No**
Pets: **No**
Children: **Welcome, over 5**
Smoking: **Permitted**
Social Drinking: **Permitted**

Located between two beaches on the ocean side, this large, immaculate home has television and reading rooms, and a spacious porch from which to contemplate the gorgeous ocean view. A quaint shopping village and the oldest carousel in America are only a short walk from the front door. Elizabeth will be happy to recommend the best values for dining in the area.

KEY TO LISTINGS

Location: As specified, unless B&B is right in town, or its location is clear from address as stated.
No. of Rooms: Refers to the number of guest bedrooms.
Double: Rate for two people in one room.
Single: Rate for one person in a room.
Suite: Can either be two bedrooms with an adjoining bath, or a living room and bedroom with private bath.
Guest Cottage: A separate building that usually has a mini-kitchen and private bath.
pb: Private bath.
sb: Shared bath.
Breakfast: Included, unless otherwise noted.
Air-Conditioning: If "no" or "unnecessary" is stated, it means the climate rarely warrants it.
Children: If "crib" is noted after the word "welcome," this indicates that the host also has a high-chair, baby-sitters are available, and the B&B can accommodate children under the age of three.
Smoking: If permitted, this means it is allowed *somewhere* inside the house.
Social Drinking: Some hosts provide a glass of wine or sherry; others provide setups for bring-your-own.

Please enclose a self-addressed, stamped, business-size envelope when contacting Reservation Services.

Remember the difference in time zones when calling for a reservation.

SOUTH CAROLINA

Salem • •Easley

•Camden

Dale • •Charleston
•Beaufort

Hilton Head Island

The Inn
1310 BROAD STREET, CAMDEN, SOUTH CAROLINA 29020

Tel: **(803) 425-1806**
Host(s): **John and Katherine DeLoach**
Location: **32 miles northeast of Columbia, 3 miles from I-20**
No. of Rooms: **8**
No. of Private Baths: **8**
Double/pb: **$65–$85**
Single/pb: **$45–$70**
Guest Cottage: **n/a**
Months of Operation: **All year**

Reduced Rates: **June 1 to September 1, $45–$65 (double); $40–$55 (single)**
Breakfast: **Continental**
Credit Cards: **M/C, VISA**
Air-Conditioning: **Yes**
Pets: **Sometimes**
Children: **Welcome, over 10**
Smoking: **Permitted**
Social Drinking: **Permitted**

Located in the center of the historic district are the two houses that comprise the inn. One was built in 1905, the other in 1890. In renovating, refurbishing, and redecorating, care was taken to adhere to the original styles. There are a multitude of sports activities as well as interesting home and garden tours. The

306

Carolina Cup and Colonial Cup steeplechase races are held in the spring and fall, respectively.

The Coach House
39 EAST BATTERY, CHARLESTON, SOUTH CAROLINA 29401

Tel: **(803) 722-8145**	Breakfast: **Continental**
Host(s): **Lorna Colbert**	Air-Conditioning: **Yes**
Location: **3 miles from I-29**	Pets: **No**
No. of Rooms: **2 suites**	Children: **Welcome**
No. of Private Baths: **2**	Smoking: **Permitted**
Suites: **$65 (for 2)**	Social Drinking: **Permitted**
Months of Operation: **All year**	Foreign Languages: **French**
Reduced Rates: **10%, December**	

The first-floor suite has a bedroom with a queen-size canopy bed, a kitchen, dining area, patio, and garden designed by Loutrell Briggs. The second-floor bedroom has twin beds, living room with a sofa bed, and piazza overlooking Charleston Harbor. There's color TV, lots of books, complimentary champagne, and a lovely view. Lorna will direct you to Fort Sumter, delightful restaurants, and shops, and will suggest other activities to make your visit special.

Holland's Guest House
15 NEW STREET, CHARLESTON, SOUTH CAROLINA 29401

Tel: **(803) 723-0090**	Reduced Rates: **Weekly, $300**
Host(s): **Betty and Wallace Holland**	Breakfast: **Full**
Location: **1½ miles from I-26**	Air-Conditioning: **Yes**
No. of Rooms: **1**	Pets: **No**
No. of Private Baths: **1**	Children: **No**
Guest Cottage: **$50 sleeps 2**	Smoking: **Permitted**
Months of Operation: **All year**	Social Drinking: **Permitted**

Betty and Wallace live in the historic district, a short distance from the downtown area. Attached to their 100-year-old house is a newly renovated guest cottage. It has a small kitchen stocked with breakfast foods and snacks, and an enclosed porch with an eating area. The bedroom, private bath, phone, and TV are perfect for travelers seeking home-style living and a little privacy. Complimentary wine and cheese are part of the southern hospitality.

Coosaw Plantation
DALE, SOUTH CAROLINA 29914

Tel: (803) 846-8225
Host(s): **Peggy Sanford**
Location: **50 miles south of Charleston**
No. of Rooms: **4**
No. of Private Baths: **3**
Double/pb: **$35**
Single/pb: **$30**
Guest Cottage: **$40 sleeps 4**
Months of Operation: **March to December**

Reduced Rates: **No**
Breakfast: **Continental**
Air-Conditioning: **Yes**
Pets: **Sometimes**
Children: **Welcome, over 12**
Smoking: **Permitted**
Social Drinking: **Permitted**
Airport Pickup: **Yes**
Foreign Languages: **Spanish, French**

This sprawling plantation offers a relaxed setting on the Coosaw River. Each guest cottage has a living room with fireplace, a full kitchen, and a bath. Your hosts will prepare a breakfast of muffins or casseroles, or will leave the fixings in your cottage. In winter, enjoy a hunting party led by an experienced guide. Boating, fishing, or a visit to Beaufort and Savannah are just a few of the local possibilities.

The Lydays
301 EAST THIRD AVENUE, EASLEY, SOUTH CAROLINA 29640

Tel: (803) 859-4176
Host(s): **Dr. and Mrs. Jim Lyday**
Location: **12 miles from I-85**
No. of Rooms: **2**
Maximum No. of Guests Sharing Bath: **4**
Double/sb: **$25**
Single/sb: **$25**
Suites: **$40**

Months of Operation: **All year**
Reduced Rates: **No**
Breakfast: **Continental**
Other Meals: **Available**
Air-Conditioning: **Yes**
Pets: **No**
Children: **Welcome**
Smoking: **Permitted**
Social Drinking: **Permitted**

This gracious home with its handsome columns is located in the foothills of the Blue Ridge Mountains. Table Rock and Keowee state parks are nearby as are several lakes for water sports and mountain trails for hiking. It's convenient to Greenville for cultural events, nightlife, and fine restaurants. Mrs. Lyday will advise you where the bargain factory outlets are to be found.

Halcyon
604 HARBOUR MASTER, SHIPYARD PLANTATION, HILTON HEAD ISLAND, SOUTH CAROLINA 29928

Tel: **(803) 785-7912**
Host(s): **Maybelle Wayburn**
Location: **40 miles north of Savannah, Georgia**
No. of Rooms: **1**
No. of Private Baths: **1**
Double/pb: **$65**
Months of Operation: **All year**
Reduced Rates: **20%, November 1 to March 14**

Breakfast: **Continental**
Other Meals: **Available**
Air-Conditioning: **Yes**
Pets: **No**
Children: **No**
Smoking: **Permitted**
Social Drinking: **Permitted**
Airport Pickup: **Yes**

Translate the word "Halcyon" and you get what is offered here—tranquility. Your hostess, an experienced tour guide, will provide information on shopping and sightseeing in Beaufort and Charleston, as well as advise on local restaurants. Visitors are welcomed with sherry; everything from cocktails to picnic baskets is available. Biking, tennis, golf, and the beach are nearby.

A Country Place
ROUTE 1, BOX 239, SALEM, SOUTH CAROLINA 27676

Tel: **(803) 944-0477**
Host(s): **Polly Medlicott, Manfred Mueller**
Location: **30 miles from I-85**
No. of Rooms: **4**
Maximum No. of Guests Sharing Bath: **3**
Double/sb: **$25**
Single/sb: **$15**
Guest Cottage: **$70–$100 sleeps 6 to 8**

Months of Operation: **February to November**
Reduced Rates: **Weekly**
Breakfast: **Full**
Air-Conditioning: **Yes**
Pets: **Sometimes**
Children: **Welcome**
Smoking: **Permitted**
Social Drinking: **Permitted**
Foreign Languages: **German**

If you have ever wanted your own place in the country, this will come close. There are 100 acres of meadows, woods, and streams, a fish pond and a cedar-shingled farmhouse with a long porch for relaxing. Polly and Manfred live next door and have stocked "your home" with fresh breakfast ingredients as well as such conveniences as a dishwasher, washer, and dryer. It's 10 minutes to state parks, lakes, Whitewater Falls, and the Chattooga River. Don't miss local activities like country music concerts, antiquing, and craft fairs.

SOUTH DAKOTA

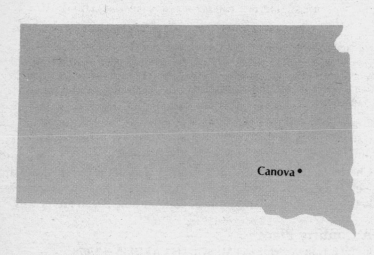

Canova •

Skoglund Farm
CANOVA, SOUTH DAKOTA 57321

Tel: **(605) 247-3445**
Host(s): **Alden and Delores Skoglund**
Location: **12 miles from I-90**
No. of Rooms: **5**
Maximum No. of Guests Sharing
Bath: **3**
Double/sb: **$40**
Single/sb: **$20**
Months of Operation: **All year**

Reduced Rates: **No**
Breakfast: **Full**
Other Meals: **Dinner included**
Air-Conditioning: **No**
Pets: **Welcome**
Children: **Welcome (crib)**
Smoking: **Permitted**
Social Drinking: **Permitted**
Airport Pickup: **Yes**

This is a working farm where the emphasis is on the simple good life. It is a welcome escape from the canned music and plastic environment of urban living. You may, if you wish, help with the farm chores, or just watch everyone else work; the family raises cattle, fowl, and peacocks. You may use the kitchen for light snacks if you can still eat after one of Delores's meals! You are welcome to use the laundry facilities or play the piano. The coffee pot is always on.

TENNESSEE

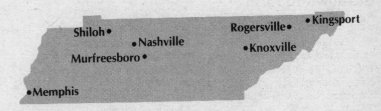

Bed & Breakfast in Memphis
P.O. BOX 41621, MEMPHIS, TENNESSEE 38174

Tel: **(901) 726-5920**	Rates (Single/Double):
Coordinator: **Helen Denton**	Modest: **$21** **$27**
States/Regions Covered:	Average: **$26** **$32**
Tennessee—Bolivar, Cordova,	Luxury: **$34–$80** **$40–$80**
Germantown, Memphis, Nashville;	Credit Cards: **MC, VISA**
Arkansas—Horseshoe Lake;	
Mississippi—Tupelo	

A sampler of Memphis sights includes the mighty Mississippi River, Mud Island, historic Beale Street, Victorian Village, Memphis Brooks Art Gallery, and Overton Park and Zoo. Helen will send you a descriptive listing of all the accommodations offered by her hosts. The $2.50 directory charge will be credited to your reservation; please note that there is a five-dollar surcharge for one-night stays.

Nashville Host Homes (a B&B Group)
P.O. BOX 110227, NASHVILLE, TENNESSEE 37222

Tel: **(615) 331-5244**	Rates (Single/Double):
Coordinator: **Fredda Odom**	Average: **$26–$32** **$26–$32**
States/Regions Covered: **Nashville**	Credit Cards: **MC, VISA**

Nashville is the home of the Grand Ole Opry and Opryland, U.S.A. Middle Tennessee offers a diversity of attractions, including Vanderbilt University and Medical School, several Civil War sites, and other historic restorations. Fredda will arrange sightseeing tours, car rentals, tickets to events, and do everything she can to assure you a pleasant stay.

Shallowford Farm
ROUTE 6, BOX 142, KINGSPORT, TENNESSEE 37660

Tel: **(615) 245-0798**
Host(s): **Jane and Bill Walley**
Location: **15 miles from I-81**
No. of Rooms: **2**
Maximum No. of Guests Sharing
  Bath: **4**
Double/sb: **$30**
Single/sb: **$25**

Months of Operation: **All year**
Reduced Rates: **No**
Breakfast: **Full**
Air-Conditioning: **Yes**
Pets: **Sometimes**
Children: **Welcome**
Smoking: **No**
Social Drinking: **Permitted**

This Dutch colonial overlooking the hills is part of a small farm with cattle, chickens, and places to fish. Guests will enjoy relaxing on the porch or by the swimming pool. A breakfast featuring fresh eggs, jams, and jellies is served in winter by the fireside, outdoors in warmer weather. The Bays Mountain Nature Center, craft shows, and Historic Netherland Inn are nearby.

Three Chimneys of Knoxville
1302 WHITE AVENUE, KNOXVILLE, TENNESSEE 37916

Tel: **(615) 521-4970**
Host(s): **Alfred and Margo Akerman**
Location: **½ mile from I-40**
No. of Rooms: **4**
No. of Private Baths: **2**
Maximum No. of Guests Sharing
  Bath: **2**
Double/pb: **$50**
Single/pb: **$45**
Double/sb: **$40–$45**

Single/sb: **$35–$40**
Months of Operation: **All year**
Reduced Rates: **No**
Breakfast: **Full**
Air-Conditioning: **Yes**
Pets: **No**
Children: **Welcome**
Smoking: **Permitted**
Social Drinking: **Permitted**
Foreign Languages: **French, German**

This Queen Anne Victorian mansion is located in an historic neighborhood near the University of Tennessee campus. The

large guest rooms are carpeted and furnished in antiques. Breakfast is served on a glassed-in porch; a magnolia blooms nearby beginning in May. Breakfast may include grits, biscuits, wheat pancakes, and southern cured bacon; the coffee pot starts perking at dawn for early risers.

Clardy's Guest House
435 EAST MAIN STREET, MURFREESBORO, TENNESSEE 37130

Tel: **(615) 893-6030**
Host(s): **Frank Clardy**
Location: **2 miles from I-24**
No. of Rooms: **8**
No. of Private Baths: **6**
Maximum No. of Guests Sharing
  Bath: **4**
Double/pb: **$17.50**
Single/pb: **$12.50**
Double/sb: **$12.50**

Single/sb: **$10.00**
Months of Operation: **All year**
Reduced Rates: **No**
Breakfast: **No**
Air-Conditioning: **Yes**
Pets: **Yes**
Children: **Welcome**
Smoking: **Permitted**
Social Drinking: **Permitted**

This Romanesque-style Victorian dates back to 1898. The 20 rooms are filled with antiques; with 40 antique dealers in town, you can guess what Murfreesboro is best known for. The world championship horse show at Shelbyville is 30 minutes away. Your host will be glad to advise on local tours and can direct you to the home of Grand Ole Opry, one hour away in Nashville.

Miss Anne's Bed & Breakfast
3033 WINDEMERE CIRCLE, NASHVILLE, TENNESSEE 37214

Tel: **(615) 885-1899**
Host(s): **Anne Cowell**
Location: **2 miles from I-40**
No. of Rooms: **4**
No. of Private Baths: **1**
Maximum No. of Guests Sharing
  Bath: **4**
Double/pb: **$27**
Single/pb: **$24**
Double/sb: **$24**
Single/sb: **$21**

Months of Operation: **All year**
Reduced Rates: **15% weekly; 10%,**
  November to March; 10%, seniors
Breakfast: **Full**
Air-Conditioning: **Yes**
Pets: **No**
Children: **Welcome**
Smoking: **Permitted**
Social Drinking: **Permitted**
Airport Pickup: **Yes**

Visiting Anne is easy and pleasant in her comfortable home furnished with a cozy blend of antiques and lots of wood and glass. Her collection of doll dishes is quite special. Breakfast features such delectables as French toast, German pancakes, and homemade raspberry preserves. Opryland, the Hermitage, and the Parthenon are all nearby.

Hale Springs Inn
ROGERSVILLE, TENNESSEE 37857

Tel: **(615) 272-5171**
Host(s): **Lola Moore, Captain Carl**
  Netherland Brown
Location: **60 miles northeast of**
  Knoxville
No. of Rooms: **10**
No. of Private Baths: **10**
Double/pb: **$35–$55**
Single/pb: **$30-$50**
Months of Operation: **All year**

Reduced Rates: **No**
Breakfast: **Continental**
Other Meals: **Available**
Credit Cards: **MC, VISA**
Air-Conditioning: **Yes**
Pets: **Sometimes**
Children: **Welcome**
Smoking: **Permitted**
Social Drinking: **Permitted**
Foreign Languages: **Spanish**

This three-story federal home dates from 1824. George Washington did not sleep here, but Andrew Jackson did, when the inn was the headquarters of the Union Army. Large, high-ceilinged rooms with fireplaces, antiques, and four-poster beds continue the hosting tradition. Guests will enjoy touring the rest of the historic district. Davy Crockett's home, Lake Cherokee, and the Smoky Mountains are nearby.

TEXAS

Sand Dollar Hospitality B&B
3605 MENDENHALL, CORPUS CHRISTI, TEXAS 78415

Tel: **(512) 853-1222**
Coordination: **Pat Hirsbrunner**
States/Regions Covered: **Corpus Christi**

Rates (Single/Double):
Modest:	**$20–$23**	**$25–$30**
Average:	**$30**	**$35**
Luxury:	**$40**	**$50**

Credit Cards: **No**

Enjoy southern hospitality in this sparkling city-by-the-sea, touted as the Texas Riviera. It combines urban life with an abundance of outdoor pleasures. There's the Padre Island National Seashore. Go crabbing in Bird Island. Visit King Ranch, with its real cowboys, or the art colony of Rockport. Shopping in Mexico is only 2½ hours away by car. Take in an evening at the symphony or participate in genuine country and western dancing. Great Mexican food, barbecue, fresh fish, and shrimp are regional specialties.

Bed & Breakfast Texas Style
4224 W. RED BIRD LANE, DALLAS, TEXAS 75237

Tel: **(214) 298-8586 or 298-5433**	Rates (Single/Double):
Coordinator: **Ruth Wilson**	Modest: **$20** **$29**
States/Regions Covered: **Austin,**	Average: **$25** **$35**
Dallas, Denison, Fort Worth, El Paso,	Luxury: **$30** **$60**
Galveston, Garland, Houston, San	Credit Cards: **No**
Antonio, Waco	

The above cities are only a small sample of the locations of hosts waiting to give you plenty of warm hospitality. Ruth's register includes comfortable accommodations in condos, restored Victorians, lakeside cottages, and ranches. To make your choice, please send two dollars for her descriptive directory.

The Bed & Breakfast Society of Houston
4432 HOLT, BELLAIRE, TEXAS 77401

Tel: **(713) 666-6372**	Rates (Single/Double):
Coordinator: **Debbie Herman Siegel**	Modest: **$25** **$35**
States/Regions Covered: **Houston and**	Average: **$25** **$35**
suburbs	Luxury: **$60** **$100**
	Credit Cards: **No**

Whether you're traveling for business or pleasure, Debbie's hosts offer the kind of friendliness and individualized care that will make your stay pleasant. The area is known for the Astrodome, Galveston Bay, NASA, and the Texas Medical Center. There are wonderful restaurants, shops, museums, and historic sights everywhere.

Bed & Breakfast Hosts of San Antonio
166 ROCKHILL, SAN ANTONIO, TEXAS 78209

Tel: **(512) 824-8036**	Rates (Single/Double):
Coordinator: **Lavern Campbell**	Modest: **$29** **$42**
States/Regions Covered: **San Antonio**	Average: **$36** **$48**
	Luxury: **$52** **$69**
	Credit Cards: **MC, VISA**

You'll find wonderful hosts waiting to welcome you and to suggest how best to enjoy this beautiful and historic city. Don't miss the Paseo del Rio (which is a bustling river walk), the Alamo, the Arneson River Theatre showplace, El Mercado (which is a restored Mexican and Farmers Market), the Southwest Craft Center, wonderful restaurants, marvelous shops, and delightful, friendly folks.

The Magnolias
209 EAST BROADWAY, JEFFERSON, TEXAS 75657

Tel: (214) 665-2754
Host(s): **Preston and Dale Kirk**
Location: **¹/₁₀ mile from U.S. 59 and Highway 49**
No. of Rooms: **3**
No. of Private Baths: 2
Maximum No. of Guests Sharing Bath: **4**
Double/pb: **$45**
Single/pb: $45
Double/sb: **$45**
Single/sb: $45

Guest Cottage: **n/a**
Months of Operation: **All year**
Reduced Rates: **10%, 2 or more weekdays**
Breakfast: **Continental**
Other Meals: **Available**
Air-Conditioning: **Yes**
Pets: **No**
Children: **Welcome, over 5**
Smoking: **No**
Social Drinking: **Permitted**
Airport Pickup: **Yes**

Return to the past to enjoy the graciousness of southern hospitality in this magnificent Greek Revival mansion, built in 1867. Relax on its wide, shady porches or enjoy the ambience of the double parlors. There's so much to see, including Jay Gould's private railroad car, the Freeman Plantation, or the McGarity Saloon. Don't miss the Living History Tour given at this special spot.

Cardinal Cliff
3806 HIGHCLIFF, SAN ANTONIO, TEXAS 78218

Tel: (512) 655-2939
Host(s): Roger and Alice Sackett
No. of Rooms: 3
Maximum No. of Guests Sharing
   Baths: 4
Double/sb: $25
Single/sb: $18
Months of Operation: All year
Reduced Rates: 15%, weekly; 15%,
   families

Breakfast: Full
Air-Conditioning: Yes
Pets: Sometimes
Children: Welcome (crib)
Smoking: Permitted
Social Drinking: Permitted
Airport Pickup: Yes

This is a suburban ranch-style home, overlooking the wooded river valley, and furnished in a Victorian style. It is located close to the Lyndon B. Johnson ranch and most major San Antonio attractions. Roger, a retired army officer, and Alice, a retired librarian, enjoy having guests and welcome you with coffee or iced tea. The washer and dryer are available for your use.

Big Thicket Guest House
BOX 91, VILLAGE MILLS, TEXAS 77663

Tel: (409) 834-2875
Host(s): Paul and Mary Betzner
Location: 30 miles from I-10
No. of Rooms: 2
Maximum No. of Guests Sharing
   Bath: 4
Double/sb: $40
Single/sb: $35

Months of Operation: All year
Reduced Rates: 10%, seniors
Breakfast: Full
Other Meals: Available
Air-Conditioning: Yes
Pets: No
Children: Welcome
Smoking: Permitted
Social Drinking: Permitted

This comfortable country home is furnished with antiques, some of which are for sale. Guests are welcome to enjoy a complimentary glass of wine. Breakfast specialties include homemade biscuits or waffles. Your hosts are happy to point the way to nearby tennis, golf, swimming, biking, and touring the Big Thicket National Forest. An Indian reservation and quite a few historic sights are within a half-hour's ride.

Weimar Country Inn
P.O. BOX 782, WEIMAR, TEXAS 78962

Tel: **(409) 725-8888**	Months of Operation: **All year**
Host(s): **Laura Smith**	Reduced Rates: **No**
Location: **85 miles west of Houston**	Breakfast: **Continental**
No. of Rooms: **9**	Meals: **Available**
No. of Private Baths: **7**	Credit Cards: **AMEX, MC, VISA**
Maximum No. of Guests Sharing	Air-Conditioning: **Yes**
Bath: **4**	Pets: **No**
Double/pb: **$38–$65**	Children: **Welcome, over 3**
Double/sb: **$30**	Smoking: **Permitted**
Suites: **$125**	Social Drinking: **Permitted**

The Weimar is constructed in the wood clapboard style of the late 19th century. The rooms are furnished with antique fans, quilts, and matching wallpaper. Your hosts welcome you to cocktails and fine dining on the premises. Breakfast features homemade jams and strudel. Nearby, enjoy a tour of the historic district, golfing, and antiquing.

UTAH

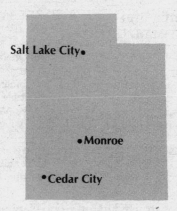

Salt Lake City•

•Monroe

•Cedar City

Bed 'n Breakfast Association of Utah
P.O. BOX 16465, SALT LAKE CITY, UTAH 84118

Tel: **(801) 532-7076**
Coordinator: **Barbara Baker, Nadine Smith**
States/Regions Covered: **Statewide**

Rates (Single/Double):
  Modest: **$15–$25** **$25–$35**
  Average: **$25–$35** **$35–$45**
  Luxury: **$35–$45** **$45–$55**
Credit Cards: **No**
Minimum Stay: **2 nights**

Utah has something for everyone, and Barbara and Nadine have a roster of hosts who delight in making you feel at home. A full breakfast is included with most of the accommodations. Location and season are taken into consideration in the rate, and discounts are offered to senior citizens, families, and for extended stays.

Meadeau View Lodge

P.O. BOX 356, HIGHWAY 14, DUCK CREEK VILLAGE, CEDAR CITY, UTAH 84720

Tel: **(801) 648-2495**
Host(s): **Harry and Gaby Moyer**
Location: **30 miles east of Cedar City**
No. of Rooms: **9**
No. of Private Baths: **9**
Double/pb: **$38**
Single/pb: **$25**
Suites: **$49**
Months of Operation: **All year**
Reduced Rates: **Available**

Breakfast: **Full**
Other Meals: **Available**
Air-Conditioning: **Unnecessary**
Pets: **No**
Children: **Welcome (crib)**
Smoking: **Permitted**
Social Drinking: **Permitted**
Airport Pickup: **Yes**
Foreign Languages: **German**

The lodge is nestled in a pine and aspen forest, 8,400 feet above sea level. In the back meadow, there's trout fishing in Duck Pond; Aspen Mirror Lake is down the road. Harry and Gaby will direct you to nearby Zion National Park and Bryce Canyon, about an hour's drive away. Coffee and cookies are always available, but if you want something stronger, bring your own; this is Utah!

Bed and Breakfast

95 NORTH 300 WEST, MONROE, UTAH 84754

Tel: **(801) 527-4830**
Host(s): **Mary Ann and Howard Peterson**
Location: **10 miles southwest of Richfield**
No. of Rooms: **2**
No. of Private Baths: **1**
Maximum No. of Guests Sharing Bath: **2**
Double/pb: **$30**
Single/pb: **$20**

Double/sb: **$30**
Single/sb: **$20**
Months of Operation: **All year**
Reduced Rates: **5%, seniors**
Breakfast: **Full**
Other Meals: **Available**
Air-Conditioning: **No**
Pets: **No**
Children: **Welcome**
Smoking: **No**
Social Drinking: **No**

This modern farmhouse, casual and comfortable, is surrounded by 10,000-foot mountains in the heart of hunting and fishing country. The Petersons have traveled extensively, and Mary Ann has just completed writing a marvelous cookbook called *Country Cooking*. By the way, if you're interested in your ancestral roots, you can use the genealogical files in Richfield for tracing your beginnings; there is no charge for this information service.

Seven Wives Inn
217 NORTH 100 WEST, ST. GEORGE, UTAH 84770

Tel: (801) 628-3737
Host(s): **Jay and Donna Curtis**
Location: **120 miles northeast of Las Vegas, 1 mile from I-15**
No. of Rooms: **7**
No. of Private Baths: **5**
Maximum No. of Guests Sharing Bath: **5**
Double/pb: **$30–$50**
Single/pb: **$30-$50**
Double/sb: **$25–$35**

Single/sb: **$20–$35**
Months of Operation: **All year**
Reduced Rates: **No**
Breakfast: **Full**
Credit Cards: **MC, VISA**
Air-Conditioning: **Yes**
Pets: **Sometimes**
Children: **Welcome, over 12**
Smoking: **No**
Social Drinking: **Permitted**
Airport Pickup: **Yes**

This delightful inn is featured on the walking tour of St. George; it is just across from the Brigham Young home and two blocks from the historic Washington County Court House. Jay and Donna offer traditional Dixie hospitality. Their home is decorated with antiques collected in America and Europe. Each bedroom is named after one of the seven wives of Donna's polygamous great-grandfather. A gourmet breakfast is served in the elegant dining room that will give you a hint of the past. St. George is located near Zion and Bryce national parks, boasts four golf courses, and is noted for its mild winters.

VERMONT

American Bed & Breakfast—New England
P.O. BOX 983, ST. ALBANS, VERMONT 05478

Tel: **n/a**
Coordinator: **Robert Precoda**
States/Regions Covered: **New Hampshire, Maine, Massachusetts, Vermont**

Rates (Single/Double):
	Single	Double
Modest:	**$18**	**$25**
Average:	**$24**	**$35**

Credit Cards: **No**

This group of B&B hosts asks the prospective visitor to select the home of his choice from a descriptive directory and to make reservations directly with the host. The directory costs three dollars and lists accommodations at farms, country villages, or ski chalets in New England and northern New York State.

Vermont Bed & Breakfast
BOX 139, BROWNS TRACE, JERICHO, VERMONT 05465

Tel: **(802) 899-2354**
Coordinator: **Sue Eaton,**
 Sheila Varnum
States/Regions Covered: **Essex,**
 Calais, Jericho

Rates (Single/Double):
 Average: **$20**   **$35**
Credit Cards: **No**

Located in the foothills of the Green Mountains in an area renowned for excellent skiing, fine restaurants, and superb shopping, Sue and Sheila's hosts will cheerfully direct you to concerts, plays, art galleries, and wonderful handicraft shops. It's not far to either the Shelburne Museum or the Kent Tavern Museum, and the fall foliage is breathtaking. A descriptive directory is yours for the asking.

Greenhurst Inn
RIVER STREET, BETHEL, VERMONT 05032

Tel: **(802) 234-9474**
Host(s): **Lyle and Barbara Wolf**
Location: **30 miles east of Rutland**
No. of Rooms: **9**
No. of Private Baths: **2**
Maximum No. of Guests Sharing
 Bath: **7**
Double/pb: **$50–$55**
Single/pb: **$50–$55**
Double/sb: **$35–$45**
Single/sb: **$30**
Months of Operation: **All year**

Reduced Rates: **15%, Sunday to**
 Thursday October 15 to December
 15, March 15 to May 15; seniors
Breakfast: **Continental**
Other Meals: **Available**
Credit Cards: **MC, VISA**
Air-Conditioning: **No**
Pets: **Welcome**
Children: **Welcome (crib)**
Smoking: **Permitted**
Social Drinking: **Permitted**

Located 100 yards from the White River, this elegant Queen Anne mansion is listed on the National Register of Historic Places. Built in 1891, the heavy brass hinges, embossed floral brass doorknobs, and etched windows at the entry have withstood the test of time. The cut crystal collection is magnificent, and the stereoscope and old Victrola add to the old-fashioned atmosphere. It's close to many points of historic interest, and seasonal recreational activities are abundant. There's tennis and croquet on the premises, and afternoon tea and snacks are served.

Green Trails Country Inn
POND VILLAGE, BROOKFIELD, VERMONT 05036

Tel: (802) 276-3412
Host(s): **Betty and Jack Russell**
Location: **6 miles from I-89**
No. of Rooms: **15**
No. of Private Baths: **9**
Maximum No. of Guests Sharing
  Bath: **4**
Double/pb: **$48**
Single/pb: **$36**
Double/sb: **$42**
Single/sb: **$33**
Suites: **$52**

Guest Cottage: **$56 sleeps 4**
Months of Operation: **All year**
Reduced Rates: **10%, weekly; seniors;
  families**
Breakfast: **Full**
Other Meals: **Available**
Air-Conditioning: **No**
Pets: **Sometimes**
Children: **Welcome (crib)**
Smoking: **Permitted**
Social Drinking: **Permitted**
Airport Pickup: **Yes**

The inn (pictured on our cover) consists of two buildings. One is
an 1840 farmhouse; the other was built in the late 1700s and has
pumpkin pine floorboards. They are located across from the
famous Floating Bridge. Furnished in antiques and "early nostal-
gia," the rooms have handmade quilts; fresh flowers add to the
cheer. The historic village is a perfect base for seasonal excursions
to the Shelburne Museum or Woodstock. Cross-country skiers
can start at the doorstep, while downhill enthusiasts can try
Sugarbush and Killington. Chuck and Betty serve afternoon tea.

The Inn at Mt. Ascutney
BROWNSVILLE, VERMONT 05037

Tel: (802) 484-7725
Host(s): **Margaret and Eric Rothchild**
Location: **8 miles from I-91**
No. of Rooms: **9**
No. of Private Baths: **5**
Maximum No. of Guests Sharing
  Bath: **4**
Double/pb: **$58**
Single/pb: **$58**
Double/sb: **$38**
Single/sb: **$38**
Months of Operation: **December 1 to
  March 31; May 1 to October 31**

Reduced Rates: **Available**
Breakfast: **Continental**
Other Meals: **Available**
Credit Cards: **MC, VISA**
Air-Conditioning: **Unnecessary**
Pets: **Sometimes**
Children: **Welcome (crib)**
Smoking: **Permitted**
Social Drinking: **Permitted**
Foreign Languages: **Arabic**

The inn is directly across the valley from the ski area where magnificent views are always in season. It was converted from an old farmhouse, parts of which date back to the American Revolution. The Rothchilds have achieved a comfortable balance between the old and the new. Their dining room and cocktail lounge feature an open hearth and kitchen with the original low wood beams from the old carriage house. After a day of skiing, tennis, fishing, hiking, or antiquing, you may dine on Margaret's continental-style country cooking, Monday through Thursday.

The Little Lodge at Dorset
ROUTE 30, BOX 673, DORSET, VERMONT 05251

Tel: **(802) 867-4040**	Months of Operation: **All year, except part of April, May, and November**
Host(s): **Allan and Nancy Norris**	
Location: **6 miles north of Manchester**	
No. of Rooms: **5**	Reduced Rates: **10%, weekly**
No. of Private Baths: **3**	Breakfast: **Continental**
Maximum No. of Guests Sharing Bath: **4**	Credit Cards: **AMEX**
	Air-Conditioning: **Unnecessary**
Double/pb: **$49–$55**	Pets: **Sometimes**
Single/pb: **$39–$45**	Children: **Welcome (crib)**
Double/sb: **$39–$44**	Smoking: **Permitted**
Single/sb: **$29–$34**	Social Drinking: **Permitted**

Situated in one of the prettiest little towns in Vermont, this delightful 1890 colonial house is perched on a hillside overlooking its own trout pond that's used for skating in winter or canoeing in summer. The original paneling and wide floorboards set off the splendid antiques. After skiing at nearby Stratton or Bromley, toast your feet by the fireplace while sipping hot chocolate. If you prefer, bring your own liquor, and Nancy and Allan will provide Vermont cheese and crackers.

Maplewood Colonial House
BOX 1019, DORSET, VERMONT 05251

Tel: **(802) 867-4470**	Months of Operation: **All year**
Host(s): **Marge and Leon Edgerton**	Reduced Rates: **Weekly; family**
Location: **On Route 30**	Breakfast: **Full**
No. of Rooms: **5**	Air-Conditioning: **Unnecessary**
Maximum No. of Guests Sharing Bath: **4**	Pets: **Yes**
	Children: **Welcome**
Double/sb: **$35**	Smoking: **No**
Single/sb: **$25**	Social Drinking: **Permitted**

This large, 20-room white colonial with green shutters is in a lovely setting. In summer, you can canoe on the pond, hike, bike, or go antiquing. In winter, it's convenient to the Bromley and Stratton ski areas. Marge and Leon will direct you to fine restaurants to suit your budget.

Blue Wax Farm
PINKHAM ROAD, EAST BURKE, VERMONT 05832

Tel: **(802) 626-5542**
Host(s): **Kenneth and Ingrid Parr**
Location: **45 miles north of White River Junction**
No. of Rooms: **4**
No. of Private Baths: **1**
Maximum No. of Guests Sharing Bath: **4**
Double/pb: **$26**
Single/pb: **$13**
Double/sb: **$24**

Single/sb: **$12**
Months of Operation: **All year**
Reduced Rates: **No**
Breakfast: **Continental**
Air-Conditioning: **Unnecessary**
Pets: **No**
Children: **Welcome**
Smoking: **Permitted**
Social Drinking: **Permitted**
Foreign Languages: **Finnish, Spanish**

If you want to ski Vermont without bedding down at resorts with bars and discos, reserve a room here. Kenneth and Ingrid have a quiet retreat adjoining the Burke Mountain ski resort. There is cross-country skiing on the property, in addition to the downhill trails on Burke. Both casual and serious hikers will find this an ideal spot too. The cordiality of your hosts and the view of the countryside is well worth the trip in all seasons.

Burke Green Lodging
RURAL ROUTE 1, EAST BURKE, VERMONT 05832

Tel: **(802) 467-3472**
Host(s): **Harland and Beverly Lewin**
Location: **15 miles north of St. Johnsbury**
No. of Rooms: **3**
No. of Private Baths: **2**
Maximum No. of Guests Sharing Bath: **5**
Double/pb: **$28**
Single/pb: **$20**
Double/sb: **$26**

Single/sb: **$18**
Suites: **$35**
Months of Operation: **All year**
Reduced Rates: **15%, weekly; 10%, seniors**
Breakfast: **Full**
Air-Conditioning: **Unnecessary**
Pets: **Sometimes**
Children: **Welcome (crib)**
Smoking: **Permitted**
Social Drinking: **Permitted**

You will enjoy the quiet country setting and spacious 1840 farmhouse, remodeled with modern conveniences but retaining the original wooden beams and old-fashioned fixtures. The view of Burke Mountain is spectacular. Sit in the family room and enjoy the warmth of the cozy fireplace. It is ten minutes from skiing and snow sports; summertime fun includes swimming, fishing, and hiking in the nearby lakes and hills. The kitchen is always open for cookies and beverages, and you are welcome to use the laundry facilities to freshen your wardrobe.

Eatonhouse Bed & Breakfast
BOX 139, BROWNS TRACE, JERICHO, VERMONT 05465

Tel: **(805) 899-2354**
Host(s): **Sue Eaton**
Location: **15 miles east of Burlington**
No. of Rooms: **2**
Maximum No. of Guests Sharing
  Bath: **4**
Double/sb: **$30**
Single/sb: **$20**
Months of Operation: **All year**

Reduced Rates: **No**
Breakfast: **Full**
Air-Conditioning: **No**
Pets: **No**
Children: **Welcome**
Smoking: **Permitted**
Social Drinking: **Permitted**
Airport Pickup: **Yes**

A charming saltbox reproduction located in a lovely pastoral setting of the Green Mountain foothills. There's skiing in winter, spectacular foliage in autumn, and spring and summer are equally delightful. Visit the Shelburne Museum to see New England's foremost collection of early Americana.

Brook-'n'-Hearth
STATE ROAD 11/30, BOX 508, MANCHESTER CENTER, VERMONT 05255

Tel: **(802) 362-3604**
Host(s): **Larry and Terry Greene**
Location: **1 mile from U.S. 7**
No. of Rooms: **4**
No. of Private Baths: **3**
Maximum No. of Guests Sharing
  Bath: **4**
Double/pb: **$28–$32**
Single/pb: **$16–$20**
Suites: **$42–$50**
Months of Operation: **November 16
  to April 24; May 16 to October 24**

Reduced Rates: **10%, Sunday to
  Thursday; 15%, April 15 to June 15,
  October 25 to December 15; 15%,
  families.**
Breakfast: **Full**
Credit Cards: **AMEX**
Air-Conditioning: **Unnecessary**
Pets: **No**
Children: **Welcome (crib)**
Smoking: **Permitted**
Social Drinking: **Permitted**

True to its name, a brook runs through the six-acre property and a fire warms the living room of this country home. Terry and Larry offer setups and happy-hour snacks for your self-supplied cocktails. You're within five miles of the ski slopes at Bromley and Stratton; it is also convenient to art centers, summer theater, restaurants, and a score of sports that include hiking on the Long Trail. Bennington College is 25 miles away.

Charlie's Northland Lodge
BOX 88, NORTH HERO, VERMONT 05474

Tel: **(802) 372-8822**
Host(s): **Charles and Dorice Clark**
Location: **60 miles south of Montreal, Canada**
No. of Rooms: **4**
Maximum No. of Guests Sharing Bath: **6**
Double/sb: **$36**
Single/sb: **$30**
Guest Cottage: **$230, sleeps 4**

Months of Operation: **All year**
Reduced Rates: **Labor Day to Christmas**
Breakfast: **Continental**
Air-Conditioning: **Unnecessary**
Pets: **No**
Children: **Welcome, over 5**
Smoking: **Permitted**
Social Drinking: **Permitted**

The lodge is 200-year-old restored log home located on Lake Champlain, in the heart of the inland sea, where bass and walleye abound. A sport and tackle shop is right on the premises. Fall and winter fishing should appeal to all anglers. Cross-country ski buffs will love the 10 miles of groomed trails. In summer, tennis, hiking, or relaxing in the reading room are pleasant activities.

Pittsfield Inn
ROUTE 100, BOX 526, PITTSFIELD, VERMONT 05762

Tel: **(802) 746-8943**
Host(s): **Tom and Sue Yennerell**
Location: **20 miles north of Rutland, Vermont**
No. of Rooms: **9**
Maximum No. of Guests Sharing Bath: **6**
Double/sb: **$46**
Single/sb: **$35**
Suites: **$56**

Months of Operation: **All year**
Reduced Rates: **No**
Breakfast: **Full**
Other Meals: **Available**
Credit Cards: **MC, VISA**
Air-Conditioning: **No**
Pets: **No**
Children: **Welcome**
Smoking: **Permitted**
Social Drinking: **Permitted**

The inn is located at the end of the village green, where it has stood since 1835. Guests are invited to the parlor, porch, or tavern, where fine food is served. The rooms are filled with antiques, and you may find your own treasures at the many craft shops in town. If you choose, professional guides will escort you from the inn to the Green Mountains. Skiing at Pico and Killington are 10 miles away.

Okemo Lantern Lodge
P.O. BOX 247, PROCTORSVILLE, VERMONT 05153

Tel: **(802) 226-7770**
Host(s): **Charles and Joan Racicot**
Location: **25 miles south of Rutland**
No. of Rooms: **7**
No. of Private Baths: **1**
Maximum No. of Guests Sharing
  Bath: **6**
Double/pb: **$30**
Single/pb: **$30**
Double/sb: **$28**
Single/sb: **$28**
Months of Operation: **All year**

Reduced Rates: **$160 per person,
  5-day, midweek rate (including
  dinner)**
Breakfast: **Full**
Other Meals: **Dinner available**
Credit Cards: **AMEX, MC, VISA**
Air-Conditioning: **No**
Pets: **No**
Children: **Welcome (crib)**
Smoking: **Permitted**
Social Drinking: **Permitted**
Airport Pickup: **Yes**

A 19th-century Victorian lodge nestled in the village, in the heart of ski country, awaits your visit. It is decorated with canopy beds, antiques, and original stained glass windows. Charles and Joan charge $38 to $43 during ski season, which includes dinner and breakfast. There are countless activities in all seasons including the gondola at Killington and the spectacular fall foliage.

Harvey Farm Country Inn
ROCHESTER, VERMONT 05767

Tel: **(802) 767-4273**
Host(s): **Don and Maggie Harvey**
Location: **35 miles north of Rutland**
No. of Rooms: **8**
Maximum No. of Guests Sharing
  Bath: **4**
Double/sb: **$56**
Single/sb: **$28**
Months of Operation: **All year**

Reduced Rates: **Families**
Breakfast: **Full**
Other Meals: **Dinner included**
Air-Conditioning: **Unnecessary**
Pets: **No**
Children: **Welcome, over 4**
Smoking: **Permitted**
Social Drinking: **Permitted**

You can find peace of mind here in this inn that combines modern country living with the beauty of mountains, open meadows, woods, and farmland. After a hearty breakfast, children are invited to help feed the small animals and ride the pony. Everyone is welcome to swim in the pool or go fishing. Picnic lunches are available and delectable dinners are served in the antique-filled dining room. Your last cup of coffee can be enjoyed on the porch or in front of the TV. In winter, the ski slopes of Sugarbush, Middlebury Snowbowl, and Killington are close by.

Hillcrest Guest House
RD 1, MCKINLEY AVENUE, RUTLAND, VERMONT 05701

Tel: (802) 775-1670	Months of Operation: All year
Host(s): Bob and Peg Dombro	Reduced Rates: No
Location: 2 miles north of Rutland	Breakfast: Continental
No. of Rooms: 3	Air-Conditioning: Unnecessary
Maximum No. of Guests Sharing Bath: 5	Pets: Sometimes
	Children: Welcome
Double/sb: $30	Smoking: Permitted
Single/sb: $20	Social Drinking: Permitted
Guest Cottage: n/a	Airport Pickup: Yes

This 150-year-old farmhouse, with a comfortable screened porch for warm weather relaxing, is furnished with country antiques. Pico and Killington ski areas are seven and 16 miles away. Summer brings one the opportunity to explore charming villages, covered bridges, and antique and craft centers. Country auctions, marble quarries, trout streams, and Sunday evening band concerts are pleasant pastimes. Bob and Peg always offer something in the way of between-meal refreshments.

Ski Inn
ROUTE 108, STOWE, VERMONT 05672

Tel: (802) 253-4050	Double/pb: $42–$60
Host(s): Larry and Harriet Heyer	Single/pb: $21–$30
Location: 47 miles northeast of Burlington	Double/sb: $30
	Single/sb: $18
No. of Rooms: 10	Months of Operation: All year
No. of Private Baths: 4	Reduced Rates: 10% January; family rates; summer rates
Maximum No. of Guests Sharing Bath: 5	Breakfast: Full

Other Meals: **Dinner included**	Children: **Welcome**
Air-Conditioning: **Unnecessary**	Smoking: **Permitted**
Pets: **Sometimes**	Social Drinking: **Permitted**

From any window you can see where you ski, and when you finish your day on the slopes, you can ski back to the inn. Stowe's Mount Mansfield offers the steepest and longest descents in the East. Cross-country skiers can start at the door. Rooms are large, colorful, and spotless, and the breakfast and dinner served in winter are generous. In summer, the breakfast is continental and no dinner is included; room rates then range from $11 to $27. The friendliness, informality, and old-fashioned hospitality hold true in all seasons.

Timberhölm Inn
COTTAGE CLUB ROAD, RR 1 BOX 810, STOWE, VERMONT 05672

Tel: **(802) 253-7603**	Reduced Rates: **10% discount for**
Host(s): **Johanna and Lee Darrow**	**5-day stay, November to April;**
Location: **2.5 miles north of Stowe**	**summer rates**
No. of Rooms: **10**	Breakfast: **Full—$3**
Maximum No. of Guests Sharing	Credit Cards: **MC, VISA**
Bath: **6**	Air-Conditioning: **No**
Double/sb: **$28**	Pets: **Sometimes**
Single/sb: **$19**	Children: **Sometimes**
Suites: **$68 (for 4); $60 (for 3)**	Smoking: **Permitted**
Months of Operation: **All year**	Social Drinking: **Permitted**

Nestled on a wooded hillside overlooking the lush valley and mountains, it is convenient to skiing at Stowe's Mount Mansfield, Vermont's highest peak. The living room is graced with antiques, an extensive book collection, and a huge fireplace where guests gather for congenial conversation. There's a recreation room downstairs with a fireplace and piano. During ski season, complimentary homemade soup is served to warm your spirit. You are welcome to stash your snacks in the guest refrigerator.

Knoll Farm Country Inn
BRAGG HILL ROAD, R.F.D. BOX 179, WAITSFIELD, VERMONT 05673

Tel: **(802) 496-3939**	Location: **22 miles south of**
Host(s): **Bill and Ann Heinzerling, and**	**Montpelier**
Ethel and Harvey Horner	No. of Rooms: **4**

Maximum No. of Guests Sharing
  Bath: **3**
Double/sb: **$72**
Single/sb: **$42**
Months of Operation: **December 1 to
  March 31; May 1 to October 31**
Reduced Rates: **Families; 5 nights;
  weekly**

Breakfast: **Full**
Other Meals: **Dinner included**
Air-Conditioning: **Unnecessary**
Pets: **No**
Children: **Welcome, over 6**
Smoking: **Permitted**
Social Drinking: **Permitted**
Airport Pickup: **Yes**

From the porch of this converted farmhouse, one can see the Mad River Glen and Sugarbush ski areas four miles away. An informal spot awaits you where you can hike or cross-country ski, swim and boat on the pond, or help care for the farm animals. Horseback riding is especially popular too. The hosts raise their own meat and eggs so chances are you've never had a fresher breakfast of bacon, sausage, and eggs; even the vegetables are grown organically. Meals are served family-style, and dinner is a candle-lit feast with wine and classical music. Picture yourself on a cold winter night sipping mulled cider and nibbling on Vermont cheese by the wood stove, chatting with your delightful hosts.

Schneider Haus
ROUTE 100, BOX 283A, WATERBURY, VERMONT 05676

Tel: **(802) 244-7726**
Host(s): **George and Irene
  Ballschneider**
Location: **13 miles west of Montpelier**
No. of Rooms: **10**
Maximum No. of Guests Sharing
  Bath: **6**
Double/sb: **$18–$23**
Single/sb: **$25–$28**

Months of Operation: **December 15
  to April 15; June 15 to December 15**
Reduced Rates: **Weekdays**
Breakfast: **Full**
Other Meals: **Available**
Air-Conditioning: **No**
Pets: **No**
Children: **Welcome, over 3**
Smoking: **Permitted**
Social Drinking: **Permitted**

This Austrian chalet is nestled in the Green Mountains. A lounge with fireplace and floor-to-ceiling windows, plus quilts, hot tub, and sauna create a warm and comforting atmosphere. Breakfast specialties include French toast and homemade muffins. Enjoy nearby fishing, hiking, fall foliage, and winter excitement on the slopes of Sugarbush and Sugarbush North.

Hunt's Hideaway
RFD MORGAU ROAD, WEST CHARLESTON, VERMONT 05872

Tel: **(802) 895-4432 or 334-8322**
Host(s): **Pat and Paul Hunt**
Location: **6 miles from I-91**
No. of Rooms: **3**
Maximum No. of Guests Sharing
  Bath: **4**
Double/sb: **$25**
Single/sb: **$18**

Months of Operation: **December 11
  to October 9**
Reduced Rates: **No**
Breakfast: **Full**
Air-Conditioning: **No**
Pets: **Sometimes**
Children: **Welcome**
Smoking: **Permitted**
Social Drinking: **Permitted**

This modern, split-level home is located on 100 acres of woods and fields, with a brook, pond, and swimming pool. Guests are served a variety of snacks; pancakes with Vermont maple syrup are featured at breakfast. Ski Jay Peak and Burke, or fish and boat on Lake Seymour, two miles away. Visiting antique shops or taking a trip to nearby Canada are other local possibilities.

Chalet Waldwinkel
P.O. BOX 364, ROUTE 100, WEST DOVER, VERMONT 05356

Tel: **(802) 464-5281**
Host(s): **Linda and Mickey Kersten**
Location: **600 feet from Route 100**
No. of Rooms: **11**
No. of Private Baths: **10**
Maximum No. of Guests Sharing
  Bath: **5**
Double/pb: **$50**
Single/pb: **$50**
Double/sb: **$45**

Single/sb: **$45**
Months of Operation: **All year**
Reduced Rates: **Groups**
Breakfast: **Full**
Air-Conditioning: **Unnecessary**
Pets: **No**
Children: **Welcome (crib)**
Smoking: **Permitted**
Social Drinking: **Permitted**

A snowball's throw from Mount Snow, this alpine-style lodge is made cozy by the warmth and geniality of Linda and Mickey. In addition to the area's famed sports and skiing facilities, they provide pool and Ping-Pong tables, games, and lots of friendship around the fireplaces. An outdoor swimming pool is a delightful summer attraction. Each room is individually decorated and some have balconies overlooking the valley.

Snow Den
P.O. BOX 615, ROUTE 100, WEST DOVER, VERMONT 05356

Tel: (802) 464-9355 or 464-5537
Host(s): Jean and Milt Cummings
Location: 30 miles west of Bennington
No. of Rooms: 8
No. of Private Baths: 8
Double/pb: $46–$70
Single/pb: $46–$70
Months of Operation: All year
Reduced Rates: April 15 to December 1, $40–$50

Breakfast: Full
Other Meals: Available
Credit Cards: MC, VISA
Air-Conditioning: Unnecessary
Pets: No
Children: Welcome, over 8
Smoking: Permitted
Social Drinking: Permitted

Located in the heart of the Mount Snow, Haystack, and Corinthia ski areas, this delightful home's guest rooms are individually and tastefully furnished with many antiques; four bedrooms have fireplaces. In spring, summer, and fall, there's swimming, golf, and tennis to keep you busy. Jean and Milt will be happy to steer you to the many diverse attractions the area offers.

The Weathervane
DORR FITCH ROAD, BOX 57, WEST DOVER, VERMONT 05356

Tel: (802) 464-5426
Host(s): Liz and Ernie Chabot
Location: 1 mile from Route 100
No. of Rooms: 10
No. of Private Baths: 4
Maximum No. of Guests Sharing Bath: 5
Double/pb: $50
Single/pb: $25
Double/sb: $40
Single/sb: $20
Suites: $54

Months of Operation: All year
Reduced Rates: 10%, March, April, November; ski-weeks
Breakfast: Full
Other Meals: Dinner (included in winter)
Air-Conditioning: No
Pets: No
Children: Welcome (crib)
Smoking: Permitted
Social Drinking: Permitted

Only four miles from Haystack, Mount Snow, and Corinthia, this Tyrolean-style ski lodge is decorated with a warm blend of authentic antiques and colonial charm. The lounge and recreation room have fireplaces and a bring-your-own bar. Winter rates range from $32 to $36 per person, including breakfast, dinner, cross-country ski equipment, sleds, and snowshoes so that you may explore the lovely marked trails. Summer brings lakeshore swimming, boating, fishing, tennis, riding, museums, and the Marlboro Music Festival.

The Colonial House
ROUTE 100, BOX 138, WESTON, VERMONT 05161

Tel: **(802) 824-6286**	Months of Operation: **All year**
Host(s): **Betty and John Nunnikhoven**	Reduced Rates: **10%, 4 days; 15%, 5**
Location: **On Route 100**	**or more days; 10%, seniors**
No. of Rooms: **15**	Breakfast: **Full**
No. of Private Baths: **9**	Other Meals: **Available**
Maximum No. of Guests Sharing	Credit Cards: **AMEX, MC, VISA**
Bath: **6**	Air-Conditioning: **No**
Double/pb: **$40–$50**	Pets: **Sometimes**
Single/pb: **$35**	Children: **Welcome (crib)**
Double/sb: **$36**	Smoking: **Permitted**
Single/sb: **$28**	Social Drinking: **Permitted**

Built in 1790, this cozy farmhouse offers you a country-living experience. Enjoy leisurely farm breakfasts, with snacks in the afternoon. There's a guest living room with a player piano, fireplace, and warm hospitality. Cross-country skiing starts at the doorstep and seasonal activities are all nearby.

Holly Tree
RD1, BOX 315A, LAKE RAPONDA, WILMINGTON, VERMONT 05363

Tel: **(802) 464-5251**	Months of Operation: **All year**
Host(s): **Norma Nadeau**	Reduced Rates: **No**
Location: **20 miles west of Brattleboro**	Breakfast: **Continental**
No. of Rooms: **2**	Air-Conditioning: **No**
Maximum No. of Guests Sharing	Pets: **Sometimes**
Bath: **4**	Children: **Welcome**
Double/sb: **$32**	Smoking: **Permitted**
Single/sb: **$18**	Social Drinking: **Permitted**
Suites: **$45 (for 4)**	

Norma operated a bed and breakfast in England, so you will find rustic New England hospitality spiced with a genuine European accent. Wilmington provides a beautiful setting in every season for swimming, fishing, hiking, cycling, skiing, skating, snowmobiling, and hunting. It is close to Mount Snow, the Marlboro

Music Festival, and historic Bennington. Whenever you wish, the coffee pot is ready.

Nutmeg Inn
ROUTE 9W, P.O. BOX 818, WILMINGTON, VERMONT 05363

Tel: **(802) 464-3351**
Host(s): **Joan and Rich Combes**
Location: **1 mile west of Wilmington**
No. of Rooms: **9**
No. of Private Baths: **4**
Maximum No. of Guests Sharing
  Bath: **9**
Double/pb: **$48–$60**
Single/pb: **$40–$50**
Double/sb: **$42–$55**
Single/sb: **$35–$45**

Months of Operation: **December 27 to April 15; June 1 to October 31**
Reduced Rates: **Ski-weeks**
Breakfast: **Full**
Other meals: **Dinner (in winter)**
Credit Cards: **AMEX**
Air-Conditioning: **Unnecessary**
Pets: **No**
Children: **Welcome, over 9**
Smoking: **Permitted**
Social Drinking: **Permitted**

Joan and Rich are proud of their home which was built in the 1700s; it still shows the original post and beams. In winter, the focus is on skiing at Mount Snow, Corinthia, and Haystack. In summer, the mountain lakes beckon. The autumn colors are spectacular. Guests always enjoy the informal atmosphere of the living room with fireplace, piano, books, and bring-your-own cocktail bar.

_____ KEY TO LISTINGS _____

Location: As specified, unless B&B is right in town, or its location is clear from address as stated.
No. of Rooms: Refers to the number of guest bedrooms.
Double: Rate for two people in one room.
Single: Rate for one person in a room.
Suite: Can either be two bedrooms with an adjoining bath, or a living room and bedroom with private bath.
Guest Cottage: A separate building that usually has a mini-kitchen and private bath.
pb: Private bath.
sb: Shared bath.
Breakfast: Included, unless otherwise noted.
Air-Conditioning: If "no" or "unnecessary" is stated, it means the climate rarely warrants it.
Children: If "crib" is noted after the word "welcome," this indicates that the host also has a high-chair, baby-sitters are available, and the B&B can accommodate children under the age of three.
Smoking: If permitted, this means it is allowed *somewhere* inside the house.
Social Drinking: Some hosts provide a glass of wine or sherry; others provide setups for bring-your-own.

Please enclose a self-addressed, stamped, business-size envelope when contacting Reservation Services.

Remember the difference in time zones when calling for a reservation.

VIRGINIA

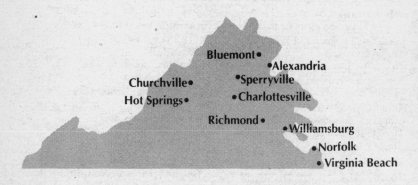

Bluemont•
•Alexandria
Churchville•
•Sperryville
Hot Springs•
•Charlottesville
Richmond •
•Williamsburg
•Norfolk
• Virginia Beach

Princely/Bed & Breakfast
819 PRINCE STREET, ALEXANDRIA, VIRGINIA 22314

Tel: **(703) 683-2159**
Coordinator: **E. J. Mansmann**
States/Regions Covered: **Alexandria**

Rates (Single/Double):
Luxury: **$50–$60 $50–$60**
Credit Cards: **No**
Minimum Stay: **2 nights**

Alexandria is eight miles from Washington, D.C. and nine miles from Mount Vernon. Mr. Mansmann, a former State Department official, has an exclusive roster of deluxe accommodations ready for you; they include an 18th-century federal-style mansion in historic Old Town Alexandria, as well as other historic houses (circa 1791 to 1838) filled with museum-quality antiques. You will be made to feel like visiting royalty, whichever place you choose.

Little River Inn
BOX 116, ALDIE, VIRGINIA 22001

Tel: **(703) 327-6742**
Host(s): **Tucker Withers**
Location: **40 miles west of Washington, D.C.**

No. of Rooms: **8**
No. of Private Baths: **4**
Maximum No. of Guests Sharing Bath: **4**

Double/pb: **$65**
Single/pb: **$50**
Double/sb: **$60**
Single/sb: **$45**
Guest Cottage: **$140 sleeps 4**
Sleeps: **4**
Months of Operation: **All year**
Reduced Rates: **No**

Breakfast: **Full**
Credit Cards: **MC, VISA**
Air-Conditioning: **Yes**
Pets: **No**
Children: **Welcome, over 11**
Smoking: **Permitted**
Social Drinking: **Permitted**
Airport Pickup: **Yes**

This tan brick house with slate blue shutters was built in 1810. Several of the guest rooms have fireplaces, and the furnishings are composed of country antiques. Located in the Virginia hunt country, it is close to Oatlands (a National Trust property) and to Manassas Battlefield. The Aldie Mill is the focal point of the historic district; Tucker is an antique dealer who will direct you to the best shops.

Blue Ridge Bed & Breakfast
ROUTE 1, BOX 517, BLUEMONT, VIRGINIA 22012

Tel: **(703) 955-3955**
Coordinator: **Sara Genthner**
States/Regions Covered:
 Virginia—Berryville, Bluemont, Boyce, Lorettsville, Purcellville, Winchester; West Virginia—Summit Point

Rates (Single/Double):
 Modest: **$18**   **n/a**
 Average: **$20**   **$30**
 Luxury: **$35**   **$45**
Credit Cards: **No**

Sara's hosts are within 25 to 75 miles of the capital, perfect for those wishing to visit rural areas near Washington, D.C. The variety includes houses on the Historic Register, mountain retreats, and traditional private homes in small towns. This area is famous for its part in American history, horses, farming, and beautiful scenery.

Guesthouses Reservation Service
P.O. BOX 5737, CHARLOTTESVILLE, VIRGINIA 22903

Tel: **(804) 979-7264 or 979-8327**
Coordinator: **Sara Reger**
States/Regions Covered:
 Charlottesville

Rates (Single/Double):
 Modest: **n/a**   **$32–$52**
 Average: **n/a**   **$36–$64**
 Luxury: **n/a**   **$64**
Credit Cards: **MC, VISA**

Charlottesville is a gracious town. The hosts in Sara's hospitality file offer you a genuine taste of southern hospitality. All places are close to Thomas Jefferson's Monticello and James Madison's Ash Lawn, as well as the University of Virginia. Unusual local activities include ballooning, steeplechasing, and wine festivals. Please note that the office is closed from Christmas through New Year's day.

The English Inn
316 14TH STREET NORTHWEST, CHARLOTTESVILLE, VIRGINIA 22903

Tel: **(804) 295-7707**
Host(s): **The Klee Family**
Location: **3 miles from I-64**
No. of Rooms: **8**
No. of Private Baths: **2**
Maximum No. of Guests Sharing Bath: **4**
Double/pb: **$40**
Single/pb: **$40**
Double/sb: **$35**
Single/sb: **$27**

Suites: **$70**
Months of Operation: **All year**
Reduced Rates: **10%, November 15 to March 20**
Breakfast: **Continental**
Air-Conditioning: **Yes**
Pets: **Welcome**
Children: **Welcome**
Smoking: **No**
Social Drinking: **Permitted**
Foreign Languages: **Greek**

This brick colonial is located in the historic district; it is close to shops, restaurants, and the University of Virginia. The guest rooms are furnished with period pieces. For relaxing, there is a large garden, a southern-style veranda, and a sitting room with fireplace. Continental breakfast includes homemade breads. Area attractions include the home of Thomas Jefferson, plus Ash Lawn, Castle Hill, and Swannanoa mansions.

Buckhorn Inn
STAR ROUTE BOX 139, ROUTE 250, CHURCHVILLE, VIRGINIA 24421

Tel: **(703) 885-2900**
Host(s): **Roger and Eileen Lee**
Location: **12 miles west of Staunton**
No. of Rooms: **6**
No. of Private Baths: **1**
Maximum No. of Guests Sharing Bath: **5**
Double/pb: **$38**

Single/pb: **$28**
Double/sb: **$28**
Single/sb: **$18**
Months of Operation: **All year**
Reduced Rates: **Groups; families**
Breakfast: **Continental**
Credit Cards: **MC, VISA**
Air-Conditioning: **Yes**

Pets: **Sometimes**   Social Drinking: **Permitted**
Children: **Welcome (crib)**   Airport Pickup: **Yes**
Smoking: **Permitted**

This vintage inn (circa 1811) has lovely open porches, and the guest rooms are decorated with fine colonial reproductions. Located in the heart of the Shenandoah Valley, in the George Washington National State Forest, it is close to the Natural Bridge as well as to an antiques mall that houses over 100 dealers. Coffee, tea, and lemonade are always available. You are welcome to use the washer and dryer to freshen your travel wardrobe.

The McGrath House
225 PRINCESS ANNE STREET, FREDERICKSBURG, VIRGINIA 22401

Tel: **(703) 371-4363**   Guest Cottage: **n/a**
Host(s): **Sylvia McGrath**   Months of Operation: **All year**
Location: **50 miles south of**   Reduced Rates: **No**
  Washington, D.C.   Breakfast: **Continental**
No. of Rooms: **3**   Air-Conditioning: **Yes**
No. of Private Baths: **0**   Pets: **Sometimes**
Maximum No. of Guests Sharing   Children: **Welcome**
  Bath: **6**   Smoking: **No**
Double/sb: **$30**   Social Drinking: **Permitted**
Single/sb: **$25**

This carefully restored house, featured on walking tours, dates back to the early 19th century and is located in the oldest part of Fredericksburg on a quiet, tree-lined street. You'll enjoy breakfast in the country kitchen that overlooks a small colonial herb garden. In the evening, you are welcome to have a drink and snacks with Sylvia before retiring. Don't miss seeing the James Monroe Law Offices, the Mary Washington House, the Rising Sun Tavern, and the Battlefield.

The Callanan House
208 MISSIONARY RIDGE, HAMPTON, VIRGINIA 23669

Tel: **(804) 851-5909**   Maximum No. of Guests Sharing
Host(s): **Patricia Callanan**   Bath: **5**
Location: **3 miles from I-64**   Double/sb: **$20**
No. of Rooms: **3**   Single/sb: **$15**

Months of Operation: **All year**	Pets: **No**
Reduced Rates: **No**	Children: **No**
Breakfast: **Continental**	Smoking: **No**
Air-Conditioning: **Yes**	Social Drinking: **Permitted**

Your personable hostess, Pat, welcomes you to her lovely home in a quiet, residential neighborhood. Historic Fort Monroe, Langley Air Force Base, and NASA are only minutes away; Williamsburg, Jamestown, Yorktown, and Norfolk are less than a 40-minute drive. Seafood restaurants are especially good in this interesting area of the Chesapeake Bay. You are invited to visit with the other guests in the den or comfortable screened porch.

Bed & Breakfast of Tidewater Virginia
P.O. BOX 3343, NORFOLK, VIRGINIA 23514

Tel: **(804) 627-1983 or 627-9409**
Coordinator: **Ashby Willcox and Susan Hubbard**
States/Regions Covered: **Chesapeake, Eastern Shore of Virginia, Norfolk, Portsmouth, Virginia Beach**

Rates (Single/Double):

Modest:	**$25**	**$30**
Average:	**$30**	**$35**
Luxury:	**$40**	**$55**

Credit Cards: **No**

The world's largest naval base is in Norfolk, as are the famed Chrysler Museum and MacArthur Memorial. It is also a cultural hub in which top-rated opera, symphony, and stage productions abound. There are miles of scenic beaches to explore on Chesapeake Bay and the Atlantic Ocean.

Cameron Residence
1605 BILL STREET, NORFOLK, VIRGINIA 23518

Tel: **(804) 587-0673**	Breakfast: **Continental**
Host(s): **Jessie Cameron**	Air-Conditioning: **Yes**
No. of Rooms: **1**	Pets: **Sometimes**
No. of Private Baths: **1**	Children: **No**
Double/pb: **$20**	Smoking: **Permitted**
Single/pb: **$15**	Social Drinking: **Permitted**
Months of Operation: **All year**	Airport Pickup: **Yes**
Reduced Rates: **No**	

This comfortable ranch home is close to Busch Gardens, historic Williamsburg, and Virginia Beach. Your hostess offers guests the use of her piano, sauna, and patio. Fishing and swimming can be enjoyed nearby.

Bensonhouse of Richmond
P. O. BOX 15131, RICHMOND, VIRGINIA 23227

Tel: **(804) 648-7560 or 321-6277**
Coordinator: **Lyn Benson**
States/Regions Covered: **Charles City, Petersburg, Richmond**

Rates (Single/Double):
  Modest: **$22–$26 $30–$34**
  Average: **$28–$38 $36–$46**
  Luxury: **$40–$60 $48–$72**
Credit Cards: **MC, VISA ($50 minimum charge)**

With a history dating back to 1607, Richmond offers a blend of the historic and contemporary. Houses on Lyn's list are of architectural or historic interest, offering charm in the relaxed comfort of a home. The hosts delight in guiding you to the best sights, and advising you on how to get the most out of your visit.

Griffin House
9601 NORTHRIDGE COURT, RICHMOND, VIRGINIA 23235

Tel: **(804) 272-2741**
Host(s): **Phyllis and Roger Griffin**
Location: **11 miles from I-95**
No. of Rooms: **1**
No. of Private Baths: **1**
Double/pb: **$35**
Single/pb: **$30**
Months of Operation: **All year**

Reduced Rates: **No**
Breakfast: **Full**
Air-Conditioning: **Yes**
Pets: **No**
Children: **No**
Smoking: **No**
Social Drinking: **Permitted**
Foreign Languages: **German**

Only nine miles from historic Richmond, capital of the Old Confederacy, this lovely private house is on a quiet street in a suburban neighborhood. Phyllis and Roger, having traveled extensively themselves, know exactly how to make visitors feel welcome. They will be happy to suggest side trips to nearby Williamsburg, Petersburg, Yorktown, and Gloucester; they will encourage you to take advantage of the new Performing Arts Center, where you can see memorable music and dance performances. You can decide what to see first while enjoying the delightful British breakfast.

Miss Blanche's Guest House
RD 1 BOX 10, ROUND HILL, VIRGINIA 22141

Tel: **(703) 338-7570 or (202) 243-4886**
Host(s): **Jonathan Dewdney**
Location: **55 miles west of Washington, D.C.**
No. of Rooms: **4**
No. of Private Baths: **1**
Maximum No. of Guests Sharing Bath: **5**
Double/pb: **$55**
Single/pb: **$45**

Double/sb: **$55**
Single/sb: **$45**
Months of Operation: **All year**
Reduced Rates: **No**
Breakfast: **Continental**
Other Meals: **Available**
Pets: **No**
Children: **Welcome, over 11**
Smoking: **No**
Social Drinking: **Permitted**

This sparkling white Victorian house, built in 1890, is located in the foothills of the Blue Ridge Mountains. The house is furnished in early 1900s fashion. It's only 13 miles to historic Leesburg. Jon is an antique collector and will be happy to recommend the best the area has to offer. You are welcome to use the washing machine and dryer, and the coffee pot is always on to refresh your spirits.

The Conyers House
SLATE MILLS ROAD, SPERRYVILLE, VIRGINIA 22740

Tel: **(703) 987-8025**
Host(s): **Norman and Sandra Cartwright-Brown**
Location: **78 miles southwest of Washington, D.C.**
No. of Rooms: **8**
No. of Private Baths: **3**
Maximum No. of Guests Sharing Bath: **4**
Double/pb: **$100**
Single/pb: **$100**
Double/sb: **$75**
Single/sb: **$75**

Guest Cottage: **$75–$90 sleeps 2**
Months of Operation: **All year**
Reduced Rates: **No**
Breakfast: **Full**
Other Meals: **Available**
Air-Conditioning: **Yes**
Pets: **Sometimes**
Children: **Welcome, over 12**
Smoking: **Permitted**
Social Drinking: **Permitted**
Airport Pickup: **Yes**
Foreign Languages: **French, German, Italian**

Built in 1770 as a country store, the house has been eclectically and elegantly restored and furnished with family heirlooms and Oriental carpets. This area is known for "the horse and the hunt," but all recreational activities are available; tennis is right on the grounds. Catering to those of sophisticated tastes, Norman, who is English by birth, is a cosmopolitan raconteur. Sandra is a warm and gracious hostess. Afternoon tea is served with applesauce cake. You are welcome to use the laundry facilities, as well as the kitchen for light snacks.

Angie's Guest Cottage
302 24TH STREET, VIRGINIA BEACH, VIRGINIA 23451

Tel: **(804) 428-4690**
Host(s): **Barbara, Garnette, and Bob Yates**
Location: **20 miles east of Norfolk**
No. of Rooms: **6**
No. of Private Baths: **1**
Maximum No. of Guests Sharing Bath: **4**
Double/pb: **$48**
Single/ pb: **$44**
Double/sb: **$38–$42**
Single/sb: **$34–$38**

Guest Cottage: **$300 sleeps 2 to 5**
Months of Operation: **All year**
Reduced Rates: **30%–50%, Labor Day to Memorial Day (without breakfast)**
Breakfast: **Continental**
Credit Cards: **MC, VISA**
Air-Conditioning: **Yes**
Children: **Welcome (crib)**
Smoking: **Permitted**
Social Drinking: **Permitted**
Airport Pickup: **No**

Just a block from the beach, shops, restaurants, and across the street from the Greyhound bus station is this bright and comfortable beach house. Former guests have described it as: "cozy, cute, and clean." They always comment about the opportunity to meet people from all over the world in it. Barbara recalls having guests from 14 different nations at the same time. The possibilities for conversation and friendship are endless. Deep-sea fishing, nature trails, and harbor tours are but a few things to keep you busy. Freshly baked croissants in various flavors are a breakfast delight.

Willow Oaks Plantation
2380 LONDON BRIDGE ROAD, PRINCESS ANNE STATION, VIRGINIA BEACH, VIRGINIA 23456

Tel: **(804) 427-9046**
Host(s): **Nancy Warren**
Location: **6 miles from routes 44 and 64**
No. of Rooms: **5**
Maximum No. of Guests Sharing Bath: **4**
Double/sb: **$50**
Single/sb: **$30**
Months of Operation: **All year**

Reduced Rates: **10%, weekly; 10%, seniors**
Breakfast: **Full**
Other Meals: **Available**
Air-Conditioning: **Yes**
Pets: **Sometimes**
Children: **No**
Smoking: **Permitted**
Social Drinking: **Permitted**
Airport Pickup: **Yes**

Situated in the farming area of Virginia Beach, this 18th-century farmhouse is in the center of historic Princess Anne County and just a short ride from the ocean. There's a warm and friendly atmosphere, and the house is tastefully decorated in authentic country style with antiques, folk art, and hunting memorabilia. Take quiet walks in the country, spend the day at the beach, or just relax in the shade of the old oak trees. Country shops, golf, and tennis are nearby.

The Travel Tree
P. O. BOX 838, WILLIAMSBURG, VIRGINIA 23187

Tel: **(804) 565-2236 or 229-4037 (call 5:00 PM to 9:00 PM only)**
Coordinator: **Joann Proper and Sheila Zubkoff**
States/Regions Covered: **Williamsburg, Jamestown, Yorktown**

Rates (Single/Double):
Modest:	**$20–$24**	**$25–$30**
Average:	**$28–$32**	**$35–$40**
Luxury:	**$40–$48**	**$50–$60**

Credit Cards: **No**

You will thoroughly enjoy colonial Williamsburg, historic Jamestown and Yorktown, Busch Gardens, and Carter's Grove Plantation. Your bedroom might be furnished with canopy beds and antiques, or tucked under the eaves in a wooded setting, or in a luxurious town house complete with swimming pool. There is even a three-bedroom condo overlooking the York River, perfect for a family planning a three-day minimum stay.

Carter's Guest House
903 LAFAYETTE STREET, WILLIAMSBURG, VIRGINIA 23185

Tel: **(804) 229-1117**
Host(s): **Mrs. H. J. Carter**
No. of Rooms: **2**
Maximum No. of Guests Sharing
   Bath: **4**
Double/sb: **$18–$20**
Single/sb: **$18**
Months of Operation: **All year**

Reduced Rates: **No**
Breakfast: **No**
Air-Conditioning: **Yes**
Pets: **No**
Children: **Welcome**
Smoking: **Permitted**
Social Drinking: **No**

This brick Cape Cod home is located in town, three-quarters of a mile from the restored area, and five miles from the popular Williamsburg Pottery. Mrs. Carter enjoys meeting people and her hobby of doing beautiful needlework is evident in the decor. She will direct you to restaurants to suit your palate and purse.

The Cedars
616 JAMESTOWN ROAD, WILLIAMSBURG, VIRGINIA 23185

Tel: **(804) 229-3591**
Host(s): **Rose deB. Harris**
No. of Rooms: **6**
No. of Private Baths: **6**
Maximum No. of Guests Sharing
   Bath: **n/a**
Double/pb: **$32**
Single/pb: **$28**
Suites: **$58 (for 4)**
Guest Cottage: **$80 sleeps 6**

Months of Operation: **All year**
Reduced Rates: **10%, January 5 to
   March 15**
Breakfast: **Continental**
Air-Conditioning: **Yes**
Pets: **Sometimes**
Children: **Welcome**
Smoking: **Permitted**
Social Drinking: **Permitted**

A guest house of distinction, attractively furnished in the Williamsburg tradition, this stately home is within walking distance of the restored area and is located opposite Phi Beta Kappa Hall of the College of William and Mary, where many cultural activities are presented. Rose, your charming hostess, exudes southern hospitality. Continental breakfast is offered from May through October.

The Chateau
330 INDIAN SPRINGS ROAD, WILLIAMSBURG, VIRGINIA 23185

Tel: **(804) 253-2323**	Reduced Rates: **No**
Host(s): **Evelyn Charbeneau**	Breakfast: **No**
No. of Rooms: **3**	Air-Conditioning: **Yes**
No. of Private Baths: **3**	Pets: **Sometimes**
Double/pb: **$35**	Children: **Welcome**
Single/pb: **$30**	Smoking: **No**
Months of Operation: **All year**	Social Drinking: **No**

The Chateau offers three separate guest units located a short walk from Williamsburg's restored district. All have private entrances and overlook a shady ravine. The house was designed by a local architect and is comfortably furnished. Shops, restaurants, and Merchant's Square are a short walk from the house. Other local sights include Busch Gardens, and William and Mary College.

Fisher's Guest Lodge
571 RICHMOND ROAD, WILLIAMSBURG, VIRGINIA 23185

Tel: **(804) 229-4320**	Breakfast: **No**
Host(s): **Marge and Bill Fisher**	Air-Conditioning: **Yes**
No. of Rooms: **2**	Pets: **No**
No. of Private Baths: **2**	Children: **Welcome**
Double/pb: **$30–$35**	Smoking: **Permitted**
Single/pb: **$30–$35**	Social Drinking: **Permitted**
Months of Operation: **All year**	Airport Pickup: **Yes**
Reduced Rates: **Available**	

Located a few blocks from the heart of the historic district, this home contains all the colonial elements. The bedrooms have either brass or canopy beds, and the period trimmings are in formal taste. Marge and Bill will direct you to the nearby College of William and Mary. The famed Busch Gardens are three and a half miles away. Coffee, tea, and cold drinks are graciously offered.

Thompson Guest House
P.O. BOX 777, 1007 LAFAYETTE STREET, WILLIAMSBURG, VIRGINIA 23185

Tel: **(804) 229-3455**	Single/sb: **$18**
Host(s): **Alma Thompson**	Months of Operation: **All year**
No. of Rooms: **3**	Reduced Rates: **No**
No. of Private Baths: **1**	Breakfast: **No**
Maximum No. of Guests Sharing Bath: **4**	Air-Conditioning: **Yes**
	Pets: **No**
Double/pb: **$25**	Children: **Welcome**
Single/pb: **$25**	Smoking: **Permitted**
Double/sb: **$18**	Social Drinking: **No**

This charming house is located close to the historic district, where you can get the look and feel of another century. Alma is a most gracious hostess and will take the time to direct you to the not-to-be-missed sights, fine restaurants, and interesting shops.

Wood's Guest Home
1208 STEWART DRIVE, WILLIAMSBURG, VIRGINIA 23185

Tel: **(804) 229-3376**	Months of Operation: **All year**
Host(s): **Lonnie and Betty Wood**	Reduced Rates: **No**
No. of Rooms: **3**	Breakfast: **Continental**
No. of Private Baths: **n/a**	Air-Conditioning: **Yes**
Maximum No. of Guests Sharing Bath: **5**	Pets: **Sometimes**
	Children: **Welcome**
Double/sb: **$22.88**	Smoking: **Permitted**
Single/sb: **$22.88**	Social Drinking: **Permitted**

This comfortable, rambling house is filled with handmade crafts and modern pieces. Relax on the screened-in porch or in the living room with a fresh cup of coffee and a cookie. Colonial Williamsburg, Busch Gardens, Jamestown, Yorktown, and Carter's Grove Plantation are just a few of the local sights.

WASHINGTON

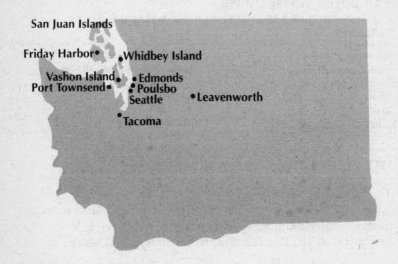

San Juan Islands

Friday Harbor • • Whidbey Island

Vashon Island • • Edmonds
Port Townsend • • Poulsbo
Seattle • Leavenworth

• Tacoma

Pacific Bed & Breakfast
701 N.W. 60TH STREET, SEATTLE, WASHINGTON 98107

Tel: **(206) 784-0539**
Coordinator: **Irmgard Castleberry**
States/Regions Covered: **Anacortes, Ashford, Bellevue, Gig Harbor, Mercer Island, Seattle, Spokane, Tacoma, Vashon Island**

Rates (Single/Double):
Modest: **$16–$25** **$28**
Average: **$25** **$35**
Luxury: **$30** **$40**
Credit Cards: **MC, VISA**

The above is but a partial list of the host homes available through Irmgard. There are Victorians, contemporaries, island cottages, waterfront houses, and private suites with full kitchens available. Most are close to downtown areas, near bus lines, in fine residential neighborhoods, or within walking distance of a beach. Many extras are included, such as pickup service, free use of laundry facilities, guided tours and more. Send two dollars for a descriptive directory.

Traveller's Bed & Breakfast—Seattle
BOX 492 MERCER ISLAND, WASHINGTON 98040

Tel: (206) 232-2345
Coordinator: **Jean Knight**
States/Regions Covered: **Bainbridge, Gig Harbor, Port Angeles, Port Townsend, Seattle, Tacoma, Vashon Island, Whidbey Island**

Rates (Single/Double):
  Modest: **$25**   **$35**
  Average: **$35**   **$45**
  Luxury: **$65**   **$65**
Credit Cards: **MC, VISA**

Jean has a roster of beautiful homes, deluxe accommodations, rooms with views of Puget Sound, and more. Rental cars and local tours can be arranged. Don't miss the Space Needle, Mount St. Helens, Mount Rainier, as well as Vancouver and Victoria, British Columbia. A ferry ride will take you to the surrounding islands and the most gorgeous scenery anywhere. Send $3.50 for her annotated listing of homes. Let Jean know your choice. She'll do the rest.

The Channel House
2902 OAKES AVENUE, ANACORTES, WASHINGTON 98221

Tel: **(206) 293-9382**
Host(s): **Sam and Kathy Salzinger**
Location: **65 miles north of Seattle, 18 miles from I-5**
No. of Rooms: **4**
Maximum No. of Guests Sharing Bath: **4**
Double/sb: **$45**
Single/sb: **$38**
Months of Operation: **All year**

Reduced Rates: **10%, September 15 to June 15**
Breakfast: **Continental**
Air-Conditioning: **Unnecessary**
Pets: **No**
Children: **Welcome, over 10**
Smoking: **No**
Social Drinking: **Permitted**
Airport Pickup: **Yes**

Built in 1902 by an Italian count, this three-story Victorian house has stained glass windows, rare antiques, gracious ambience, and is in mint condition. The guest rooms have beautiful views of Puget Sound and the San Juan islands. It's an ideal getaway for those who want to relax in the "cleanest corner of the country." Kathy serves gourmet breakfasts in front of the fireplace, and Sam's 23-foot sloop is ideal for sailing. The communal hot tub is a treat after you've been salmon fishing, playing tennis, or golf. And it's only minutes from the ferry in case you want to visit Victoria, British Columbia.

Phoenix Inn Bed & Breakfast
4569 LYNWOOD CENTER ROAD N.E., BAINBRIDGE ISLAND, WASHINGTON 98110

Tel: **(206) 842-0341**
Host(s): **Diane Moser**
Location: **2½ miles from Island City of Winslow**
No. of Rooms: **4**
No. of Private Baths: **2**
Maximum No. of Guests Sharing Bath: **4**
Double/pb: **$38–$42**
Single/pb: **$38**
Double/sb: **$38**

Single/sb: **$34**
Suites: **$49 (for 2)**
Months of Operation: **All year**
Reduced Rates: **No**
Breakfast: **Continental**
Air-Conditioning: **No**
Pets: **No**
Children: **Welcome, over 12**
Smoking: **No**
Social Drinking: **Permitted**

A view of Puget Sound and the warm English cottage furnishings gives the Phoenix Inn its charm. Tea carts, marble washstands, old pictures, and handmade pillows are some of the personal details in each room. You can browse in small, village shops, walk along Puget Sound, or just enjoy the beautiful surroundings.

Palmer's Chart House
P.O. BOX 51, ORCAS ISLAND, DEER HARBOR, WASHINGTON 98243

Tel: **(206) 376-4231**
Host(s): **Majean and Don Palmer**
Location: **50 miles north of Seattle**
No. of Rooms: **2**
No. of Private Baths: **2**
Double/pb: **$60**
Single/pb: **$45**
Months of Operation: **All year**
Reduced Rates: **No**

Breakfast: **Full**
Other Meals: **Dinner (included)**
Air-Conditioning: **No**
Pets: **No**
Children: **No**
Smoking: **No**
Social Drinking: **Permitted**
Airport Pickup: **Yes**
Foreign Languages: **Spanish**

It's just an hour's ride on the Washington State ferry from Anacortes to Orcas Island. This is an adult, private paradise—quiet and informal. Seasoned travelers, Majean and Don know exactly how to make your stay special. The guest rooms are carpeted, spacious, and spic and span. Each has a private deck from which you may survey the harbor scene. Majean loves to cook and local seafood often provides the basis for her special dinners, included in the rate. *Amante*, the 33-foot sloop, is available for sailing when Don, the skipper, is free.

Evergreen House
22606 87TH AVENUE W, EDMONDS, WASHINGTON 98020

Tel: **(206) 771-5536**	Reduced Rates: **No**
Host(s): **Marion and Sidney Snow**	Breakfast: **Continental**
Location: **15 miles north of Seattle**	Air-Conditioning: **No**
No. of Rooms: **1**	Pets: **No**
No. of Private Baths: **1**	Children: **No**
Double/pb: **$25**	Smoking: **No**
Single/pb: **$20**	Social Drinking: **Permitted**
Months of Operation: **All year**	

Your hosts have traveled widely and welcome you warmly to their comfortable contemporary-style home. Edmonds is often called the Gem of Puget Sound and offers fine restaurants, a fishing pier, excellent shopping, and ferry connections to the Olympic Peninsula and Canada. Marion is well known for her excellent home canning and preserves, which are evident at breakfast time.

The Harrison House
210 SUNSET AVENUE, EDMONDS, WASHINGTON 98020

Tel: **(206) 776-4748**	Reduced Rates: **No**
Host(s): **Jody and Harve Harrison**	Breakfast: **Continental—$2**
Location: **15 miles north of Seattle**	Air-Conditioning: **No**
No. of Rooms: **1**	Pets: **No**
No. of Private Baths: **1**	Children: **No**
Double/pb: **$25**	Smoking: **Permitted**
Single/pb: **$20**	Social Drinking: **Permitted**
Months of Operation: **All year**	

This new, informal, waterfront home has a fine view of Puget Sound and the Olympic Mountains. It is a block north of the ferry dock and three blocks from the center of this historic town. Many fine restaurants are within walking distance. The Harrisons' special interests are golf, mountain climbing, hiking, and travel.

Heather House
1011 "B" AVENUE, EDMONDS, WASHINGTON 98020

Tel: **(206) 778-7233**
Host(s): **Harry and Joy Whitcutt**
Location: **15 miles north of Seattle**
No. of Rooms: **1**
No. of Private Baths: **1**
Double/pb: **$25**
Single/pb: **$20**
Months of Operation: **All year**

Reduced Rates: **No**
Breakfast: **Full—$3**
Air-Conditioning: **Unnecessary**
Pets: **No**
Children: **No**
Smoking: **Permitted**
Social Drinking: **Permitted**
Foreign Languages: **French, German**

This contemporary home has a spectacular view of Puget Sound and the Olympic Mountains. The guest room has a comfortable king-size bed and opens onto a private deck. Joy and Harry are world travelers and enjoy visiting with their guests. The homemade jams and syrups for French toast and pancakes are delicious. You can work off breakfast by walking a mile to the shops, beaches, and fishing pier.

San Juan Hotel
50 SPRING STREET, FRIDAY HARBOR, WASHINGTON 98250

Tel: **(206) 378-2070**
Host(s): **Joan and Norm Schwinge**
Location: **50 miles north of Seattle**
No. of Rooms: **10**
Maximum No. of Guests Sharing
  Bath: **6**
Double/sb: **$38**
Single/sb: **$29**
Months of Operation: **All year**
Reduced Rates: **10%, October 15 to
  May 1**

Breakfast: **Continental**
Credit Cards: **MC, VISA**
Air-Conditioning: **Unnecessary**
Pets: **Sometimes**
Children: **Welcome, over 5**
Smoking: **Permitted**
Social Drinking: **Permitted**
Airport Pickup: **Yes**

Built in 1873, the San Juan is 100 feet from the ferry dock and steps away from restaurants and shops. Each guest room has quaint wallpaper, antique furnishings, and overlooks the harbor or the gardens. Norm and Joan provide bike rentals and will direct you to boating, fishing, national parks, a whaling museum, and the marine laboratory. In crisp weather, a crackling fire in the old nickel-plated parlor stove makes it a cozy spot to relax with the other guests.

Hillside Bed and Breakfast
6915 SILVER SPRINGS DRIVE N.W., GIG HARBOR, WASHINGTON 98335

Tel: **(206) 851-5007**
Host(s): **Carol and Dick Unrue**
Location: **10 miles from Tacoma, 3 miles from Route 16**
No. of Rooms: **1**
No. of Private Baths: **1**
Double/pb: **$30**
Single/pb: **$20**
Months of Operation: **All year**

Reduced Rates: **10%, 3 nights; 20%, weekly**
Breakfast: **Continental**
Air-Conditioning: **No**
Pets: **No**
Children: **Welcome, over 12**
Smoking: **No**
Social Drinking: **Permitted**

This comfortable home, set on a hillside, is surrounded by trees and flowers. Guests are welcome to relax by the fireside or in the garden or sun rooms. Arriving guests are greeted with wine and cheese. Fresh fruit muffins, blueberry pancakes, and eggs are served for breakfast. Gig Harbor and Point Defiance Park are nearby.

Mauss' by-the-Sea
8419 104TH STREET, GIG HARBOR, WASHINGTON 98335

Tel: **(206) 858-3171**
Host(s): **Tom and Karol Mauss**
Location: **2 miles on Sehmel Drive from Highway 16**
No. of Rooms: **1 suite**
Suites: **$35 for 1; $45 for 2**
Months of Operation: **All year**
Reduced Rates: **Weekly**

Breakfast: **Continental**
Other Meals: **Available**
Air-Conditioning: **No**
Pets: **No**
Children: **Welcome**
Smoking: **Permitted**
Social Drinking: **Permitted**

There is a half-mile of private beach to explore and a view of the Olympic Mountains to enjoy. There's a bedroom with a queen-size bed, a living room with a fireplace and hide-a-bed sofa, a full kitchen, and a private bath. Add to this a patio, picnic table, and private entrance, and you have a good picture of your home away from home. Puget Sound is 30 feet from the door.

The Olde Glencove Hotel
ROUTE 4, BOX 4616A, GIG HARBOR, WASHINGTON 98335

Tel: **(206) 884-2835**
Host(s): **Larry and Luciann Nadeau**
Location: **20 miles from Tacoma,**
6 miles from Highway 302
No. of Rooms: **2**
No. of Private Baths: **1**
Maximum No. of Guests Sharing
Bath: **2**
Double/pb: **$40**
Single/pb: **$40**
Double/sb: **$30**

Single/sb: **$30**
Months of Operation: **All year**
Reduced Rates: **15%, weekly**
Breakfast: **Full**
Other Meals: **Available**
Air-Conditioning: **No**
Pets: **Sometimes**
Children: **No**
Smoking: **Permitted**
Social Drinking: **Permitted**

This 1896 residence, listed on the National Historic Register, is located in a quiet cove on Puget Sound. Larry and Luciann have been restoring it to its original appearance, and they have decorated it with antiques and handcrafted stained glass. There's biking, boating, badminton, and croquet. Larry is known locally for his horseshoe game and backgammon expertise. The breakfast is special, and champagne and *hors d'oeuvres* are offered for your pre-dinner enjoyment.

Wauna Hide-a-Way
14416 GOODRICH DRIVE N.W., GIG HARBOR, WASHINGTON 98335

Tel: **(206) 851-4832**
Host(s): **Carolyn K. Harrison**
Location: **15 miles north of Tacoma.**
No. of Rooms: **2**
Maximum No. of Guests Sharing
Bath: **4**
Double/sb: **$35**
Single/sb: **$35**

Months of Operation: **All year**
Reduced Rates: **No**
Breakfast: **Continental**
Air-Conditioning: **Yes**
Pets: **No**
Children: **Welcome, over 10**
Smoking: **Permitted**
Social Drinking: **Permitted**

Overlooking the water, this modern home features a living room with a fireplace, a family room with a pool table and wet bar, and a barbecue on the patio. Guests are offered wine, champagne, and snacks. Breakfast includes homemade breads and jams. Henderson Bay, Horseshoe Lake, historic Purdy Bridge, and state parks are nearby.

Brown's Farm
11150 HIGHWAY 209, LEAVENWORTH, WASHINGTON 98826

Tel: **(509) 548-7863**
Host(s): **Steve and Wendi Brown**
Location: **115 miles from Seattle**
No. of Rooms: **2**
Maximum No. of Guests Sharing
  Bath: **4**
Double/sb: **$40–$45**
Single/sb: **$40–$45**

Months of Operation: **All year**
Reduced Rates: **No**
Breakfast: **Full**
Air-Conditioning: **No**
Pets: **Sometimes**
Children: **Welcome (crib)**
Smoking: **No**
Social Drinking: **Permitted**

It's like visiting Bavaria, because Leavenworth overlooks the snowcapped Icicle Ridge, the Wenatchee River, and is filled with European-style shops. The farm boasts a wooded setting for the delightful home built with love by Steve and Wendi and their children. It is furnished with antiques, handmade stained glass, lovely quilts, and a collection of family treasures. Breakfast is a feast. Children love the farm because there are eggs to gather, rabbits to hug, and a pony for rides. Children under four stay free, and you are requested to bring sleeping bags for older children.

Edel Haus Bed 'n' Breakfast
320 9TH STREET, LEAVENWORTH, WASHINGTON 98826

Tel: **(509) 548-4412**
Host(s): **Betsy and Mark Montgomery**
Location: **2 blocks from Route 2**
No. of Rooms: **4**
No. of Private Baths: **1**
Maximum No. of Guests Sharing
  Bath: **6**
Double/pb: **$43–$50**
Double/sb: **$38–$45**
Single/sb: **$28–$37.50**
Months of Operation: **All year**

Reduced Rates: **November, March,
  April; Sunday to Thursday; weekly**
Breakfast: **Full**
Other Meals: **Available (off-season)**
Credit Cards: **MC, VISA**
Air-Conditioning: **Yes**
Pets: **No**
Children: **Welcome**
Smoking: **No**
Social Drinking: **Permitted**
Airport Pickup: **Yes**

Located in a Bavarian-style village in the central Cascades, this white stucco two-story home was built in 1930. The rooms are light and airy, and are furnished with antiques. The view is of the riverfront park. In winter, the accent is on skiing, and Mark and Betsy offer cross-country ski instruction as well as high camp adventure in the Scottish Lake area. In summer, they will arrange bike tours, river rafting, and hay rides. In all seasons, relaxing in the hot tub is fun.

Lake Pateros B&B
206 WEST WARREN, BOX 595, PATEROS, WASHINGTON 98846

Tel: **(509) 923-2626**
Host(s): **Bob and Charlene Knoop**
Location: **19 miles north of Chelan**
No. of Rooms: **2**
Maximum No. of Guests Sharing
  Bath: **4**
Double/sb: **$33**
Single/sb: **$25**
Months of Operation: **All year**

Reduced Rates: **25%, October to April; 10%, seniors**
Breakfast: **Full**
Air-Conditioning: **Unnecessary**
Pets: **Sometimes**
Children: **Welcome**
Smoking: **No**
Social Drinking: **Permitted**

This white Dutch colonial has a red roof, red shutters, and is furnished with oak, wicker, and plants. The beds have handmade quilts and fluffy down pillows. Each room has a private half-bath and shares the full bath. It is located in the north central part of the state, known as the heart of Apple Country. Columbia River provides fabulous year-round fishing and water sports. Bob and Charlene want you to feel at home; you can use the kitchen for light snacks, and the washing machine and dryer are also available to you.

Lizzie's
731 PIERCE, PORT TOWNSEND, WASHINGTON 98368

Tel: **(206) 385-4168**
Host(s): **Thelma Scudi, Gabrielle and Charlie Ross**
Location: **10 miles from Route 101**
No. of Rooms: **7**
No. of Private Baths: **2½**
Maximum No. of Guests Sharing Bath: **5**
Double/pb: **$59–$79**
Single/pb: **$53–$73**
Double/sb: **$45–$69**
Single/sb: **$39–$63**

Months of Operation: **February 11 to November 28; December 16 to January 2**
Reduced Rates: **No**
Breakfast: **Full**
Credit Cards: **MC, VISA**
Air-Conditioning: **No**
Pets: **No**
Children: **Welcome, over 12**
Smoking: **Permitted**
Social Drinking: **Permitted**
Airport Pickup: **Yes**
Foreign Languages: **Japanese**

History has been beautifully preserved here. Relax amid fireplaces, leather sofas, and Parisian wallpaper; try your hand on the rosewood piano. Sandy beaches, charter and surf fishing, galleries, book and antique shops, hiking, and bicycling are close by. The famous Olympic Peninsula warrants closer inspection. There are breathtaking views of the Olympic and Cascade mountains, as well as Puget Sound. The coffee pot is always on. Lizzie's is a state-licensed, fire-safe facility.

Palace Hotel
1004 WATER STREET, PORT TOWNSEND, WASHINGTON 98368

Tel: **(206) 385-0773**
Host(s): **Liz and Bill Svensson**
No. of Rooms: **11**
No. of Private Baths: **8**
Maximum No. of Guests Sharing Bath: **6**
Double/pb: **$33–$54**
Single/pb: **$28–$49**
Double/sb: **$28**
Single/sb: **$23**
Suites: **$45 (for 4)**

Months of Operation: **All year**
Reduced Rates: **No**
Breakfast: **No**
Credit Cards: **MC, VISA**
Air-Conditioning: **No**
Pets: **No**
Children: **Welcome (crib)**
Smoking: **Permitted**
Social Drinking: **Permitted**
Foreign Languages: **Danish**

This three-story Victorian hotel, located on the downtown waterfront, is listed in the National Historic Register. The comfortable rooms are spacious, with 14-foot ceilings, and are furnished with antiques. Liz is an artist, Bill's an architect, and their professional talents are obvious. Although no breakfast is offered, the individual guest rooms are equipped with electric pots for making tea or coffee. Each suite has a fully equipped kitchen.

Burton Residence
P.O. BOX 9902, SEATTLE, WASHINGTON 98109

Tel: **(206) 285-5945**
Host(s): **Brenda Burton**
Location: **2 miles from I-15**
No. of Rooms: **3**
Maximum No. of Guests Sharing
  Bath: **5**
Double/sb: **$30–$35**
Single/sb: **$25**
Months of Operation: **All year**

Reduced Rates: **15%, after 3 nights,**
  November to April
Breakfast: **Continental**
Air-Conditioning: **No**
Pets: **Sometimes**
Children: **Welcome, over 3**
Smoking: **Permitted**
Social Drinking: **Permitted**

The Burton House was built in 1911 and has the high ceilings, massive brick fireplace, and wainscoting of that era. A buffet-style breakfast enables guests to help themselves whenever they like. The atmosphere is informal and comfortable. Downtown is a five-minute ride away, and the sights of Seattle include the aquarium and Pike Place Market.

The College Inn Guest House
4000 UNIVERSITY WAY N.E., SEATTLE, WASHINGTON 98105

Tel: **(206) 633-4441**
Host(s): **Gladys Louise Fred**
Location: **3 blocks from I-5**
No. of Rooms: **27**
Maximum No. of Guests Sharing
  Bath: **5**
Double/sb: **$37–$44**
Single/sb: **$26–$31**
Months of Operation: **All year**

Reduced Rates: **No**
Breakfast: **Continental**
Credit Cards: **AMEX, MC, VISA**
Air-Conditioning: **No**
Pets: **No**
Children: **Welcome**
Smoking: **Permitted**
Social Drinking: **Permitted**

Built in 1909, the inn is now on the National Register of Historic Places. Recently refurbished, this English Tudor building is an old-fashioned place within a cosmopolitan city. It is next door to the University of Washington and within walking distance of shops, theaters, parks, restaurants, and museums. Each guest room has a sink in it. Coffee and tea are always available.

Seattle Bed & Breakfast
2442 N.W. MARKET # 300, SEATTLE, WASHINGTON 98107

Tel: (206) 783-2169
Host(s): I. Pokrandt
Location: 1 mile from I-5
No. of Rooms: 3
No. of Private Baths: 1
Maximum No. of Guests Sharing
  Bath: 3
Double/pb: $34
Single/pb: $27
Double/sb: $28
Single/sb: $18
Suites: $34 (for 2)
Months of Operation: All year

Reduced Rates: 10%, weekly; 10%, seniors
Breakfast: Full
Other Meals: Available
Credit Cards: MC, VISA
Air-Conditioning: No
Pets: No
Children: Welcome
Smoking: No
Social Drinking: Permitted
Airport Pickup: Yes
Foreign Languages: German

Located in a quiet, residential neighborhood, this is a most comfortable home. The private, one-bedroom suite has a kitchen, so you can help yourself to breakfast, with fixings provided by your host. For houseguests, a full German breakfast of cold cuts, German specialties, and coddled eggs is served. The Pokrandts are world travelers and enjoy art, music, and good books.

The Shelburne Inn
P.O. BOX 250, SEAVIEW, WASHINGTON 98644

Tel: (206) 642-2442 or 642-4142
Host(s): David Campiche and
  Laurie Anderson
Location: 145 miles south of Seattle
No. of Rooms: 14
No. of Private Baths: 1
Maximum No. of Guests Sharing
  Bath: 6
Double/pb: $50
Single/pb: $50
Double/sb: $26–$32
Single/sb: $27

Months of Operation: All year
Reduced Rates: Groups
Breakfast: Continental
Other Meals: No
Credit Cards: MC, VISA
Air-Conditioning: Unnecessary
Pets: No
Children: Welcome (crib)
Smoking: Permitted
Social Drinking: Permitted
Foreign Languages: German, Spanish

This comfortable inn is operated by the husband and wife team of David and Laurie. It is furnished with lovely antiques, and all the guest rooms have individual charm. Most of the antiques you see are for sale. There's a marvelous seafood restaurant on the premises featuring home-baked breads and delightful desserts. From Sunday through Thursday, October 1 to April 15, a marvelous dinner, delicious breakfast, and lodging for two costs $75 per night.

Keenan House
2610 NORTH WARNER, TACOMA, WASHINGTON 98407

Tel: **(206) 752-0702**	Months of Operation: **All year**
Host(s): **Lenore Keenan**	Reduced Rates: **No**
Location: **2 miles from I-5**	Breakfast: **Full**
No. of Rooms: **5**	Air-Conditioning: **No**
Maximum No. of Guests Sharing	Pets: **No**
Bath: **4**	Children: **Welcome**
Double/sb: **$30**	Smoking: **Permitted**
Single/sb: **$25**	Social Drinking: **Permitted**

This spacious Victorian house is located in the historic district near Puget Sound. It is furnished in antiques and period pieces. Afternoon tea is served, and ice is available for cocktails; fruit and croissants are served each morning. Local possibilities include Puget Sound, Vashon Island, the state park, zoo, and ferry.

The Swallow's Nest
ROUTE 3, BOX 221, VASHON, WASHINGTON 98070

Tel: **(206) 463-2646**	Reduced Rates: **$30, 2 or more**
Host(s): **Kathryn Brown Keller**	**nights; $150, week**
Location: **15 minutes from Seattle by**	Breakfast: **Continental—$2.50**
ferry	Credit Cards: **MC, VISA**
No. of Rooms: **2 cottages**	Air-Conditioning: **Unnecessary**
No. of Private Baths: **2**	Pets: **No**
Guest Cottage: **$40 sleeps 2**	Children: **Welcome**
Months of Operation: **All year**	Smoking: **No**
	Social Drinking: **Permitted**

The "nest" actually consists of two lovely cottages overlooking Puget Sound and Mount Rainier. Fresh flowers and a basket of fruit help welcome guests. There are 20 acres of forest, fruit trees, and open fields to explore. Your breakfast is brought on a tray to the cottage.

Guest House Bed & Breakfast

835 EAST CHRISTENSON ROAD, GREENBANK, WHIDBEY ISLAND, WASHINGTON 98253

Tel: **(206) 678-3115**
Host(s): **Don and Mary Jane Creger**
Location: **49 miles northwest of Seattle**
No. of Rooms: **6**
No. of Private Baths: **5**
Maximum No. of Guests Sharing Bath: **4**
Double/pb: **$45**
Single/pb: **$40**
Double/sb: **$30–$35**
Single/sb: **$30–$35**

Guest Cottage: **$85 sleeps 5**
Months of Operation: **All year**
Reduced Rates: **Weekly, $245 for 2 in cottages**
Breakfast: **Continental**
Credit Cards: **MC, VISA**
Air-Conditioning: **Unnecessary**
Pets: **No**
Children: **Welcome, over 14**
Smoking: **No**
Social Drinking: **Permitted**

It is a delightful 15-minute ferry ride from Mukilteo to this lovely island. A variety of accommodations are offered, including two charming country guest rooms in the 1920 farmhouse, with shared bath; three self-contained private guest cottages cozily furnished with antiques, stained glass, fireplaces, and petite kitchens; and the luxurious log lodge that sleeps up to five. Continental breakfast is included with farmhouse accommodations. A full breakfast set-up in the cottages is $2.50 per person per day for a maximum of two days. Vancouver and Victoria, B.C., are an easy reach from Whidbey.

WEST VIRGINIA

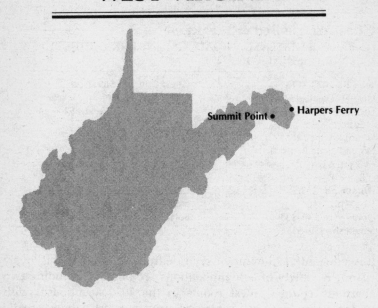

Summit Point • • Harpers Ferry

Summit Point Bed & Breakfast
BOX 57, SUMMIT POINT, WEST VIRGINIA 25446

Tel: **(304) 725-2614**
Host(s): **Lisa and Daniel Hileman**
Location: **8 miles from routes 7 and 50**
No. of Rooms: **2**
No. of Private Baths: **2**
Double/pb: **$35**
Single/pb: **$30**
Months of Operation: **All year**

Reduced Rates: **10%, December to April; after 3 nights**
Breakfast: **Continental**
Air-Conditioning: **No**
Pets: **Yes**
Children: **Welcome**
Smoking: **Permitted**
Social Drinking: **Permitted**
Foreign Languages: **Spanish**

In the Shenandoah Valley of the Eastern Panhandle, only 20 minutes from Harpers Ferry, this country home with white shutters, large yard, and patio is on a quiet street in a charming old village. It is furnished with country oak furniture, antique quilts, and original art. Lisa and Daniel offer an escape from stress, and hospitable touches of fruit and candy are placed in each guest room. Snacks, beverages, and cookies with ice cream are offered in the evening.

WISCONSIN

Seven Gables
215 6TH STREET, BARABOO, WISCONSIN 53913

Tel: (608) 356-8387
Host(s): **Ralph and Pamela W. Krainik**

Location: **13 miles from I-90**
No. of Rooms: **1 suite**

No. of Private Baths: **1**
Suite: **$50**
Months of Operation: **All year**
Reduced Rates: **10%, seniors**
Breakfast: **Continental**
Credit Cards: **MC**

Air-Conditioning: **No**
Pets: **No**
Children: **Welcome**
Smoking: **No**
Social Drinking: **Permitted**

Seven Gables is a restored 1860 Gothic Revival home. It is on the National Register of Historic Places as one of the best examples of Gothic Revival architecture. The 17 rooms are furnished entirely with Civil War–period furnishings. Pamela and Ralph will be happy to direct you to the activities, restaurants, and shops that make their area special.

Old Birnamwood Inn
425 MAPLE STREET, BIRNAMWOOD, WISCONSIN 54414

Tel: **(715) 449-2883**
Host(s): **Penelope Mordeu, Thomas Opper**
Location: **21 miles east of Wausau**
No. of Rooms: **14**
Maximum No. of Guests Sharing Bath: **20**
Double/sb: **$18.50**
Single/sb: **$13.50**

Months of Operation: **All year**
Reduced Rates: **Groups**
Breakfast: **Full**
Other Meals: **Available**
Air-Conditioning: **No**
Pets: **No**
Children: **Welcome (crib)**
Smoking: **Permitted**
Social Drinking: **Permitted**

In the scenic north woods of Wisconsin, this restored turn-of-the-century hotel is furnished with antiques. Penelope and Thomas are interested in restoration, preservation, carpentry, and craftsmanship, and the house looks it. It's close to Rib Mountain for skiing, Wolf River for white-water rafting. Free tennis, swimming, fishing, hiking, biking and hunting are nearby. A relaxing sauna is on the premises and arrangements can be made for hayrides and box lunches.

Village Guest House
P.O. BOX 98, LAKE DELTON, WISCONSIN 53940

Tel: **(608) 254-6568**
Host(s): **O. J. and Lois Thompto**
Location: **50 miles from Madison on Highway 12**

No. of Rooms: **2**
No. of Private Baths: **2**
Double/pb: **$50**
Single/pb: **$50**

Months of Operation: **All year**
Reduced Rates: **No**
Breakfast: **Continental**
Air-Conditioning: **Yes**

Pets: **Sometimes**
Children: **Welcome, over 12**
Smoking: **No**
Social Drinking: **Permitted**

Located midway between Milwaukee and The Twin Cities, this brand new house was built especially for B&B. It is situated on a major waterway; there's access to an enchanting creek and lake for fishing, swimming, and boating. It's five miles from the International Crane Foundation where you can watch cranes from Africa, Asia, and America. O. J. and Lois look forward to greeting you, and will arrange for discounts to many restaurants and shops.

The Duke House
618 MAIDEN STREET, MINERAL POINT, WISCONSIN 53565

Tel: **(608) 987-2821**
Host(s): **Tom and Darlene Duke**
Location: **48 miles southwest of Madison**
No. of Rooms: **3**
Maximum No. of Guests Sharing Bath: **6**
Double/sb: **$35**
Single/sb: **$25**

Months of Operation: **All year**
Reduced Rates: **No**
Breakfast: **Continental**
Air-Conditioning: **Yes**
Pets: **No**
Children: **No**
Smoking: **Permitted**
Social Drinking: **Permitted**

This colonial corner house is furnished with antique beds and hardwood floors. Tea and pastries or wine and cheese are served in the afternoon. Breakfast features homemade breads and coffee cakes. Local possibilities include House-on-the-Rock, Frank Lloyd Wright architecture, Governor Dodge State Park, and the Wisconsin River.

Farmhand Cottage
ROUTE 1, BOX 216, PRAIRIE DU SAC, WISCONSIN 53578

Tel: **(608) 643-4258**
Host(s): **Robert and Joan Weiss**
Location: **1 mile west of Highway 12**
No. of Rooms: **1 cottage**
No. of Private Baths: **1**

Guest Cottage: **$25–$35 sleeps up to 4**
Months of Operation: **All year**
Reduced Rates: **Available**
Breakfast: **Full**

Air-Conditioning: **No**
Pets: **No**
Children: **Welcome**

Smoking: **Permitted**
Social Drinking: **Permitted**
Foreign Languages: **German**

Joan and Bob have a working beef-hog farm located halfway between the Dells and the House-on-the-Rock in Mineral Point. The self-contained guest cottage is 90 years old and furnished with antiques and an up-to-date water bed. The fixings for a do-it-yourself breakfast are supplied and include freshly laid eggs, homemade bread, and jam from homegrown strawberries.

The Lake House
515 ELM STREET, RR2, BOX 217, STRUM, WISCONSIN 54770

Tel: **(715) 695-3519**
Host(s): **Florence Gullicksrud**
Location: **20 miles south of Eau Claire**
No. of Rooms: **2**
No. of Private Baths: **1**
Maximum No. of Guests Sharing Bath: **4**
Double/pb: **$20**
Single/pb: **$15**
Double/sb: **$20**
Single/sb: **$15**

Suites: **$35**
Months of Operation: **May 30 to Labor Day**
Reduced Rates: **No**
Breakfast: **Continental**
Air-Conditioning: **No**
Pets: **Sometimes**
Children: **Welcome, over 4**
Smoking: **Permitted**
Social Drinking: **Permitted**
Airport Pickup: **Yes**

This lovely lakeside home is surrounded by parks and hills. There are miles of hiking trails through scenic farm country as well as a nine-hole golf course and free tennis. Or, you can just stay "home" and use the canoe, rowboat, and picnic table. Florence is a retired nurse, is interested in art, and devotes herself to making her guests feel at home. The two-bedroom suite is best suited to a couple with children or friends traveling together. It's a half-hour to the University of Wisconsin, theater, and concerts.

White Lace Inn—A Victorian Guest House
15 NORTH FIFTH AVENUE, STURGEON BAY, WISCONSIN 54235

Tel: **(414) 743-1105**
Host(s): **Dennis and Bonnie Statz**
Location: **175 miles north of Milwaukee**

No. of Rooms: **10**
No. of Private Baths: **10**
Double/pb: **$45–$54**
Single/pb: **$40–$49**

Months of Operation: **January through March; May through October**
Reduced Rates: **15%, January to March, 3 or more days**
Breakfast: **Continental**
Credit Cards: **MC, VISA**

Air-Conditioning: **Yes**
Pets: **No**
Children: **Welcome, over 6**
Smoking: **Permitted**
Social Drinking: **Permitted**
Airport Pickup: **Yes**

This elegant Victorian guest house is beautifully furnished with quality antiques, Laura Ashley fabrics and wallpapers, down pillows, cozy comforters, brass canopy beds, lace curtains, and fine rugs. Located in a residential area close to the bay, it is near shops and historic sites. Winter features great cross-country skiing, snow sports, and hot chocolate in front of the fireplace. Summer offers boating, tennis, and swimming with iced tea served on the front porch.

The Serendipity Farm
ROUTE 3, BOX 162, VIROQUA, WISCONSIN 54665

Tel: **(608) 637-7708**
Host(s): **Suzanne Garrett**
Location: **30 miles southeast of La Crosse**
No. of Rooms: **1 cottage**
No. of Private Baths: **1**
Guest Cottage: **$50 sleeps 6**
Months of Operation: **All year**
Reduced Rates: **Weekly**

Breakfast: **Continental**
Other Meals: **No**
Credit Cards: **No**
Air-Conditioning: **Unnecessary**
Pets: **No**
Children: **Welcome, over 11**
Smoking: **Permitted**
Social Drinking: **Permitted**

You will find tranquility and privacy in this lovely stone cottage on a 200-acre dairy farm. While you are relaxing, the Garrett family is busy working sunup to sundown, tending the cows, hogs, chickens, and ducks. Suzanne stocks your kitchen with all the necessary staples, delicious Wisconsin cheese, and freshly laid eggs so you can fix breakfast at your leisure. Try the Kickapoo River for exciting rapids and canoeing.

WYOMING

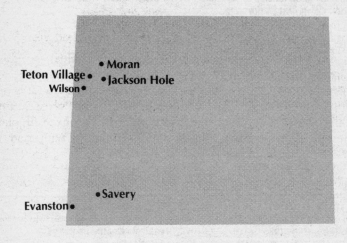

Teton Village •
Wilson •
• Moran
• Jackson Hole

• Savery
Evanston •

Captain Bob Morris
BOX 261, TETON VILLAGE, JACKSON HOLE, WYOMING 83025

Tel: (307) 733-4413 (mornings, please)
Host(s): **Captain Bob Morris**
Location: **7 miles from Highway 22**
No. of Rooms: **2**
No. of Private Baths: **1**
Maximum No. of Guests Sharing
  Bath: **3**
Double/pb: **$30**
Single/pb: **$25**
Double/sb: **$25**

Single/sb: **$20**
Months of Operation: **December 1 to**
  April 15; May 30 to October 15
Reduced Rates: **Non-smokers**
Breakfast: **Continental**
Air-Conditioning: **Unnecessary**
Pets: **Yes**
Children: **Welcome**
Smoking: **Permitted**
Social Drinking: **Permitted**

There's room for you in a fabulous contemporary house with the only red roof in the village. It's just 400 yards from the longest tram in the U.S. Skiing is the keynote here but the other wonderful things to do include visiting Yellowstone or Grand Teton national parks, experiencing Snake River in a raft, or riding western-style.

Pine Gables Bed and Breakfast Inn
1049 CENTER STREET, EVANSTON, WYOMING 82930

Tel: (307) 789-2069
Host(s): **Jessie and Arthur Monroe**
Location: **85 miles east of Salt Lake City**
No. of Rooms: **6**
No. of Private Baths: **2**
Maximum No. of Guests Sharing Bath: **4**
Double/pb: **$28.50**
Single/pb: **$26.50**
Double/sb: **$28.50**
Single/sb: **$26.50**
Suites: **$32.50**
Months of Operation: **All year**
Reduced Rates: **15%, November to April; 20%, seniors**
Breakfast: **Continental**
Credit Cards: **CB, DC, MC, VISA**
Air-Conditioning: **No**
Pets: **Sometimes**
Children: **Yes**
Smoking: **Permitted**
Social Drinking: **Permitted**
Airport Pickup: **Yes**

This antique-filled inn is one of the sites on the tour of Evanston's historic district. Each of the six bedrooms is furnished with collectibles and decorated using different woods—oak, cherry, mahogany, and walnut. Your hosts operate an antique shop on the premises. They prepare a breakfast of homemade breads and pastries. Hiking, fishing, skiing, and hunting are nearby.

KEY TO LISTINGS

Location: As specified, unless B&B is right in town, or its location is clear from address as stated.

No. of Rooms: Refers to the number of guest bedrooms.

Double: Rate for two people in one room.

Single: Rate for one person in a room.

Suite: Can either be two bedrooms with an adjoining bath, or a living room and bedroom with private bath.

Guest Cottage: A separate building that usually has a mini-kitchen and private bath.

pb: Private bath.

sb: Shared bath.

Breakfast: Included, unless otherwise noted.

Air-Conditioning: If "no" or "unnecessary" is stated, it means the climate rarely warrants it.

Children: If "crib" is noted after the word "welcome," this indicates that the host also has a high-chair, baby-sitters are available, and the B&B can accommodate children under the age of three.

Smoking: If permitted, this means it is allowed *somewhere* inside the house.

Social Drinking: Some hosts provide a glass of wine or sherry; others provide setups for bring-your-own.

Please enclose a self-addressed, stamped, business-size envelope when contacting Reservation Services.

Remember the difference in time zones when calling for a reservation.

Canada

Note: All prices listed in this section are quoted in Canadian dollars.

NOVA SCOTIA

Bute Arran
P.O. BOX 75, BADDECK, NOVA SCOTIA, CANADA B0E 1B0

Tel: **(902) 295-2786**
Host(s): **Donald and Margot MacAulay**
Location: **2 miles from Trans Canada Highway 105**
No. of Rooms: **4**
No. of Private Baths: **1**
Maximum No. of Guests Sharing Bath: **5**
Double/pb: **$30**
Single/pb: **$30**
Double/sb: **$25**

Single/sb: **$20**
Months of Operation: **May 16 to October 14**
Reduced Rates: **No**
Breakfast: **Full**
Credit Cards: **AMEX, MC, VISA**
Air-Conditioning: **No**
Pets: **Sometimes**
Children: **Welcome (crib)**
Smoking: **Permitted**
Social Drinking: **Permitted**

This rambling Cape Cod cottage is on the shore of the Bras d'Or Lake. It is convenient to the famed Cabot Trail, a scenic 185-mile drive around northern Cape Breton. It is one mile east of the Alexander Graham Bell Museum. It is furnished in a comfortable blend of antique and modern pieces, with lots of books and games for guests of all ages. Breakfast features hearty oatcakes and scones. The MacAulays serve tea in the evening.

Confederation Farm
RR3, PARRSBORO, DILIGENT RIVER, NOVA SCOTIA, CANADA
B0M 1S0

Tel: **(902) 254-3057**
Host(s): **Bob and Julia Salter**
Location: **45 miles south of Amherst**
No. of Rooms: **4**
No. of Baths: **2**
Maximum No. of Guests Sharing
  Bath: **4**
Double/sb: **$25**
Single/sb: **$19**
Months of Operation: **May 1 to
  November 15**

Reduced Rates: **No**
Breakfast: **Full**
Other Meals: **Available**
Air-Conditioning: **No**
Pets: **Sometimes**
Children: **Welcome (crib)**
Smoking: **Permitted**
Social Drinking: **Permitted**
Airport Pickup: **Halifax—rates on
  request**

This peaceful berry and fruit farm overlooks Cape Split on the Bay of Fundy. The farmhouse is homey, comfortable, and immaculate. Julia sets a table fit for royalty, featuring the seafood specialties that the area is famous for. Prices are modest and portions are hefty. Be sure to ask to see Bob's Horse and Buggy Days museum containing a collection of family memorabilia from way back when. The highest tides in the world may be viewed here, and it is a rockhound's paradise. The Salters have three housekeeping cottages as well as a picnic park on their property.

ONTARIO

Ottawa Area Bed & Breakfast
P.O. BOX 4848, STATION E, OTTAWA, ONTARIO, CANADA K1S 5J1

Tel: **(613) 563-0161**
Coodinator: **Suzan Bissett, Al Martin**
States/Regions Covered:
  **Ontario—Kanata, Nepean,
  Gloucester, Ottawa; Quebec—Hull**

Rates (Single/Double):
  Modest: **$18**   **$20**
  Average: **$25**   **$30**
Credit Cards: **No**

If you are seeking an interesting but inexpensive holiday, then Canada's capital, Ottawa, is the place for you. The city is packed with free activities including museums, the House of Parliament, art galleries, and historic sites. You can skate on the Rideau Canal or bike on miles of parkways and trails. The variety of homes include those located in the heart of the city, suburban homes with pools, lovely farms, and beach houses. There is a $25 membership fee to join the organization.

Toronto Bed & Breakfast
P.O. BOX 74, STATION M, TORONTO, ONTARIO, M6S 4T2

Tel: **(416) 233-3887 or 233-4041 (call evenings & weekends)**
 Coordinator: **Randy Lee**
 States/Regions Covered: **Toronto**
	Rates (Single/Double):
	   Modest: **$25** **$35**
	   Average: **$30** **$45**
	 Credit Cards: **No**
	 Minimum Stay: **2 nights**

Toronto, located on Lake Ontario, is a sophisticated city, but the hosts in Randy's network of homes are warm, friendly, and helpful. Accommodations vary from a bedroom in a British colonial to a terraced penthouse suite in a luxury condo; full breakfast is included. All homes are convenient to public transportation, so that you can easily visit the CN Tower, the Ontario Science Centre, Fort York, and the exciting Harbourfront with its craft galleries and ethnic restaurants. Send two dollars for the descriptive directory and make your reservations directly with the host of your choice.

Oppenheim's
153 HURON STREET, TORONTO, CANADA M5T 2B6

Tel: **(416) 598-4562 or 598-4063** Host(s): **Susan Oppenheim** Location: **Downtown Toronto** No. of Rooms: **4** Maximum No. of Guests Sharing Bath: **3** Double/sb: **$40** Single/sb: **$20** Months of Operation: **All year**	Reduced Rates: **No** Breakfast: **Full** Air-Conditioning: **No** Pets: **No** Children: **No** Smoking: **No** Social Drinking: **Permitted** Foreign Languages: **French**

Susan is a singer-lyricist, and you are welcome to accompany her on one of the four pianos in this restored Victorian house that is furnished with memorabilia, warmth, and humor. She shops at the international Kensington Market, so breakfast often features seasonal specials like banana buttermilk pancakes, glazed maple syrup pears, or dilled Havarti omelets. It is served in her huge kitchen whimsically decorated to resemble a turn-of-the-century country store. It's located three blocks from the Art Gallery of Ontario, the Royal Museum, Parliament, and the University of Toronto. A three-day minimum stay is preferred.

Bed & Breakfast—Kingston
10 WESTVIEW ROAD, KINGSTON, ONTARIO, CANADA K7M 2C3

Tel: **(613) 542-0214**
Coodinator: **Ruth MacLachlan**
States/Regions Covered:
  **Ontario—Bath, Gananoque,
  Kingston, Perth, Westport**

Rates (Single/Double):
  Average: **$23**   **$31**
Credit Cards: **No**

Situated at the eastern end of Lake Ontario, at the head of the St. Lawrence River, Kingston has much to offer besides gorgeous scenery. There's Old Fort Henry, boat cruises through the Thousand Islands, historic sites, museums, and sports activities of every sort; the Rideau Nature Trail starts here and heads northeast towards Ottawa. Send one dollar for the detailed directory.

Jakobstettel Guest House
16 ISABELLA STREET, ST. JACOBS, ONTARIO NOB 2N0

Tel: **(519) 664-2208**
Host(s): **Ella Brubacher**
Location: **75 miles west of Ontario**
No. of Rooms: **12**
No. of Private Baths: **12**
Double/pb: **$55–$85**
Single/pb: **$40–$80**
Months of Operation: **All year**
Reduced Rates: **10%, weekly**

Breakfast: **Continental**
Other Meals: **Available**
Credit Cards: **AMEX, MC, VISA**
Air-Conditioning: **Yes**
Pets: **Sometimes**
Children: **Welcome**
Smoking: **Permitted**
Social Drinking: **Permitted**

Elegant individuality is the main feature of each guest room. This Victorian mansion lends itself to the ultimate in relaxation and is ideal for seminars and meetings. A swimming pool and tennis court are found in the backyard. For quiet moments, read a good book in the library, stroll in the woods, or enjoy casual conversation in the common room. This is Mennonite Country, famous for arts-and-crafts shops and fine restaurants. Ella offers snacks and beverages as part of her warm hospitality.

Bed & Breakfast Heritage Homes of Stratford
266 ONTARIO STREET, STRATFORD, ONTARIO, CANADA N5A 3H5

Tel: **(519) 271-5385**
Coodinator: **Pat Wilson and Grace Brunk**
States/Regions Covered: **Stratford**

Rates (Single/Double):
Modest:	**$25**	**$30**
Average:	**$30**	**$35**
Luxury:	**$35**	**$40**

Credit Cards: **No**

Stratford's Shakespearean Theatre is world renowned, and the beautiful parks, art galleries, excellent restaurants, and the Mennonite country will keep you busy and happy. Pat and Grace have hosts who look forward to sharing their knowledge of their hometown with you.

The Maples
220 CHURCH STREET, STRATFORD, ONTARIO, CANADA N5A 2R6

Tel: **(519) 273-0810**
Host(s): **Lina and Ed Morley**
Location: **18 miles from Highway 401**
No. of Rooms: **5**
Maximum No. of Guests Sharing Bath: **5**
Double/sb: **$25–$30**
Single/sb: **$20–$25**
Months of Operation: **All year**
Reduced Rates: **Groups**

Breakfast: **Continental**
Air-Conditioning: **No**
Pets: **No**
Children: **Welcome, over 10**
Smoking: **Permitted**
Social Drinking: **Permitted**
Airport Pickup: **Yes**
Foreign Languages: **French, German, Polish**

This 90-year-old red brick house is surrounded by a lovely garden, large maple trees, and a veranda. It is tastefully furnished with a warm blend of the old and the new. Your hosts are particularly hospitable. It is convenient to the famed Shakespear-

ean Theatre, summer music, Kitchener Farmer's Market, and the
African Lion Safari.

Glenbellart House

**285 MARY STREET, P.O. BOX 445, WIARTON PROVIDENCE,
ONTARIO, CANADA N0H 2T0**

Tel: **(519) 534-2422**
Host(s): **Sally and John Wright**
Location: **120 miles northwest of
    Toronto**
No. of Rooms: **3**
Maximum No. of Guests Sharing
    Bath: **8**
Double/sb: **$30**
Single/sb: **$25**
Months of Operation: **All year**

Reduced Rates: **No**
Breakfast: **Full**
Air-Conditioning: **No**
Pets: **No**
Children: **Welcome, over 10**
Smoking: **Permitted**
Social Drinking: **Permitted**
Airport Pickup: **Yes**
Foreign Languages: **French, German**

Built in 1886, this magnificent Victorian mansion has hand-
covered rosewood fireplaces, stained glass windows, oak floors, a
library, spacious bedrooms, and a full veranda overlooking
flowers and lawns, with a view of Colpoy Bay. It's close to sandy
beaches, clear water swimming, sailing, and fishing for salmon
and trout. John will happily describe outings and activities for all
seasons, while Sally prepares a hearty breakfast.

ALBERTA

Alberta Bed & Breakfast
4327 86TH STREET, EDMONTON, ALBERTA, CANADA T6K 1A9

Tel: **(403) 462-8885**
Coordinator: **June Brown**
States/Regions Covered: **Calgary, Edmonton**

Rates (Single/Double):
Modest:	**$15**	**$20**
Average:	**$20–$25**	**$30–$35**

Credit Cards: **No**

Try a bit of Canadian western hospitality by choosing from June's variety of lovely homes in the majestic Rocky Mountains. Make a circle tour of Calgary, Banff, Lake Louise, the Columbia Icefields, Jasper, and Edmonton and stay in B&Bs all the way. Send one dollar for a descriptive list of the cordial hosts on her roster, make your selections, and June will do the rest.

QUEBEC

Montreal Bed & Breakfast
5020 ST. KEVIN, SUITE B, MONTREAL, QUEBEC, CANADA H3W 1P4

Tel: **(514) 735-7493 or 738-3859**
Coodinator: **Marian Kahn**
States/Regions Covered: **Montreal, Ste. Adele (Laurentian Mountains), Sutton**

Rates (Single/Double):
Modest:	**$25**	**$35**
Average:	**$28–$30**	**$40–$45**
Luxury:	**$35**	**$50**

Credit Cards: **No**

Marian has a list of lovely homes in Montreal and Quebec City. Many hosts are French Canadian and the full breakfasts included in the rate often reflect a gourmet's touch. Visit Old Montreal and The Harbor for a glimpse of history, the Museum of Fine Arts, Place Des Arts for a touch of culture. McGill University, Mount

Royal Park, St. Helen's Island, and the Laurentian Mountains are all worth a visit too. There are marvelous restaurants, wonderful shops, and the people are warm and friendly.

PRINCE EDWARD ISLAND

Woodington's Country Inn
RR 2, KENSINGTON, PRINCE EDWARD ISLAND, C0B 1M0 CANADA

Tel: **(902) 836-5518**
Host(s): **Marion and Claude "Woody" Woodington**
No. of Rooms: **5**
Maximum No. of Guests Sharing Bath: **5**
Double/sb: **$27**
Single/sb: **$25**
Months of Operation: **All year**

Reduced Rates: **10%, after August 25**
Breakfast: **Full**
Other Meals: **Available**
Air-Conditioning: **No**
Pets: **Welcome**
Children: **Welcome**
Smoking: **Permitted**
Social Drinking: **Permitted**

Relax on the spacious lawns surrounding this immaculate Victorian farmhouse or stroll to the private beach. Your hosts are unusually hospitable and you'll feel at home immediately. Marion is a fabulous cook and her table reflects all that is fresh and wholesome. The charge is $25 per adult for three robust meals;

that includes your room too of course. Woody hand-carves the most realistic duck decoys you've ever seen. Marion's spare time is spent making gorgeous quilts. A wood carving or quilt would make a memorable souvenir to take home.

Sea Breeze
KENSINGTON RR #1, PRINCE EDWARD ISLAND, CANADA C0B 1M0

Tel: (902) 836-5275
Host(s): **Fran and Leslie Harding**
Location: **40 miles north of Charlottetown**
No. of Rooms: **3**
Maximum No. of Guests Sharing Bath: **6**
Double/sb: **$27**
Single/sb: **$13.50**
Months of Operation: **May 1 to October 30**

Reduced Rates: **10%, May 1 to July 10, August 20 to October 30**
Breakfast: **Full**
Other Meals: **Available**
Air-Conditioning: **No**
Pets: **Sometimes**
Children: **Welcome**
Smoking: **Permitted**
Social Drinking: **Permitted**

This modern home overlooks the harbor of a quiet island community. For those who like to fish, deep-sea or tuna excursions can be arranged. The beaches, shops, and Cabot Provincial Park are nearby.

Dyment Bed & Breakfast
RR 3, WILMOT VALLEY, SUMMERSIDE, PRINCE EDWARD ISLAND, CANADA CIN 4J9

Tel: (902) 436-9893
Host(s): **Earle and Wanda Dyment**
Location: **34 miles west of Charlottetown**
No. of Rooms: **3**
Maximum No. of Guests Sharing Bath: **6**
Double/sb: **$17–$18**
Single/sb: **$17**

Months of Operation: **May 20 to October 31**
Reduced Rates: **No**
Breakfast: **$1.50–$3.00**
Air-Conditioning: **No**
Pets: **Sometimes**
Children: **Welcome (crib)**
Smoking: **Permitted**
Social Drinking: **Permitted**

This spanking clean house is set in a picturesque farming area overlooking the Wilmost River. Wanda delights in having people stay, and allows you to use her kitchen for light snacks. There is much to do and see, including swimming, golf, deep-sea fishing, and going to the race track.

PUERTO RICO

Buena Vista Guest House
2218 GENERAL DEL VALLE, OCEAN PARK, SANTURCE, PUERTO RICO 00913

Tel: **(809) 726-2796**
Host: **N. Mondin**
Location: **Suburb of San Juan**
No. of Rooms: **11**
No. of Private Baths: **7**
Maximum No. of Guests Sharing
  Bath: **4**
Double/pb: **$35**
Single/pb: **$29**
Double/sb: **$32**
Single/sb: **$26**
Months of Operation: **All year**

Reduced Rates: **10%, April 15 to
  December 15**
Breakfast: **Full**
Other Meals: **Available**
Air-Conditioning: **Yes**
Pets: **No**
Children: **Welcome**
Smoking: **Permitted**
Social Drinking: **Permitted**
Airport Pickup: **Yes**
Foreign Languages: **French, Spanish**

You won't miss an ounce of sunshine on the terrace, patio, or porch of this comfortable tropical home. You're welcome to strum the guitar, play the piano, use the kitchen for light snacks, and generally make yourself at home. It's on the beach and all water sports are available. In the evenings you can visit the hotel casinos and clubs for glamorous excitement.

Appendix:
STATE TOURIST OFFICES

Listed here are the addresses and telephone numbers for the tourist offices of every U.S. state. When you write or call one of these offices, be sure to request a map of the state and a calendar of events. If you will be visiting a particular city or region, or if you have any special interests, be sure to specify them as well.

Alabama Bureau of Publicity
  and Information
532 South Perry Street
Montgomery, Alabama 36130
(205) 832-5510 or (800) 252-2262
  (out of state) or (800) 392-8096
  (within Alabama)

Alaska Division of Tourism
Pouch E
Juneau, Alaska 99801
(907) 465-2010

Arizona Office of Tourism
3507 North Central Avenue, Suite 506
Phoenix, Arizona 85012
(602) 255-3618 or (800) 352-8432
  (within Arizona)

Arkansas Department of Parks
  and Tourism
1 Capitol Mall
Little Rock, Arkansas 72201
(501) 371-7777 or (800) 643-8383
  (out of state) or (800) 482-8999
  (within Arkansas)

California Office of Tourism
1030 Thirteenth Street, Suite 200
Sacramento, California 95814
(916) 322-2881

Colorado Office of Tourism
Division of Commerce
  and Development
1313 Sherman Street, Room 500
Denver, Colorado 80203
(303) 866-2205

Connecticut Department of Economic
  Development
Tourism Promotion, 210 Washington
  Street
Hartford, Connecticut 06106
(203) 566-3948 or (800) 243-1685
  (out of state) or (800) 842-7492
  (within Connecticut)

Delaware State Travel Service
99 Kings Highway
Dover, Delaware 19901
(302) 736-4254 or (800) 441-8846
  (out of state) or (800) 282-8667
  (in Delaware)

Washington, D.C. Convention
  and Visitors' Assoc.
Suite 250
1575 I Street, N.W.
Washington, D.C. 20005
(202) 789-7000

Florida Division of Tourism
107 Gaines Street
Tallahassee, Florida 32301
(904) 487-1462

Georgia Department of Industry
  and Trade
Tourist Division
Box 1776
Atlanta, Georgia 30301
(404) 656-3590 or (800) 241-8444

Hawaii Visitors Bureau
2270 Kalakaua Avenue, Suite 801
Honolulu, Hawaii 96815
(808) 923-1811

Idaho Division of Tourism and
  Industrial Development
Capitol Building, Room 108
Boise, Idaho 83720
(208) 334-2470 or (800) 635-7820
  (out of state)

Illinois Office of Tourism
620 East Adams
Springfield, Illinois 62706
(217) 782-7139 or (800) 252-8987
  (within Illinois) or (800) 637-8560
  (neighboring states)

Indiana Tourism Development
  Division of Commerce
1 North Capitol, Suite 700
Indianapolis, Indiana 46204
(317) 232-8860

Iowa Development Commission
Tourist Development Division
600 East Court
Suite A—Capitol Center
Des Moines, Iowa 50309-2882
(515) 281-3251

Kansas Department of Economic
  Development
Capitol Plaza Tower, 22 Floor
Topeka, Kansas 66603
(913) 296-3481

Kentucky Department of Tourism
Fort Boone Plaza
Frankfort, Kentucky 40601
(502) 564-4930 or (800) 372-2961
  (within Kentucky)

Louisiana Office of Tourism
Inquiry Department
P.O. Box 44291
Baton Rouge, Louisiana 70804
(504) 925-3860 or (800) 535-8388
  (within Louisiana)

Maine Publicity Bureau
97 Winthrop St.
Hallowell, Maine 04347
(207) 289-2423

Maryland Office of Tourist
  Development
45 Calvert Street
Annapolis, Maryland 21401
(301) 269-2686 or (301) 268-3517

Massachusetts Division of Tourism
Department of Commerce and
  Development
100 Cambridge Street—13th Floor
Boston, Massachusetts 02202
(617) 727-3201 or (800) 343-9072
  (out of state) or (800) 632-8038
  (within Massachusetts)

Michigan Travel Bureau
Department of Commerce
525 W. Ottowa
Lansing, Michigan 48933
(517) 373-1195 or (800) 248-5700
  (outside Michigan) or
  (800) 292-2520 (in Michigan)

Minnesota Tourist Information Center
240 Bremer Building
41 North Robert St.
St. Paul, Minnesota 55101
(612) 296-5029 or (800) 328-1461

Mississippi Division of Tourism
P.O. Box 849
Jackson, Mississippi 39205
(601) 359-3414 or (800) 647-2290
  (out of state) or (800) 962-2346
  (within Mississippi)

Missouri Division of Tourism
P.O. Box. 1055
Jefferson City, Missouri 65102
(314) 751-4133

Montana Vacation Information
1424 9th Avenue
Helena, Montana 59620
(406) 444-2654 or (800) 548-3390
  (out of state)

Nebraska Division of Travel and
  Tourism
P.O. Box 94666
Lincoln, Nebraska 68509
(402) 471-3796 or (800) 742-7595
  (within Nebraska) or
  (800) 228-4307 (out of state)

Nevada Commission of Tourism
Capitol Complex
1100 East Williams
Carson City, Nevada 89710
(702) 885-4322

New Hampshire Division of
   Economic Development
Office of Vacation Information
P.O. Box 856
Concord, New Hampshire 03301
(603) 271-2343

New Jersey Division of Travel
   and Tourism
C.N. 826
Trenton, New Jersey 08625
(609) 292-2470

New Mexico Travel Division
Bataan Memorial Building
Santa Fe, New Mexico 87503
(505) 827-6230 or (800) 545-2040
   (out of state)

New York State Division of Tourism
99 Washington Avenue
Albany, New York 12245
(518) 474-4116 or (800) CALLNYS

North Carolina Travel and Tourism
   Division
P.O. Box 25249
Raleigh, North Carolina 27611
(919) 733-4171

North Dakota Tourism Promotion
State Capitol Grounds
Bismarck, North Dakota 58505
(701) 224-2525 or (800) 472-2100
   (within North Dakota)

Ohio Office of Tourism
P.O. Box 1001
Columbus, Ohio 43216
(614) 466-8844 or (800) BUCKEYE
   (within Ohio)

Oklahoma Division of Tourism
   Promotion
500 Will Rogers Building
Oklahoma City, Oklahoma 73105
(405) 521-2646 or (800) 522-8565
   (within Oklahoma)

Oregon Travel Information Office
595 Cottage Street, N.E.
Salem, Oregon 97310
(503) 373-7501 or (800) 547-7842
   (out of state) or (800) 233-3306
   (within Oregon)

Pennsylvania Bureau of Travel
   Development
Department of Commerce
415 South Office Building
Harrisburg, Pennsylvania 17120
(717) 787-5453 or (800) 323-1717

Rhode Island Department of
   Economic Development
Tourism Division
7 Jackson Walkway
Providence, Rhode Island 02903
(401) 277-2601 or (800) 556-2484 (out
   of state from Maine to Virginia)

South Carolina Division of Tourism
1205 Tendleton Street
Columbia, South Carolina 29201
(803) 758-2536

South Dakota Division of Tourism
Joe Foss Building
Pierre, South Dakota 57501
(605) 773-3301 or (800) 843-1930
   (within South Dakota)

Tennessee Tourist Development
P.O. Box 23170
Nashville, Tennessee 37202
(615) 741-2158

Texas Tourist Development
P.O. Box 1200A Capitol Station
Austin, Texas 78711
(512) 475-4326

Utah Travel Council
Council Hall
Capitol Hill
Salt Lake City, Utah 84114
(801) 533-5681

Vermont Travel Division
134 State Street
Montpelier, Vermont 05602
(802) 828-3236

Virginia State Travel Service
Ninth Street Office Building
Ninth and Grace—5th Floor
Richmond, Virginia 23219
(804) 786-4484

Washington State Department
  of Commerce and Economic
  Development
Travel Information
General Administration Building,
  Room 101-AX-13
Olympia, Washington 98504
(206) 753-5630

West Virginia Travel Development
  Division
Room 564, Building 6
1900 Washington Street East
Charleston, West Virginia 25305
(304) 348-2286 or (800) 624-9110

Wisconsin Division of Tourism
P.O. Box 7606
Madison, Wisconsin 53707
(608) 266-2161 or (800) 362-9566
  (within Wisconsin) or (800)
  ESCAPES (neighboring states)

Wyoming Travel Commission
Frank Norris, Jr. Travel Center
Cheyenne, Wyoming 82002
(307) 777-7777

BED AND BREAKFAST RESERVATION REQUEST FORM

Dear _____
    Host's Name

I read about your home in *Bed & Breakfast USA,* and would be interested in making reservations to stay with you.

My name: _____

Address: _____
     street

_____
     city   state   zip

Telephone: _____
     area code

Business address/telephone: _____

_____

Number of adult guests: _____

Number and ages of children: _____

Desired date and time of arrival: _____

Desired length of stay: _____

Mode of transportation: _____
(car, bus, train, plane)

Additional information/special requests: _____

_____

_____

_____

_____

_____

I look forward to hearing from you soon.

Sincerely,

WE WANT TO HEAR FROM YOU!

Name: _____

Address: _____
        street

_____
        city   state   zip

_____

Please contact the following B&Bs; I think that they would be great additions to the next edition of *Bed & Breakfast USA*.

Name of B&B: _____

Address: _____
        street

_____
        city   state   zip

Comments:

Name of B&B: _____

Address: _____
        street

_____
        city   state   zip

Comments:

_____

The following is our report on our visit to the home of:

Name of B&B: _____ Date of visit: _____

Address: _____ I was pleased. ☐

_____ I was disappointed. ☐

Comments:

Just tear out this page and mail it to us. It won't ruin your book!

Return to:
Tourist House Association of America
Box 355A, R.D. 2
Greentown, Pennsylvania 18426

INFORMATION ORDER FORM

We are constantly expanding our roster to include new members in the Tourist House Association of America. Their facilities will be fully described in the next edition of *Bed & Breakfast USA*. In the meantime, we will be happy to send you a list including the name, address, telephone number, minimum rates, etc.

For those of you who would like to order additional copies of the book or perhaps send one to a friend as a gift, we will be happy to fill mail orders. If it is a gift, let us know and we'll enclose a special gift card from you.

ORDER FORM

To:
Tourist House
Association
R.D. 2, Box 355A
Greentown, PA
18426

From: _____
(Print your name)
Address: _____

_____
City   State   Zip

Date: _____

Please send:
☐ List of new B&Bs ($1.50)
☐ _____ copies of *Bed & Breakfast, USA* @ $6.95 each plus $1 for 4th class mail; $3 for 1st class mail.

Send to: _____

Address: _____

_____
City   State   Zip

☐ Enclose a gift card from:

Please make check or money order payable to Tourist House Association.

APPLICATION FOR MEMBERSHIP
(Please type or print)

Name of Bed & Breakfast: _____

Address: _____

City: _____ State: _____ Zip: _____ Phone: (   ) _____

Host(s): _____

Located: No. of miles _____ Compass Direction _____ of

Major City _____

No. of miles _____ from Major Route _____

Accommodations: Total number of guest bedrooms: _____
Total number of private baths: _____
Maximum number of guests who must share
one bathroom: _____

Room Rates:
$_____ Double—private bath $_____ Double—shared bath
$_____ Single—private bath $_____ Single—shared bath
$_____ Children 12 or under $_____ Suites
Separate Guest Cottage $_____ Sleeps _____

Are you open year-round? ☐ Yes   ☐ No
If "No," specify when you are open: _____

Do you discount rates at any time? ☐ No   ☐ Yes   If "Yes,"
specify (ie., 10% less during March, April, November; 15% less
than daily rate if guests stay a week; $10 less per night Sunday
through Thursday).

_____

Do you offer a discount to senior citizens? ☐ No   ☐ Yes: _____%
Do you offer a discount for families? ☐ No   ☐ Yes: _____%

Breakfast: Type of breakfast included in rate:
☐ Full ☐ Continental
Breakfast is not included: ☐ cost: $ _____
Are any other meals provided? ☐ No   ☐ Yes
Lunch ☐ cost: $_____   Dinner ☐ cost: $_____
Meals are included in rate quoted with room ☐ Yes   ☐ No

Do you accept Credit Cards? ☐ No   ☐ Yes:
☐ AMEX   ☐ DINERS   ☐ MASTERCARD   ☐ VISA

Do you have household pets? ☐ Dog ☐ Cat ☐ Bird

Can you accommodate a guest's pet?
☐ Yes ☐ No ☐ Sometimes

Are children welcome? ☐ No ☐ Yes If "Yes," any age
restriction? _____

Do you object to smoking? ☐ Yes ☐ No

Do you object to social drinking? ☐ Yes ☐ No

Guests can be met at ☐ Airport ____ ☐ Train ____ ☐ Bus ____

Can you speak a foreign language fluently? ☐ No ☐ Yes

Describe: _____

GENERAL AREA OF YOUR B&B (i.e., Boston Historic District;
20 minutes from Chicago Loop):

GENERAL DESCRIPTION OF YOUR B&B (i.e., brick colonial
with white shutters; Victorian mansion with stained glass
windows):

AMBIENCE OF YOUR B&B (i.e., furnished with rare antiques;
lots of wood and glass):

THE QUALITIES THAT MAKE YOUR B&B SPECIAL ARE:

**THINGS OF HISTORIC, SCENIC, CULTURAL, OR GENERAL
INTEREST NEARBY** (i.e., 1 mile from the San Diego Zoo;
walking distance to the Lincoln Memorial):

YOUR OCCUPATION and SPECIAL INTERESTS (i.e., a retired
teacher of Latin interested in woodworking; full-time hostess
interested in quilting):

If you do welcome children, are there any special provisions for
them (i.e., crib, playpen, highchair, play area, baby-sitter;
books and games)?

Breakfast is prepared by ☐ Host ☐ Guest

Breakfast specialties of the house are (i.e., homemade breads and
jams; blueberry pancakes):

Do you offer snacks (i.e., complimentary wine and cheese; pretzels and chips but BYOB)?

Can guests use your kitchen for light snacks? ☐ Yes ☐ No
Do you offer the following amenities: ☐ Guest Refrigerator
☐ Air-conditioning ☐ TV ☐ Piano ☐ Washing Machine
☐ Dryer ☐ Sauna ☐ Pool ☐ Tennis Court Other _____

What major college or university is close by?

_____

Do you offer a discount for other B&B hosts in our Association?
☐ No ☐ Yes: ____%

Please supply the name, address, and phone number of three personal references from people not related to you (please use a separate sheet).

Please enclose a copy of your brochure, if possible, along with a photo of your B&B. If you have a black and white line drawing, send it along too. If you have a special breakfast recipe that you'd like to share, send it along too. (Of course, credit will be given to your B&B.) Nobody can describe your B&B better than you. If you'd like to try your hand, please do so. We will of course reserve the right to edit. As a member of the Tourist House Association of America, your B&B will be described in the next edition of our book, *BED & BREAKFAST, USA,* published by E. P. Dutton, Inc. and distributed to bookstores and libraries throughout the U.S. The book is also used as a reference for B&Bs in our country by major offices of tourism throughout the world. Note: If the authors or publisher receive negative reports from your guests regarding a deficiency in our standards of CLEANLINESS, COMFORT, and CORDIALITY, we reserve the right to cancel your Membership.

This Membership Application has been prepared by:

_____
(Signature)
Please enclose your $15 Membership Dues.   Date: _____

APPLICATION FOR MEMBERSHIP FOR A
BED & BREAKFAST RESERVATION SERVICE

NAME OF BED & BREAKFAST SERVICE:_____

ADDRESS: _____

CITY: _____STATE: ____ZIP: ____PHONE:(   ) _____

COORDINATOR: _____

Names of State(s), Cities, and Towns where you have Hosts (in alphabetical order, please, and limit to 10):

Number of Hosts on your roster: _____

THINGS OF HISTORIC, SCENIC, CULTURAL, OR GENERAL INTEREST IN THE AREA(S) YOU SERVE:

Range of Rates:
Modest:	Single $_____	Double $_____
Average:	Single $_____	Double $_____
Luxury:	Single $_____	Double $_____

Do you accept Credit Cards? ☐ No ☐ Yes:
☐ AMEX ☐ DINERS ☐ MASTERCARD ☐ VISA

Briefly describe a sample Host Home in each of the above categories: (e.g., A cozy farmhouse where the host weaves rugs; a restored 1800 Victorian where the host is a retired general; a contemporary mansion with a sauna, swimming pool, and tennis court):

Please supply the name, address, and phone number of three personal references from people not related to you (please use a separate sheet of paper).

Please enclose a copy of your brochure.

This Membership Application has been prepared by:

_____
(Signature)

Please enclose your $15 Membership Dues.   Date: _____

If you have a special breakfast recipe that you'd like to share, send it along. (Of course, credit will be given to your B&B agency.) As a member of the Tourist House Association of America, your B&B agency will be described in the next edition of our book, *BED & BREAKFAST USA*, published by E. P. Dutton, Inc.